From The Women's Press Ltd
34 Great Sutton Street, London EC1V 0DX

D0417275

The letters and diaries published here were originally researched by Tierl Thompson for a stage play entitled *Dear Girl*, co-devised with Libby Mason and performed by The Women's Theatre Group in 1983–4. The same material formed the basis of a radio dramatisation broadcast as *Friend to Friend* by the BBC in 1984.

Tierl Thompson co-edited, with Janie Grote and Andrea Webb, a feminist songbook, *Sisters in Song,* published in 1979. From 1978–84 she worked for The Women's Theatre Group. She currently teaches drama and directs productions on the Drama Foundation Course at the South-East London College. She is on the Management Committee of Gay Sweatshop Theatre Company. She lives in London.

TIERL THOMPSON (EDITOR)

Dear Girl

The diaries and letters
of two working women
(1897–1917)

The Women's Press

First published by The Women's Press Limited 1987
A member of the Namara Group
34, Great Sutton Street, London EC1V 0DX

British Library Cataloguing in Publication Data available

Typeset by Reprotype Ltd, Peterborough
Printed and bound in Great Britain by
Hazell Watson & Viney Ltd, Aylesbury, Bucks.

Contents

*For Margaret Johnson
and Nicolle Freni*

'*I do not know how I would have felt if your new friendship had
made a difference to us, but it has not – you are just the same
dear girl and I am so delighted for you altogether.*'
(Eva to Ruth, November 1906)

Acknowledgments

Firstly I want to thank Margaret Johnson for permission to use the material, and for entrusting it to me, for all her own initial work on the diaries and letters, and for her generosity and support over the last five years; Cris Wilson for getting me involved and also for initial valuable input; and Nicolle Freni for all her love and ten years' never-ending enthusiasm for my work.

For help with research and the work itself, I want to thank: Sue Davies for access to her background notes, for *Friend to Friend*, a Radio 4 dramatisation of some of the material, produced by Sue in 1984; Eileen Yeo for her useful material on the religious background, again for *Friend to Friend*; Jim Moore for the use of his personal library, particularly the religious and social history sections; Catherine Hall for talking to me about the links between Nonconformism and feminism; Margaret Johnson for lessons in Quaker history and loads of talks about Ruth; François Lafitte for talks about his mother Françoise, for permission to use any of her material, and thanks to him and Eileen Lafitte for their encouragement; Christina Lawson the Woodbrooke librarian for the photo of Eva and a helpful day in the Woodbrooke library; Peter Loach for looking up Eva's family tree after hearing *Friend to Friend*; Noël Greig for chats about Edward Carpenter, sexuality and writing; Carol Smith for information on health issues; Molly Richardson for transforming and typing my manuscript and for positive feedback; Jen Green at The Women's Press for helpful editing; and The Women's Theatre Group and Libby Mason for producing 'Dear Girl' in 1983.

Lastly I want to thank all the people who helped in different ways to get me through such a vast amount of work: Dorigen Caldwell, Jo Smith, Nicky Simpson, Jo Richler, Gay Sweatshop Theatre Company, Sue Baynton, Jo Hudson, Lucy Shalgian and Diveen Henry, Trisha Ziff, David Benedict, Jane Harper, Sheila and Tony Ingall, Joy and Peter Barker, my mum and dad, Marg Yeo, Andrea Webb, Carol Smith, Lesley at Garbanza's for all the coffee and Ann Day.

Introduction

'Kate said to Gertie she often wondered if our lives would ever be written about in a book, and how interesting they would be.' (Eva's diary, 20 April 1915.)

'Women have no history', said Virginia Woolf in 1929. This quotation (at the beginning of Dale Spender's book *There's Always Been a Women's Movement this Century)[1]* seems particularly appropriate to *Dear Girl*. While men have been encouraged to 'gloriously' leave their mark on the world, women's history, Woolf said, lies 'at present locked in old diaries, stuffed away in old drawers, or half obliterated in memories of the aged.' History has mainly been a record of the achievements of male-dominated society, concerned with the public and governing side of life from which women are largely excluded. History has also traditionally represented the dominant class, race and sexuality, so that the experiences of working-class people, black cultures, and anyone outside the 'norm' of heterosexuality, are equally marginalised and misrepresented.

While a few, mostly white, middle-class women have transcended the roles imposed on them to join the ranks of the famous, others have fought unsuccessfully for recognition, and too many women have internalised the idea that it is not the stuff of their lives which makes up social history or culture; that what they have to say about themselves or the world is insignificant. Women, if they write, have tended to write out their thoughts in private or have told stories about the past which people may or may not have listened to, and for all their battles and campaigns have remained only on the fringes of history.

Thanks to the recent and determined excavations of feminists

1

into the past, we now know a great deal more about women's lives. A new definition of history has emerged, in which the public and private sides of life are more equally represented. We now know that not only the mundane, domestic aspects of women's lives – or what Ruth would have called 'the events of my ordinary, very ordinary life' – can be fascinating and full of political struggle, but that women have made extraordinary achievements in the outside world and many more women's battles were being fought than has been thought. We have also learned that the Women's Movements of the past concerned themselves not only with particular issues but with many aspects of personal and sexual freedom. Many of us associate women's liberation and its ideas with the 1970s. This book shows that there has been an active Women's Movement throughout this century, not just the campaign for the vote, or the few most 'outrageous' suffragettes that we might have learned about in school.

Dear Girl takes us into the heart of the early twentieth-century Women's Movement in Britain, which was part of a great, international movement for women's emancipation. It takes us into the context of feminism as it specifically affected a group of white working women in London; much of it has a universal significance.

The wealth of history in this book did indeed lie locked away in old diaries for many years, and it was probably not felt by its authors to be the wonderful and inspiring contribution to history that it is, for precisely some of the above reasons. Admittedly, the diaries and letters were written for personal reasons and not for publication, but it is the difference between the content and the writers' confidence that is so striking. While in moments of optimism Ruth and Eva could express a desire to write their own or each other's lives, or even write for a living, and while they were so obviously good at it, they all too frequently, with the 'lack of confidence' which Ruth called the 'curse' of their lives, doubted their creative efforts, or simply lacked the opportunity to pursue them.

Ruth was particularly self-effacing about her writing, but her diaries give a fascinating account of the period. Even though friends encouraged her to write, she dismissed her diaries as being 'as full of detail and self-interest as Pepys – but without its interest'. With her characteristic admiration of Eva's 'noble' and 'superior' qualities and devaluation of her own, she won

2

dered 'If I could see Eva's diary, would it be like this of mine, full of horrid things, rubbish and stupidity, personal animosities. I don't think so. I imagine rather that it would prove to be a record of large thoughts, careful judgements, beautiful dreams for the future...'[2] Yet the 'personal animosities' are interesting now. Ruth felt a strong need to write about domestic struggles and conflicts, much of which revolved around her need for independence, and for which she could find no expression elsewhere. With her sound Christian upbringing, and its emphasis on uplifting moral thoughts, the recording of personal complaints seemed spiritually weak and even wicked, but there were complex and strong emotions that could not be purged so easily. It was the Women's Movement which eventually gave Ruth the confidence to take her troubles seriously and feel less guilty about expressing them.

The diaries are valuable because they do record personal feelings as well as great social events. They describe the effects of sexism and political oppression and the growth necessary for true political change. Much of this parallels the modern Women's Movement and is strikingly familiar.

The writings show the impact of the Women's Movement on everyday life. They were written, not by prominent members of the movement, or women from artistic or literary circles who may have had some leisure in which to write, but by women who wrote during a hard-working day, in time snatched after rounds of home and Chapel duties, and later, political activities. While there was a tradition of journal writing amongst some middle-class women in the nineteenth century, for the purposes of 'spiritual self-improvement', Ruth and Eva aspired to, rather than belonged to, this category.

Both Ruth and Eva came from lower-middle-class Nonconformist Methodist families, and were brought up in an atmosphere where respectable honest labour, a sober and earnest commitment to the Chapel and responsibility towards the family were expected. Ruth was born in 1884 and Eva in 1882. While neither of them faced the desperately underprivileged world of the labouring classes, neither family was financially very secure or comfortably placed. Ruth's father was a commercial clerk whose employment was not always stable. Eva was illegitimate and was adopted by her grandparents, who similarly had a trade (her grandfather was a master baker) but who ended up deeply in debt. It was typical for girls of Ruth's and Eva's class to leave

3

school early, as Ruth did at 13, to contribute, and in Ruth's case become essential, to the family wage. Her first job was a manual packing job and she progressed to clerical work. Eva had been a domestic servant but had managed to learn 'shorthand and typing when her grandparents were better off' and become a typist.

While Ruth and Eva benefited from families who encouraged some education for girls (Ruth's parents considered she had been 'well-studied') and from the educative atmosphere of the apel, writing and studying was frowned upon if it took a direction not compatible with family and Chapel ideology.

The women, however, cherished their dreams of a fuller life through 'long years of dreary labour' and they took what opportunities they could for 'expansion'. The diaries were vital places where they could express their most private feelings, attempt to sort out their ideas, or simply enjoy describing their 'doings and sayings' as Ruth said, 'so that I shall know, even when my memory fails me'. While Ruth might have wondered at her 'occasional scribble' (which filled seventeen thick note-books), she admitted that 'the habit of recording the outside details of my life has a wonderful hold upon me' and often soothed her in times of difficulty. Eva, displaying the intellect-ual abilities which Ruth and others admired so much, particu-larly used her journals to review her 'mental position' on current 'troublous problems' and to analyse political ideas. Minna, who formed a close relationship with Eva after 1911, and who 'never wrote a line' in her life – 'even letter writing was a trouble to me' – was prompted by her grief after Eva's death to write for the first time. Once started, she could not 'let it alone'. Writing with frequent interruptions from her children, she was desperate to write Eva's life, put down her own experience 'in marriage, in soul consciousness, in friendship' and 'write and speak on the Sex Question, for it would be worth reading'.

The letters between the women were a basic means of communication and essential to the development of their ideas on paper. Significantly, after Eva's sudden death in 1917, Ruth's journal-writing stopped, though this may also have been affected by her marriage, the fragmentation of the Women's Movement and the general loss of idealism that came with the First World War. Ruth kept her own and Eva's diaries and letters and Minna's writings, and some painstakingly typed pages of Eva's journal suggest that Ruth, consistent with her idea that Eva

4

possessed 'great gifts', might have been trying to write her life.

When Ruth's husband Hugh discovered and read her diaries after her death in 1953, it was like opening a door to a forgotten world, some aspects of which he found he knew very little about, despite having known Ruth since 1910. Ruth, who had always had 'big reserves' about confiding her deepest feelings, particularly to Hugh, had obviously kept some of her most precious thoughts to herself.

Hugh was impressed with the diaries, and regretted that he had not encouraged Ruth more. He asked Margaret Johnson, a mutual friend whom he and Ruth had met through pacifist work, if she would one day 'do something' with Ruth's writing. When Hugh died, more than twenty years later in 1976, Margaret inherited a veritable archive of material – not only Ruth and Eva's diaries and letters, but letters from many other women friends and political colleagues, and a large collection of books, newspaper cuttings and political pamphlets. Many of these were collected by Ruth in the early 1900s and show a wide range of feminist, socialist and progressive religious activity in those years which envisaged a radical personal and political transformation of society. Margaret began to piece together the details of Ruth's early life, much of which she knew nothing about, having never, for example, heard of Eva. She then gave permission for the writings to be used in the Women's Theatre Group's production, *Dear Girl,* and for this book.

The bulk of the book consists of Ruth Slate's diaries (written mainly between 1897 and 1909), Eva Slawson's diaries (written later between 1913 and 1916), and Ruth's and Eva's letters to each other (1903 to 1916). The first half is mostly Ruth's diaries, the second mostly Eva's, with their letters providing a continuous thread, although far fewer of Eva's letters have survived. Extracts from Minna's letters to Ruth written in 1916 and 1917 appear in the Appendix and throw new light on the relationships between the women. Ruth started her diary when she was 13, and the early writing records her life in Manor Park, East London, where family and Chapel formed the focus of her life. In 1903 she met Eva at Chapel and they became devoted friends, corresponded regularly and developed a relationship which Ruth was to call 'the foundation' of her life. Finding they had many thoughts in common, they shared their religious difficulties, personal problems and their aspirations for something beyond what was offered to them. From 1906 the great movement for women's emancipation and the campaign for the vote intensified, and opened up new possibilities for women. Its ideals connected up with Ruth's and Eva's longings, suppressed feelings and things 'they had long felt the seeds of', and the diaries show the transformation they experienced. In 1911, Eva met Minna through the Walthamstow Chapel, was immediately impressed with her as 'a type of woman of the future', and they formed a close and passionate friendship which is well documented in Eva's diaries.

The early 1900s were a momentous time in women's history, when over a thousand women went to prison for 'The Cause' of the vote, when thousands more upturned the whole notion of the Victorian womanhood and developed militant campaign tactics, the like of which have not been seen over any women's issue in England since. Their determined actions and the very demands of the movement caused the debate about the 'New Woman' and the 'Sex Question' (all aspects of the roles and relations of the sexes) to rage up and down the country. It was a time when Charlotte Despard, the much admired President of the Women's Freedom League, to whom Ruth wrote for advice in 1909, replied to her that 'every woman of thought and determination should at the present moment, so *critical* as I believe in our history, try to do something for the woman's cause.'[3]

Ruth's and Eva's accounts give us a sense of what it must have felt like to be there at the time when the Women's Movement was emerging. When they discovered feminism and radical politics, the diaries are full of accounts of rallies, meetings, and demonstrations, which show that their contemporaries wanted change in many areas of their lives, not only legal equality. The suffrage campaign both regenerated interest in older issues and created new ones. Ruth and Eva themselves were not militant suffragettes and did not particularly focus their energy on the vote but on a wide range of women's issues and on the ideals of socialist and progressive religious groups. Just as women's lack of political power had thrown up a great movement, the onslaught of industrial capitalism and British imperialism at the end of the nineteenth century had produced a revival of socialism and groups concerned to establish a new and 'nobler' life, based on equality and co-operation. Many wanted, as Eva put it, 'to harmonise all sections of life'.

The diaries show women in various groups organising them-

6

selves around women's working conditions and sweated labour, engaged in all manner of State reforms, doing battle with the chronic poverty of the early twentieth century and fighting the abuse of prostitutes and children. They were discussing marriage, the free union and sexuality, issues of birth control and the 'condition of Motherhood'; were falling in love with each other, running girls' clubs, working in settlements, living in experimental communities. They were interested in vegetarianism, the 'modern trend of mystical thought', arts and crafts and a host of 'alternative' activities.

The situation in the late nineteenth century which prompted the fervour of the Women's Movement, and which formed Ruth's and Eva's background, was one in which there were few opportunities for women to support themselves as independent beings, or to do remotely interesting work. For middle-class women, devotion to others, service and self-sacrifice and a dependent existence within families and marriage, was the order of the day. For working-class women there was poverty and deprivation. Women were disenfranchised people with no 'rights of citizenship'. A half century of reform and the pioneering activities of middle-class women in the latter part of the nineteenth century had gone some way towards improving the situation.

Many women had helped to open up new professions and justify activity for women by transforming their passive servicing role into one of active service – by doing philanthropic social work, or by using women's special influence to tackle particular areas, such as temperance and prostitution, often issuing political challenges to the authorities. By the turn of the century a few jobs had been created in teaching, nursing, social work, and in 'business' (the growing area of commercial, secretarial or clerical work).

Ruth and Eva could be said to have benefited from some of this, for they could earn a living in 'business', but their jobs were still poorly paid for the labour involved, monotonous and uncreative. Kearley and Tonge's, the firm that Ruth worked with for 12 years, was known 'to be a firm of sweaters' and 'had a bad name in the City for overworking its employees'; Ruth was one of those 'indispensable' secretaries, vital to the firm, but not given full credit for her role.

Both she and Eva longed for 'lives of wider service and development' and in their earlier years, the ideal of a mission in

7

life, of going out into the world to do 'noble self-sacrificing work', much like some of the nineteenth-century women had done, had great appeal. But while this had been immensely facilitating for those women because it took them out of the domestic sphere, it was ultimately limiting if women could have no say in the way things were organised, if they could not vote or make the political decisions which affected the social conditions they were grappling with. In Ruth's and Eva's case, imagining 'noble work' was more a way of being active that seemed compatible with the religious beliefs they were trying so hard to live up to. In reality, activity and self-sacrifice militated against each other and caused conflict, and even 'worthy work', if it involved training or independence from home, was discouraged by Ruth's family. It also involved money they didn't have.

By the turn of the century the true position of women was becoming apparent. Middle-class women could get no further with the progress they had made in the previous century, whilst working-class women were still in dire poverty. Independence of spirit, of wanting things for oneself, in Ruth's case, could be seen as 'downright wicked' or abnormal. Through the Women's Movement which erupted in the early 1900s, after decades of pioneering initiatives from individual women, and patient constitutional attempts to win the vote, women as a body demanded an equal share in the structuring of society, in which they were to be free and independent beings. For Ruth, Eva and many others, the vote was not only a right due to women but an instrument for change. In the words of Isabella Ford, the Leeds feminist and socialist who spoke at a meeting which Ruth attended in 1909, 'the Meaning of the Women's Movement', was that '... women were going to improve the condition of things and they were of one mind that it was not going to be done by philanthropy. They were going to have the same freedom as men who did not know how to use it. This movement was a thorough one; they were desirous of getting down to the foundation of things, and women must be at this foundation.'[4]

It was the transition to this new spirit that was so crucial to Ruth and Eva, for while they never lost all the 'humility' which Ruth realised was fostered in herself and Eva by 'hard circumstances and mistaken religious training', and while devotion and self-sacrifice to the new cause was often the tenor of the Women's Movement, they could at last consider their own needs and feel justified in looking for better things. The changes

8

did not however involve an absolute break between religion and feminism. One of the striking phenomena in the diaries is the presence of religion in the 'new' politics; the links between religion and feminism, or religion and socialism, which are absent from present-day movements. For while different religions and cultures may be acknowledged in Britain today, religion is not generally upheld as a radical force for change. At this time, religion formed the fabric of most people's lives and a spiritual imperative – that spiritual and as well as material change was necessary to transform society – often formed a part of radical politics.

There were already links between Ruth's and Eva's Nonconformist background and socialist and feminist ideas. Nonconformists had a tradition of dissent and resistance to the Established Church. Unlike the High Church, they had always been concerned with the mass of the people and social conditions, and were less evangelical than the main body of Methodists. In the late nineteenth century, great Nonconformist preachers did much to awaken complacent bourgeois consciences to desperate social conditions. One of Ruth's problems with her Chapel background was that it both encouraged a certain amount of independence in her and subdued it. The United Methodist Free Church to which she belonged was a lively body and encouraged activity and participation from its members from an early age, although the male ministers held ultimate authority. Ruth was a prominent Chapel member and she was one of many feminists and labour supporters who received an early training in organising in Methodist Sunday Schools and Chapels.

In order to progress, however, she and Eva needed to move away from the more orthodox and oppressive aspects of Nonconformity. The patriarchal concept of God as an all-powerful judge to whom they felt accountable, was not easily compatible with the new idea of a free-thinking woman; nor was the idea of submitting to suffering as a religious necessity, for suffering came to be seen as the result of circumstances that needed to be changed.

Significantly, the move to feminism and progressive religion was almost simultaneous. In January 1907, shortly before she attended her first women's suffrage meeting, Ruth wrote in her diary that 'the religious world is being stirred to its depths by the Reverend Campbell's New Theology' and she was immediately taken with his ideas, for which she was almost ostracised at home. R. J. Campbell was a Nonconformist Congregational minister, and his ideas – that 'love and broad human sympathy' should form the basis of Christianity rather than the institutions of the Church, or the 'moral God figure' – caused a national uproar, for they challenged much conventional doctrine.

Eva was also interested in the New Theology, but her religious changes took a different direction. While Ruth, whose nature was more 'restless and cynical', moved towards a broadly spiritual philosophy, staying closer to the Quakers, Eva remained essentially religious, and developed a basic 'Christian Socialist' faith. Her ideas also showed connections with the late-nineteenth-century Utopian socialists. She seemed in fact to have made the break with the Old Chapel as Ruth had, taken up more social activity with the Independent Labour Party and other groups, and then to have moved back to seeing religion as the 'fundamental power'. In July 1914 she wrote, after a discussion on 'Syndicalism' with a neighbour, 'How my views have changed! I believe all these theories and methods, political and otherwise, have great things to do for the future, but the power of religion seems to me to supersede all and to be the only force which can produce the *greatest* development and growth ... '

For Eva the true Christian spirit was a socialist one of love and comradeship which she considered a great force for change. It was the task of Nonconformists to 'keep the flag of Christ and labour, flying' as the rebels, the real representatives of the Church, had done 'through the centuries'. It was also 'the urge of the spirit which should make woman desire and claim equal opportunities with man', to 'compel him to recognise her as a personality, a soul, with a right to freedom'.[5]

Eva's stress on spiritual force is interesting, because where she is not referring specifically to God, she is often stating her belief that the 'inner soul' has to change for real progress to take place; that economic change is not enough, which parallels modern feminism and the idea that the 'personal is political'. Although sometimes confined by her philosophy of 'love and toleration', and by her reliance on God to console or guide her in difficult times, Eva saw her religious philosophy as essentially active. Unlike the old gloomy punishing aspects of Christianity, it upheld 'redemption', liberation and joy of life, not 'renunciation' and repression.

The areas of overlap between religion and feminism in the Women's Movement are interesting. Ruth first came into contact with feminist ideas through her Quakeress friend, the 'unorthodox' Miss Brown. (Quakers had long-established connections with women's emancipation.) Her first suffrage meeting was held at St Ethelburga's, an Anglican Church in Bishopsgate, where her friend May was Superintendent of a girls' club, and whose minister, Dr Cobb, was an ardent socialist and supporter of women's suffrage (as was R. J. Campbell). Many churches supported the suffrage campaign, although almost all took a non-militant line, and several Church 'Leagues for Women's Suffrage' were formed. (They were predominantly Christian, but the Jewish League for Women's Suffrage was formed in 1912.)

The atmosphere of the Women's Movement approached one of religious fervour at times, and devotion to 'The Cause' reached martyr-like proportions. Much of the language and propaganda had a religious or moral tone: women were going to be 'world redeemers' and 'Man's idea of freedom needed to be purified'. The Biblical images of darkness and light – light representing progress or good, and darkness representing evil or lack of progress – which are now rejected for their racist implications, were pervasive metaphors in all radical groups. Above all, women relied on spiritual strength, for with no material or economic power, spirituality was seen as a great force to be pitted against men's physical authority, against 'those who, by the brutality of mere physical power, are trying to crush us, who must know that there is behind us the spiritual force of a great and splendid vision, that the women of Britain after generations of servitude are awake, and that nothing, no material force that can be brought against them, can make them pause.'[6]

Ruth's and Eva's politics revolved around these areas of feminism, religion and socialism. They tended towards groups which had a free-thinking, undogmatic approach, which recognised the stark realities of the under-privileged side of life, which worked constructively and co-operatively towards change, but which also presented dreams and visions of better things. Neither was attracted by the militancy of the Women's Social and Political Union, and would not have been capable of their actions, although Eva admired 'those bold reckless souls who destroy not only their own peace but the fictitious peace of society'. But by 1913 she felt dissatisfied that the concentration on the vote meant that 'the suffragettes so *seldom discuss the*

11

fundamentals of progress amongst women', which to her included all aspect of the Sex Question. Both she and Ruth joined the Women's Freedom League, which had split from the WSPU in 1908 to form a more democratic organisation. Although not as militant as the WSPU, the Women's Freedom League took direct action and did not use merely constitutional methods. The WFL saw itself as 'highly educative, forming a centre for the strong and ardent faces that will be needed to make the woman's vote effective one the Vote is won ...'[7]

Eva joined the Independent Labour Party and its women's section, the Women's Labour League, in 1909. The Women's Labour League gave some support to 'Votes for Women', but focused its activity on getting Labour representation of women in Parliament, and on the domestic and industrial conditions of working women's life. Although she continued to support the WLL, Eva left the ILP in 1912 (it is not clear why), and became more involved in the activities of the Walthamstow Chapel, which had been shaken up by the arrival of Mr James, a Congregational minister, 'much persecuted' for his radical religious views. Eva was attracted by 'SBJ' himself, by his 'strongly social preaching' and the Chapel's debating circles, the 'Parliament' and 'Conference'. She eventually became Superintendent of its Girls' League and Women's Conference. (Congregationalists were Nonconformists who believed in the powers of the Congregation, not just the ministers.)

Ruth joined the Progressive Thought League, which was formed to promote the ideas of the New Theology, and both she and Eva taught at the Hoxton Adult School, which combined religious and social teaching. Adult Schools had existed for over a century and the early 1900s saw a widespread revival of the Adult School movement, which provided education for working people. In 1912 Ruth attended the Freewoman Circle, a newly-formed group which attracted women and men interested in social problems besides the vote, and took a keen interest in sexuality.

Ruth's and Eva's politics were also internationalist and essentially pacifist. For many women, the suffrage cause strengthened feelings of internationalism because it linked them to 'all disenfranchised persons and nations'. When the First World War broke out, Ruth and Eva joined pacifist organisations which promoted 'friendly understanding and co-operation between people of all nations'. Woodbrooke College,

12

which they both attended, finally realising their ambitions to study, was an international settlement which combined social and religious study and taught the basics of modern social work.

Throughout all their political activities personal struggles continued. Above all, the material bears witness to the love between the women themselves: their relationships with each other were fundamental to all they managed to achieve. Ruth, Minna and Eva supported and encouraged each other when their desire for independence met with resistance from families and men friends, and in not infrequent periods of depression, and they had a capacity for emotional closeness that did not seem to exist as a reliable factor between men and women. Ruth felt her relationships with men were 'disappointing things', although she had successive deep involvements. Eva did not have any relationships with men (although she was attracted to Mr James), and Minna, who had been married 'in mated loneliness' to Will, 'simply couldn't have borne her life' without Eva and Lily (a close friend who helped to support Minna and her children). They were each other's 'dear girls', 'precious loves', and their friendships were full of warmth, intensity and freely expressed declarations of love. Friendship in itself was a great ideal, was as important and as enriching as marriage or free union; it was not incompatible with them, and could mean a number of things.

For Ruth, friendship was the 'breath' of her life, and 'Eva was its crown'; their relationship deepened over 13 years. For Eva, friendship and fellowship formed the basis of her politics, for it was a 'City' or extended community of friends who would work together to change the world. On an individual level, 'where we have once really loved', friendship for Eva became deeper all the time. 'Old friends are like old books,' she wrote to Ruth in January 1913, 'we read them early and grasping with our crude young minds the story, we *think* we know, but after experience and growth, we go back, we read again and are amazed at the gems which sparkle before us.'

Minna and Eva experienced a physically passionate friendship which caused Eva to expand her ideas about physical expression and relationships generally. While their relationship did not seem to be explicitly sexual, or was not seen as sexual by them, it was obvious that sexual desire and affection were experienced. Their relationship did not fit easily into the

13

category of 'romantic friendship' (passionate but not sexual, and therefore acceptable) but revealed all the contradictions and complexities surrounding sexuality, as did their relationships with men.

In the early 1900s women's choices about sexual relationships were determined by a number of factors, one being that the new debate on the Sex Question, focused on marriage and the heterosexual Free Union. Sexuality therefore was synonymous with heterosexuality and sexual activity was only envisaged by Eva within a heterosexual 'union'. Women were not seen to have an active independent capacity for sex. At the same time women far outnumbered men in the population (by three-quarters of a million in the late nineteenth century) and for many women this meant there seemed no prospect of a sexual relationship at all or of fulfilling longings to have children. The problem of the so-called 'surplus' or 'odd women' was something that was much debated and something the Women's Movement fought by demanding an independent role for women.

Independent work or activities and a greater sense of dignity, did not, however, resolve the Sex Question, and many women, Eva included, felt stranded by the lack of sexual possibilities, and frustrated by sexual longings. For Eva, celibacy was not a positive choice, because it was physical union that she wanted. With very few men sympathetic to women's emancipation, too many men were using the 'old argument of there being too many women' to their advantage. The difficulties for women of throwing off their conditioning and forming 'free unions' (where they would still get a 'reputation' and men would not), meant that the sexual prospects were fraught with difficulties. Eva, despite her longings, had definite demands to make of relationships with men for which she would not subdue her independence.

The women's relationships with each other were not seen as having a sexual potential; but what is interesting about Eva's and Minna's relationship is that their experiences together suggested something other than even their broad notion of friendship. In the absence of an adequate label for their experiences, they used what concepts they had and added their own, creating a language for their feelings – which in itself began to widen the existing categories. Eva's and Minna's experiences together were 'rare' and 'sacred'. Eva wondered at

14

them and felt as though a 'miracle' had 'been performed' on her life. Her relationship with Minna led her to think that 'too much spiritual and physical love is reserved for sexual union. We ought to be able to mingle soul and body, woman with woman, man with man – glorifying, caressing, embracing with the whole body – not simply the touch of hands and lips.' In the absence of a sexual factor, their love was at least exclusively defined as between *women,* not affected by the stereotypes of masculinity and femininity as were the sexologists who could only later see same-sex relationships in terms of the coupling of a 'masculine' woman and a 'feminine' woman, or a 'masculine' man and a 'feminine' man.

Minna in particular seemed to want to break through boundaries and conventions. Having been married, she no longer thought it was 'the most important thing to be oneself to one', enjoyed an affair with Mr James, wished she had been more demonstrative with Eva, had plans for a women's colony where women might 'if they wanted to, obey a divine impulse and have a child'. She felt a great urgency about solving the Sex Question. After reading Edward Carpenter's *The Intermediate Sex,* which argued for same-sex relationships, Gertie (Eva's half-sister) decided Minna was an 'Urning' (someone capable of being attracted to their own sex).

At the very point that Minna was most preoccupied with the Sex Question, the writing stopped, and the period of absorbing relationships between the women and of intense idealism appeared to be over. After sharing their experiences for a period of over 20 years, we are left, at the end of it all, inspired, informed, and warmed by the writings, by the women's strength and commitment to each other, and by the hopefulness of their political dreams and their determination to work for change. Equally it is frustrating that the story ends when it does.

The writing raises some tantalising questions. How exactly can we interpret Ruth's silence and lack of writing after 1916? Did the warmth go out of her life after Eva died, as she feared? How did Minna resolve the Sex Question? How did those women relate to their own past and how did the great days of the Women's Movement relate to life in the 1920s and beyond? What became of those ardent suffragettes? We know something about the smaller campaigns that followed the suffrage period, but little is known of the personal dimension of women's lives.

In Ruth's case we do know that her desire to write was not

realised, nor were her hopes of a 'great work with Eva', although we can see the continuing application of her beliefs in the social work and pacifist activities which continued throughout her life. Perhaps, as in this telling entry from her diary in 1909, when she felt overwhelmed by work and domestic problems and her ambitions seemed impossible to realise, she might somewhere have nurtured greater ideals:

'Awoke in a worse mood than ever. Nodded all the while in the train, and crawled along after like an old woman, my mind busy all the time with ridiculous notions of writing a touching story, founded on the events of my own life. The story was to move the hearts of the people so that justice and happiness should reign quite easily and all should be roused to usher them in. Myself was to fade quietly away – an unrecognised genius, starved mentally and morally, yet clinging to the last to an exalted ideal!!'

With the publication of this book, Ruth's and Eva's writing has at last been recognised, and Ruth's desire to write something which would 'move the hearts of the people' has surely come true. Hopefully it will encourage women to delve deeper into the past, to be confident about what we have to say about ourselves and to struggle to keep our own dreams alive and well.

1

'A Hard-hearted Wicked Girl'
July 1897-July 1903

This chapter consists of extracts from Ruth's early diaries, started when she was 13. While they give a fascinating account of the period in a general historical sense, they also show the influences that formed Ruth, the dominant ideology for a girl of her class and religion, growing up in the late Victorian era.

In the diaries Ruth describes her immediate world, the 'goings-on' in a lower middle-class area of Manor Park, East London, her family life and Chapel activities, her work experiences (from her first job at 14, in a 'druggist's sweatshop', to clerical work in the City), her preoccupations with boys, and her five-year relationship with Ewart Johnson. She records the beginnings of her friendship with Eva, her secret longings 'to study and to learn', and her ongoing struggle to subdue many of her own desires in order to 'live the life worthy of a Christian'.

Ruth and her family were Nonconformist Christians and staunch members of the local Chapel, which was part of the United Methodist Free Church. Family and Chapel were the foci of Ruth's life, and the two were so inter-connected that maintaining independence from either could be extremely difficult. Both had their contradictions. While she enthusiastically involved herself in the Chapel, enjoying the 'bright meetings', educative atmosphere and social activities typical of Methodism, the religious morality of duty and service and the earnest sense of propriety often seemed hard, and many of Ruth's more spirited characteristics were narrowed down in the process. At home, the family was close-knit, and Ruth's mother and father considered themselves 'kind and indulgent parents' who gave their children a certain amount of freedom. They could nevertheless subject Ruth to severe criticism, particularly when she had ambitions for

17

herself, expressed independent opinions, or displayed strong emotions. The diaries record bitter conflicts between Ruth and her mother, who relied on her as elder daughter to take an exemplary domestic role in relation to sister Daisy and brother Tom, and seemed herself threatened by Ruth's behaviour. The overriding morality was to accept a humble position in life, and for girls to be a 'cheer and comfort to those at home'. However, despite being conscientious and dutiful, Ruth was independent-minded. In the struggle to please everyone, and yet remain true to herself, she often grew 'reserved and unhappy', not knowing how or when to express herself.

The self-image Ruth began to develop, of being 'faulty' and 'selfish' if she showed signs of self-interest or emotion, she was never quite able to throw off. As she approached young woman-hood she tried to conform, to be more 'sober' and less 'frivolous', looking up to others like Ewart and Eva as more 'noble' than herself. But in her diaries she was able to show the 'old spirit of rebellion', express her private thoughts, and pursue her interest in what she called 'recording all my deeds'.

These diaries show the remarkable powers of expression she possessed from an early age. The following are extracts from what were often long narratives, or from accounts which she wrote up retrospectively from notes when she was trying to catch up. (Occasionally the dates become confused.)

Ruth's Diary 21 July 1897
90 Carlyle Road, Manor Park
On today 21 July 1897 I am going to start and write all that I do so that I shall know even when my memory fails me. Before I start with today I am going to write all the important things that have happened during the past year. This day last year our Sunday School excursion to Southend took place. I am rather fond of taking notice of boys (most of my companions do it) and the boy I liked then was Fred McDowall.

Nellie Smith my chief friend liked Fred even better than I did and I think he liked her. I thought that I would have a good game. It was so hot that we hardly knew what to do with ourselves best after paddling. But in the afternoon while we were sitting on the cliffs he came along. We talked but gradually got inclined for fun. He dragged us up and down the cliff and we when free chased him to the great amusement of our elders. After tea we had more fun and then went to the station.

18

Early in October Nellie moved to Palmers Green and I hear from her sometimes. In the summer holidays all August we went over to the Flats[1] a good deal and when Dad had his holidays to Clacton by boat. In October I am at Manor Park School Board. (I go to Little Ilford and am in the Standard 6th at the time of which I am writing.)

On the 6th, 7th and 8th of April our Chapel held a bazaar. Mother superintended the Sunday School stall and Daisy and I stayed from school to help her. As they were going out Harry and Fred kissed me. I struggled I can tell you. I did not like Fred so much and was fascinated by a pair of brown eyes belonging to a boy named Ernest Round. Nothing particular happened at the bazaar. I never went to Chapel in the evening until on the 18th of April, Easter Sunday. Mother said I could go on condition that I behaved myself for twice before when I had been Mr Gurnett had threatened to put me out for almost nothing.

All this while I had been trying to serve God, having enlisted in his army some time. Whenever I went anywhere where boys were I used to make up my mind to take no notice of them but always failed miserably. On 30 July we broke up at school for a month. Daisy and I each had a prize for attendance. We went to Grace's for tea and after to singing class. On giving out the anthems Ernie had to give me a light knock on the cheek (for fun of course). I payed him out by treading on his toes whenever I could. This does read silly to me but in my heart it is kept as warm and joyful recollections.

Description of Ernie. He is very dark and has lovely brown eyes. Cannot yet be called good looking though mother said Monday she thought he was improving. Like us girls shows off in the presence of the opposite sex and perhaps rues it after. Why I like him is because he has such a wistful sorrowful look when thinking. I think he wants to be good and like me loses control.

31 August 1897

On Sunday morning Daisy and I stayed away from Sunday School but went to Chapel. The Minister in his sermon spoke about some people and boys and girls and how they are like an apple. Very beautiful to look upon but containing a maggot inside. How those boys all turned and looked at me! Oh dear! I do not think I am beautiful though everywhere I go I am told I am good-looking and better-looking than my sister. What rubbish this is, I must keep on. Hope tomorrow to have better things to talk about.

29 October 1897

Dear me! It seems as though I am never going to get time to write in here again. Have conquered my weakness for Ernest Round and am in love with another boy. Ewart Johnson by name. This boy along with Harry and Fred McDowall followed Maggie and I who were going for a walk after Chapel. On 24th October, another talk ended in getting a *kiss*. A gentleman minister came to our Chapel and held three mission services. Ewart came and sat directly in front of me. He is very fair and has come from Manchester. His speech does sound funny. He is so different from the other boys. He is a Christian, therefore as he and I are both trying to serve God there is no harm in having one another. My liking for him is not flighty as it was for the others, but steadfast. Mr Poppleton's words stirred us up so that we stayed and gave in our names as Christ's disciples. There was such a lot of us. As I have made an open declaration I must strive more earnestly.

22 December 1897

Such a long while has past since I last wrote in here. The past few weeks have been entirely taken up with operetta practices and evening classes. Five weeks ago we started a Christian Endeavour [CE][2]. It is very nice. We have a paper read by a member each week, and a text is said by each one on the subject. We must all take part in the meetings. I am on the committee and so is Ewart. My duty is to look after the others and bring new members. Daisy is on the social and Dad the prayer meeting committees. Ewart comes in late on account of work.

10 February 1898

I really have had no time to come here before, and as usual, now I am here have forgotten all my deeds. On Sunday Ewart and his sister Nellie came to ask us to tea in the afternoon. It was a very long way to the house which is 108 Heigham Road, East Ham. There are six of them alive and six dead. Mrs Johnson is very nice.

On Monday afternoon I went up to the day school[3] to tell Mrs Osborne that Daisy and I had left. I have not been for weeks. I have been to the Doctor's four times and he says I am not strong enough for teaching and so I am going to stay at home and help Mother for a little while with the blouse work she sometimes does for a friend. Daisy is going as an apprentice to a dressmakers next week I think. Mrs Osborne was sorry and said all the nice girls were leaving. Also that she would be pleased to see us any afternoon we had to spare. In the evening we went to Night School.

26 September 1898

It is such a long time since I wrote in my diary and I have been making notes all this while. In March our great friends the McDowalls moved to Southampton. We miss them very much but often write. Good Friday I went to Hornchurch [where Ruth's grandparents lived and ran a Post Office], it was unbearably hot. All day Easter Monday we wandered about the Flats. On 19 May it was Ewart's birthday. Mine on 27 February was very wet. I did not even wish Ewart Happy Returns of the day. He did me. I have been very disagreeable with him. I always am it seems. I wonder he puts up with it. There is no cause only that I feel like it. In the evening of 24 September I went to prayer meeting and Ewart came home with me. I began having fun but seeing he looked grave, I soon ceased. He then began his trouble by saying 'We shall never live with Father again.' I stared and he went on. 'He's been going about with other women, one especially as his wife, and she has two children by him.' He looked upset and it came upon me all of a sudden that I had been treating him in that foolish way all the while. I felt as if I could have cried there and then but did not even say I was sorry. Perhaps he saw. On the next Sunday Mother went up to see Mrs Johnson. Mrs J. cried bitterly all the while. She could not bear the thought of living with him again. He had done the same thing again about three years before when she had forgiven him and trusted him. Then they had gone bankrupt and nearly starved.

9 December 1898

Did not go out at all with faceache till Friday when I came up to the City with Mother after a place. Daisy was apprenticed to a Mrs Pettifer to learn dressmaking. Mother was speaking to Mrs Kinnear (a neighbour) and telling her I wanted to go to work when Mrs K. said they wanted girls up at Mr Kinnear's place. The work she said was clean, only they had to be there at 8 sharp

21

and it was half an hour's walk from Liverpool Street Station.

Mr Kinnear spoke for me and I was to go and see the manager. Dad tried hard to persuade me not to go, but I would persist and in spite of faceache, Friday saw Mother and I at Davy, Hill and Son, Yates and Hicks, wholesale and export druggists of 60 Park Street, Southwark, SE. We were not prepossessed with the appearance of the place. It looked quite different to other places of business. It is Spurgeon's old Chapel enlarged. We went in and saw Mr Edwards the manager, who said I was to start following Monday with eight shillings a week. It seemed a vast amount to me.

The next day I went to Wanstead Park with Ewart and told him that I was going to work, which news he could hardly believe. He said that he did not think I should stop there long. On the Monday morning I felt very nervous and my first impressions were far from favourable. The forewoman was a Mrs Clark, a very nice old lady, and the names of the girls were as follows: Beatrice Taylor, Ada Allison (or Tiny), Ada Rust, Rosa Greenfield, Ethel Garrett, Agnes Ingram, Alice and Ada Fullock and Mary and Maria Farrell. I did not like it a bit but would not say so.

Worked till 8 o'clock for the first time on 13 January and then pretty frequently, not getting home till 9 and getting nothing extra. In the beginning of February, while things continued the same with Ewart, Daisy having to leave her place, came up to the City with me. Warnings from me of no use,

23 February 1899

Ewart was angrier than I had ever seen him and said he was not going to be played by anyone not even me. Whenever he asked me to go out I had refused and not even answered when he spoke. If I cared for him at all (and he thought I must do, a little) we would be alright again and if I did not care to say so he would say 'brake it off' though what the 'it' was I always failed to comprehend. At last I said 'I did not care' and then he wouldn't believe me, so I said no more till I got home, bounced in the gate and got safely in.

On 18 March, I went a walk to Ilford and such a way with Ewart. I think of all our walks that was the best. We seemed to understand one another better than we had ever done, for since our last disagreement, I had felt a difference in Ewart. He gave me such a searching look and we both felt alright once more. I have put all this down which may be very silly of a girl just sixteen, but I know that Ewart has done me a lot of good, made me more thoughtful and affectionate, for I have always been very reserved and cold in manner. He as well as myself spoke of that walk as the best we had, yet we spoke of nothing particular, except discussing *John Halifax, Gentleman,* which we were both reading and enjoyed.

On Sunday 4 June, after school in the afternoon, I was walking along with Bertha Holliday when E.J. caught me up (while Bertha vanished). He said it would probably be their last Sunday in Manor Park. More he would explain in the evening. How funny did I feel. But I only said 'Oh!' quite calmly, and I do not think I changed colour. In the evening I heard all the particulars from Mother who said they would be at Manor Park four more days, and were going back to Manchester, but Ewart was to stay until his Mother found him a place.

7 July 1899

Ewart came to say he had had a letter from his Mother saying he was to go down to Manchester Saturday week. I felt myself going white or some funny colour, so I ran upstairs with some excuse. Ewart seemed very miserable and when I was out of the room asked Mother if she minded us writing to each other. She of course said 'No'. The place E.J. is going to is a cloth place, just like his present one and was obtained for him by his old Manchester Sunday School Teacher. I am getting terrible downcast. I am trying now to be better in every way. If only I had my time over again I would not be so silly as I was last summer.

11 July 1899

I went out and bought E.J. a Bible. It is a nice one and cost 1/9. Ewart says he supposes when he comes up to Manor Park he will see my hair taken right up.

Saturday Ewart said 'Goodbye' and that is all I wish to write, as memory will not fail for the rest. As I went to walk away something happened, I will not write what. Sunday went to Chapel I could not sing a note, for a most tremendous lump seemed to form in my throat and I am sure they chose all the miserable hymns. In the park on Saturday I made up my mind to serve God and I hope Ewart has done the same.

Mother went to see Aunt Amy and found her nearly starving, children filthy and husband not caring a bit. On Saturday Daisy and I came straight home and did not go out again, but put my boxes in order. Mother and Daisy went up to the library and Dad to see Auntie Amy. He with the father-in-law went all round in search for a Parish Doctor. Sunday I went to Sunday School. It was exceedingly hot and I had such a bad headache. Dad, who has commenced his holidays, proposed that we should go to Clacton. I am pleased we are to go, though expect to be very lonely, having no one to go with. Must grin and bear it I suppose, though I do wish Ewart was here. I miss him more every day and quite get into a fever while waiting for letters.

19 August 1899

This morning, Mrs Robinson (our forewoman) began to show signs of being intoxicated, and very much so. She kept shouting and hugging till Mr Kinnear and Mr Edwards came up. Mr K. made some remarks about dirty bottles laying about, and she went on something dreadful to Mr Edwards. Said *she* would not clean bottles. Did her *dooty* etc. Dooty was about all you could hear; at last presently a summons came for her to go down to Mr Edwards. She was there a long time and when she came up she said she had received notice to go from next Saturday. She raved at Alice, Daisy and I more than at anyone. Said we should all go through it before she went. She felt inclined to send Mr Edwards through the window etc. From then on till we went home we heard nothing but Forewoman Dooty and Bottles. We shook when we met Dad at dinner time, he was shocked at the news.

12 September 1899

On Sunday went to School and Chapel in morning. Mrs Hummerton gave us a lesson on going with young men in the afternoon. She did not think it wrong, only we should be modest. Everyone looked at poor Ada. In the evening Mr Sunderland preached a very nice sermon on heroes and heroines. Last night when we got home Mother was rather out of temper. Saturday evening Mother said that if Daisy and I wanted new places we are to find them, as she will not have us at home.

25 September 1899

Last Monday evening went to Harvest Festival Meeting. The

fruit etc. is always sold after the meeting by auction and the money spent on poor people. We always liked to stop, it is such fun to watch the bidders. Thursday bad fire at a rag and oil place back of us. Girls tore about like maniacs. When I got home, found that Mr Sunderland had been round requesting me to read my paper at CE (Temptation). I was to sing as well.

16 October 1899

Did not have to work late after all last Monday. So was able to go to meeting of the British Women's Temperance Association.[4] Miss G. Collier sang and the speaker was a Mrs Jenny Walker. The meeting was very nice and Daisy and I joined the Association. When I got home Mr Moxham was there, having come to see if Daisy and I would like to work at a Cigar place he knew of. Wednesday we met Dad at the Bank and went to see this place. It was a new business, just starting, and we were to label cigar boxes. The only nice thing about it was the hours, which were from nine to six. Dad was mad for us to go, but on thinking it over Daisy and I thought it was jumping from the frying pan into the fire, and declined. No more sympathy from either Mother or Dad. On Thursday had to work late again; not a penny extra do we get. I had a letter from Ewart last Monday (best one as yet) and had to answer it in dinner hours as best I could. On Saturday caught train from East Ham and went to Hornchurch. Grandpa wants me to go down and work in office. Wages five shillings per week, board and lodging. I could come home on Sunday. Aunt Minnie is going be married at Christmas, that is how G.Pa is in want of an assistant. Do not like leaving CE, meetings etc. I am to think it over and let him know.

23 October 1899, 1 pm
City

On Friday Grandma came up with the news that Aunt Minnie has taken a house and will be married earlier than we thought. I am to go down there and Daisy and I gave notice on Saturday. Alice asked us to write to her and all the girls said they were sorry. Yesterday was our Sunday School anniversary. Mr Luther Hinton spoke, taking as an illustration a beehive and five bees. Bee just, Bee earnest, Bee self-sacrificing, Bee useful and Bee steadfast. Saw some soldiers on Saturday afternoon that are going out to war with the Boers. Hundreds and thousands are leaving and they say the price of everything will go up. They have put me on the Guild committee this year. The society is to be called Literary instead.

31 October 1899, 2.20 pm
Hornchurch

Yesterday morning I arrived here about 9.30 am. Grandma got me a nice hot cup of coffee and a piece of cake, which I did justice to, being hungry. I have a good deal of time to myself, not getting up until 8 am and going to bed about 10 pm. In the afternoon there is very little to do. I am getting on alright. A great number of telegrams to send, which are sent through a telephone. I also receive a good number. Grandad wrote to Dad and said he was very pleased with me and that I would make an excellent clerk. Tom has been to CE and they brought forward the subject of taking my name off the register. The majority would not hear of such a thing, so it is to remain on and I am to send my texts.

10 February 1900

I feel very lonely down here sometimes. Three weeks ago, I went for the first time to the Christian Endeavour here, which is held on Monday evenings. There were about a dozen people present, and they mostly grown up. They repeated no texts, had no solos, and on the whole did not seem to take much interest in the meeting, as we do at home. On Thursday 8 February I went home and went with the others at home to the Teachers' and Elder Scholars' Annual social. I do not think I enjoyed myself better. Everyone said how well I looked and indeed I am getting quite fat. Dad was Master of Ceremonies and quite gay for him. We (Daisy and I) wore our pretty blouses, that Mother made us out of the skirts of our bridesmaid dresses, and she and Dad bought us each a nice pair of slippers to wear and to serve as birthday presents. Yesterday, as a damper on our enjoyment, George, Aunt Amy's husband, came to our house in rags. He ate as though starved and cried like a baby. He asked where was Amy and said he was going to be different etc. Mother was upset of course.

Saturday, 10 March 1900

This week has passed in much the same way as usual. Last Saturday evening Mother met me at Woodgrange Park Station. Dad did not get home till gone twelve pm. Some of the clerks were to work all night and part of Sunday. It is all to do with the taxes, which are to be raised on everything to pay for this war.

I have opened a banking account for Mother, she is to let me put one shilling a week by. I have not been outside the front door this week, so all has been very quiet. Am doing plenty of needlework, and this week made a start at Geography, which I never learnt at School. I find I am an ignoramus but will try to improve. Have now got £1-4-0 in the Bank, for myself, and keep Mother up with her shillings.

7 April 1900

Have just been reading back in my diary and am surprised at the difference between me, then and now. I think I was happier this time last year. But I must only complain in my book, as I grumbled when up in the City. Indeed, I would not go back, but what I miss are my friends, meetings and companions.

Saturday, 14 April 1900

Wednesday and Thursday arose as usual at six and went out with Jessie [Ruth's aunt]. Am feeling much benefit from these walks. Yesterday (Friday, Good) we had to get up at five, as Jessie was on duty at 7 am.

20 April 1900

I continue rising at six. These last days have been perfect. So warm and bright. Some girls have donned their white blouses already. I am reading *Babylonian Life and History* by E. A. Wallis Budge, MA, and *The Story of the Nation* (Chaldea) by Lenaide A. Ragozin The latter belongs to Grandad. Interesting though dry at first. I have, and always have had, a craving to be clever and to learn. Therefore I read these books. My ambitions may never be satisfied, thwarted by circumstances, but they remain in me. Naturally reticent, I seldom shew these feelings and am thought very discontented. I must read while I can.

21 May 1900

Great things have been happening since I made my latest notes. Last Sunday evening, we all went to the Forest Gate Chapel, to hear Joseph Hocking preach.[5] How shall I describe the beautiful sermon we heard ? I have never listened to anyone to compare with him. You feel that you cannot lose one word he utters. He quoted Lord Byron, Robert Burns and Ruskin. He also spoke of

Cecil Rhodes. How after the relief of Kimberley he made a speech about the wealth and grandeur of England, not even mentioning the orphans, widows and bereaved parents. The people stamped and shouted Hear! Hear! even though it was Sunday. We were all sorry when he had finished. This morning I had quite a task to get up White Post Lane. They are laying down lines for the electric tramway. The Boer report that Mafeking is relieved has been confirmed today. In London, the excitement was dreadful, we heard.

13 June 1900

June 6 being Whitsun I was at home. Daisy did my hair right up. It looked beautiful. Mother thinks I am too young to keep it up always so I have promised to keep it tied behind until the Autumn. May came and we went to Wanstead Park. The trees and everything looked splendid. We met Ernie Round who still slouches along.

On Saturday I arrived at East Ham 7.40 pm. I met Bertha and Grace who thought me very disagreeable. I was too. Tired out. After supper I went up to bed. When Mother came in to say 'Goodnight,' she anxiously enquired what was the matter with me, and losing control over myself, I commenced to cry. She repeatedly asked what was wrong, but I only said 'Nothing,' till she went away. I felt very small, as it is a very unusual occurrence for me to cry in front of *anyone*. Dad brought me a cup of tea next morning. In the evening Mother and I went to call for May, to go Church with her. Bertha had her hair up. The Minister endeavoured to explain the Trinity. I am no wiser than formerly. Highly amused at bow, kneel, and get up again.

Monday, 2 July 1900

Wet and miserable today. Very unlike July but harmonises with my present mood. I seem to get more dull and disagreeable inwardly every day, though I keep a smooth surface still. It is wrong to upset my Grandparents with a display of my evil nature. I commenced some weeks back to read a portion of the Bible daily. I began at Genesis, and intended reading it all the way through, but cannot make up my mind whether it is right to do so. That in a small way worries me, but no one can imagine how trying Grandma is, and Grandfather is so vulgar. If something nice would only happen.

Dad has proposed that he and Daisy should go to Southampton while Mother brought forward the Manchester project. Dad agreed to Mother and I going. Mrs Johnson wrote to Mother last week and said if I could go Ewart *would* be pleased.

The Grand Christian Endeavour Convention is being held at the Alexandra Palace this week. Delegates coming from all parts of the world, thousands from America. A young lady belonging to the CE down here has just been in and says the crush is shocking. People fainting away and no food to be procured. We all wanted to go but cannot afford to. I have a lot of needlework to do for Aunt Minnie this week.

21 July 1900
I read my diary from the beginning in the afternoon, and was shocked to see how foolish, frivolous and conceited I was in the days of long ago. It has been hot again; 88 degrees in the shade. On Monday it was 90. Grandpa came back last night and said it was dreadful up in the City; the Omnibuses had to keep stopping to get fresh horses, as the others would suddenly be taken so ill, that they could get no further. Most of them wore large straw hats and presented an amusing sight.

2 August 1900
Mother and I are to go to Manchester on Saturday. We catch the twelve forty train from St Pancras. The fare is sixteen shillings each and I have taken twenty five shillings out of the Bank. We shall come home next Thursday. Grandfather informs me that Manchester is a most doleful place and that I cannot expect to enjoy my visit. (Does he think I go to see the place?) Grandma says 'What an expense!' I take no notice of them however, but am just beginning to feel nervous over it.

13 August 1900
What a lot has happened since I last sat here at this table and penned the events of life. The morning to go to Manchester came at length. Mother and I got our luggage together and also some sandwiches to eat in the train. I wore my fawn dress and best hat. The feather in the latter was a great source of worry. There was no bother about getting into the train and off we started. The scenery was grand, especially about Matlock. The train reached Manchester Central at 7.40 pm. We got out and

looked round but could see no one. I then heard Mother say, 'There he is,' and on turning beheld her talking to the individual I had hoped, yet feared, to see. He looked very white, and far from well, and was also taller; but still it was Ewart. He took the bag, etc., from my hand and led us down Oxford Street to his home. Giddy and headachy from travel, I wondered whether he was disappointed or not. Whether I had grown plainer, and all manner of things. Mother chatted most complacently. Presently we turned into a narrow street, and down a little blind place where there were about four houses. Mrs Johnson was near one, and after warmly greeting us, took us in No. 2. I had not imagined quite such a small house. Only four rooms and a scullery, but it looked so comfortable and homelike. Mrs Johnson looked older and thinner but seemed very cheerful.

15 August 1900

Such a glimpse of homelife we had last week. Poor Mrs Johnson must have an awful struggle, yet neither she nor any of the children let a word of complaint drop. Nellie especially deserves praise, for needlework and long hours must seem hard to her after her dream of being a teacher. Ewart's opinion always seemed needed, and the children obeyed him just as they would a father. Tonight after dinner I put all my letters in order and numbered them. From Ewart I have yet received fifty-six. Just fancy! While I was doing this, which task lasted all the afternoon, Mother told me what Mrs Johnson said about Ewart and I. She said it was most amusing to see how Ewart rushed off every Sunday night to write to me. She had told him there was to be no engagement till he was eighteen, as we were both young enough to change our minds. Ewart said he would not change his. I felt rather dismayed to think I had been spoken of like that, such thoughts scarcely ever entering into my mind. Yet it proves that Ewart still cares for me, and I think I do for him more than I used.

Sunday turned out a beautiful sunny day. I went to Chapel in the morning and Mr Dunn preached. He was a staunch Radical, and Dad thinks he is rather inclined to Socialism. At Chapel in the evening the Rev. Dunn *almost* came up to Joseph Hocking. All he said was so startlingly true. He has seen much distress in Bermondsey, where he comes from, and told us some very sad cases.

I resumed my old duties here on Monday again, but am only

just beginning to settle down. I received yesterday morning the longest letter I have ever received from Ewart, with a piece of heather enclosed. I feel very dissatisfied with myself in every way. I do so want to be good and noble, yet my thoughts often dwell on such things as looks, etc. Mother said a short time back that I was plainer than I used to be, and the remark haunts me a little. It is for Ewart's sake that I want to be nice-looking, in fact he is seldom out of my thoughts. No one knows what an influence for good he has been to me, and is. With God's help I intend to crush every particle of wickedness out of my nature, and live a life worthy of the name of a Christian. It is very hard sometimes, I am so lonely here, but a thought comforts me. It is the idea that this is to train me for some work God has for me to do, and I must not complain.

22 August 1900

Ewart's letter came yesterday, and he said that an agent of his firm had recently seen Mr Johnson on the Manchester race-course posing as a bookseller. Ewart did not say much, but I read through the lines how much he felt it. I could cry when I think how hard their life is, and what trouble is always behind them, mocking their happiness and spoiling their brief moments of joy. I wished too, that I could write some comforting word, and overcome my reserve and pride. After a long struggle I managed after writing the ordinary letter, doings of the week etc, to say: 'I am very sorry indeed to hear that your Mother has heard anything to upset her. More sorry than I know how to express. It is very hard to forgive, but your Father must suffer, while he has a conscience. Yours is a heavy cross, but you know where to go for strength. With love and sympathy. Ruth.' What a time before I could bring myself to write those words, which read so bare and cold, and yet my heart aches, and has done so ever since I received that letter. It should be natural to be sympathetic but to me it is more often an effort which ends in failure. I do try, oh so much, to be different. Mother said some time ago she thought I possessed no power of feeling; she cannot guess that each feeling that comes to me is deep, even my loves are painful. May's friendship has helped me a great deal, but I have much to fight against. I should not care for anyone to see this, it is quite sacred to myself and I could not tell anyone what I have just written.

31

Saturday, 15 September 1900

I have been thinking how nice it would be, if I could go to some evening classes this winter. I have been up and about with Jessie each morning this week and the weather has been splendid. Jessie went to Earl's Court Women's Exhibition yesterday. I stayed in and scrubbed the office floor this morning. I still feel far from well, my teeth are so bad. Ewart also has been ill, with inflammation of the lungs. I am going to try to be better-tempered. I think that, and a habit of dwelling on the past, is a great deal the cause of my indispositions, such as they are. I am getting quite a skilled hairdresser.

Saturday, 29 September 1900, 3.00 pm

Very busy week, in telegram way. Coming election rendered it especially so. Louis Sinclair is the Conservative candidate and Lionel Holland is the Liberal. Jessie stayed at Aunt Minnie's all week. It has been dull without her. I went for a solitary ramble Thursday morning having risen at six. I got back in time to sweep and tidy kitchen, and go into office at nine. I am reading *Pickwick Papers* by Charles Dickens, which I rather like.

Monday, 8 October 1900, 3.00 pm

I was so very busy last week that I could not find time even to come to my diary. The coming election gives us such a lot of extra work, and I felt tired out each day. As a rule I do not like to keep a record of family jars, but this one concerns myself and I have no one to speak to at all. The Saturday before last when I arrived at East Ham Station May and Mother were awaiting my appearance. I had made up my mind to be good-tempered, and do them all good. We talked about the election, the different candidates, their merits and failings as shown by the daily papers. May said Goodnight at our gate. Just before tea the trouble commenced. Though I had kept control so far over my bitter temper, I had noticed how Mother took up and miscon-strued the meaning of my remarks and Daisy always helped her along. At last while setting the tea table, I exclaimed, 'I believe there is a conspiracy between you two. You must think over, during the week, what you can say against me on Sunday.' No need to utter another syllable. Mother did go on at me. At last I took up a book and went into the parlour to read. Dad came in, and we sat down to tea and Mother began to cry. Dad looked first at her, then at me. He then said, 'Have you been upsetting your Mother again?' I had no answer and Mother burst forth in a whole torrent of my misdeeds. How ungrateful I was, etc, etc. I sat with my lips closed until upstairs I went.

Then I could hear Mother giving vent to her feelings. Impelled by curiosity I walked to the top of the stairs and listened. I, who generally loathed the idea of eavesdropping. I heard Mother say, 'Going away and coming back in this temper. The worst of it is, that when she is disagreeable with me, she is to everyone else.'

'Yes,' I heard Daisy's weak voice reply, and that one word of hers did me more harm than anything else. What had I done to Daisy, that she should help keep open a breach, which she might have tried to smooth over. I crept back, got into bed, and covered up my head with the clothes.

15 October 1900
Jessie noticed there was something wrong when I arrived back at Hornchurch, and glad to unburden my mind, I told her every word that has been uttered by every party, sparing no one. On Tuesday Jessie informed us that she had paid Mother a visit. Mother did not tell her anything, except that I was uppish, came home in awful tempers, that she would not put up with. She also said that they slaved for me all the week and I scarcely thanked them. Jessie said that she told Mother it was all nonsense, and that the work here was very hard.

On Wednesday all went well, till the results of the election became known, leaving Sinclair with a majority of 3,062 which surprised everyone.[6] Grandfather was having his sleep when the rush of telegrams of congratulations came pouring in. I managed to keep afloat until just before 4, when I had to give in and wake Grandfather. A torchlight procession, band and tar barrels paraded the village.

Saturday evening it poured with rain as I went home. But feeling restless and finding no one at East Ham to greet me, I went for a walk then wended my way home. Daisy opened the door in answer to my knock, and did not say a word of greeting. I walked into the kitchen and found that they had finished supper. Mother said, 'So you've come home in the same spirit', and finding she received no answer, repeated the question. 'How did you think I was coming?' I asked. Then the combat began. I said I was not going to give in where I did not think I was entirely in the wrong and Mother replied that no matter

33

what she had done, or if she was the worst Mother on the face of the earth, I had no right to behave as I did and that it was always the children's place to give in. I sat down and leisurely ate my supper. No one then spoke to me except Tom. On Monday morning I dressed as usual to come away. Dad came and kissed me before he went out and said, 'I hope you will come home in a different spirit next week.' Without a thought I answered, 'I shall not come home any different, you only know one side of the case.' Mother called me wicked and a whole host of hard names, concluding with the remark that I had better keep away altogether and not come home at all. Utterly wrought up I said that I would keep my money then. 'Keep your money', was what she answered, and out I came. At dinner time I could not keep in a few tears.

Monday, 22 October 1900, 2.00 pm
I am sorry I have to again record quarrelsome words. But now it is so lonely with no one to speak to that to write things is sometimes a relief. I went home by my usual train on Saturday. After treating me to a prolonged stare, Mother said, 'Good evening Miss Slate', and bowed mockingly. At last I mustered up enough courage (or as Mother would term it, impudence) to ask whether in future I was to keep myself, or go on as we previously had done. 'Please yourself, I want nothing more to do with you', was all she would say about it, but she went on at me more than ever, and I am afraid I answered back much that I should have left unsaid. Mother said I was a thoroughly bad, hard hearted and wicked girl, and that my bad nature was stamped on my face. She said that she saw people looking at me in amazement.

As a grand final, she said I was utterly without affection or feelings, like Grandma Bond [Ruth's father's mother] and a she-devil. This has cost me something to write, but I feel so very strange and unlike myself. Because I stood like a statue without displaying feeling, did that prove I had none? This morning I placed my money on the table, with the exception of one shilling, which I said I would keep toward my jacket. There is always a dreadful struggle when we want anything new, and I thought by saving that way to make it easier. As usual, she put another reason to it, making me appear selfish and calculating, where I had thought but of her. She seemed to think I was afraid I would not get a jacket. I left without saying any more and was beset with questions directly I reached here. I avoided answering as many as possible as I do not like taking things out from the circle of action.

Friday, 2 November 1900, 3.30 pm

On Saturday with various feelings I knocked at the house door. Judge my astonishment when Dad opened it, and greeted me most affectionately. He got my supper ready, for all the others were round at the Chapel attending a concert. We had been seated some time before the subject was broached. Little was said, and Dad did not grumble at me at all, guilty as I was beginning to feel. He said Mother was often very aggravating, but like him, I must learn to give and take. I stared at him in amazement, for I had never heard him say one word like that about Mother before. He then said that when the others came home, I had better open the door and kiss Mother. I sat and pondered the matter over, and concluded that if I did, it would be for Dad's sake only. It was late before I heard the dreaded knock, and went in answer. There was no need for me to do anything, for Mother bent forward and kissed me. I felt glad all was serene once more, and it was late before we got to bed.

I must not forget the Evening Classes that began on Monday. I obtained Grandfather's permission to go, and at seven pm, set out. Arrived at the School entrance some minutes before I could summon up enough courage to venture in. The number of ambitious students including myself was eight. The fees are to be two pence a week, and the lessons, on Mondays drawing, composition and arithmetic, on Wednesdays, drawing, bookkeeping and mensuration. On Wednesday there was an improved attendance of 24, the village policeman bringing up the rear.

Monday, 31 December 1900, 2.45 pm

Here I am, on the last day of the last year in this century. We were nearly at our wits' end getting ready for Christmas, and the endless number of parcels, letters and telegrams seemed wonderful. At last I was free to go home.

Christmas morning dawned, fairly bright. Daisy and Dad went to Church, while Mother and I cooked the turkey, mince pies, etc. The postman brought a budget of letters from Manchester, McDowells and other friends. May and Florry came to tea, and we spent a pleasant if quiet evening round a big log fire. I felt particularly cheerful, with Ewart's letter in my pocket.

35

This morning I came away here.

This evening, to please Grandma I went to bed quite early. I was wakened by the village band, which paraded the street, and hearing through the wall our neighbour's clock strike twelve knew that the new year and century had begun.

5 January 1901

This week has been very dull, and I find it difficult to put on even a semblance of cheerfulness. We get busy in the office and I have given up Evening Class. Grandfather did not say anything, but I know he had a difficult task to cope with the work in my absence. This morning I got up at six, and went across to Aunt Minnie. The first thick frost this season covered the ground, and the trees and hedges looked lovely.

Monday, 7 January 1901, 2.30 pm

Last Saturday I went home as usual. It is proposed that we give a party and provide provisions and amusements ourselves of course. We shall have to get some boys to come. Dad thought the idea alright, when told, for really our soirees are very tame. In the evening Mr Sunderland preached on the needs of the new century.

I thought a lot about Ewart and made a resolution that I would in future be more cheerful. To not only bear my cross, but carry it patiently and loyally. Daisy had been to a party during the week and grown dissatisfied because she can not play or sing. So I am to commence and teach her to play, as far as I can, on Saturday evenings.

Tuesday, 29 January 1901, 2.30 pm

How much has happened since I last wrote in here. On Tuesday evening 22 Jan last at half past six , England's greatest sovereign Queen Victoria passed away. The papers are full of the late Queen's doings and saying, and the goodness expressed throughout her marvellous career.

The remains of the Queen will be carried through London on a gun carriage. Most places of business and shops will be closed, but I doubt if we shall. The order for all loyal subjects to wear mourning came into force yesterday, and we first of all went to purchase new black hats. I said I should like to see the great procession in which the Queen's coffin would be displayed, but Dad said it would mean being crushed to death, and so the idea

36

had to be given up.

Wednesday, 20 February 1901, 2.15 pm

Grandfather let me go home on Thursday for the social. The soiree did not commence till seven, and while I waited at home, I was musically entertained by the people next door. The Kinnears have moved, and some Salvation Army people reign in their stead. Judging from the doleful sounds proceeding through the wall, I should imagine they are caretakers for the army's instruments of torture, as we distinguished a cornet, trumpet, harmonium and concertina in that brief period. Arrived at the soiree. A good many old faces were present. The first part of the evening passed away in stupid games. On Saturday I disgusted myself and everyone else, and declared I would not spend another winter here. Poor Mother seemed very worried. Is it my duty to stay at Hornchurch or not, is the tormenting question which holds sway.

On Monday I came down as usual, and yesterday morning received Ewart's letter. Somehow I fancied it breathed weariness of writing, and I pondered as to whether I ought to tell him to give it up if he wished. But that he promised to do, before he left Manor Park, and my letters too have been rather distant. So I concluded to let it pass for a while, and strange to say felt very near to him tonight. We are having a lot of snow and cold weather.

Monday, 1 April 1901, 2 pm
Hornchurch

Little did I think last time I wrote what trouble would overtake me, and yet my heart aches so, that I can scarcely bear it. Grandma had cheered me very much, by telling me to ask May down on Good Friday, but a letter I received from Mother upset all. She wrote that Tom had had a letter from John Johnson [Ewart's brother] to say that Ewart was ill. We knew that he had been suffering with a bad cough, ever since last summer, but he had never said anything in his letters to make us think seriously about it. Oh the shock I had when I came to the following sentence: 'The doctor told Ewart that he had consumption.' It seemed, and still seems, impossible to me, but the agony is there still. All at home have been worrying too, and Mother wrote to Mrs Johnson. I have prayed constantly since I heard, prayed that he will soon be well and strong, and also that we may soon

37

see each other. I deserve all these punishments I know; for his Mother's sake, God grant that he will be restored to health.

Tuesday, 9 April 1901

I did not get Ewart's letter till rather late last Tuesday, and I saw to my great grief, it contained confirmation of John's tidings. He tried to write in a way to make me think it was very slight, but somehow the heavy feelings of depression would not be shaken off. The right lung, he said, was affected, but he was taking all kinds of medicine, and hoped soon to be well again. I answered the letter, when I was supposed to be in bed, and sat up till about twelve. I said all kinds of things, I have never before written, but I hope I did not overstep the bounds of maiden delicacy.

Monday, 15 April 1901, 6.30 pm.

Ewart's letter contained more favourable news, and he thinks he will be able to come up this summer. Last night I resolved not to be conquered by depression. Am I failing already? I do so want to be good, and instead of that I seem to get worse. But I will live in hope.

It was over a year before Ruth recorded any more 'doings and sayings', and then her entries were much less frequent. In May 1902, she wrote that 'nothing much has happened since I left off my diary last summer'. The writing, though, showed her to be busier, happier, and in a livelier state of mind, having left the isolation of Hornchurch for home and a new job in the City at Kearley and Tonge's (a well-known firm of grocers).

The anxieties about Ewart's health had abated, although on another holiday visit to Manchester in July she wrote that since she saw him a year ago he 'looked no better, and terribly thin'. She assumed he would get better though, and encouraged his plans to obtain a place with a firm in Egypt, 'where the warmer climate may cure him,' adding that this made her feel 'rather lonely, but there seems small chance of him getting better in Manchester'.

Her work at Hornchurch had stood her in good stead, for she had a responsible job as a clerk in the saleroom at 'K & T's' 'among the principals', which sometimes caused a 'deal of jealousy on the part of the other girls'. She stayed at 'K & T's' for the next 12 years. Thrown back into the activities of the Manor

38

Park Chapel, she had joined the choir, had been elected organist at the CE, and was taking a Sunday School class. Her diary, for the moment, was less a place where she confided her private thoughts and troubles, than somewhere to jot down a few significant events.

On 30 May 1902, Ruth mentioned Eva for the first time. Eva had just moved to Manor Park with her grandparents, William and Emma Slawson, who had brought her up as their adopted daughter. (Eva was the illegitimate child of their eldest daughter Mary; she had some contact with her mother who had married a Mr Gallop and had two more children, Gertie and Cecil).

Ruth wrote that because of an argument with the minister at the Chapel, her father wanted her to leave the choir, but, she wrote, 'I want to think it over first. Last night I had to go, because I had promised my friend Eva Slawson ...'

On 3 June, she 'met Eva Slawson at Bow Road Station, and together we went to join a class for shorthand and typewriting. Eva is a shorthand typist, but she wants to improve speed, and I want to learn altogether.' When Ruth gave a paper at the CE on 'Eden and its inmates', 'in fear and trembling,' she wrote, 'Eva Slawson took the chair, and felt nearly as nervous as I did.'

Almost a year later, after another break in the writing, she reflected on her work, her developing friendship with Eva, and her increasing feeling of optimism and interest in life.

23 March 1903

This is the third day of spring and quite warm and beautiful enough for a summer one. We have been very quiet since Christmas. I suppose we must not expect every year to be as eventful and exciting as 1902 was. I am still working at Kearley and Tonge's, and though it has a bad name throughout the City for overworking its employees, I manage to get on very comfortably there. There are now other girls besides myself in the saleroom, Miss Panting, Miss Williams and Miss Cook. They are wonderfully nice, sensible girls, and we get on famously together. We have some rather hot arguments occasionally, on subjects religious, political and social, and it is strange, but somehow we do not seem to agree on any one point. May is still my staunch, trusty friend, but I am rather afraid that a young man is about to appear on the scene. What shall I do then? Eva and I are also great friends. She has an uncommon character, and I think sometimes will become a writer or something great. I suppose being with elderly people, and having made so few friends has helped her to make her so staid and grave, but she has such lofty ideals and noble thoughts that one cannot help liking her. Somehow I have felt happier lately. I feel like a child just awakening, and longing to know all the splendour of God's earth, and to do my little to help others to believe that everything good is not dead, and that it rests largely with themselves as to whether their lives are things of triumph or disappointment.

Ruth's optimism, however, was short-lived, for at the end of May, Ewart's health suddenly deteriorated, and she suffered the unexpected shock of his death. With her mother she made a frantic journey to Manchester and helped to nurse Ewart through the final harrowing stages of consumption. The disease was widespread at the turn of the century, particularly affecting the poor working-class communities. Later Ruth recorded the experience.

Wednesday, 17 June 1903

What a long dreary time it seems since I last made any note in my diary and what a lot has happened since then. How can I write that Ewart is gone where we shall see him no more in this life, or express the gnawing lonely pain at my heart. Sometimes I feel it cannot be true. How often do I find myself making mental notes of things I think interesting for my next letter, or find him creeping into my dreams of the future. It seems to me that I can never get used to the idea, that I have not fully realised my loss. But I want to have a written record of all that happened as far as possible.

On Saturday, 23 May, a letter had come from John to say that Ewart had been taken suddenly ill. On Tuesday 26th, on getting to Manor Park Station I found Mother awaiting me. She had come to tell me a telegram had been received saying 'Come at once, won't last long.' I never wish to go through such a journey again. I could do nothing but think and think, and pray God to spare him if only for a time to say Goodbye.

On the morning of that day Ewart had asked his Mother, 'Aren't I going to get better?' And she had to tell him she was afraid not. After being quiet for a few minutes he said he would like them to send for me, and for some time had asked repeatedly 'Have they come?' 'Have they come?'

When we were taken up to see him I could feel my heart going thump thump thump. Mother went first to the bedside, so giving me time to attempt to steady my nerves. He was lying propped up a little on some pillows, and I saw how changed he was. For the first time since I had known him, I stooped and kissed him of my own accord. Somehow it all seemed so sudden to me, I could not grasp it properly and when they shut the door, leaving me alone with him, I felt I could say little for the choking feeling upon me. For a moment he looked at me, then said with an effort, 'Has Mother told you, Ruth?' and upon my saying 'Yes', took my hand and told me oh so gently not to fret. 'I had hope things would be different' he said, 'but it is not to be.' Then he went on to speak of the happy times we had spent together in Wanstead Park before all this trouble came. I shall never forget him saying that if people who love each other very much are always near one another, we should never be far apart.

The next time I went into the room, Ewart was asleep, and then I saw fully, with a sudden pang how strangely different he looked. His eyes were half opened and he made a strange sound every few minutes, caused by the difficulty he had in breathing. He never slept for long, seldom more than ten minutes. They told us he was different altogether after we came. I was seldom out of the room, and as I found it impossible to eat, had an egg and milk or cup of tea up there. He noticed it so whenever I was out of the room and seemed more peaceful when I was there. Sometimes as we sat watching, Ethel [Ewart's mother's friend] would tell me what Ewart had so bravely withheld from his letters, how he suffered during the winter. She told us of the struggle they had had, and the insufficient food with which they had to content themselves during the first few months after their return to Manchester. Ewart himself said, if it had not been for the kindness of his fellow workers, he would not have been able to keep at work so long.

That night Mother and I sat up, and it was the best Ewart had spent, for he dozed on and off all through the night. I seemed unable to keep my eyes off him, each time he opened his own, they met mine. But through that night I had a hard, hard struggle for composure. I can see it all now. The small room and big bedstead in the middle, and Ewart's white face propped up on the pillows. The gas was low to keep the light from hurting his eyes. He seemed to be gradually sinking away. Mrs Johnson was crying and I felt it impossible to control myself any longer.

41

The tears came rolling down my cheeks and I tried to hide them, but it was useless, Ewart had seen them and said so gently 'Don't cry, Ruth.' That made me worse and it was only by nearly choking myself that I kept from sobbing aloud.

Mother and I sat with him all through the next day. He was constantly bringing up some nasty brown stuff, and needed someone to hold him and raise his head all the time. Mother did it nearly all morning and then I took her place. It was wonderful how thoughtful he was, each time I moved the towels or wiped his mouth, he always thanked me. He said that he had not said anything to me, he did not think he had a right to, but he should not like me to keep single all my life through him. He then kept repeating 'whatever she does is right, whatever she does is right' and 'Poor Ruth'.

Later he grew more restless. Together we had to move him almost every minute, but nothing seemed to ease him. He could only speak with great difficulty, and sometimes the words seemed to be shouted out in his efforts. It was agony to watch him. I sat as on the previous day, propping him up with my arm and we had to listen while he rambled on all sorts of subjects. Suddenly he almost shouted, 'Aren't you coming Ruth? If we don't go to this exam there won't be another, oh you can't mean to say you don't understand, Ruth.' Those were the last words he said, and he sank back exhausted. He began to gasp. While I stood there right in front of him, warned by Ethel's fingers not to move, though longing to get closer if only to hold his hand, he passed away. A cry went from me – I could not have stopped it.

There was still much to be done and I felt it was better to leave the room. Presently they let me in and when I saw how lovely he looked and what a beautiful smile was on his face, I felt that truly he must be 'resting in peace'.

2

'Better for an Exchange of Confidences'
July 1903–December 1904

Ewart's death was a setback for Ruth, for as well as being the loss of a friend, it plunged her back into a conflicting set of intense emotions that were difficult to resolve or express, given her usual home difficulties and constraints. The attempt to keep outwardly composed and accept it all as God's will caused 'times of agony'. It was Eva who provided a welcome, unstinting and new kind of sympathy and support. They soon became devoted friends, keeping in close contact when Eva moved away to Leyton.

As well as understanding each other's emotional difficulties, they shared the longing to do more fulfilling work. (Eva had become a secretary in a solicitor's office in Walthamstow, where she stayed until 1915.) While they earnestly envisaged 'noble unselfish work', 'heroic deeds' and 'lives of service', for which they would be rewarded for doing good, they nevertheless encouraged each other's interest in reading, studying and developing ideas. They also began some practical work in their own community by teaching Emma, a disabled child. Eva, who had left her grandparents to live with her mother's sister, her 'beloved' Aunt Edie, had a freer home life than Ruth with less demands on her time. She was an avid reader, and suggested that she and Ruth discuss books in their letters, often sending her pages of edifying quotations or full-length reports of inspiring sermons she had heard (all painstakingly copied by hand). One, which she thought Ruth would like, stated that 'we should reasonably conclude that Jesus encouraged a certain freedom for women and independence in the conduct of women, such as would excite criticism in the present day'. Ruth's and Eva's encouragement of each other, and their genuine ambitions for one another, were to be enduring features of their relationship.

In May 1904, almost a year after Ewart died, Ruth reported in her diary that a Mr Walter Randall had taken an interest in her, and despite her reluctance at first, by the end of the year she had decided to be 'friends' with him. This began a long and complicated relationship.

In July 1903 Ruth confided to Eva her deepest feelings about Ewart's death.

Ruth to Eva   13 July 1903

When I promised to tell you everything on Friday evening, I knew it would have to be a written account, for it is *impossible* for me *always* to speak of my deepest feelings. I have been going to write for some time, I guessed you thought me a little strange, but do please try to understand me now. I have been feeling that terrible 'Aloneness' peculiar to reserved natures like my own and I know that even at home here they do not know what to make of me. The subject of Ewart's death is a closed one, and I am thinking Mother is rather afraid of me.

Somehow I never could speak of my feelings even to her and the moment anyone commences to make advances I seem to shrink into myself. I think though, if I saw anyone suffer in a like manner, I should be able to overcome this peculiarity, and fully sympathise with them. Some lines of George Eliot's have been ringing in my ears: 'May I reach that highest heaven, be to others the cup of strength in some great agony.' I wonder will that privilege ever come to me. We can never really understand another's grief unless we too have been through the deep waters. You can scarcely know all that Ewart was to me. It is six years and over since we first knew each other. Then we were quite children and it was not until their great trouble through their Father that we grew so necessary to each other. You know how we corresponded each week and what a comfort those letters were, quiet and simple as they were. It was a great blow when Ewart found out he was consumptive. The idea of him ever being other than the model of health and strength had never occurred to me. Just think only three months ago or even less than that, if anyone had told me Ewart was going to die, I should not have believed them, so firm was my idea of his getting well and strong again, as indeed was his own. When the letter came telling us it was hopeless (just after a cheerful one from Ewart himself), I felt petrified. When you hear of people being taken without warning or time to say farewell to their

44

loved ones, have I not a great deal to be thankful for? I was able to help and soothe him during those last few days and we managed to say a good deal. He always said my influence for good over him was very great and I know that I should have been very different if I had never known him.

I am beginning to think more calmly of what has happened, though at times it still seems strangely unreal. I have tried hard to be bright and cheerful, for have not people enough sorrows of their own without me adding mine?

But I shall be wearying you soon, and I want your advice. Do not think what I am about to tell you is a new idea for it is not. I should like very much to be a nurse. I want some occupation where I can serve others. I am sure I should be happier. When I was little I always used to say I should be a missionary when I grew older, and I think this is the same wish modified. Do you advise me to see a doctor and ascertain whether I am strong enough before I go any further? I am inclined to think it would be wisest. I should like to live a noble self-sacrificing life, and without any conceit, I think I am able to endure a good deal. You must not let any thoughts of me disturb your holiday. Come back brown and well. This is intended for your eyes only. I know you like to show your Auntie everything, but please do not give her this. Tell her, if you like. I am unable to write any more now. I remain your loving friend, Ruth.

Ruth's Diary   12 August 1903

There is just a little to record since last I made any entry here. On the Sunday before last I saw Eva again after her stay at Yarmouth. We had a nice walk and talk together after the Evening Service which did me a great deal of good. She spoke to me so nicely about Ewart. I gave her one of my photos, which she liked, but did not think was good enough. We talked about many serious things. About my wish to be a nurse for instance. She is rather afraid I am not strong enough, and I have some fears myself. Ever since our return from Manchester, Eva, May and the girls in the City have been telling me I do not look well, and have told me I should see a doctor, but I think I have been worrying a little too much and will soon be alright again. After tea, as we sat resting our weary feet, the topic of conversation somehow turned upon religions. It is really wonderful to hear Eva speak, she is so very clever and has such an impartial way of looking at things. I felt freer to speak when it was to Eva only

45

and we told each other of the different doubts and fears which at times had come over us. I feel that it is a great honour to me to have such a friend as Eva, for I know she is much better and nobler than I. She has said the same of me and I was so surprised and shall I say pleased, but I am sure she has the nobler nature.

One evening I went a long long walk alone in Wanstead Park. The sky overhead was black and threatening and whichever way I looked I seemed to be utterly alone, for it was not an evening many would have chosen for walking. The wind rustling through the branches of the trees made a weird accompaniment to my thoughts. I was thinking of Ewart and the great influence for good he exercised over me. I walked home trying to see more clearly that God's will is best and fixing more deeply in myself the determination to be better, stronger, sweeter and more self-sacrificing. For some days the feeling kept with me and then the old spirit of rebellion and unrest returned and has not really gone yet. I have lain awake thinking bitter thoughts and saying to myself, 'It is hard and cruel', and at times, oh it seems too wicked to write even, longing to die gently and silently to myself. These thoughts seem to come in spite of me and cause times of agony.

Ruth's Diary   Monday, 17 August 1903
Yesterday was a most eventful day for the Chapel. Mr Ratcliffe, our long looked for new Minister, preached his first sermons and they were splendid. I am afraid though, that many of the extremely matter of fact, practical Chapel folk will think him too poetical and dreamy. I went home to tea with Eva after school. We had plenty to tell each other and plenty to talk about. Eva was some years ago a servant in the Duke of Westminster's house, her Grandma thinking that kind of work the best for girls. But it did not suit Eva and made her so ill that she had to give it up and as they were better off then, she was able to learn typewriting and shorthand and became what she is now, a typist. She has been wondering if she had remained in service she could have earned more to help her Grandparents now they have such a task to make ends meet. I told her then how I had been worrying in the same way about ever leaving Hornchurch, and offering to go back, and we had to laugh to think of us both having done similar things which had cost each of us great efforts. We are beginning to find we have many feelings and thoughts in common.

46

Ruth to Eva   20 August 1903
My dear,

Many, many happy returns of your birthday and I hope you had plenty of presents and will not think mine a very foolish one. I wondered for a long while what to give you and knowing you had several picture postcards, I thought you might like an album for them. Hence my choice! You will be thinking too what a foolish girl I am to be writing now when I shall be seeing you this evening and tomorrow as well, but I think you will bear with my peculiarities. I want to ask you once again to forgive me for worrying you last night with the details of my Hornchurch life. I want you to know, Eva, that I am not half so noble and splendid as I can see you are and promise to be, so you must not get disappointed in me for I value your friendship very, very much and feel that it is something for which to be grateful. I like to hear you express your thoughts, mine seem so crude and half-formed. I feel already that it is easier for me to tell you things and I shall be better able to soon, I hope.

   Your Loving Friend, Ruth.

Ruth's Diary   Saturday, 22 August 1903
This week has passed quietly without anything of great importance happening. On Wednesday evening Eva and I went a long long walk, first as far as Ilford and then turning round by Cranbrook Lodge and Wash into the long country lane. We told one another of the religious troubles we had met with. I told Eva how troubled I used to be because I had never felt any great change, like the people in the books are supposed to feel. I had never cried for days and called myself a terrible sinner and then suddenly felt I was 'Saved'. When I was little, that used to worry me and I felt that something was wrong, but that has gone now. We told each other of the strange ideas we used to have of things we ought to do, such as trying to 'Convert' those around us and telling others we were 'Saved'. These notions on my part were nearly all derived from books and Eva's from very much the same source. We laughed together as we went, but felt better for an exchange of confidences. This afternoon Eva, May and I are going to the British Museum. Miss Panting and the other girls are laughing at me for wanting to go so much and Mother said this morning, that Eva and I would be kept there as examples of imprisoned angels, compelled to walk this earth, though with unwilling feet. It was scarcely kind of her to be so sarcastic.

47

Ruth's Diary   Wednesday, 20th October 1903

What a long time it seems since I wrote anything in my diary. So much has happened that I have almost forgotten. I have had the four days remaining to me from my fortnight, and the rest did me good. The good done me by those few days of recreation did not last very long, and a few weeks ago, after being admonished by friends and relatives, I went with Mother to the Doctor. He said my circulation was very,very bad indeed, indeed ejaculations of 'dreadful, dreadful' freely mingled themselves with his remarks. He said I should massage my legs for an hour every night and morning as they were inclined to swell. He seemed horrified when I told him I had 96 stairs to run up and down several times a day and half suggested a change of employment. I asked him one time if it would be advisable for me to join some evening classes this winter, but he was emphatic in his disapproval, and said I should simply be killing myself. I am taking his advice and am only going to Evening Class on Wednesdays. It is a grammar and literature class held at Latham Rd Board School, East Ham.

I am giving up the choir for it seems almost impossible for me now to get up in front of the whole congregation when so much reminds me of Ewart. Mr Ratcliffe charms me as much as ever. After his sermons I feel like a new creature.

A Saturday or two ago, May, Eva and I went to the British Museum. We paused with awe before Cleopatra's mummy. Some exquisite ivory work claimed our admiration, it seemed that the closer we looked at it, the more wonderful it became, and then the autographs of great writers and poets. I almost danced with joy when I discovered George Eliot's. May made us laugh very much in the Museum, she kept saying such quaint, practical things.

I have been reading one of George Eliot's books, *Middlemarch*. Her books are a great favourite of mine, there is so much food for thought in them. I want to get a Life of George Eliot and find out a little how she understood human nature so well.

Ruth's Diary   Monday, 16 November 1903

My heart is filled with such a wondrous calm, such a deep peace this morning! It seems that I am going to be useful at last, and I am so glad. Eva and I are to have a little class between us, one evening a week, where we can read and talk to some girls. I have a little deformed girl in my Sunday School class now. She is a dear little child. Her people are very poor and Eva wheels her to school in such a funny old bassinet perambulator. She is just nine years old. Eva goes to see her almost every evening and is teaching her to write, read and sew. She has to be very patient, for Emma Clover, that is the child's name, has scarcely any fingers on the right hand and has to use the left, which is also very deformed, for everything. I want to do some good oh so much, it is the only thing which brings true happiness I am certain.

Ruth's Diary   Monday, 11 January 1904
I have been struggling with my tears almost all today and have felt almost heartbroken now Eva has gone. Oh my friend, my friend, you little know how I shall miss you! Things have been getting worse and worse at the little baker's shop in Greenhill Grove where Eva has been living and at last they got deeply into debt and the old people have been obliged to make application for entries into the Baker's Almshouses at Leyton. In the meantime Eva and her Aunt Edie have gone to Leyton. Aunt Edie has taken a little general shop there and a flat. Eva's Aunt Priscilla has been taken to the Infirmary, from there I expect she will be removed to an Asylum. Eva felt her Aunt's going very much, she wished so much that they would have been able to keep her. Yesterday was a sad day. At School in the afternoon there were many farewells to be said and some of the girls begged Eva to write to them. I went to every service for I wanted to be with Eva as much as possible. Then, after the evening service, though it was a wet evening, we went a long walk together and had a beautiful talk. We *shall* miss each other. I have never known anyone like Eva and after Ewart's 'home-going' I seemed to cling to her and gained so much good from being with her. Today I have been very lonely. I am to go on teaching little Emma Clover and I feel the task will be a sacred one to me. On Wednesday I went with Eva and watched her as she taught and thought how gentle and patient she was.

Ruth's Diary   18 January 1904
On Thursday I went to the Teacher's and Elder Scholar's Soiree. We had some tableaux and to please the young lady who got them up, I took part in some. In the Three Graces I was 'Faith' and in another picture I was the 'Peacemaker'. In one or two of the tableaux, a young man named Walter Randall took

part with me. Some time ago I took rather an interest in him for the reason that I was astonished at Christmas time to receive a beautiful card from him. Since then numerous little episodes have occurred which have made me feel uncomfortable, but I hope he will soon forget all about me and see someone better to like. At May's Christmas Party he was there and seemed very willing to help make the evening pass enjoyably.

Ruth to Eva   19 January 1904
My dear,

You were right in supposing I was looking for a letter from you. I have felt so desolate without you, and your words, 'When we next see each other, do not seem ever so far away from me', have recurred over and over again to my mind. What made you say that? I feel that as long as I try to grow better and nobler, I shall always be near you, for you have helped me so. You seemed to come when Ewart died, and in your quiet way strengthen me. In looking back I am ashamed to think how little I deserved your companionship, for I was very self-absorbed, indeed I felt more numbed than anything. On Monday I had hard work to keep back the tears once or twice, as I thought of the loss I was experiencing and of the dreams I had been having of future pleasant intercourse and work you and I could have had together. Once I thought your going away showed I was not worthy of your friendship, but that mood has passed and I feel that we *can* always be friends. I am right am I not? I shall be wearying you soon with all these plaints of mine, and I want to ask you before I proceed any further, Eva, do not be afraid to tell me about your troubles and difficulties. I know you usually keep them all to yourself and bear them in silence, but I shall know you indeed think of me as a friend if you confide in me some of your sorrows as well as your pleasures.

I do hope you will be very happy and comfortable where you are. It is sure to be strange for a little while, but who knows, before long you may meet a kindred spirit and do many heroic deeds ... I have a presentiment Eva (you will perhaps shake your head here) that you will be no ordinary woman when you grow up, but I know you will never forget those whom you have known and cared for. I am pleased to hear you think of coming to the Church 'At Home' as they are calling it, we must seize the precious chances of meeting now. You must tell me what you read. I am reading one of three volumes of the *Life of George*

Eliot by her husband. I have enjoyed it so far, but have not got really into it yet. I shall be thinking of you and know you will of me. Distance will not sever our friendship I am sure.

I remain your loving friend, Ruth.

Eva to Ruth   22 January 1904
                                        177 Albert Road, Leyton
My dear,

Thank you so much for your nice letter, it was such a pleasure and I felt brighter and better after it arrived. I do not think I quite realise the change in my life yet – you know Ruth, before we came to Manor Park we were living in Edmonton and I had no companion there and I think I grew to live very much within myself and at last I became very melancholy and morbid – it's painful to me even to write of that time. Then we moved to Manor Park and I came to the Chapel and grew to know you, and it has made oh, such a difference to me. Do not think like that about my going away, dear Ruth, oh, if only you knew me as I know myself (and I do not know myself as I hope to do), you might wonder whether I were in some respects worthy to be your friend. It has been good for me to know you Ruth, you have taught me lessons in self-control and truthfulness, although you may not have known this and I know it will strengthen me only to think of you when I am at all depressed and troubled. I do feel that you are able to understand my peculiarities (for so they would seem to some people) better than most.

You do not know, dear Ruth, how often I have travelled with you in thought all through that sad time last year, and how often I have tried to share your grief – I know I cannot fully understand and enter into it all – and I think sympathy sometimes gives one great power of understanding in a measure. You know that a new life is often only given to the world through pain and suffering and sometimes even by the loss of a life – may it not be that every loss and sorrow we experience will, if we will only let it, give rise to some sweet and noble new life – may not this be the meaning of sorrow and sacrifice? I hope Ruth, you will be able to understand my meaning.

Now Ruth, I must tell you I went to evening service at a Primitive Methodist Chapel last Sunday. It seemed so different, so many strange faces – I kept thinking of the Manor Park Chapel and missing it all.

Miss Richardson has lent me the first volume of *The Stones of*

Venice by Ruskin, and I am reading one of Aunt Edith's books, *Gertrude* by E. M. Sewell, which I like very much. We must have a little talk about the books we are reading in our letters, Ruth. I hope you will enjoy George Eliot's life. I too should like to read it.

About next Thursday, I am looking forward to coming, it will be such a pleasure to be together. And now really I must say 'Goodbye' until we meet, for it is getting late.

Your loving friend, Eva.

Ruth's Diary   Monday, 25 January 1904
We are having bitterly cold weather now, and I feel chilled mentally and physically. My hands are sore with chilblains, some of which are broken, and my brain is in a terrific whirl. I have had a beautiful letter from Eva, and it has stimulated my sluggish disposition to somewhat higher things, and I am grateful to her.

I feel better for having little Emma to teach, though Mother hurt my feelings very much with regard to her. I had thought she would understand how the work would take off in some measure the desolate feeling I experience without my friend. I only spend three hours of the week with Emma and the rest of my spare time is spent chiefly in Chapel work. But last week Mother was saying how little I did, especially to help her, and that I spent nearly all my time at the Clover's. If she only knew how willing I am to help her in every way – but it seems to me rather that my every effort is repulsed or attributed to some selfish motive. I have been wanting to tell Mother of my wish to become a nurse or, if I am not strong enough, to work among poor and afflicted people, but somehow my courage failed me, but I must not be such a coward.

I have thoroughly enjoyed what I have read of the life of George Eliot. But I am appalled at my own ignorance as I read some of her letters. Indeed I do not understand everything she says.

The meeting on Tuesday evenings of which Eva and I had expected such great things, has dwindled into an ordinary sewing class conducted by Mother. In November next we are to have an enormous bazaar at the East Ham Town Hall, which means hard work for everyone, hence our sewing class! Tonight I am going to Mr and Mrs Ratcliffe's 'At Home' at the Chapel and – *Eva is coming.*

52

Sunday was my twentieth birthday. Eva and May came to tea
and we spent an agreeable afternoon and evening. At eight
o'clock May, Eva and I went to the prayer meeting (to please
Dad) and I am afraid derived more amusement from it than
anything else, and really it was not to be wondered at. There
were about twenty of us seated around a table, and between the
prayers, we had Sankey's hymns. One lady, Mrs Wales, during
the singing of the hymns went through such contortions and sang
in such an agonised tone. Then the long pauses between the
prayers, made one feel almost hysterical and the creaking boots
and asthmatical voice of one old gentleman wrought one's
nerves up to an alarming extent. But we did really lose our self-
control when Mr Randall stood up and with much stammering
and gasping prayed for those who had 'backslid' or 'slidback'
and asked that 'fleshy hearts might be turned to stone', no, 'our
stony hearts turned to flesh'. A peculiar gurgling sound escaped
me, much as I strove to repress it and with feelings of shame I
acknowledged my relief when the meeting was over.

We have been enjoying such beautiful Springlike weather this
last week and if it were not for the worry I have been feeling
over Mr Randall, I should be feeling much calmer and in a
measure happier than I have been since Ewart's death. How I
dislike writing that word, and how my heart aches when I think
of the loss. It sometimes seems, even more frequently of late,
that I have grown morbid and terrified. Such a sense of shame
and depression comes over me when I think how wicked I am,
what displays of passionate temper and cruel cutting remarks
have been mine. In looking back it does seem to me that my life
has been a long series of follies and mistakes, and I wonder if
many at my age have sinned so grievously. I think first of all of
the falsehood I told when at School, from fear of my Mother's
anger. Then, when Daisy and I were up in the City, I made my
home miserable with complaints and fault finding. Further on,
my going to Hornchurch and the bitterness that consumed me
there. Oh how wrong it seems now! But in looking back on that
period I can see that it was not the hard daily trials that made me
most unhappy, it was the lack of home sympathy. I used to build
such fairy visions of home, and idealised it to such an extent that
the disappointment of the reality caused me much bitterness. I

hope I have learned some lessons from it which will always be useful to me.

Mr Randall has ventured to accompany me home from one or two meetings – I *do* feel so worried and vexed too, for I have had some very uncomfortable things said to me. The boy Randall (as I usually speak of him) has said nothing to me at any time beyond commonplace stuttering remarks on the weather or the sermon and yet every boy and girl in the school seems aware of his feelings. I wonder if he supposes I am ignorant. Last Sunday afternoon I was especially annoyed by some familiar remarks of Mr Smith's. He was wheeling Emma out of the schoolroom for me, when he suddenly turned round and said, 'How are you and young Randall getting on?' I think Mr Randall might have kept silent, if only out of respect to other people's feelings. Almost every morning for months past I have either met him on the way to business, or in Liverpool St. At first he used to rush frantically to a book-shop close by and gaze earnestly in at its windows. Was there ever such a nervous being? I do not know what to do.

Ruth's Diary   4 April 1904
I have enjoyed such a feast of Nature's beauty this morning that I feel impelled to write of it. Daisy and I, with little effort, jumped out of bed at a quarter to six and were soon dressed and out in the beautiful sunshine. Naturally we turned our steps Wanstead Park-wards and walked quickly across the Flats. The wide stretch of wavy grass, growing in peculiar little clumps and sparkling with dew, the delicate foliage of the newly-dressed trees, the beauty of the plantations, and the sweet warbling of the skylarks, impressed us deeply. We were soon nearing the Park Gates and where three or four years ago the ground was bright with cornfields and poppies, we saw red-brick villas standing, and the sight made me feel sad, perhaps a selfish feeling. Inside the park all was beauty and I thought, 'How glorious is this place!' We were soon back amid the busy haunts of men and away to our different occupations.

Ruth's Diary   24 May 1904
Last week passed very quietly, the sole exciting event being the commencement of spring cleaning, since when, before coming to business in the morning and whenever I can spare time in the evening, I have been surrounded with furniture polish, dusters

54

and pails of water. Now I feel quite sore and bruised with the unusual exertion. On Thursday I went up to meet Eva as usual and we had a nice walk and talk together. She is a little more at ease at her new place, at first she found it very difficult.

Yesterday morning Daisy and I went out over to Wanstead Park and enjoyed the quiet and beauty as much as ever. After dinner Dad, Mother and I decided to go over to the Park for a walk. Some very curious sights met our eyes. Hundreds of people flocked from Beckton and other places of stifling atmosphere, the electric trams making a now cheap and pleasant journey for them. Good-natured fathers and mothers, cross fathers and mothers, weeping children, laughing children in gay or ragged attire, all helped to make a very varied scene. At first I felt a little vexed that people should come to my loved Wanstead Park and defile it. Then I felt ashamed of myself and thought perhaps the occasion was a very rare one, when these hard-working and weary-looking men and women could come and gaze upon so fair a spot.

On Saturday afternoon, Aggie Fairfax [a neighbour] called, bringing me a paper on 'Heaven' to read. Before going she asked if I would go for a walk with Eleanor and herself on Whit Monday. After mentioning the request to Mother, I went upstairs and on coming down again was surprised to find her crying. I immediately guessed the cause was Eleanor's invitation and sat with a sore heart listening as she told me I was getting away from them all at home, going beyond my station and a lot of things too painful to dwell on. One remark especially painful was that I made friends with impossible affected girls, who wanted all the nonsense knocking out of them, like Eleanor and Eva.

Ruth's Diary   Monday, 24 October 1904
We were observing at breakfast time yesterday that it is only nine weeks to Christmas, and the year seems to have sped along. Of late, my life has seemed one rush, and the constant attempt to do impossible things has left me no time to think. I have been obliged to abandon all schemes of evening studies for a time, at least. It is just seven weeks today since Mother became really unable to do anything but what was absolutely necessary and she seems not a bit better yet. She has a varicose ulcer on her right leg and is obliged to sit on one chair all day with her foot up on another. Poor Mother! It is very hard for her to be kept in all

day; she has become so used to an active life. Daisy has taken over Mother's needlework for the Bazaar, whilst I have done the housework getting up at half past five or six and finishing on getting home in the evenings. I am getting quite fat and muscular, so the work must be doing me good. We could manage splendidly, but for this ever more closely impending 'Bazaar'. Already I, as secretary, have attended numerable Committee meetings of my own calling together, and have written receipts and business-like letters, visited wholesale toy-dealers in my brief lunch hour, made calls and arrangements, superintending sewing meetings until my brain is in a whirl. On Saturday we shall have a houseful of helpers, pricing goods and wrapping toys, whilst the following Saturday I expect will find us wearily murmuring how thankful we shall be when it's over.

Ruth to Eva   12 December 1904
My dear,
Just a few brief lines to let you know how often I have thought of you during the past week. I would have written sooner, but spare time seems to get more and more a rarity and I feel ashamed to think how seldom I write to you. And now Eva, how have you been getting on? I have felt so much for you and yet I can say so little without fear of hurting you. You are very brave in trying to bear all your troubles alone, but I have been thinking of what our favourite George Eliot says, 'until we know our friends' private thoughts and emotions we hardly know what to grieve or rejoice over for them', and Eva, it lightens burdens so much to share them with another, if that other is lovingly prepared to help. I shall not be able to come tomorrow, needless to say I shall be on 'Chapel' duties bent, but if Wednesday is convenient for you, I will come then.

There is something I must not longer delay in telling you, and I do trust it will not make even the least bit of difference to us. I thought long and earnestly about the matter and I do pray I have done right in promising to be 'friends' with Mr Randall. Something seemed to impel me to do it, I cannot explain how, and then he is so different to what I had, perhaps hastily, imagined. I trust I have done right and yet I am still always thinking of Ewart. I gave my promise a fortnight ago and fully intended telling you last Tuesday, but we had other things to say.

I must tell you all further news when I see you. I do hope you

will be looking better, and do talk to me *all* about *yourself*.
    With very much love, Ruth.

Eva to Ruth   December 1904
My dear,
A little note to wish you a very happy Xmas and a New Year full
of new joys, hopes and pleasant friendships.
    Thank you for your last letter, Ruth, and for telling me about
Mr Randall. At first I felt a wee bit as if I were losing my friend
but I believe that the bond between us is too strong to be
severed by any new or even dearer friendship. Keep a place
always for me in your heart, dear Ruth, I shall be all the better
for it. Your friendship with Mr Randall is, I feel, perfectly
natural and right, so do not worry about it Ruth – I quite
believe what you tell me of his character and disposition and I
think he is full of promise. You will never forget Mr Johnson,
but that is no reason why other love should not come into your
life, although perhaps never quite the same, for you were very
young Ruth, and although grief and love in youth are sharp and
strong yet I do not think they have the same power over us later
on in life. Time is a great physician and we can live down so
many things that at first we may have thought almost impossible
and although scars are left, yet wounds heal and we learn to be
happy again.
    You asked me, dear Ruth, to tell you my troubles and
thoughts: so many of the former are purely imaginary and so
many of the latter far from edifying, that I do not think it would
be right to be always dwelling on them. Still I feel I can tell you a
great deal, my dear Ruth, and will you not also confide in me.
    I hope all will soon be well. Write to me soon Ruth.
    With fond love, Eva.

Eva to Ruth   22 December 1904
I feel I must thank you again for the CE Hymn Book. I spent
yesterday evening and some little time on Wednesday playing
them over. In giving me this you have given me much pleasure,
Ruth. I expect we have not said all that we would to each other
lately, there has seemed so little time. One thing I must tell you,
I have lately read *Villette* and think it splendid. Lucy Snowe, the
heroine of *Villette,* is a lonely woman of about two and twenty,
and Charlotte Brontë vividly depicts her mental struggles and

57

sufferings. Have you been able to read at all lately? My present library book is *The Light of Asia* and I am pleased with it (on the life of Buddha – he being the light of Asia). What with this book and that book, this opinion and that opinion, Ruth, I really feel in a most confused state of mind. I think I am a wee bit wiser than at one time; I *used* to want all questions answered and difficulties smoothed away at once, but now I am more content to leave much to time and experience.

Oh to be wise! I have been feeling my mind is not nearly so large or so clear as I would wish – I cannot seem to grasp new thoughts as I wish. Have you ever felt knowledge to resemble a high mountain: one can see the summit but in order to view the surrounding country, how one must climb!

You are troubled I know at present Ruth – how difficult all these worries seem to bear sometimes, do they not? One feels so overwhelmed, I have thought sometimes: 'When shall I learn to live *only* in today, when cease to bear the burdens of tomorrow?' But it is just that which is so difficult. May there be a very bright lining to your cloud, Ruth, and the New Year be one of happiness and peace. Shall be expecting you Tuesday.

Your loving friend, Eva.

3

'Begun some Good Work'
1905

In 1905, a significant shift took place in Ruth's thinking. She became more aware of social conditions outside her own circle and saw more of the poverty that existed in the Manor Park community. By the end of the year, rather than being dissatisfied with herself, she was suddenly critical of the Chapel for not addressing itself more to outside problems.

Meanwhile she had become involved in the fervour of the Chapel's 'Revival', which provided an immediate outlet for her energies, and itself fostered some of the changes. In February the local paper reported that 'the religious Revival which commenced in South Wales, seems to be reaching South Essex generally ... ' Several of Nonconformist Chapels in Ruth's areas were holding special mission services, making instant conversions, and increasing their membership. Ruth's own Chapel decided to 'go out to the people', and combined their mission with a Temperance Campaign in the working-class areas of Manor Park. Temperance was a major issue in the nineteenth century, uniting all denominations. Pledges of abstinence from drink (which was seen as spiritually weakening) were made at the same time as the conversions. The campaign brought Ruth into contact with 'awful looking men and women', she wrote, 'such as I had never imagined lived in Manor Park'. She became aware that women were often the victims of men's drunkenness. The sense of moral superiority she showed at first towards her neighbours changed to a genuine social concern.

The extra Chapel activities, her developing relationship with Walter Randall ('Wal'), and her continuing home responsibilities, made it difficult for Ruth to keep abreast of her study plans with Eva (who was also undergoing some change), and she con-

cluded, reluctantly, that she 'must not aspire too much'.

Ruth's Diary   Thursday, 5th January 1905
Five days have gone by and I have not yet been able to re-
commence my diary, and I meant to be so methodical in the
New Year! I am glad 1904 is gone, it has seemed such a
stagnatory year to me. We awaited the birth of this New Year as
usual, at the Midnight Service. The service did not seem so
solemn and impressive as in Mr Sutherland's time, indeed to my
shame be it written, I slept soundly through the sermon and
dreamt of Fred McDowall and days gone by. The hand-shaking
and good wishes exchanged outside were enough to make one
adhere more than ever to good resolutions if one made any. Of
course Mr Randall and I shook hands and wished each other a
Happy New Year.

On the 12th of January, we held the Teachers' and Elder
Scholars' Social, and had some more tableaux. Mr Randall took
me home again. We had almost reached the gate, when he asked
me in nervous tones, whether I would go to the Albert Hall with
him the following Saturday. An alarming silence followed, but
at length I managed to muster up sufficient voice to say I would,
and then rushed in the gate and knocked at the door with
unusual vigour. I dreaded the approach of Saturday morning,
and as the time for leaving K & T's drew near I felt in my usual
foolish condition – nearly sick with excitement. However I
enjoyed it very much after all, it was such a novel outing for me.
It was a splendid band (Sousa's) and the music was pretty and
lively, but I do not enjoy that kind of music nearly so much as a
string band. Mr Randall had a pocket edition of *Adam Bede*
with him, and that led us to talk a little of George Eliot. On the
26th January we went to the Church 'At Home' and Daisy and I
agreed then and there that Socials are altogether a bore and a
waste of time.

The following Sunday Mr Randall came to tea. When he rose
to go, Dad amused and embarrassed me by looking at me and
saying, 'You go to the door.' Thus admonished I had to see Mr
Randall to the door and I shall never forget how pale he went,
and how difficult it seemed for him to speak, as he asked if I
would let him see me sometimes in the week. It ended in our
arranging Wednesday as an evening to be spent together.

Eva to Ruth   24 January 1905
My dear,
You will smile at receiving a letter from me so soon after our
meeting, but I have written asking if it would be convenient for
Emma to come to tea this Saturday. *Can* you manage to come?
It is so long since you took tea with us.

I do enjoy my French lessons. My last was taken in a room
with such a delightful bookcase in it – it ran the whole length of
one wall and contains many books. My present library book is
How to Become a Journalist by Ernest Phillips, but although I
like most of the work allocated to the reporter, I do *not* seem to
relish all allotted to the lady journalist, which seems to consist of
writing descriptive articles of dresses worn by distinguished
ladies at balls etc. (I fear I have no very good memory for the
names of trimmings), answering correspondence through journals (hateful task), and interviewing distinguished personages
which would, I think, be rather pleasant. But there seems a lack
of depth in it all somehow.

I think I'll come over to the Social, Ruth, perhaps we might
have one of our 'specially nice evenings', only I must not be
selfish. We do not seem to have talked much lately of books and
subjects which interest us both. Do not worry – I think all must
come right presently. Eva.

Ruth to Eva   28 January 1905
I have thought of you such a lot since Thursday, that I felt I *must*
write, if only a very little.

I am afraid you did not enjoy the Soiree very much: to me the
best part was our closing conversation at the station. It may have
been melancholy, but it soothed me wonderfully and I have felt
less restive ever since. Yesterday I had a good think about many
things, and it was then I resolved to write to you. I think I may
have told you how from my earliest years I have longed to study
and learn, how it has been my fairy dream often, and occasionally such dreadful moods overcome me, that I feel fit for no one's
company. I want to read and study, and yet at the same time to
be helpful at home, and spare Mother all the work I possibly
can, and between the two feelings I am often sorely vexed. You
know dear, how I should like to astonish you each Tuesday with
proofs of the week's diligence, and yet I seem at a standstill.

Mr Barnett preached on Sunday, such a helpful, comforting
sermon. I resolved after all that little offices of comfort and

61

cheer to those about us bring us more true happiness than all the knowledge could give. I do wish you could have heard the sermon for yourself.

There seem to be such stirring events taking place just now, enough I should think to move the coldest natures. First of all the War, then the Revival, and lastly this awful Revolution. How confusing it all is! I do believe though that when it is over (the Revolution I mean) it will be better for the poor, crushed Russian peasantry, if only all this suffering and misery could be spared.

I have been reading one of Rosa Carey's books. They are so refreshing, and full of sweet simple home life. In reading this letter over, I am ashamed to find it is all about myself. Enclosed is a little letter from Emma. She has only just commenced to write with pen and ink, and in the effort to excel herself has not done quite so well as usual. I am looking forward to the Saturday afternoon we shall spend together, and I know Emma is.

And now Goodbye until Tuesday next, when I hope my 'ego' will not be so much in evidence. With love from Ruth.

Eva to Ruth   *undated*
I have another letter of yours to answer, Ruth. I can so understand your wish to study – I think I shall always enjoy gathering knowledge and it is a special pleasure to impart it to others. But I do not think Ruth, our woman's nature will ever be entirely satisfied with this, delightful as it is: God has formed us for greater pleasures and joys, and although I am *very, very* grateful that the paths of learning are open to us (the wider the better) yet do I feel the great crown to a woman's life is not a successful career in a profession or occupation, not a coveted scholarship, title or prize, but the noble life of a wife and Mother, made great by spiritual and earthly wisdom. Still I am glad that for single women there are now so many varied occupations and all honour to those who fill them worthily.

In your letter you mention the 'Revival', Ruth, and it does seem wonderful. In her last letter to Grandma, Aunt Emily says she has heard a lady give her experience of one of the meetings conducted by Evan Roberts, and she said it seemed as though heaven itself must open and God come down.

I do also like Rosa Carey's book, Ruth. I have lately read *A Houseful of Girls* by Sarah Tytler. Last night I went to a

62

Limelight lecture on 'Essex' held in the schoolroom of the Chapel and I did enjoy it. I actually had the audacity to ask if I might have a class in the Sunday School – they expressed themselves *pleased,* and I was introduced to the Superintendent who asked me if I would mind a class of *boys.* Ordeal of ordeals! Imagine me, separated from female intercourse, adrift in a male Pacific; I am sure I don't know what my feelings would be. The lecture was very enjoyable and wound up with some nice specimens of coloured photography. Don't get *too* excited about the piano. Please remember me kindly to Mrs Slate and your sister. I shall be expecting you next Tuesday in a very delightful and exalted state of mind (not *me* but *you*) caused by harmonious melodies.

And now 'Goodnight'. Your loving friend, Eva.

Ruth's Diary   Thursday, 16 March 1905
I am still a long way behind with my entries but I think they come in better order now. On Wednesday 1st February Dad and I went to a Quakers' meeting in the lunch-hour, and found it a very curious experience. I had long wished to go to one, for since reading Elizabeth Fry's life, I have felt greatly interested in 'The Friends'. We met outside Devonshire House in Bishopsgate, and entered a fair-sized room plainly furnished, with a good many people (mostly gentlemen) sitting with bowed heads on low forms. For a quarter of an hour we sat, hearing no sound but the ticking of the clock. At length a gentleman went on his knees, and began to pray aloud, and immediately everyone else rose. Last of all a young lady spoke a few words on the nobility of work with a clearness and calmness I quite envied. They have no music or singing, except when an individual feels called upon by the Spirit to sing a verse. It was all very peculiar after our own bright meetings, yet I enjoyed it and felt the better for it.

On Wednesday 15th February I went to the Albert Hall with Mr Randall to hear the famous American Revivalists, Dr Torrey and Mr Alexander. We went on the top of a bus and the inelegant scramble to get up there over, I enjoyed the ride and the novel sightseeing. At the hall there were crowds waiting and we had to take our places at the end of the long line the police were keeping in position. I was amazed at the sight of so many thousands of people, and my brain was quite staggered to take in the size of the hall and its splendour. The singing was beautiful and everyone felt compelled to join in. The Glory

Song was sung of course.

On Friday the 17th February I met Dad after business, and we went to Moorgate Street to choose my piano. Dad, in a moment of daring, proposed a scheme to Mother, whereby they could purchase one for my twenty-first birthday, and they had paid part of the money before I knew anything about it. I was silent with surprise and joy, and then I began to think of the many things they could get for themselves for the money they were spending on undeserving me. I remonstrated with them but to no purpose.

The next evening, the 18th, we had a record Prayer meeting in preparation of a Mission we were starting, to last a week. Weeks before, preparations had been started for this Mission and Dad, as Secretary, had worried us nicely at home. As Mr Randall and I walked home from the meeting, I remarked that the Mission excitement must be contagious, as I was feeling quite excited myself. He replied that it had not affected him as yet, and then we shook hands and parted. The next day Mr Ratcliffe asked if there were any boys or girls who would like to stand up and so declare their young lives to Christ. A good many did so, among them three of my girls, and I felt singularly touched. I spoke to them after the close of School and tried to encourage them, though I do not know that I am altogether in favour of these methods with such young children. Before the evening service, I found myself joining lustily in what I had rather scorned the idea of, viz., a good 'sing' outside the Chapel from six to half-past. People looked astonished as they passed along the street, but an enormous linen poster told them what was about to take place. Inside we had a fine meeting.

Saturday the 25th, though, was the day of 'never-to-be-forgotten' events. The morning at business seemed unusually long and irksome, and I have seldom felt more pleased at the arrival of 1.30. Miss Panting [a colleague] and I met two of her friends at Vauxhall, from whence we walked to the Tate Gallery. I know Miss Panting had described me to her friends as somewhat of an oddity, born a century after my time, and at first I felt too awkward and constrained to enjoy the pictures much. On the whole we had a nice time in spite of my agonies of nervousness. I got home and arrived at the Chapel for the open air meeting and sung heartily till eight. About a quarter past ten, the Salvation Army came round, with their band, and we formed a huge procession, the longest of the kind ever before

64

seen in Manor Park, I am sure. We marched first of all to 'The Three Rabbits', singing as we went, and gazed at by crowds of amazed spectators, who thronged the paths and shop doors. The proprietor, evidently fearing the effect of our approach on his trade, had the lights put out, but nothing daunted, we sang from memory, and by the time we left there our numbers were swelled by some of the half or wholly intoxicated men and women. We marched on to 'The Earl of Essex', which was just closing, and from there the men came out and shouted 'Sing Onward Christian Soldiers', 'Sing The Glory Song', though many were swearing dreadfully. We sang one hymn after another, and as we marched away almost all our young fellows held someone by the arm, helping them along the road. It was getting late, so we could not stay long outside the 'William the Conqueror', but there the groups of awful looking men and women (such as I had never imagined lived in Manor Park) standing about, watching us half in wonder, half in derision, roused me fully, and dragging Daisy along with me, we broke away from the procession line, and going first to one and then to another, begged them to come to our meeting. Some laughed, some hesitated, and a good many *did* come in. We found the women hardest to persuade. One man, with whom we pleaded hard, said to me, 'It's no use you talking to me Sally, talk to our employers, them as overworks and underpays us, mate, talk to them.' Such a sight as that which met our eyes had never been seen in our Chapel before, and the change which had come over its dignified members was equally amazing. The smell of spirits was almost overpowering, and hymn books and sheets were receiving no gentle treatment, but what did it matter? The Chapel was packed and it seemed as though they would never tire of the music and singing. At the close of his address, Mr Ratcliffe asked if any would sign the pledge, and immediately a young fellow sprang up saying, 'I will', bringing from his pocket a bottle of beer, and putting it on the table. He was heartily clapped, and soon in ones and twos (for it was astonishing how one did as his companion did), fifteen went into the vestry and signed the pledge. It was almost a quarter past one am before they left. It had been a glorious meeting. I am glad we have at last begun some really 'good' work, but I am not sure what is the attitude of my mind towards missions.

Ruth's Diary   23 March 1905

I suppose I shall get up to date one day! Monday 27th February
was my twenty-first birthday, and a very happy one. I had some
nice presents. First of all the piano, then a splendid Teacher's
Bible from Daisy, Mendelssohn's *Song without Words* from
Miss Panting, a dressing bag, sound and strong, from practical
May, a picture from Eva, silver spoons, a brooch and salt cellars
from Aunt Minnie.

But the day had a sad ending. We were sitting quietly, about
ten o'clock, Mother and Dad had just come in from a Band of
Hope Meeting,[1] when there was a knock at the door which
startled us. Daisy answered it, and found Hebe a [neighbour's
child] standing with a white agonised face on the step. The next
thing we heard was a shriek from her, and then, 'Aggie's killed
Father – she's cut his head open with a chopper.' We got her
some water, and by degrees she grew calm enough to tell us how
her father had come home drunk, and was just going to cut his
wife's throat when her sister Aggie, to save her Mother seized a
chopper and struck him on the back of the head. He rolled on
the ground dead, as they thought, but the poor wife knew better,
and unaided bathed and bandaged the wound, while the others
ran terrified into the street. Hebe and a little sister came on to
our house. We sat up and felt so shaken that we could not sleep.
Crime and tragedy seem so much more real when they take
place close at hand. For days the man hovered between life and
death, and we hoped he would get better for Aggie's sake. He is
now almost recovered, and spends his evenings at 'The Earl of
Essex' with the woman who has been his undoing. It is terrible!

Ruth's Diary   Saturday, 8 April 1905

On Thursday evening I went up to Eva's, but we did little else
but talk. Trade seems a little brighter at the shop now and the
old people are very comfortable in their almshouses. Last night
Daisy and I went to a Mission Band Committee meeting, which
was not over till gone ten. It is going to mean working very hard.
I am in a very strange state of mind: I am drawn in many ways. I
cannot think it is right to spend so much time at the different
prayer-meeting and services. Surely there are home and social
duties! It seems one continual whirl of excitement and I cannot
think what is right. I am going to commence reading my
Pilgrim's Progress again today; perhaps I shall get some little
stimulating aid from that. At present, 'melancholy has marked

me for his own', and I cannot overcome him.

Ruth's Diary   Tuesday, 18 April 1905
Saturday evening was a very eventful one for me; indeed it was a
rush to get to the Open-air meeting. We were out about nine. I
knew Mr Randall wished to speak to me, but I could not
imagine about what, and was rather puzzled when he led the
way across the Flats. What he wanted to know was whether I
cared for him or not, and I found an answer impossible to give. I
could not help but think of Ewart, and I knew that if I
encouraged Mr Randall, that would be wrong, and yet I do care
for him. After what seemed a long time, he very gently put his
arms around me and kissed me, and said he supposed he must
take it for granted. We walked back in silence and I felt happy,
miserable and bewildered all at the same time.

I felt quite a different being as I went to School that morning;
and I dreaded the thought of having to meet his eyes in the
afternoon. I did all I could to avoid it, and I am afraid my girls
wondered what was the matter, I moved them about so and
desperately implored them to sit bolt upright. I enjoyed Mr
Barnett's sermon in the evening. One thing he said especially
struck me: it was that as a country, collectively, we do things
that would shame us individually. I had not thought of it before.

Tonight I went up to Eva's and as she was feeling worried and
troubled we had one of our 'nice' talks together. She was in
charge of the shop and I found great amusement in watching her
weigh up sugar and soda with no very certain hand.

Ruth to Eva   29 April 1905
Having nothing very much to do this morning, I will endeavour
to fulfil at length my promise of writing. You must not expect
either a long or nice effusion, for my brains are in their usual
Saturday morning condition – one of blissful inanity.

I do not think you will guess what I did! On Good Friday I
spent the morning dusting and sweeping, etc., and in the afternoon I went with the redoubtable Mr Randall to Barkingside.
We could not talk much for the wind was terribly high. I will just
tell you the mental vision I conjured up of myself. Complexion
varying between beetroot and lobster red, nose of rubicund hue,
head surmounted by hat of rakish demeanour, hopping from
side to side in a manner truly alarming, fur blowing out in all
directions, and occasionally striking my companion caressingly;

skirt *almost* up to my knees, so that inches of (I blush to write it) 'leg' filled my eyes with horror. Altogether it was too boisterous to be pleasant, though the country round about was very pretty. I was thoroughly glad to get back for tea.

I had to stay at home from business on Thursday with Mother. She was very queer indeed.

I am ashamed when I think of the Shorthand and French, but I do not think you quite know how hard it is to get any spare time at home. Now Mother's foot is worse and there is Hebe to look after, and it is more difficult than ever. It seems as though I must learn not to aspire too much, also to be content if I can be useful only in a simple homely way. I see a far different career for you, *ma chère*, but you will always keep a warm corner for your friend, will you not?

This is just a silly little missive, but there is much I could say with my tongue. Remember me to your Grandparents and Aunt and accept much love yourself, from Ruth.

Ruth's Diary   Monday, 8 May 1905
On Wednesday I went to Emma's, and was afterwards met by Mr Randall. We went our usual walk and somehow seemed to understand one another better that evening. I felt a little depressed after, and have done ever since. I discovered Mr Randall has an unusually high ideal of woman, and I would not like to lower it. What great responsibilities there are in our friendships!

On Saturday afternoon I actually went to a Theatre, the first I have ever been to. I met Mr Randall outside the Royal Exchange, and was quite surprised at the agility with which I mounted and dismounted buses, as we sped away – first to have some lunch, then on to the Haymarket Theatre. The Comedy we saw was entitled *The Dictator*. I suppose it is my prim, old-maidish nature that made me think the embracing love-making part rather cheapening. We got home to Chapel and stayed to the open-air service. I felt beautifully tired by bed-time.

Ruth's Diary   Saturday, 20 May 1905
This last fortnight has been a very trying time for us home folk, and we have Hebe staying with us now for an indefinite period. On the Tuesday before last we had our usual fortnightly 'Musical Evening' – a quieter one than our wont, for Hebe was feeling worried about her Mother, who had left home that

68

afternoon taking the two little ones with her, and gone no one knows where. Daisy and I saw Eva to the Station, and then escorted Hebe home. We were talking at the gate when we saw a dreadful fight between a man and his drunken wife, which ended in the man striking such a blow that the woman reeled over into the road. I was sure she had struck her head on the kerb, and rushed to her at once, but some other rough-looking neighbours raised her, and seeing she was not greatly hurt, I went back to Hebe and Daisy. Daisy and I walked up and down the road, after Hebe had gone in, we hardly knew why, and saw Hebe's father lurch into the house, highly intoxicated. Realising that we could not do much good, we walked home. The sight of the fight, which I know is of common occurrence, made me feel sick, and I thought of the unhappiness and misery going on under our very eyes, which has been going on for years, while the Chapel and Churches are blindly concerned with their own petty bickerings. It is terrible!

How things will end with Hebe we do not know. Daisy and I have been dreading another coming into our home, though we have striven to overcome such selfishness.

These last two Friday evenings, Daisy and I have been to the CE, and have returned in a state of disgust. Such pitiful, small strivings among themselves, seem to be all they achieve, and if I knew what to do, I would take up some work independently of all these Societies. I do not wonder at the sneers we receive from those who refuse to attend our places of Worship.

Ruth's Diary   Thursday, 13 July 1905
What an age it seems since I made any record in this little book, and how much has happened! The event uppermost in my mind this afternoon is Wal's removal, with his family, to Balham. That is why I feel rather sad. But we understand each other better now and I think he knows I care for him, but the meeting and Sunday School will seem bereft of something that made them much more precious to me.

This week has been a very trying one to us all. Hebe is still with us, and until last Friday we had heard nothing of her Mother, but as she came home from work that evening, her father met her, and told her Mrs Styles [Hebe's mother] was coming back to him. On Sunday there was knock on the door and we let in Mrs Styles, who had fled in fear of her life, and having had to borrow a neighbour's hat and coat to come in. I

69

had never seen her before, but I liked her face directly. It was refined and gentle, but so terribly thin. After the evening service, we were just seated at the supper table when another knock startled us, and this time we admitted Edie and Ivy, [Hebe's sisters] looking like scared street Arabs. They had escaped from their Father and guessed where their Mother would be. What a strange suppertime that was! Each of us seemed to speak with bated breath, and to be wondering what next would happen. We put the poor fugitives up for the night, and saw to it that every door was well fastened. They were to catch a train a few minutes after five the next morning and get up to the City. They were soon gone and none too early, for Mr Styles arrived just after eight, and upset Mother further by arguing at the street door. In the evening he came again and I went to the door, but did not manage to get rid of him. Mother came, and together we had to listen to some comforting threats. We have heard nothing since, nor received any further visits from the troublesome one.

There are pleasant events to write about however. Mother is very much better, which is a relief to us all. On Saturday 17 June we had our Sunday School Excursion to Southend, the following Saturday we went to the Band of Hope outing to Grange Hill. The heat was overpowering. Last Saturday we *did* enjoy ourselves. It was a glorious afternoon and Wal and I went to Richmond, and strolling by the riverside in the sun we watched the gay throng of people boating; then mounting an electric car we went to Hampton Court. Before concluding, I must note that I sang at the CE, 'I have read of a Beautiful City'. Strange to say, the room was not empty when I had finished.

After this entry in her diary, Ruth did not write until January of the following year (1906). There were not many letters between herself and Eva, but those that exist show their increasing concern with social issues, and some worries over 'great questions'.

Eva to Ruth   3 August 1905
My dear,
According to promise I am writing to tell you a visit next Tuesday will be very welcome, as I'm not going away until the 17th of this month.

Now, my dear Ruth, I hope you are taking great care of yourself. I want to see you looking more robust, Miss, so just take everything as easily as possible and don't do too much or get mixed up with those spiritual parties at the Chapel.

I very much enjoyed our walk together on Tuesday – such conversations seem to help us to know and understand each other better. I came home to wish that I had a mighty pen wherewith to show the world the sin and evil lying around – to wish for a spirit of fire that I might kindle others into such zeal that a great reformation might take place; and then one finds awaiting 'The daily round, the common task', which after all is the world one must fill, the world one must conquer (and oh! how poorly I do it sometimes) and there comes at times such a wish to get away into the fields and quietness and rest, just to get fresh strength and courage to go on, to make and strengthen our resolutions to draw into closer knowledge of God.

My kind wishes to all for this bank holiday and come over if you can this Tuesday, when we must discuss some arrangements for study. How is little Emma? Your loving friend, Eva.

Ruth to Eva   16 August 1905
The very first thing I must do is to wish you 'Many Happy Returns' of your Birthday. If trying to do some good in the world, especially in our own little corner, brings happiness, then I have no fear for you. I often wonder what we shall be doing ten years hence, but wondering does not tell me, though it suggests, and I conclude by thinking our duty lies in making the most of the present. I am afraid my little token must wait until I see you again, but you will not mind that I know. I shall think of you often during the holiday, and do not forget that I expect to see you very brown and well-looking after.

I did not tell you there is a remote chance of getting Emma away for a fortnight. The money to pay for it all we shall have to raise between ourselves. It would be nice if we could do a little, wouldn't it?

How delightful to think of getting away from the din and bustle, the never-ceasing sound of telephone bells and irritable voices for two whole weeks!

And now, *ma chère,* wishing you a *truly* happy birthday, and bon voyage. Your loving friend, Ruth.

Eva to Ruth   15 November 1905
My dear,
As I did not have the pleasure of seeing you yesterday evening, I

concluded you were busily engaged overcasting, hemming and sewing etc., or otherwise usefully occupied.

Sunday afternoon I had such a large class – I was pleased, but it was harder to teach such a number. I have been reading the *Daily News* lately, and it makes one's heart sad to think of the distress amongst the unemployed; I am glad a fund is being started, but I think it should be used to provide work, rather than as a sort of Relief Fund. If only we would live more simply. Why, I wonder, are we in such haste to be rich, such haste to accomplish our different tasks? We might learn something I think from the slow workings of nature who grudges not a century to the perfection of some small object; yet we hurry, rear our jerry-built houses, our electric railways, as though all the world depended upon our haste.

I hope, Ruth, that you are keeping well. Do not worry so over these great questions – we cannot possibly understand all that these things mean. What to us seems often so distressing and inexplicable may be the necessary birth pangs of some great blessing. How much wisdom, patience and endurance we all need. We need to form our opinions slowly, for there are many sides to every question.

How is little Emma progressing? Let me know about the Bath chair, I should like to help with that. I was busily at work on my dress yesterday evening (by the way, what a deal of work there is in a dress!).

Are you satisfied with the way our Tuesday evening study is progressing? Do you think we could make any better arrangement? I think we had better read something we can understand and not waste time over paragraphs that require an Encyclopaedia to be even ordinarily intelligible. Don't you?

How very soon Xmas will be here. Let us hope by that time something will have been done to relieve and help the unemployed. Your loving friend, Eva.

4

'A Creed of our Own, from our Own Experiences'
January 1906–June 1907

In the period following Ruth's rumblings of discontent with the 'missions' and the Chapel, enormous changes took place. The beginning of 1906 found her sticking a list of resolutions on the cover of her diary, noting that she should still think less of herself and 'do more for others and help Wal more', but by February she wrote that 'some change has begun – I am really waking up!'

Reflecting critically and more objectively on her development so far, Ruth gradually began to question her basic beliefs, and place more faith in her own perceptions. By the middle of the following year she had taken the considerable leap of moving away from religious dogma. She was interested in socialist and psychological thought, and was now writing confidently about 'conventional ideas that retard women's emancipation'. The transformation did not happen without a struggle, but it was worth risking the pain and the criticism of others (family and Wal) in order to 'live and learn'. The process was facilitated by new influences, and new ideas.

From 1906, the Women's Movement became a much more public and militant force, motivated by the indifference of the new Liberal government, and the majority of the new Labour MPs, to the 'Votes for Women' issue. The general election, reported by Ruth in January, brought Labour MPs into Parliament for the first time, but the suffragettes (many of whom were Independent Labour Party members) did not get the support they expected from them. The very demands of the suffrage campaign, and the upsurge of militant tactics in particular, challenged the firmly entrenched notions of female submission, and the 'Suffrage' and 'Sex' Questions were hotly debated. After 1906, with increasing labour unrest in Britain and a 'ferment' of socialist thought, there were great socialist and liberal preachers to be heard in London. In January 1907 an uproar broke out when the young Rev R. J. Campbell of the City Temple in Holborn (the 'Mecca' of Nonconformity), expounded upon his 'New Theology' in the national press. An Independent Labour Party member and suffrage supporter, Campbell pointed 'to the unequal distribution of the means of human existence on this planet', challenged Church doctrine and the power of ministers, and claimed that God 'reigned in the hearts of men', not in the institutions of the Church.

These events had crucial implications for Ruth and Eva. Ruth's diaries show how these external political events related to her own personal feelings and frustrations. They also provide the background in which those changes took place. The process of change was stimulated by the appearance in March of her new Quakeress friend – the unorthodox Miss Elizabeth Foster Brown – who understood Ruth's difficulties, encouraged her independence of thought, and introduced her to new ideas.

Ruth became increasingly assertive and was now in a better position to challenge some of the problems in her relationship with Wal, to whom she had become engaged in 1906. But while she was prepared to fight her own passivity, and put the relationship on a more equal, honest footing, Wal, with his unreliabilities, his 'masculine' evasions and defences, and his disagreements with Ruth on the suffrage question, consistently undermined her efforts.

For Eva, it was a more isolated and restless time, when she was 'longing to get to work properly', was less in contact with new influences, and had to make do with 'small opportunities for unselfishness'. Ruth too was determined to find more fulfilling work, but material opportunities were few and far between and unemployment was high.

Eva did not see Ruth as much as she would have liked, but new friends and activities did not threaten their deepening friendship or cause jealousy. As Eva wrote to Ruth in November 1906, 'I do not know how I would have felt if your new friendship [with Miss Brown] had made a difference to us, but it has not – you are just the same dear girl and I am so delighted for you altogether.'

Ruth's Diary   8 January 1906
On Monday, New Year's Day, I spent the evening at Mrs Fairfax's. It was very nice, and I was enjoying a quiet talk with Eleanor when Aggie, now entitled to cap and gown, and I fancy

74

ambitious for a BA, came in with her friend, Miss Dunn. I did not feel so much at ease after the arrival of these awe-inspiring damsels, feeling indeed too insignificant and humble to offer a remark before them! They had been to a matinee – *A Midsummer Night's Dream* – and I found it extremely interest-ing to listen to their remarks. Is it necessary, I wonder, for a girl with such a classical face, such refined tastes and ideas, to show her college connections by calling one person a 'fool', and speaking cynically of mankind as a whole? I am beginning to realise that with a little encouragement I should have been a worshipper at the shrine of knowledge, and have been in danger in using that great gift wrongly, allowing myself to become patronising and contemptuous. No! There are things even better than knowledge, and now my daily prayer is rather for 'the wise and understanding heart' than for the ready and brilliant intellect.

Still, I am so easily influenced that instead of seizing the good obtainable from intercourse with people of refinement and culture, I let it make me discontented and unsettled, I am afraid.

Ruth's Diary   Friday, 12 January 1906
On Tuesday this week it was the poor children's Christmas Party, given in the Schoolroom, and it made one's heart ache to watch the poor, ragged little mites. They all appeared to enjoy themselves for the time being. By the time the parcels had been given out, and the toys from the tree distributed, it was past ten o'clock, and the vestry was filling with mothers and elder sisters, mostly ragged and untidy, some even gaunt. Daisy and I escorted a few bairns to Bessborough Road, and learned much from their chatter. Though it was so late, the street seemed full of children, some bare-footed, looking as if they had no thought of going home, and the sight made one shudder. What can or ought to be expected from these neglected little ones, brought up in such horrid surroundings? I had never imagined there were places quite so bad in Manor Park. The few we had tried to help – what were they compared to the whole?

Last night Eva came over, and we went a long walk together. I wanted her advice as to what I ought to do with regard to the Chapel. We had a serious talk over our Sunday School classes and what to teach. I have long worried because I fear I teach morals rather than religion, and yet the Christian code is the purest and highest. I mean I do not talk to the children about

75

being 'saved', yet I am anxious they should grow up noble Christlike women. I am puzzled over many things, that I do not feel *sure* in teaching them. Eva said much that was helpful; she always does, though I know she has the same difficulties herself.

Ruth's Diary   Monday, 22 January 1906
Last week was not altogether uneventful. On Wednesday I rushed off to dressmaking class, back to tableaux rehearsal, then met Dad at Stratford at ten o'clock, where we stood on the Green until some time after eleven, watching the limelight reports of Election results. That reminds me that I have said nothing of what is causing such excitement everywhere. The Liberals are gaining the day, and Dad is jubilant. I have just heard that our Liberal candidate has been returned with a huge majority. Dad has been so far roused that with a neighbour's aid he has done some canvassing and had many funny little incidents to relate in consequence. How will it be I wonder a few months hence? How will the promises, the glowing pictures of better things in store, appear against results?

Ruth's Diary   Saturday, 27 January 1906
This is a different Saturday to all others for I shall not see Wal this evening. On Tuesday I received a letter from him telling me about some spiritualist meetings he had been to. He appeared very much impressed by what he had seen and heard, and somehow as I read his account, I felt very depressed and concerned. I have always felt strangely adverse to spiritualism as something unnatural and unhealthy. I wrote back, and asked if he could tell me its aim, and say what good it does in the world. I told him too, what I begin to believe more and more, that the best life is possible apart from all creeds. I am so weary, so utterly weary of the petty differences which prevent so much good – and yet my perplexity on many subjects does not grow less. My longing for the 'wise and understanding heart' increases daily, but wisdom has to be sought through the oft-times painful paths of experience. I would have a simpler creed than this [spiritualism], which fills me with morbid thoughts and uncanny suggestions. Do we not, each one for ourselves, build up a creed of our own, from our own experiences?

Some paralysing influence seems at work. I cannot think, cannot expand, and terrible moods of depression seize hold upon me. But somewhere I feel there is peace, and after a long

76

conflict, how sweet the finding will be.

Eva to Ruth   31 January 1906
My dear,
This is to say I shall not be coming over to Manor Park
tomorrow. I have been blaming myself for disappointing you
and breaking my appointment, but I have been finding out lately
what a very weak spot I have in my composition. Desiring to
please almost everyone, I make a promise here and a promise
there, and am dismayed afterwards when I realise what I *ought*
to have said and done. Will you pardon me this dear? I am going
from a feeling of 'duty' to our Sunday School gathering tomorrow evening. I am looking forward to it with some dread, and
wish so much that I might be with you instead.

How are you my dear, with your Chapel troubles and busy
evenings? I hope you are not wearing yourself out in the pursuit
of duty and knowledge.

Last Wednesday was our election day at Walthamstow and
very amusing I found it. People hurried along, adorned with
blue or yellow bows – motors dashed with flying ribbons,
meteor-like through the town – small boys hooted, and even
the doggies boasted bows of bright yellow or blue. Our Liberal
candidate won the day. I was pleased – I know not why –
having no very clear idea of the opinions of either Conservatives
or Liberals, but I have a kindly feeling towards Liberalism. How
do you feel about it?

I must thank you, Ruth, for the pretty Post Card of 'The
Needles', also for one of 'Dover Cliffs'. Both look nice in my
album. Are your albums full yet?

My dear Ruth, it is getting late. Goodnight now dear, with
fond love and an imaginary 'kiss' from Eva.

Ruth's Diary   Friday, 9 February 1906
We are at last experiencing some real wintry weather. Darkness,
hail, and thunder and lightning doing their best to make us
realise what insignificant little pigmies we are!

Some change has come over me of late, and I am only just
learning of its nature. I see the selfishness of the self-centred
existence I have lived these last few years, priding myself on
eccentric ways, and fostering the idea that I really am superior
to my neighbours, indeed so much above them that I must walk
through life ill-used and misunderstood. I see now that I

77

estrange myself from those who would love and help me and now I would be different. I am thinking of Wal, who I am sure has altered very much since he moved to Belvedere, has become despondent and moody, when I might have tried with a little sympathy to stop it. I, who surely after my experience at Hornchurch, should have known what to do. I know I have held back often because it is natural to me. I am determined to make one big attempt to make our fellowship what it should be.

On Monday evening I went to Emma's and was much cheered by the progress she at last seems to be making. On getting home I read some of Ewart's letters, especially the last one or two in which he spoke so hopefully. I think they did me good, for I began to feel more myself. I look back at the time between leaving Hornchurch and Ewart's death, and see myself quite a buoyant creature, living up in the clouds, with highflown notions of 'missions' in life, scarce treading on earth, and believing that in some miraculous way Ewart would get strong and all go well. When the trouble came, I still lived in this ethereal world, had visions of becoming a second Florence Nightingale and I know not what beside. I see now it was a phase of development, not to be scoffed at as useless and futile. From then till now I seem to have been fighting against myself, stifling myself, and walking in dark places. What will happen now I wonder? I must waken, be myself, and surely do something to make someone glad they knew me, some spot the better for my having been there!

Ruth's Diary   Wednesday, 21 February 1906
Sunday the 11th was a red letter day, for Daisy came of age! She had some very nice presents.

I met Wal the following Wednesday, and we had a most odd conversation – my fault, I think. I had been reading over some of Ewart's letters, and could scarce believe I am the same girl as the one who received those simple hopeful loving little epistles. Wal seemed to think it was only with him I am so 'unnatural', but I told him I am the same to everyone. He prophesied that I should be different soon, while I inwardly commented the change had begun, I am really 'waking up'. I told him I had been reading Ewart's letters, and he said he knew more about Ewart than I thought he did – it had struck him that I was sorry for a great deal, and imposed a kind of penance on myself. More followed which I cannot remember, but I thought, after, he had taken a wrong impression. On Sunday some genius, evil or otherwise, prompted me to scribble to Wal explaining what I had meant. Strange to say, I dreamt of that letter the next evening, and then an answer came to the effect that Wal's impression of the person I liked best in this world and always should was *myself* was confirmed. That dream was evidently the outcome of my own train of thought.

Ruth's Diary   Saturday, 10 March 1906
Somehow I feel unusually happy this morning, whether because I plucked up the courage and had a troublesome tooth drawn yesterday, or whether because spring seems to have come with its sunshine and flowers, or whether it is Saturday and I can look forward to seeing Wal, I do not know. So much has happened. I continued to worry as to what was causing Wal to be unable to meet me, until a letter came that for a little while at least roused my anger. It very coolly and curtly stated that he was 'rather busy' and was not sure that he would be down on the following Saturday. The letter went on to state, in the coolest, making quite sure manner, that he would like to buy me a ring – would I accompany him to Stratford the next Monday, or should he find out the size in some way when he came on Sunday? I learnt after that he was actually at Syd Hoffman's house that evening, just at the top of the street, and yet did not take the trouble to call. My indignation grew higher and higher. I knew they thought it strange at home, but I avoided mentioning anything, and above all always endeavoured – I think fairly successfully – to assume an indifferent manner. But on this occasion I felt I must tell Daisy – I could endure it no longer. It seemed as though almost ever since I have known Wal, I have been stretched on a kind of mental rack, expecting right up to the last *moment* to hear he was not coming. Lately it had become the usual thing for him to say he was 'not sure', 'would let me know', and then at the eleventh hour a postcard would come after I had endured silent agonies. I began at last to dread the Postman's visits and would start at every knock, thinking, 'I know that's a postcard', while if we arranged to meet anywhere, I dreaded the long wait I should surely have. I told Daisy and she agreed it should not go on. I could not sleep that night of course, but tossed about trying to solve the problem. I remembered Mrs Suckling [a Chapel friend] telling me once that men do a lot of hurtful things just from want of thought, and decided that this once I would conclude that as the cause, but tell Wal

79

about it so as to prevent future occurrences of like trials.

Sunday dawned, and thoughts of the dreaded interview I had planned sadly interfered with my lessons, I am afraid. I will not enter into details, but just record that during the evening I *did* manage to say much I had intended, allowing myself womanlike to be pacified and caressed into a different frame of mind. Wal confessed that there was justice in my rebukes. I told him I had hoped it would have occurred to him without my mentioning it, but I felt it was upsetting me too much. How easily we women are satisfied! I really was no wiser at the end of our talk, yet I was prepared to go on again.

After making a big silly of myself, I lent Wal the ring Grandma had given me and said I would not go with him to select it.

Now I have written so much I wonder if I am right in keeping such an account of little unpleasantnesses. Ought I not rather to forgive and forget? Yet something forces me to write the painful as well as the joyous, else I should scarce be truthful. The very real suffering of the past few months cannot fail to have left its mark. I hope different times are in store.

Ruth's Diary   Tuesday, 20 March 1906
The Saturday following, Wal brought the ring. I felt strangely shy, happy and all kinds of things at once, with that ring on my finger. As we said Goodnight, Wal said he wondered if I should get tired of him, for one day he would want me all to himself. I asked what made him think such a thing, and he said perhaps I would wonder the same about him. 'Yes,' I said, 'I think I could do that very well.' Putting my arms for the first time round his neck I said, 'And I think the same.' So it was settled. I missed what I had scarcely dared hope to receive – some words of counsel or pleasure from Dad and Mother.

Next morning, when I arrived in the City with my latest present, there was great excitement. No one would believe it – I seemed so quiet, they all said, that they had never associated 'that kind of thing' with me. I felt greatly flattered, and heartily thankful when I could take my embarrassed self home.

Ruth to Eva   30 March 1906
My dear,
I do not remember a birthday when I have had so many evidences of kindly thought from my friends – Tuesday found

me quite bewildered with pleasure. Thank you dearie for the share you took in causing that to be my condition. I was very pleased when I opened my precious parcel and saw its contents. I sat down to play some of the pieces on Wednesday evening. Miss Panting gave me a music-case, and three favourite pieces, so I should surely strive to become proficient now! My other presents I must show you when you come. On Tuesday I am to see my Quakeress friend, so perhaps I shall have something interesting to tell you.

Among my presents is one the nature of which you must guess. Do not be vexed because I have said nothing about it before – several times I have intended mentioning different things, and then have not done so. I am all embarrassment this morning: everyone is so surprised at 'prim Miss Slate', and remarkably candid about it too. Will you be surprised, I wonder? Do not be afraid dearie, to tell me just what you think – I hope you will be pleased. Believe me when I tell you I feel very happy. Can I say more?

Thanking you again very much, my friend, for indeed you are a friend who will be constant ever, I feel sure. I say Goodbye until Thursday. Love from Ruth.

Eva to Ruth   7 April 1906
My very dear,
Although late, I feel I must scribble a little note. I felt so grieved tonight when I got in the train to think of the somewhat abrupt way in which I left you. I should have liked so much to have kissed you dear, and to have wished you the happiness you so well deserve, but a railway station is not the nicest place in which to express one's feelings.

I am so glad for you, my dear, dear Ruth–because I believe the love of a good man, little children and a home are amongst the most precious things life has to give us. I shall think of you so of-ten–it is so good to know you have now someone to take care of you–this need be nothing more than a fresh bond between us.

And now I must say 'Goodnight', with loving, loving wishes for a very *blessed* and happy future for both you and Mr Randall. Your very loving friend, Eva.

Ruth to Eva   15 April 1906
My dear,
Did you not indignantly exclaim, 'Just like her!' when you

81

received my postcard on Tuesday, and indeed I can scarcely plead for mercy on this occasion, the fault being entirely mine. On Tuesday morning I found myself in a fix, and so sent off that card to you. I would have come this evening instead, but was not sure whether it would be convenient to you; and then too, I have been out such a lot, and tomorrow I am to see my Quakeress friend.

The Reception for Sunday School Teachers was disappointing, after all, and my thoughts kept reverting to the pleasant time we should have had.

Thank you dearie for your sweet little letter, it was just like you to write so kindly.

Now prepare for some doleful news! You know we have long thought of moving from Manor Park, and now I am afraid the much dreaded event will take place shortly. Dad thought Higham's park, Walthamstow, would prove a suitable spot for our next sojourn, but was obliged to relinquish the scheme on account of expensive railway fares, etc. His latest idea is Hither Green, Lewisham, or a place near those suburbs, and I think that is the most likely place. Already I feel weighted down with grief at the prospect: it will mean giving up so much. I feel much as a tortoise would if it were dragged away from its shell alive.

Can I come on Monday next week? If I hear nothing I will come. Much love from Ruth.

Ruth's Diary   Saturday, 16 June 1906
Nearly three months have elapsed since I made any record of the events which make up my ordinary, very ordinary life! I wonder sometimes why I take so much pleasure in dwelling on little incidents, and think them of sufficient importance to write about. Is it because I think too much of myself, or because I do not want to forget all that passes between myself and others? I do not know, only that I enjoy an occasional scribble.

To commence again, I shall have to start with a memorable evening I spent on Friday 16 March, at the office of my Quakeress friend, at Devonshire Chambers, Bishopsgate. We stayed there by our two selves, until quite late, and I found myself able to talk to her about things that had long perplexed me, as I had never spoken to anyone before – she seemed to understand me at once. I was rather awed to find her quite a clever personage, and acquainted with 'real, live authors'. She is secretary to a certain Mr Grubb MA, who is editor of *The British Friend*[1] and I believe she sometimes writes articles for the said periodical. It was strange how little we spoke of 'Quakerism' – Miss Brown (her name is Elizabeth Foster Brown) informed me at the outset that she is not an orthodox Friend. She seemed immediately to divine my difficulties, and because she had been through a bitter struggle herself was able to help and sympathise. I do not think I am likely ever to forget our conversation, and I went home that evening in a most happy frame of mind, hugging some books she lent me, but too excited to read. I had been reading Anna Buckland's *History of English Literature* but now I turned to a book by Mr Grubb himself called *Social Aspects* as viewed from Quaker standpoints. It was a book full of practical suggestions, and spoke hopefully of a *gradual* improvement of the existing order of things, with its extreme wealthy and its degraded poor.

The 13 April was Good Friday. Wal came to dinner, after which we betook ourselves to Ilford to see the spot chosen for our new home. We were a little alarmed to find we should have nearly half an hour's walk to and from the station every day, but thought the house pleasantly situated, and very comfortable and convenient in itself. Sunday 22 April was Mother's birthday, and my last Sunday at School. I shall never forget it! All my class were present in the afternoon. The children hugged me, and promised to write often, and then the teachers came one by one and shook hands sympathetically. Mr Smith came up and, seizing my arms, said he felt my going more than anything that had happened before, and that the School would not seem the same without me. I felt at last my heart must burst, and hurried away to take Emma home – for the last time!

Arriving home, something was said which upset me again and I wept so violently that Mother grew frightened. But I had to be made as presentable as possible, for Daisy and I were to take tea with the Chesters. After much bathing and applications of powdered starch, I began to resemble my usual self again, and we set out.

All the week following we were busy packing. On the last Monday morning we were up before five; there was still much to be done. At eight I had to leave for business, and took a sad farewell of the house of so many associations, mostly happy ones. It was strange 'going home' to Ilford, and the long walk from the Station I began to liken irreverently to Windsor's Long Walk, which seems near when it is afar off. It seemed as though we should never get things in 'home order'. Mother was queer also and Dad had taken a week of his holiday so that he might help, but he is not a useful man in the house, though he does his best. All the next week I was busy cleaning furniture and getting it in its place.

Monday 4 June – Whit Monday! I met Wal early in the morning at Stratford, and we spent the day at Epping. Somehow we got in a part of the forest which no one else seemed to frequent. I rather liked it, though the quiet seemed almost eerie – then it was just lovely to look through the cool green of the trees! Then we walked to Ongar, where we stood in the Churchyard watching the sunset, which was glorious. Wal asked what I was thinking so deeply about. I told him it was the anniversary of the day when Ewart was buried, and I could not help but think of it. He was very kind and patient with me, though I fear I spoilt the day for him. The next day, he said he would meet me after I left business in the evening. We walked to one of the London Parks, I don't know which. One of us must have been in a contrary mood, I expect it was me, and before long we had succeeded in making each other thoroughly miserable. Wal said I would not be natural with him, and I said I was nearly always conscious of something between us which would not let me be natural. Talking in this strain we returned to Liverpool St, and Wal said, 'Well, you must tell me what you were going to, when there is a chance; perhaps that will make a difference.' (I had promised to tell him about Ewart.) I could feel then that he thought Ewart still held first place in my heart, and I said, almost passionately, 'You *mustn't* think I think more of Ewart than of you.' But there was no smile on his face. I felt utterly wretched as I returned home.

The next day I wrote all I was feeling, making sure he would understand, and that it would put everything right. I told him of Ewart's influence over me, and that I had cared for him as much as it was then possible for me to care for anyone, for I felt I must be truthful about it. 'But', I added, 'Could I not care for you more because I had once known Ewart? And could we not remember him together and speak of him sometimes?'

I received an answer on the Friday which seemed to freeze me. 'Do not expect me to be strong, for you will be disappointed', he wrote, or words to that effect; also, 'If I have ever done any good, it has been entirely overshadowed by the evil of later days.' He will never know how that letter hurt me. It seemed as though I had laid bare my very soul before him, and received an insult in return. I met Miss Brown in the evening, and went with her to Queen's Hall to see the Sweated Industries Exhibition.[2] The things we saw made our hearts ache, if it were possible that mine could ache more. Oh, the terrible injustice meted out to hundreds and hundreds! Miss Brown seemed to know the history of all the workers (there were some working in the hall): brushmakers, artificial flower-making, hook and eye sewing on cards, umbrella making – everything seemed tainted with this terrible thing. She had a kind word and smile for each one. I did admire her that evening! We came away feeling such an exhibition could not but bear fruit, though it may take ages to ripen. We noted with astonishment that expensive articles were paid at as poor a rate for making as cheaper ones.

No one at home knew of my trouble and heartache. I was almost glad when it was time to go up to the Station on Saturday. Wal and I met calmly, and walked in the direction of Wanstead Park. Presently I tried to make him see how his letter hurt me, but I think I only partially succeeded.

Ruth to Eva   15 July 1906
                                                        22 Eton Road, Ilford
My dear,
It is Sunday afternoon. I can scarcely believe that I have left business behind for a whole fortnight, but I am glad to have the little change, for of late we seem to get so very busy. Just fancy! This time next week we shall be at Hove, probably by the sad sea waves.

I am afraid I shall not be able to come to Leyton this week, much as I should like to see you. What with Grandmas and Aunts and a certain other person, I foresee some difficulty in planning out the time so as to please them all. But you shall see me in all my red-Indian glory either on the Tuesday or Thursday after my return. Please write to me while we are away, and say which evening I am to come. Then you must come to Ilford soon and judge for yourself the charms of our new residence. We are in better order now. We have not settled at any Chapel, not one seems like our own.

This morning we were at the Wesleyan. The Rev. Taylor from Forest Gate preached. His text was 'And they asked each other's welfare'. He spoke of the joys of the small seemingly commonplace things of life. But we are reticent, and though we talk of the weather, the events of the day, we bury the deep things and speak to no one of them. There is a gold mine in us which is not being worked.

It was strange, but I had been thinking myself of this unwillingness to speak of the deep and sacred. I feel it, myself, and I know I have closed myself up most abruptly sometimes because I feared an intrusion on what I preferred to hoard miser-like. It is wrong, don't you think, and must impoverish and dwarf one's growth?

I was much struck by something you said in your last letter about the effects of day-dreaming, and I am sure you are right. We are in great danger of drawing ourselves apart, of shirking the battle, for the fancied Utopias, where all has been already accomplished.

I have thought often of our last conversation, and felt grateful for it. I do hope you have not been reproaching yourself for anything you may have said. I am thankful indeed to have a friend so ready to help as you are. Do you know I think I have always had good friends, and that is a rare joy, isn't it?

I hope you are not being overworked and shall be glad to know you are on holiday and recruiting your health. I have quite finished Renan's *Life of Jesus*[3] if you like to read it; it has been a help in many ways.

Please remember me to your Auntie and Grandparents, and accept your own share of love from Ruth.

Eva to Ruth   10 September 1906
My dear,
I meant to write earlier, Ruth, but for one thing we have been busy at business the last few days, and for another I felt in a queer, restless mood last week – almost incapable of settling to anything for long. Saturday it would have been a relief to have been able to spring from the floor to the ceiling – to have waved one's arms wildly or ... but I will stop or you will be alarmed!

My new music I am very pleased with, Ruth, and 'thank you' again and again. There is no need to tell you how much kind wishes are valued. So I am four and twenty. Another year and the quarter of the century is reached! How aged it sounds, does it not? Then the aims and ideals that one had in abundance in

86

very early youth – do they seem to you easy or difficult to attain? To me difficulties seem to abound; I remember at one time few things seemed impossible, but now I find to do anything or be anything is uphill work indeed. Not that I mind uphill work, but there is a strange loneliness in life – don't you think? – that grows on one with increasing force as the years go by.

Well, I must say, Ruth – this is a nice letter to be writing you; but I feel in a very mixed mood today. A bundle of letters arrived this morning, accompanied by a young woman, and a breach of promise case is now in hand. Fancy exposing to the unsympathetic eye of a solicitor her love (??) letters!! But I had better leave this young woman alone. You cannot imagine how indignant I am feeling at the present moment. Horrible notions of the revival of the ducking stool punishment being good for some people are occurring to me!

Ruth, take great care of yourself. Come, oh do come, if you possibly can on Thursday. I will come and meet you at Leytonstone Station. Oh the foolish things I have said in this letter: but come and see me – a visit from you does me an immense amount of good. With love, dear, Eva.

Eva to Ruth   11 October 1906
My dear,
I *did* mean that my letter to you should have been written in the week this time, but here is Thursday evening and you still without the promised epistle. It is a great pleasure to me to write to you, my dear – you know so much about my surroundings, that I can tell you all the little incidents that mark time, feeling that you will take interest in them. Then too I know you would not be shocked or grow cold if I expressed sentiments or beliefs opposite to your own.

Did you think me a 'cold-hearted wretch' last time we met? I met you in a somewhat damp and depressed condition, and you received the low-spirited one with kindly cheerfulness – I feel ashamed.

You and I have had so little time for conversation lately. You must tell me more about the wonderful book you are reading, also the result of your visit to the Phrenologist.[4] I have finished reading *Mistress Dorothy Marion,* and I enjoyed it, Ruth, and often think of it. It had been translated from old English, so you may know it was not at all a modern book. The hero I thought somewhat weak in character – the heroine, however, was a perfect *mountain* of courage and had quite a bracing effect on me: she made one sigh for opportunities of physical valour. But alas! few ladies fair nowadays have the opportunity of receiving on their own white arm the sword thrust intended for their lover, of rescuing him by means of a rope from a dreary hole, or of performing a necessary but harrowing operation upon the aforesaid victim during a dangerous illness! No, maidens have to be contented (in these prosaic times) with a quiet walk, a ring, a birthday gift, a letter, little opportunities for unselfishness. I *did* wish a little of *old* England was left to us – don't you feel dissatisfied with modern architecture sometimes, and wish for a little more solidity and picturesqueness?

My present library book, *The Birds* of Aristophanes, translated from the Greek by Rev. H. Cary, I am not greatly interested in. Did you enjoy *Tale of Two Cities*. It is very tragic, is it not? With love, Eva.

Ruth to Eva   25 October 1906
My very dear,
I have been longing all this week for an opportunity to chat with you. When I read your kind, unselfish letters and compare them with my own, I feel overcome with shame; but between friends who understand each other there is no need for comparisons, is there?

Was I wrong in telling you the trouble I experience at home sometimes? I hope not, for I am going to tell you more – I feel I must tell someone. I had arranged to go to Miss Brown's on Sunday with the full knowledge of all at home. Judge my dismay then, when on Saturday reproaches came thick and fast, and I was told I ran after people unnecessarily. That night I sat down and wept bitterly. It was foolish, but I lost control of myself when they would ask why I was looking miserable. In a few minutes I had recovered and was laughing gaily in order to evade questionings, but Mother in her own mind decided I had 'quarrelled' with Mr Randall.

I wish, oh I wish, that I could introduce you to Miss Brown. Sunday was a red-letter day to me, because it brought us in contact again. I will begin at the beginning. Leaving home at nine in the morning I proceeded to Liverpool Street, from there to Purley. Miss Brown joined the train at Croydon. At first

to him to confide in another. I tried to explain that it seemed the most natural thing in the world that between two persons like ourselves there should be perfect openness, and added that I could not be happy and natural with him until this confidence came about.

But before knocking at the door, one of those impulses came over me to make yet one more attempt at reconciliation, so touching his arm, I lifted my face for him to kiss me. In a moment everything seemed right.

Ruth's Diary   14 December 1906
Thursday Eva came over. Eva was rather concerned because Miss O'Dell [the phrenologist] urges 'Foreign Mission' work as specially adapted for her. Failing that, educational work of some kind, probably lecturing. There would be heavy expenses to meet, and keen competition, in taking up educational work, while of course Eva would not dream of entering on a missionary career without feeling strongly drawn to it, which she does not just now. I understand her longing to get to work properly, and I hope the way will clear for her soon. I believe she has a genius for something.

Eva to Ruth   14 December 1906
My very dear,
I shall not be writing again before Xmas, so felt I must slip a little note in with my gift to wish you a *very, very* happy Xmas and glad New Year. I thank you so much for telling me what you did on Thursday – I could sympathise deeply with you, and I wanted you to know, only it was difficult to put it into words, how very much your friendship is to me. I cannot exactly explain it, but you satisfy a certain *want* in me, and I feel when with you as I have never (I do not think) felt with anyone else in my life. That is saying a good deal is it not? Always keep a corner for me, dear, even when perhaps you are surrounded with closer ties and dearer – I really feel as if there is something stronger than usual in our friendship, and I have a greedy craving feeling about you sometimes. But how you will smile at me!

I do so hope there is going to be for you a *great, great* deal of happiness in the future – I should so rejoice to see you happy and richly blessed!

My love to you dear, and wishes most sincere. Eva.

Xmas is over once again, and we are trying our hardest to settle into ordinary ways, but a restless spirit seems abroad which makes it very difficult. And the weather! Snow, snow everywhere!

From our windows at the back we gaze upon a stretch of white country – truly a pretty sight. The City presents a spectacle far from picturesque – mud, slush and grease everywhere!

The Saturday before Xmas we had visitors, and Wal came to tea. The visitors were Mrs Newcombe and Mrs Masters; the widowed sisters for whom Daisy works. We spent a pleasant and fairly musical evening, Mrs Newcombe being a good pianist, and her sister a good singer. These sisters interest me wonderfully – I used to hear about them from Eleanor Fairfax, who worked for them at one time. Mrs Newcombe, she has often told me, more nearly approaches her ideal of a woman than any other she has met, her mother excepted. I fancy the lady would irritate me considerably. She is very calm and placid, and is never heard to say a harsh word of anyone. 'We must not judge,' 'We do not know what led them to do it,' are frequent remarks – charitable and tolerant; yet I preferred the sister whom Eleanor thought a heartless creature – Mrs Masters. A splendid woman physically – superb in build and carriage, full-throated, her shapely head crowned with masses of tawny hair, eyes tawny also. There is nothing small about her – loves, friendships, animosities – all I feel would be strong from her. She is whimsical too, and rather likes to appear indifferent when feeling otherwise. It would be impossible to find two more opposite types of character, yet the sisters are bound together by strong affections, one sees. At suppertime Mrs Masters made a remark which aroused my attention. She said we often 'wrangle' most with those we love best – we should not take the trouble with other people.

On Xmas Eve we left business early, so Miss Panting proposed we should walk down to Cheapside and Ludgate Hill to 'see the sights of London'. It was very dirty underfoot, and before long began to rain, but that did not matter – we struggled on amid the crowds. Ludgate Hill impressed me much, but the cries of the hawkers made me think sad thoughts. Old and bent men and women, and pinched children, selling toys that perhaps had never brought pleasure to them – it was a pitiful sight to me! It seemed also as if we passers by regarded them as beings not possessed of feelings like ourselves – what joys had Xmas in store for these poor souls? We get so accustomed to the sights of poverty that sympathy and love are in danger of becoming dulled.

I woke up early on Xmas morning and opened a package Eva had left with strict injunctions that I was not to open it till then. Its contents filled me with delight – a beautiful little seascape in a fumed oak frame, and a loving letter; I believe I enjoyed the letter even more than gazing on the picture – it was so strong and true in its sentiment. But I am forgetting to record one incident. I was rather troubled to learn through some conversation Wal and I had during the Xmas revelry that he is acquainted with the secret of Eva's birth. How could Mother, for it must have been her, betray my confidence? But then how came I to betray another's in the first instance? Oh! I shall ever regret it.

Ruth's Diary   15 January 1907
This is my first New Year entry. The last time I entered up my journal was on the Saturday after Xmas, when Wal and Nellie were coming to stay the night with us. After exchanging our wishes for each other that the New Year would be a happy one, I suggested that perhaps we should understand one another better than we had done in 1906. Wal assented, and then told me he had resolved to try to help me more this year as I (so he said) had helped him. He insisted then on what I know is not true, namely that I am above him in every way. Yet it was sweet to hear him say I had helped him. I then told him how I would like to just be 'myself' with him, because I love him. We parted conscious of our love at last, it seemed.

Ruth's Diary   Sunday, 20 January 1907
I did not get far after all the other night. On 3 Jan I felt very poorly on getting home from business. All night I was racked with severe pains, and in the morning Dad would have a Doctor sent for. We learnt that my complaint was influenza and I was at home all the week after. It was a wretched week – I could not shake off a heavy fit of depression. Perhaps my one solace was the perusal of *Jane Eyre*. I had read the book before, but this time it charmed me out of myself. I only read a few lines – then fell a-thinking! I concluded that much of our depression arises because we have not enough time to think – we are strangers to our best selves! How much calmer and stronger I am sure we

would grow if only we thought sufficiently to realise our own dimly felt inner strength.

Last Sunday we had arranged to go to Miss Slawson's [Aunt Edie]. Most of the evening we spent in talking. I have never heard anyone talk like Eva – it is just wonderful to listen to her, and I felt more than ever my unworthiness of the love and friendship she gives me. We spoke of many things – books, and our favourite characters in them; childhood days and early friendships, and then – here Eva was at her best – of social problems. Eva put forward her idea that if we could open our homes more to the outcast and degraded, we could more easily show our love and sympathy, and win them to higher things. I am more than ever certain that Eva possesses unusual powers: surely the opportunity of putting them to the test will come!

We have been worried about Dad, who is uncertain of his situation continuing, and has been poorly in health, also about Tom, who appears indefinite as ever in his plans. These troubles add to my load considerably, for I do not know what would become of us should Dad get 'out of work'. Yet how many are already suffering – men who would gladly work if they could only 'get some' to do – why should we expect to be exempt?

Ruth to Eva   17 January 1907
Let me tell you first and foremost how much we 'all' enjoyed ourselves on Sunday. Last night I read over your Christmas letter – I felt in need somehow, of an assurance of someone's steady love. Suppose one day I disappoint you – will you try still to keep a place for me in your affections. But I hope I shall not do that, only I wonder if you realise that I am not nearly so good, strong, or clever as you? You must not contradict me, but just let me say what I feel to be true.

I have been a little worried about business. You know I am not earning a great deal, and railway fares and lunches make away with a goodly part of my wage. It is now about three months over the time when I should have had an increase, but I have been as good as told that I shall not receive one, it being inferred that as an 'engaged' girl, I should not expect it. I know that I am better off than many of the girls there – but it is unfair, don't you think?

On Monday I went to Emma's and I do believe we made more progress than usual. There is some talk of her going to school – I think it would do her good if they could manage it, don't you?

Yesterday I lunched with Miss Brown and enjoyed very much the short time we had together. Perhaps there will be an opportunity of introducing you one day. I told Miss Brown I had just read *Jane Eyre* and she informed me she read it three times straight away – it so fascinated her.

Here is the passage from *Jane Eyre* I referred to on Sunday: 'Women are supposed to be very calm generally; but women feel just as men feel; they need exercise for the faculties, and a field for their efforts as much as their brothers do; they suffer from too rigid a restraint, too absolute a stagnation, precisely as men would suffer; and it is narrow-minded in their more privileged fellow-creatures to say that they ought to confine themselves to making puddings and knitting stockings, to play-ing on the piano and embroidering bags. It is thoughtless to condemn them or laugh at them, if they seek to do more than custom has pronounced necessary for their sex.'

I must tell you too when I see you about the sermon I heard preached by Dr Campbell Morgan[5] at Bishopsgate Chapel in the lunch hour of New Year's Day.

And now dear friend, I may say Goodbye until next Thursday. Look well after yourself, or I shall have to scold you severely. Please tell your Auntie how much we enjoyed our-selves, and give her my kindest regards. Your loving Ruth.

Eva to Ruth   31 January 1907
My dear,
It seems quite a long time since you and I had a really 'good talk' together – I feel the necessity of it very much, for one seems to get such an accumulation of subjects in one's brain, and what an 'exceeding great relief' it is to look into these with a friend upon whose toleration, sympathy and understanding one can count. I have read just a *very* little this week about Mr Campbell's 'New Theology' but should require to know a great deal more before I could form a decided opinion. I cannot help feeling, though, that there is still in the world a great want of toleration. I think when a man or woman has thought and studied deeply and is convinced that the conclusions he or she has arrived at are right, they ought, at any rate, to be given a hearing, free from prejudice, and honoured for the courage in stating their convic-tions. This, I think, we should hold to through all time with regard to all things. If we could only go with free, unfettered minds to different subjects and books! Do you know Miss

Brown's opinion on this subject?

Now dear, I have rambled on and on without asking you one question about yourself, and here is your last dear letter too, at my elbow. A certain very eulogistic paragraph therein I will say nothing except that 'I renounce it all'. I am not worthy of such words, Ruth.

I am so sorry about your 'business worry'. I think, as you say, that it is unfair – the expense of going to the City is too great. I do hope you may hear of something more lucrative and congenial – I have told you my salary has been risen to 23/- per week, and Mr Cunningham said, 'I don't say it will stop there Miss Slawson', so I am really as well off as if I were taking about 28/- in the City, as I have no railway fare or lunch to pay.

I am expecting to see Emma this week. I think with you, that it would be *very* good if they could get her to school. Don't forget to tell me Miss Brown's remarks on *Jane Eyre*. It is very unselfish of you Ruth to wish that I might know your new friend too, and I should very much like one day to see and speak to her, only I am afraid she would not feel so towards me. We have not had much opportunity lately to talk of books, but my reading has been very varied. I have commenced another huge volume on Africa, also on America, and am now reading *Lives of the Queens of England,* which interests me much. I have felt lately something like a traveller on a voyage of discovery – books have lately been opening up to me new worlds. I believe our hearts and minds are so formed for the *infinite* that things *finite* cannot possibly satisfy us.

I am growing envious of your luncheon hour opportunities of hearing great preachers, and fearful lest you should feed the spiritual at the cost of the physical; now *do,* Ruth, this dreadfully cold weather, have a good luncheon; you *must* take care of yourself.

I have 'a desire for thy presence', dear friend – so come next Thursday if you can. Eva.

Ruth's Diary   Wednesday, 23 January 1907
This has been a happy week – most happy! The religious world is being stirred to its very depth by what great numbers have chosen to call the Rev. R. J. Campbell's 'New Theology'. I have watched the newspaper reports of the controversy with great interest, indeed I am making a collection of as many cuttings as I can get. I have found myself almost 'ostracised', however, at

home and abroad, for daring to sympathise with him. On Monday, after getting home from Emma's in the evening, I sat down with a newspaper in my hand, intending to read, but somehow we began a discussion. To the amazement of Dad and Mother, and also to myself, for it seemed some foreign voice spoke through me, I declared with vehemence that what the revival people had been praying for had come, though not in the way they expected. Mother was cross, Dad surprised, but I grew more excited, and spent a sleepless night in vain attempts to still the inward tumult.

Ruth's Diary   Saturday, 26 January 1907
The papers had announced that Mr Campbell was to preach on Thursday the 24th, at the City Temple lunch-hour service, for the last time before a rather long holiday – his health having been impaired by the great strain he is undergoing. I determined to be present, and reached the Temple about a quarter past twelve. A policeman stood in the lobby, where a large notice informed late-comers like myself that the downstairs part was full. Mounting the stairs to the gallery, I was dismayed to find that full, or overfull, if such a thing is possible. What a sea of eager faces! However, being but a small person, I contrived to find room on a narrow window ledge. I could not see his face and, strain as I would and did, I could not hear much of the sermon which followed. It appeared he was refuting the charge of 'preaching new doctrines'. What he *is* trying to preach, he said, is the simple truth, as Christ preached it, getting back, away from the dogmas and creeds which have hampered our spiritual growth. Love, and a broad human sympathy, not theology, is what men need. He seemed to think that the time will come when we will not need our Churches. 'A quickening spirit', he said, 'is passing over and stirring men's souls' (my Monday's thought). Now and again there was a burst of applause – sometimes mingled with a slight hissing – as when he spoke of 'the humanity of God' and the 'divinity of man'. Near by me a man would call 'Order! Order!', but I was so carried away by my own emotions that calm thought was impossible. My hour being already up, I hurried back to the office. It seemed I had travelled far away from business; all the afternoon I sat on my stool trembling with suppressed excitement. Miss Panting I knew viewed my opinions with disfavour, and my action in going to the City Temple quixotic – therefore

I could not speak to her of the service.

Eva came in the evening, but as it was bitterly cold, and the ground snow-covered, we could not have our usual walk. Eva told of the pain she feels over the frequent conflict between her emotions and intellect. Sometimes she fancies intellectual occupations could fill her life, she said; at others there comes a strong feeling for love, and the touch of baby fingers. Is it wrong to feel this last longing, she wondered? Surely this must be evidence of the true woman-nature growing, as I think it is meant to grow, in all of us and it means pain when it has to go unsatisfied. We spoke of Charlotte Brontë who, with her passionate nature, married an 'ordinary' man, and we wondered if this longing had been hers, proving itself stronger than the love of intellectual pursuits after all. I could wish Eva a good man's love above all things else – but love seems half pain too.

I was made glad that day also by a letter – a wonderful little letter, from Miss Brown, in answer to one I had written her, in which I tried to explain without Uriah Heep-like humility, my real ignorance of much that has become, through study and experience, real to her. I shall ever value that letter! To my amazement she seems to value my friendship. I was pleased to read a favourite quotation in it from George Eliot – 'Those who trust us, educate us.' Yesterday I again lunched with Miss Brown. Just before we separated she quoted some words to me – I only remember they began with 'It hurts being made', and went on to say it is better to be 'made' even though it 'hurts'. I felt encouraged and happy, and feel so still. What impulse made her press my hand, and say so warmly, 'Goodbye dear'? I wonder if I can ever repay her for the good she has done me? I hope so!

Ruth's Diary   Monday, 28 January 1907

On Saturday I walked with joyous steps to meet Wal. At length he arrived – he had missed the train. This was disappointing, for 20 minutes is a long time to hold evenly the pleased anticipation of a loved one. A remark now and then was all either of us ventured, until we had turned homeward, when Wal asked if I was thinking deeply, or was there something I wanted to say. In the course of the conversation that followed, Wal said I was different to most girls – they had a way of making you tell them everything, but I had not, or apparently failed with his sex. Surely that is not true – either way it hurt terribly! We parted as

98

usual, Wal saying that we seemed only to understand one another when we were saying Goodnight. I would be content if he never touched me, if only we understood each other. Until we do, caresses seem almost a mockery. Yesterday Wal spoke of next year – of our marrying. It seemed to me he spoke from an idea of Duty and it did not relieve my heartache.

Ruth's Diary   Thursday, 7th February 1907
All last week I thought, and wondered, about Wal and myself. At length I resolved to tell Wal when he came that I too have an ideal before me, though perhaps I have thought singularly little of marriage for myself – it has seemed remote, almost improbable. But I know that I should feel it wrong to marry him next year, or at any time, unless things were very different between us. To go on as we have done would kill me, or would kill all that is best in me, and worthy of being kept alive, and I feel my life is not my own to do as I like. I understand myself better than I once did, and have a clearer outline of the needs of my nature – I know what I could, and *would* do without, whatever it cost, if I felt I ought. I want to do *something good* with my life, and I cannot do anything with this load on my mind, breaking my spirits and sapping my energies. 'Yes', I thought, 'I will tell him this', and let him know that I too expect, and would give much! If we cannot live our life *together,* sharing ideals, nay uniting them – thoughts, joys and sorrows – of what use is it all?

On Monday I spent a bitter-sweet kind of evening. After leaving business, and partaking of tea at Lyons', I walked to St Ethelburga's[6] where I had promised to join May at the 'Guild' to which she belongs. There were fewer girls present than usual, but it was fascinating to watch May – she seemed the 'life' of the little party. After a while she beguiled me into joining in the games, and I was to be seen skipping, jumping, running and swinging the clubs like a great tomboy. Some ghost of my old self, or from my younger days, seemed to rise up and reproach me for having become so morbid and grave. 'This innocent recreation', it seemed to say, 'keeps the mind well-balanced.' But my spirits suddenly sank in proportion as they had risen and I was not altogether sorry when it was time to leave.

My depression increased as I walked from the station home – I longed to spend the night out of doors, pacing up and down, battling with the foe. My attempts at dancing, too, had made me feel rather ill. However, home I went, contriving with difficulty to present a gay front to the others and keep it up until safely in bed. I could not sleep – indeed my brain seemed to reel when I laid my head on the pillow – and soon I began to experience what must surely have been a kind of delirium. It was horrible! I think everything that has ever happened to cause my unhappiness, either through my own misdeeds, or through estrangements with others, rose up in clear image before my mind, and it seemed without will or intention on my part. I seemed in fact to lose all control of my thinking powers. The arrival of morning after this night of pain was welcome – very welcome! Miss Panting was away from business unwell, so I had double work to attend to next day. It was better so, for whenever I was still and quiet, this 'unhinged' sensation returned.

In the evening I went to Leyton. Here my depression returned threefold and I felt I was puzzling Eva very much. We started on a walk and by degrees it passed off – in the end we had a more than usually helpful talk and seemed to get knit even more closely together.

Ruth's Diary   Monday, 11 February 1907
Yesterday I took the train to Balham. After dinner, the younger members of the family went out, and Wal and I were left in solitary state in the parlour. For a time we said nothing worth recalling, and then some sudden impulse led me to tell him a little of the strange mood which o'ercame me last week. It seemed to trouble him, for I fancy he thought I had been tormented (as I had in great part) by thoughts of my wrong doings and he said how much the thought of this should trouble him, if my 'little mistakes' so upset me. He then spoke of my marrying him before next year, and I told him I thought we should first feel sure we could 'unite' our ideals. He seemed confident that 'unity' would follow.

After tea we set out for the Unitarian Chapel in Great Portland Street. My attention was absorbed throughout the sermon, 'the Real Jesus', more so than Wal's, I fancy, for he grew restive. 'The Real Jesus', the Minister said, was a socialist, a friend of the oppressed. Afterwards we talked of many things. We mentioned Miss Brown, and afterwards, Eva. I told him my belief that the future holds in store for her no ordinary lot, and he seemed inclined to agree.

On Tuesday the 19th I spent a very pleasant evening with May at a Women's Suffrage meeting, held in the hall at the back of St

100

Ethelburga's. The speaker was an elderly lady, Mrs Stope, but she put forward the splendid arguments or reasons why women should have the vote, clearly and skilfully. Dr Cobb, whom I am beginning to admire very much, also spoke for the cause – the only opposition came from a young and self-satisfied youth, and an elderly gentleman whose ideas I should imagine to be very conservative. Dr Cobb was for limiting the Franchise. This was a new idea to me, and I saw much sense in it. He thinks voters should be put through an examination or test before being allowed to exercise their privilege. I really believe May, in her inmost heart, became a 'Suffragette' that night.

Saturday evening brought a trial. On arriving at Emma's I learned she had been attending school nearly all the week previous and was now looked upon as a regular pupil, therefore my teachership must be resigned. The news came like a shock and it was with difficulty that I kept back some troublesome tears. Mrs Clover thanked me for all I had done. But Emma will be happier I feel sure – I alone am the loser. Let me not be grudging, but seek to be useful wherever I find the opportunity.

Ruth's Diary   Saturday, 9 March 1907
On Saturday I met Eva in Ilford. She brought me two pictures for my birthday – they are so beautiful. We left about six and I saw her onto a tram, then walked on to the station to meet Wal. Would he miss his train, I wondered? Yes, and the next one as well. I felt free to give expression to vexed remarks when he *did* appear, after I had waited for nearly an hour. He did not appreciate them, and punished me by refusing to explain the cause of his lateness, and so we started out on our walk in no very amiable mood. I was then soundly berated on my obstinacy and independence – the latter quality I intend ever to cultivate and Wal must learn my intention. I am sure it would be better for many, many people if conventional ideas concerning women's dependence upon men could be altered – they are a hindrance to the true progress of women, and are not altogether good for men. I believe so strongly in the possibilities and powers of my own sex, that I deprecate all customs, though rooted in ideas of chivalry once admirable, that would retard their emancipation. Wal would shield and shelter, where I do not desire that he should. We were soon home, and as Wal stayed the night, sat talking after supper until quite late.

The following Saturday I met Wal as usual, and as is now

becoming usual, he missed his train. I said nothing, so to Manor Park we went, or rather were blown, for the wind was unusually high. We walked across the Flats, and if it had not been for those feminine articles of clothing which make one dread the healthy breeze, that walk would have been delightful. As it was I enjoyed myself as much as possible with a hat and skirts to look after.

Wal left me a gift, and a pamphlet to read, entitled *Woman – or Suffragette!* written by Marie Corelli.[7] This pamphlet was in its author's usual style, and did not shake my convictions one bit, though it roused me so that I found myself composing replies which I was vain enough to think would entirely vanquish the enemy, stir and awaken the inane, and strengthen the weak.

Ruth's Diary   Thursday, 2 May 1907

I have just returned from the City Temple! A longing to see Mr Campbell again possessed me, so I have done without lunch for once, in order to get to hear part of his sermon. But perhaps a trouble which is weighing heavily on my mind just now – a problem to which I can find no solution – prevented me giving him my whole attention. I have written very little, or nothing, in my diary, about business, but a climax has come, and the course of my life may be altered by it. I have not written previously, because I knew if I started I should want to say so much, moreover it would be difficult to express the disgust and indignation I daily feel. The whole system is so abominable, and so unjust – its influence so crushing – that I wonder it does not bring about revolt; but the crushing, I suppose, prevents that. The most terrible instance of the effect this slave-driving process has, is the case of the Brentwood manager, who threw himself under a train and was decapitated; and of another, who went mad. The firm is universally spoken of as a firm of 'sweaters', and the experience proves the name truly given.

Numbers and numbers of office staff, male and female, have been trying to get the small increase in salary which in most cases, including my own, has long been overdue. Yesterday we were told it is vain to ask and that if we are not satisfied we had better look for something else. It is only the thought of the home folk which has kept me there so long, and prevents me leaving on Saturday, but I have finally determined to do as they suggest and 'look out for something else'.

In addition to the unjust treatment, there is the terrible

depression to which I so often fall a prey, in consequence of being in the department for dealing with all questions of competition. The meanness of tactics adopted for the baffling of tradesmen and their ultimate undoing, is beyond description. The unfortunate managers, whose business it is to flog them up well, and be flogged themselves by Head Office for not being drastic enough, all come into our little office before Mr Bray, who is certainly a splendid 'bully'. But to listen to this bullying, day after day, makes the heart sick.

But the bitterest drop in my cup, I know, is the knowledge that whereas I might have been fitting myself for some higher order of work, I have drifted along, absorbed in my trouble over Wal, or in day-dreaming. I know myself to be ignorant and incompetent, and the knowledge *is very bitter*. What shall I now turn to?

Sunday 28 April I was up betimes and away to Purley, where Miss Brown met me. We went to the Friends' meeting, and very interesting I found it. By the time Miss Brown and I had reached her 'diggings', and eaten heartily of the tasty dinner spread before us, the afternoon was well advanced. Miss Brown took up some needlework. She was putting the finishing touches to a 'reform' dress, which was donned after Wal's arrival just before tea. It pleased me royally – it was so classic, simple and graceful. Its hue was a soft shade of green – its trimmings a pointed yoke of white canvas, whereon was worked in orange and pale yellow silks the quaintest of Japanese designs. Perhaps I *was* shocked to learn Miss Brown is a cigarette smoker! During the afternoon she asked my opinion on a very delicate matter. I gave it unhesitatingly, and she almost sprang from her chair in astonishment. She had intended acting as I said, but could hardly believe I would have done so, as she, a short while ago, would have deemed such a course unwomanly. Strange!

On Monday the 29th I went with Miss Brown to Caxton Hall to the meeting held in commemoration of the life and work of Mrs Josephine Butler,[8] where my hero-worship cravings found food in plenty and my interest ever since in a movement that *must* do some good. Over tea I heard the romantic history of the meeting at Windermere, and subsequent friendship between Miss Brown and Joan Fry. The meeting itself was splendid! The chairman, to my surprise and pleasure, called upon Mrs Fawcett to speak.[9] Perhaps her chief point was that the question was one of equal concern for men *and* women. She also quoted from a

103

minister who said that what we most have to trouble about is the getting of heaven into men, not men into heaven (applause).

She was followed by the Bishop of Southwark, who pointed out that 'discernment' as well as courage was largely possessed by Mrs Butler. Many great and good people were at first difficult to win over to her side, among them Mr Gladstone, but her case was won eventually because she appealed to the heart of the *people*. It was a moral movement, resting for its strength on moral motives alone.

After him spoke Mrs Bramwell Booth,[10] and I think I might say her speech was the most stirring and inspiring of them all. Her clear, ringing voice, and fearless delivery were splendid! She said there was present a great principle in her work, a feeling that a great element was lacking in government. This made her work largely political. She saw that force, law, religion, were already powers in government, but it was *she* who brought into politics the *mother*. The principles of motherhood have a right to speak and act in the government of nations. Second, her work came from the impulse of a Divine call. She was a *Prophetess of Love!* We left early, as the journeys before us were long.

Ruth's Diary   Monday, 13 May 1907

Since my last entry I have been weathering mental storms, and I rather think there are many more before me. My resolution to leave the employ of Messrs Kearley and Tonge's remains firm.

On Thursday 2 May I went over to Eva's and enjoyed the evening very much. One of Eva's half-sisters – Gertie – has come to live with them; a bright girl of fourteen. We spent most of the time looking through her school books, and wishing we had had the chance to learn much of their contents. Eva was very excited, for she is going to take up painting, and besides is trying to teach Gertie shorthand and general office work.

On Thursday I paid that long deferred visit to Eleanor's and heard some tidings she has been waiting impatiently to communicate, namely, that she is going as a sister[11] to Dr Steven's Home, Bonnar Road, NE. This so nearly approached the subject occupying the attention of my own mind that I told Eleanor about it, and of course she was delighted. The more we talked, the more excited I became, and the more feasible the plan appeared, and I came away fully determined to speak about it to Wal on Saturday, and to get him to say what would be best for both of us.

On Saturday I met Wal, as arranged, at Liverpool St. The weather had suddenly become very hot, and everyone was in summer attire. The evening was a beautiful one, and instead of getting out at Ilford, we went on to Fairlop, and walked to the Forest. Espying a fallen tree-trunk, we sat down, and I began, stammeringly and falteringly, to tell my story. Wal seemed rather pleased at the idea than otherwise, and thought it would act as a 'test' between us. I felt, as I have often felt, that I had put my deepest and best before him, he realising only the surface.

Ruth's Diary   Friday, 17 May 1907
It is bitterly cold today, and numberless folk are sneezing and coughing in evidence of the colds they have caught as a result of donning summer garb at the beginning of the week, when it was truly hot.

In the lunch hour, Dad met Miss Panting and I, and escorted us through Tower Gardens to see the flags and pansies, just now making the spot really beautiful. Little attentions as we walked along filled me with warmth, and I realised a little how I should miss the father I have always more or less idolised, if I actually left home. Whether that will come to pass is still very uncertain; my way is obscure and darkened, though I have earnestly pleaded for light. On Monday I told Mother all about it, and she was both upset and angry, and said some things which hurt me terribly. Dad had nothing to say against it – his only reproach was that I am too secretive about matters.

On Wednesday I spent a very unhappy evening at home. Mother accused me of selfish motives in thinking of taking up Deaconess work, and said I was altogether unfit for it.

Ruth's Diary   Friday, 14 June 1907
Yesterday brought an agreeable surprise in the shape of a bulky package, addressed to me in Mr Sunderland's handwriting, an application form for me to fill in, a little booklet explaining the work of a Deaconess (I do not like that term, 'sister' is much better). There is much that does not quite appeal to me, both in the booklets and in the style of the application form. I still think that if I had the necessary style and courage I should prefer to take up 'nursing', where religious opinions are left unquestioned, better far would I like to take up a branch of purely

social work among the poor and degraded, with those who allow free religious thought, but for carrying out my last confessed wish, I should greatly need experience. If I speak frankly and fearlessly, and I trust I shall, I am afraid the committee appointed to examine me will find me lacking in many respects.

Acting on impulse I wrote to Wal, and forwarded the booklet with my letter. What will he say after all?

The next day Wal had promised to be down by seven, and in spite of the rain I went to the Station to meet him. I waited patiently – watched three trains come in, but he did not appear, and sick at heart I turned away home. On getting indoors I quickly escaped upstairs, where I could weep at will. How tired I felt of it all! Disappointment upon disappointment, weary waitings and anxieties, and cool indifference and surprise that I should feel any [disappointment] from Wal, when he finally chose to come.

Ruth's Diary   Monday, 24 June 1907
The weighty question of my becoming a Deaconess has been finally settled – and in the negative. On Thursday I wrote to Mrs Sunderland. It was very difficult, for I feel I have troubled them unduly, but for all the love I feel towards them, I could not possibly have entered that sphere in the spirit they would have desired.

5

'A Sudden Rebellion to our Old Ways of Living and Thinking'
November 1907–December 1909

Ruth's decision not to become a Deaconess showed that she was acting according to her new ideas, despite being desperate for a change of occupation. It was ironic that just as she was 'waking up to the powers and possibilities' of her sex, her family suffered a crisis when Daisy became ill and, two years later, died from consumption. Not only did this cause Ruth great personal distress, as she was close to Daisy (and it must have awakened painful memories of Ewart), but the strain it put on her family's resources drew her further into a situation that she was finding almost impossible. With her mother's frequent ill health, her father's hopelessness when it came to household duties, the increased load of domestic work fell to Ruth (the same responsibilities were not expected of her brother Tom). While she did her utmost to please everyone, she was often in conflict with her mother for pursuing her own interests. It was significant that as she became more involved with the ideas of women's emancipation, the tirades on her 'faults, follies and weaknesses and the accusations of selfishness' increased. Single women were not expected to conduct a life away from home, and if not married, had duties to their families.

By the end of 1908, Ruth felt exhausted and demoralised. Although she knew her mother's accusations were unjust, she was easily debilitated by guilt and self-doubt. It was no light matter 'throwing off the chains' of duty and service that had been so deeply instilled.

Despite the domestic troubles, the years 1908-9 were ones of great political activity and personal development. When things improved at home, Ruth's diaries were suddenly full of descriptions of women's meetings, demonstrations, socialist rallies, great sermons, cultural events and lectures of all kind. Often she only had time to make brief notes. Just as the times of isolation at home brought depression, the contact with 'splendid' and inspiring events (many of which were the major political events of the day) brought increased confidence.

In June 1908 Ruth attended two 'Votes for Women' demonstrations which were two of the greatest suffrage events in history. They were organised to show the extent of the movement and its support, while Prime Minister Asquith procrastinated about including 'Votes for Women' in the proposed Reform Bill. The Women's Social and Political Union demonstration in particular, held on Midsummer's Day, was a feat of organisational ability, with 80 women speakers and 20 platforms in Hyde Park, and most of the women dressed in the suffragette colours of white, mauve and green. The Daily Express described it as 'one of the most astonishing sights since the days of Boadicea ... It is probable that so many people never before stood in one square mass anywhere in England', and The Times estimated the numbers at up to half a million.

Ruth's ideas were more in sympathy with the non-militant suffragettes and groups which had links between women's emancipation, socialist ideas and spirituality. She also began to tackle the more personal areas of the Sex Question and the difficulties surrounding it. She joined the Woolwich branch of the Progressive Thought League, which had been formed to promote the ideas of the New Theology. In July 1909 she wrote to Charlotte Despard, President of the Women's Freedom League, for advice on the best course of action to take 'in the women's cause', and received a helpful and sympathetic reply.

Eva went to many of the same events as Ruth, and was clearly happier and more active than in the previous year. In July 1908 she joined the Leyton branch of the Independent Labour Party, and in January 1909 was attracted by the 'strongly social' preaching of the Rev. James of Walthamstow–'a Congregational Minister and a much persecuted man' (presumably for his radical religious views). By the summer she was attending lectures, services and the Women's Conference at his Trinity Chapel. Mr James was to become an important figure in Eva's and Minna's life, for they were both attracted to him.

For Ruth, the 'old ways of living and thinking' finally became incompatible with the new. By the summer of 1909, she was drained by the continual ups and downs in her relationship with

Wal, who seemed to make every attempt to undermine her need for independence. Discovering also that she had been 'duped and fooled' by him, although it is never clear exactly what happened, she broke off her engagement. At the end of 1909, after much heart-searching, she finally left home.

In November 1907 Ruth took up her diary after a six-month gap, recollecting the events since Daisy became ill, and wrote to Eva.

Ruth to Eva   8 November 1907
                                              46 Chancelot Road
                                             Abbey Wood, Kent

My own dear friend,

Are you wondering *when* my letter is coming? It has been uppermost in my mind during the last two weeks but work, never-ending inexorable work, at home and in the City, has prevented me from getting even one word written. And there is so much to tell you – little things in the main – yet I would pour them all in your sympathetic ear!

We have been in our new home now just upon three weeks – such strange weeks. Do you know what it is to seem to lose your own identity? I am only just beginning to believe that 'I' am actually 'I'. That is badly expressed, but I think you will understand what I mean. I am such a one to get attached to certain persons, places and things. It is very foolish, I know, but I seem to get worse instead of better, as the years roll on.

I wondered how Woolwich would impress you. We have to go into Woolwich for most of our shopping, and I always come away with a heartache. The poverty and squalor – oh it is dreadful! Close by the Station there is a large square where stalls are erected – the haunt of 'cheap Jacks', open air speakers, hooligans – a motley multitude! Abbey Wood itself is popu-lated solely, as far as our observations tell us at present, by people of the Artisan type. (Do not think I mean any disrespect to them.) Poverty seems rampant here also – chiefly brought about I expect by the lack of employment at the Arsenal.[1] The only redeeming feature about the place is the beautiful country which lies at the back. How your artistic sense would revel just now in the glorious autumnal tints of the trees which crown the hill-tops! Then the Pine Woods – there is something very weird about them! Oh, you must come soon and see it all for yourself! Wait till you see our wallpapers and prepare for shocks!

Gorgeous pinks, mauves, greens, with which our humble furniture clashes painfully!

The reports of Daisy's progress have been reassuring, this last week or two, and she keeps very bright.

Dear, you make me feel a poor creature indeed, when you say I have been an example to you in *any* way. I am most faulty at home, though I do try hard to make myself helpful. If I ever did leave home dear, it would be because I thought they would be happier without me. This was in mind much at the time I purposed taking up Deaconess work – the difficulty of doing right, and pleasing those at home seemed so great.

I feel anxious in many ways about Dad. He seems to get more melancholy, and less inclined than ever to mix with people, filling Mother and I with fears we scarce admit, even to ourselves. He does not like Abbey Wood, finds the railway journey irksome, and says he would never stay in the place but for Daisy. To make matters worse there is a dearth of Chapels and Churches in the neighbourhood.

I am giving you the worse view of things – grumbling, because it is a relief – but there are compensations! I find the extra time at the office very useful for shorthand practice. I go twice a week to shorthand classes at Plumstead and am getting on famously. I get home about 10.30. Mother now goes to bed and does not wait up, so I am free from qualms which would otherwise torture me. The first time I went the old arguments had all to be gone through again.

About our meeting dear. You know how much I want to see you, and you know too how difficult it is for me to get an evening's outing. Next week I shall be quite unable to manage it. Can you come up to the City on Saturday the 23rd instead? Do say 'Yes'. I wonder if we could come to any arrangement like that we used to have, about writing? The only reading I can contrive to do now is the paper which I share with Dad every morning, and shorthand matter. I took out from the library Walt Whitman's *Democratic Vistas* but had to return it unperused.

Are you getting tired of my chatter? Write soon if you have time, and let me know all about yourselves – how *you* are, and Gertie and your Auntie, and accept your own big share of love.

Your friend, Ruth.

Ruth's Diary   31 December 1907
This has been a year of great stress and strain, yet I can scarcely

110

realise that a few hours more will see the birth of 1908. Pain and worry and bewilderment seem to have dazed our senses so that we were hardly conscious of the passing of time. A few *big* events and happenings stand out very clearly as I look back – the rest is blurred and confused.

In August was our holiday in Folkestone – a week of much pleasure and pain. One night I felt almost certain about what was the matter with Daisy – a night when I sat up in bed battling with terrible thoughts and fears, and Daisy sat up coughing fearfully. Immediately after, visits to Victoria Park Hospital followed. One dreadful Sunday when the Doctor told Dad there was very little hope for her, consumption having taken such a strong hold, I shall never, never forget. Daisy was away thirteen weeks, and during that time we removed to Abbey Wood, hoping the pine air would prove beneficial to her.

We were not sorry to get away from Ilford, though Abbey Wood is a depressing sort of place, with nothing but the woods to recommend it. Dad and I leave home at seven every morning in order to catch the last workman's train, for we could never pay full fare on this line. We have a long, comfortless journey, and are never sure what time we are going to arrive home, punctuality being a virtue altogether unknown to the SE railway. We are not far away from where Wal lodges, and I see him a *little* more frequently, but we have not been the happiest of couples.

I joined shorthand classes soon after we came here, hoping to get on quickly so as to get another place and more money, for we are very pinched at home. My progress is dismally slow, for I am generally tired out before I get to the class, and when it is over I feel scarcely able to crawl home. Before Xmas, I began to feel ill and exhausted, and became the victim of a horrible depression, but the holiday has done me a world of good, and I hope to accomplish more shortly. I must struggle on somehow.

I have seen May twice, and Eva once, since we moved – Miss Brown not at all.

We are doing our best at home for Daisy, but her cough continues to be troublesome, and she is often very sick. *Rest* is most essential, so she sits by an open window upstairs, and inhales the air that way. She is very bright and cheery now, but before she went into the hospital we could do nothing with her, she was so strangely silent – altogether unlike herself. How could this cruel complaint come to *her* ? What – what will this coming year bring forth?

My dear,
If you will excuse this assortment of notepaper, I will commence
my letter to you, having a few moments to spare. News I have
none! The week which has elapsed since our meeting passed
quietly and swiftly.

I had been looking forward, I could not say how much, to a
walk on Saturday, but 'the rains descended and the winds blew',
you will remember, and prevented our stirring from the house.
However, Daisy and I had a very nice time together. We read,
and talked, and sang – you should have heard Daisy singing –
and my heart warmed to her as it does somehow when we are
alone. We seemed to realise then how precious is sisterhood.

Many things seem to point to a marked improvement in
Daisy; she has not been sick, and on Saturday was wondering
what she could do to 'earn something'. Of course we should not
let her do anything, but it is a favourable sign.

I am not sure yet about the Saturdays in March, but as soon as
I can I will send you word. I do feel, often, that all the giving,
the unselfishness of our friendship is on your side – one day I
hope to serve you.

I am still undecided about those classes, thinking it best to see
how things are going at home. I really must learn something
thoroughly, dear – a woman needs a profession or trade as
much as a man and I know nothing well.

What interesting book are you reading now? I have recently
read a little book entitled *The Woman Socialist*.[2] It has given me
much to think about – you must read it! There are four verses
of a poem by an anonymous writer quoted, which I will cite, if I
can, from memory.

> Oh, to be alone!
> To escape from the work, the play!
> The talking every day;
> To escape from all I have done
> And all that remains to do;
> To escape – yes, even from you, my only love, and be
> Alone and free.
>
> Could I but stand

112

Between grey moorland and grey sky
Where the wind and plovers cry
And no man is at hand
And feel the wind blow on my rain-wet face and know
I am free – not yours – but my own
Free and alone.

For the soft firelight
And home of your heart, my dear,
They hurt, always being here,
I want to stand upright
And see how my back can bear
Burdens, to think, to know,
To learn, to grow.

I am only you!
Part of you, yours, your wife.
And I have no other life.
I cannot ...
I cannot see, cannot breathe
There is us, but there is not me,
And worse, at your kiss I grow,
Contented so.

Will this strike you as the natural cry of a growing woman soul, I wonder, or as the cry of an egoist? Perhaps I should not have given it you apart from the book. But I do think dear, the Sex Question, or instinct, should I say, is made too much of, is treated unhealthily in so many books and plays (that play I saw gave form to ideas I have long been arriving at). Do not, do not think I would belittle the wonder and greatness of love, but should not we women be so trained that we *can* live independently if need be? Would it not prevent much misery and ruin if women lived *their own lives* – had *their own* interests?

I met this idea first in Tolstoy, when it gave me a great shock. (I mean the idea of the sex instincts being made too much of.) But dear, I ought not to have touched upon a subject like this – it is one of the things I have wanted to talk over with you.

How have you been keeping through this very trying weather? With so much sickness about one feels many apprehensions as to the welfare of loved ones, especially those out of sight.

Give my kindest regards to Aunt Edie and Gertie, and accept

your own huge share of love. Ruth.

Ruth's Diary   Tuesday, 28 January 1908
Home to tea with Miss Nimmo [a co-employee] at Lewisham.
Went with her to a drawing room Suffragette meeting (twelve
present). Miss Macauley, of the Women's Social and Political
Union, gave an address which was most enthusiastically
received.

Ruth's Diary   Tuesday, 11 February 1908
Went to High Holborn in the lunch hour to be interviewed by
Miss Spencer, of the Women's Employment Association. She
advised a course at the Cusack Institute.

Ruth's Diary   Thursday, 27 February 1908
My birthday, so had heaps of cards and letters and some lovely
gifts. Wal round in the evening. Ended miserably with a big 'M'.

Ruth's Diary   3 March 1908
Called at Cusack's. *Trouble* at home, sense of misery deepened.

Ruth's Diary   4 March 1908
Met Wal. Told him I think of leaving home.

Ruth's Diary   6 March 1908
Met Wal. Wet evening so came home. Wal said he had 'no
feelings'. Said he had once cared too much – no, not too much,
but it had been dangerous for him, but he cared as much as he
was capable of caring now.

Ruth's Diary   9 March 1908
Stayed at home with Daisy. Met Wal in the evening. Long, long
talk. Said he had tried religion – it had failed to satisfy and he
was now determined to try pleasure. Also told me he could not
marry as he had saved no money. I will not say anything of my
own heartache and weakness.

Ruth's Diary   14 March 1908
Wal round. Walk and talk. Tried to tell him never to think of
marrying for my benefit, as when I marry, if ever, it will be to a
man who would feel it a joy – it was a poor attempt, but we
agreed not to think of the subject again until things are quite

different between us.

My dear,

You will be surprised when I tell you in what high style I am
writing this letter. It is Monday afternoon, yet I am seated
upstairs in Daisy's room, at her table. We have the windows as
wide open as they will go, and the sunshine is streaming in
beautifully (likewise the wind). Daisy is stretched right across
the window in her lounge chair, reading the paper – I am a little
further back. To please her I have enveloped myself in a great
white shawl, as the air is certainly keen.

I was very grateful dear for your birthday gifts, the thought
behind them, and your letter.

So you have fresh anxieties about home. I am sorry for that
dear, for it is so hard to keep from worrying about these
troubles, and the worry does such harm. After painful mental
struggles I have relinquished my scheme of going to the Cusak
Institute – at least for the time being. I fear the money I should
have wanted to spend will soon be wanted for other things.
Dear, do you know I wonder sometimes what *is* to become of
us. It must seem to you that I am always forming plans and
dropping them – it seems so to myself, and I get very
disheartened about it, but I do try. This time I had even been to
the Institute and been interviewed by the good Doctor. Heigho!

I had a treat last week though. On Thursday evening I met
Miss Brown and went to a lecture with her. It was on the
Treatment of Child Criminals and was given by Miss Adler
(Secretary of the Committee on Wage-Earning Children). She
pleaded for separate Courts for children. I think a Bill is now
before Parliament, dealing with most of these questions.

I have had one or two inspiring lunch hours. On Wednesdays
I have been going to hear Dr Cobb at St Ethelburga's – he is a
noble and brave thinker and, I believe, doer. The other
Thursday I heard a remarkable old man, famed for his work in
social matters, the Rev. Boyd Carpenter. These sermons have
cheered and helped me greatly, but I find despondency hard to
conquer.

Can you meet me next Thursday, the 19th, at the usual time
and place? Remember me kindly to your Aunt Edie and Gertie.
I hope to see them soon. For yourself there is my heartfelt love.

Thy friend, Ruth.

Ruth's Diary   Sunday, 19 April 1908
Took Daisy a short walk in the morning. Went alone to Young
People's Conference at City Temple. Cosy surroundings – nice
people. Brief papers with discussions after each – Sympathy,
Art and Religion, Christian Science, Esperanto, Women's
Suffrage. Lively argument after last mentioned. Chairman's
trite 'I should like my wife to have a vote.' Met Wal Cannon St.
Made me have tea at an 'Italiano' shop.

Ruth's Diary   Wednesday, 29 April 1908
Bond St in evening to help May with a girls' Club. May's dainty
workroom – dinner at restaurant. Busy evening – home with
May. Tired out – had my first glass of 'ale'.

Ruth's Diary   Wednesday, 6 May 1908
New Cross. Suffragette Meeting with Mrs Nimmo (heard sad
story of her early married life). Meeting rough. Miss Pankhurst
not present. Liked Mrs Pethick-Lawrence.[3]

Ruth's Diary   Friday, 8 May 1908
Commenced Mary Wollstonecraft's *Rights of Women*.[4]

Ruth to Eva   11 May 1908
Mine own dear friend,
If you will excuse these scraps of notepaper, I will write a brief
reply to your letter.
   Both Walter and I will be *very* glad to spend Sunday with you,
and as for our long Saturday afternoon and evening together,
my spirits bubble over at the thought! If it is a fine, glorious
afternoon, it would be nicest, don't you think, to stay out in the
open? – the free fresh air I have begun to revel in! We could
journey on the top of the bus to Hyde Park, and there sit and
talk to our heart's content. If it *should* be wet, we must visit a
Museum or Picture Gallery.
   Do not let me ever receive a self-abusive letter from you
again! A cow-like appearance indeed – whatever next? Do not
take Mr Wilson's words too much to heart, dear. Do you know,
I am often really frightened at my own impressionableness – I
have known a few unflattering words, lightly or even jokingly
spoken, to rankle long and bitterly.
   Your description of the Quaker meeting made me smile. I
must not stop to remark anything about the Quakers, except

116

that I could not make a habit of attending their meetings either. Have I ever told you that Miss Brown herself is far from being an orthodox Quaker? It would not be possible for *her*, I know, to be an orthodox *anything*.

I feel so delightfully alive this morning – dangerously so, in fact, and it seems impossible to settle to writing. If I were *with* you, I should probably be talking with wild haste and excitement, but I cannot write. Yet I am always fearing the reaction of this particular mood. Heigho!

We are still unsettled and rather miserable at home, but shall I tell you some 'practical' good news? I am to have a 'rise' at business – a whole half-crown per week. Miss Panting and I have come under the notice of Mr Tonge lately, and so our good fortune seems assured. It is almost too good to believe.

How we *will* talk on Saturday. All further news when we meet. With all love dear, Ruth.

Ruth's Diary   Tuesday, 19 May 1908
Commenced morning studies – Algebra, French and Geography. Went for a walk with Wal in the evening. Unsatisfactory talk on 'Suffragettes', through an article in the *Mint* which accuses them of undermining family life.

Ruth's Diary   Thursday, 28 May 1908
Read *The Story of an African Farm*[5] in lunch hour. Am I presumptuous in feeling that *much* of what I have been thinking and feeling so strongly is here expressed? Met Eva in the evening. Journeyed on a motor bus to Hyde Park, seeing many of the decorations put up in honour of the French President's visit on the way. Both of us feeling strongly a sudden rebellion to our old ways of living and thinking – which though expressing itself suddenly has, I think, been growing a long while; we had much to say.

Ruth's Diary   Tuesday, 9 June 1908
Wal did not put in an appearance, as is usual when he says he might, so wrote to Eva, read, etc.

Ruth's Diary   Wednesday, 10 June 1908
Wal round for an hour. Walked with him to Woodhurst Rd. Learned he had been to the Holborn Empire the previous evening. Walked backed alone. Accosted by man, lost way, but

117

kept calm. Would accompany me right the way home – anxious
for me to see him again. If I had had an umbrella with me he
should have received the best thrashing I could give for *daring* to
say the things he did to me. Could not sleep – Wal, the man –
is there one worth trusting?

Ruth to Eva   9 June 1908
My dear,
As usual I begin with apologies, first for not writing sooner, and
second for brevity and scribble; but then we shall soon be
together! We are having a great rush at business this week – I
cannot seem to get any spare time, but you know the difficulty as
well as I. How glad I am dear, we can understand so well in each
other this longing that has come upon us for a larger way of
living. I found so much of what I have been feeling interpreted
in *Story of an African Farm*. I was almost frightened sometimes
as I read it – I felt it so intensely.

Like you I feel the want of recreation – that outlet for
overcharged feelings. I must see if I cannot find a bargain in the
bicycle way, and oh, I should like a holiday by the sea. Daisy
still keeps well. You *will* be surprised when you see her. Don't
forget the 'Ghost Melody' and my other favourite. May is
bringing a song she is learning, and I am endeavouring to revive
an almost forgotten recitation.

Well dear, I must say Goodbye for a day or two longer. Give
my kindest regards to your Auntie and Gertie and accept your
very own share of my love. Ruth.
(Liverpool St. 2.30. Energy – high spirits – music!)

Ruth's Diary   Saturday, 13 June 1908
Met Eva and May Liverpool St. Station 2.30. Took bus to
Charing Cross – saw 'Votes for Women' procession – a *really
marvellous sight*. Thousands upon thousands of women, carrying
small banners and large – some exceedingly beautiful. Most of
the notable women were represented – George Eliot, Charlotte
Brontë, Josephine Butler, Madame Curie, Black Agnes of
Dunbar, Joan of Arc, Boadicea, Vashti – I could not name
half.[6] The smaller banners showed us the class to which each
group belonged – clerks, typists, scriveners, lace-makers,
doctors, nurses, painters etc. There were some splendid bands
too. The entire procession took exactly an hour to pass, and
there was no halting. The crowd stood through it all, cheering

118

and applauding often, but I did not hear one sound of mockery or contempt. It was a most impressive sight. We came home, had tea, and then went a little walk, taking Daisy with us. Some music – and bed.

Ruth's Diary   Sunday, 21 June 1908
Up to City 12 o'clock. Met by Wal at Charing Cross. Hyde Park Demonstration by Women's Social and Political Union. *Most* marvellous sight, outreaching the procession of the previous week in numbers – I should think by thousands – but my sympathies are more with the others. We joined the throng around Miss Pankhurst's stand for a time, but the crush was becoming very dangerous, so we fought our way out. Miss Pankhurst was wearing her robes and college cap, and made an inspiring figure in an inspiring spectacle. I should very much have liked a picture of her as she stood, a smile on her almost beautiful face, a slender arm outstretched, appealing for an audience, which a gang of roughs, stationed right in the front, refused for some time to give her. It was all very wonderful, but I could not help thinking their object would not be half-attained – the crowd seemed more intent on amusement than anything else.

I went on with Wal to Ealing. His friend Mr Reynolds and the young lady he is marrying in September came to tea, and we spent the evening in talking and music. I had been curious to see this pair, but strive as I would to keep them away, some bitter and jealous thoughts tormented me and toned my impressions. They knew so much more about Wal than I did. I felt all out in the cold, and felt too that Wal is often needlessly and thought-lessly cruel. It hurts me almost more than I can bear, that he should treat me so affectionately one time and so coolly another – I cannot understand it.

Ruth's Diary   Tuesday, 23 June 1908
Have nearly cried myself silly this morning – very foolishly. Later – learned that some orange coloured pamphlets displayed in the window of Wal's lodgings, offering to explain the case *against* Women's Suffrage, had been placed there by him.

Ruth's Diary   Wednesday, 1 July 1908
Met Eva. Went to Victoria Embankment Gardens, where sat and talked of many things. Happy evening. Eva's *life* beginning

– *how* glad I am. She has joined ILP. Told her a few difficult thoughts concerning my own life. Was struck by the unusual loveliness of the sky as came down in the train.

Ruth's Diary   Saturday, 4 July 1908
Hampstead Meeting House, Friends' Quarterly Meeting – most interesting. Listened to conversation on the Strand nude statues and discussion now going on in the daily papers concerning them. Arrived home accompanied by Elizabeth [Miss Brown] just before ten o'clock.

Ruth's Diary   Sunday, 5 July 1908
Elizabeth and I sat in woods and talked during the morning, mostly on women and the Sex Question. Could not express my own thoughts. Sat indoors and talked all the afternoon. I should have been happy but for an undercurrent of worry through Mother's coolness to me.

Ruth's Diary   Tuesday, 7th July 1908
Out with Wal. Told him I want to see Isadora Duncan dance at the Duke of York's Theatre, on Saturday. Said he might be able to go with me and promised to call in the evening before and make final arrangements.

Ruth's Diary   Friday, 10 July 1908
Sat sewing all evening – no Wal appeared. About ten found a curiously jumbled note under the door; would be going to garden party instead, could I not put off the theatre? The casual tone of the note hurt me. This dancer was, as far as I know, making her last appearance in London this season. I felt in some strange way that I *was meant to go* to the Theatre that evening. Sitting down I wrote a note saying that he could either meet me after, or join me before at 8.15 at Charing Cross.

Ruth's Diary   Saturday, 11 July 1908
Left, as arranged, but saw nothing of Wal at Charing Cross, so proceeded alone to the theatre. I could not write in cold words an account of that evening – or what it meant to me. I do not think I have ever seen anything more exquisite than Miss Duncan's dancing and my heart went out to the woman herself and loved her. The children too were the most beautiful – like little sprites and fairies. Sometimes they gambolled round in a

simple ring-a-roses, and Isadora would join in. Then they frolicked with ferns and flowers – once with some beautiful white lilies, which they threw among the audience. Alas! I was not near enough to catch even a petal. *And* the audience – the tribute of perfect silence during each dance – the enthusiasm at its close! The whole thing was a revelation to me. I had felt that somewhere must be the dancing that expresses the emotions – and here at last it was found! No tawdry drop scene disturbed the effect – nothing jarred – just neutral tinted curtains, carpeted stage, soft light lovely music – and this exquisite figure and face crowned with warm chestnut hair.

The lady I sat next to and myself soon got into conversation and this added to my enjoyment. She was alone and had come much in the same way as I had. Both of us had read the articles in *The Daily News* and *New Age*,[7] and both felt we *were to go*. I fancy she was on the staff of some newspaper or journal from the way she spoke. She told me all she knew of Isadora Duncan's life. She had been very poor, and conceived this idea of dancing to earn the money which was so much needed at home. But at first she could get no engagements. If she would dance in the ordinary style, managers said, they would take her on. But not even to earn means of living would Miss Duncan debase her art. Presently she came to Europe, and there proved a great success.

The lady had a good pair of opera glasses with her, which she would insist on my using frequently, thereby enabling me to see the face of this woman I really loved because she had shown me something so wondrously beautiful. When it was over no one stirred, so she came back and danced again. Still people only rose, and cries of 'Bravo' rent the air and deafening clapping – so she danced yet again. My new-found friend and I walked out together, and were turning in the direction of Charing Cross, when I suddenly espied Wal a little way in front. A hasty adieu, and this kind lady and I had parted. I *would* like to have known her name, and to have parted a little less hurriedly.

Wal and I walked on and I soon became aware of a great coolness in his manner. My note had upset him. I then learned he had left the garden party early and had been at the Theatre all the while. How he could still be angry after so much beauty passed my comprehension, but he did not share my enthusiasm – or would not. I was taken to Ealing like a naughty child and felt too tired to rebel.

Once again will you excuse my improvised notepaper, as I write
from the City, where the supply is 'nil'. I have much to tell you,
but I must save it mostly till we meet. And there, dear, I have to
crave a boon. Could you meet me on Wednesday week, instead
of next Wednesday? And I must tell you *why* I want to put off an
evening's pleasure to which I have been looking forward even
more than usual, for our last talk together drew us closer, don't
you think? Well, it is this way. Miss Brown has somehow
dispelled all my scruples about accepting Mr Grubb's invitation
to Guildford. After all my inward strife, I am *going*. This last
week has seen me needleworking with a will (also with dim eyes
and aching limbs). If I work with the same will next week I shall
only *just* manage to get done, so you will readily understand I
ought not to go out on Wednesday. Vanity of vanities; all is
vanity! I am trying to make a blouse, pinafore dress and a top
for this holiday. Miss Panting – always a friend in practical
needs, is stitching up the seams of the latter for me. Isn't she
kind?

Are you quite disgusted with me? Then picture what a change
it is to have two holidays to look forward to, when I expected
none. It is not yet settled where we (Walter and I) shall spend
the second week. (I fancy it is permissible for unmarried couples
to stay at Boarding Houses.) I wonder if I have ever looked
forward to a holiday so much before? There *are* sore points! I
feel abominably selfish when I think of home and Daisy etc.,
etc. Mother has had the 'nettle-rash' and seems poorly
altogether, whilst we had news from Hornchurch yesterday that
Grandma is queer again. I wonder when our sun is going to rise?

How I have rambled on, all about myself. But my thoughts
have been much with you, and of you, dear, and I am so glad
that a way of life is opening before you. I do not know much
about the ILP, but you must enlighten my ignorance as you
learn yourself. Walter said this morning he would get some of
the Fabian Society 'Tracts' sent on to you. I too am to have
some to read. They should be interesting.

I wish I could write you a long, long letter but oh dear, the
work – how it does increase. This commences the fifth week of
what I may call downright 'slogging'.

Your friend now and always, Ruth.

122

My dear,

It had become quite an unusual thing for me to finish work at business now, but this morning, at any rate for a time, such is the case, and I hasten to commence the letter for which you must long have been looking.

Oh, the weather!! It is just raining, raining today, and yesterday too was most damp! I am wondering how it is affecting Daisy – I often think of her. Please give her my kind regards.

And you Ruth – are you feeling well? I thought, last time we met, you looked somewhat in need of sea breezes – I did not after all hear much about your holiday arrangements – I am afraid I monopolised the evening! I am just beginning to feel the need of the holidays.

I am sending you a letter to read, received from ILP Secretary – on Monday evening I attended their meeting, and was the first in the room. Imagine how I felt, Ruth, when a long string of *men* filed into the room! However, finally three married ladies came with their husbands – greatly to my relief. I was made a member amidst much clapping. This branch has only been in existence for a year – there are 90 odd members – ten of them ladies.It was so interesting, Ruth, again I noticed the peculiarity of expression on many faces that I had noticed in the London procession – there were men of varied class and age – the labourer, clerk, man of thought and refinement, the youth of eighteen and the man well advanced in years. One man interested me particularly, and I have heard more about him since. He is between thirty and forty years of age and unmarried – I am told he has had a very eventful life, starting as a miner and boy agitator. He is an agnostic and his principal literature is fairy lore. I wonder if I shall ever be so fortunate as to know him.

It was a business meeting, and there was some quarrelling over the selection of a candidate for a seat on the County Council. After the meeting a number of people spoke so kindly to me, then I made my way to the table covered with books and pamphlets for sale – I could not resist them, but bought *Unto This Last,* by Ruskin, a booklet on Socialism, and *The Woman Worker!*[8] *What* a splendid paper that is! Did you have last week's? Those articles on 'The Slum Mother', 'Ellen May Brett', and 'Baby's Heritage' – are they not fine, and are you not interested in Ethel Carnie, the new poetess?

I must tell you the members of the ILP call each other 'Comrade'! During the week I had the enclosed post card from *Comrade Mrs Shimmins* (it sounds strange to me yet). I went to her house, wishing to know the women members better. Only two others attended, the wives of working men, and I could not help remarking how enlightened and thoughtful they were compared with the women one generally meets. Mrs Shimmins, however, has been a teacher and has passed through college. I am not sure yet whether I like her. She is young and very bright – talks with ease (which I do not) and has a decided manner. She told us some of her experiences as a teacher at Harrow Green – they were terrible, Ruth – the poor children; to think there is such ignorance and vice in England. I cannot here tell the sad tales she told – it would take too long. Perhaps when we meet I can relate them.

Aunt Emily came to see us the Sunday before last – she had heard from Grandpa of my recent escapades, but said little. She is much against women speaking in public – why allow them to sing?

We have only bad news from Kingston – Mr Gallop [Eva's stepfather] is again out of work – it is very worrying. There are some, Ruth, who never know the pang of anxiety – 'What shall we live on next week? ' – it is easy for such to be thankful for their blessings.

Let us turn to a more cheerful subject – in August, my dear friend, I am to take a whole 26/- per week !! I felt very wretched over it, but like Oliver Twist, screwed up my courage and asked for 'more'. I hope you won't think I was *greedy*. This is my fifth year with Mr Cunningham and I honestly think, Ruth, the work is worth 26/-. I have my slack times, I know, but oh, the difficulty of dragging one's mind through a legal maze – even now I sometimes feel it is too difficult for me.

Have you been out 'scorching' [bicycle riding] again lately? At last I have mastered my cycle – I can now get on it, ride, and get off alone! On Saturday I went to the library on it, but I generally dismount whenever I see an extra large cart or a small hill – my courage not being equal to either.

Ruth, I so *much* enjoyed our evening in the Embankment Gardens – how marvellously light it was that night. Did you read about the Aurora? Ruth dear, I have made such a muddle of our evening! The ILP meet on Mondays, so I asked Wallie Goodwin if we could alter our lesson night to Wednesdays –

now I suddenly remember that is *our* night! I am *so* sorry Ruth. Tuesdays and Thursdays I remember you see Mr Randall – could we meet on Friday this week?

My kind regards to Mr & Mrs Slate and much love to self. Your loving friend, Eva.

P.S. Have just received your dear letter – I am *delighted* that you are going to Guildford. *Mind* you have a good time. How I wish I too could assist with all that sewing – I would most gladly if near you. Much love and warm wishes for a happy week.

Ruth's Diary   Friday, 17 July 1908
Left early in the morning for Guildford, arriving in time for morning lecture. Walked to Compton Watts village in the afternoon through pouring rain. Lovely country – interesting company. Enjoyed it all thoroughly. Joan Fry (Elizabeth's friend and daughter of Sir Edward Fry) insisted on my accompanying her. More lectures etc. in the evening. After getting to our lodgings about ten o'clock, we sat talking, and Elizabeth weaned from me a confession of my trouble. I could not tell her everything – how at times I seem to feel on my own shoulders the burden of those poor, poor women – how personal it grows – but I think she guessed. I did tell her I would try to face what comes bravely, nor shirk the suffering it may bring. She asked me not to think of marriage until I was more settled in mind. She told me I was wrong to cherish the romantic idea of the one man for one woman. Am I? I cannot let it go yet. Helped in many ways, yet with an aching heart, I finally got to bed.

Ruth's Diary   21 July 1908
Wal met me in the morning and together we went to Hornchurch. Wal left after dinner to go to a meeting of the Anti-Suffrage Society[9] held at the Westminster Palace Hotel, while I returned home.

Ruth to Eva   Sunday, 2 August 1908
My dear,
If only you knew how much I have thought of you during the holiday you would forgive very heartily any seeming slackness I have shown with regard to writing. Last week passed in a maze, a delightful one, true, but still a maze. We stayed at a very comfortable Boarding House. I cannot think why I was so lazy – I know I enjoyed it and it certainly did me a world of good.

We were agreeably surprised by Margate altogether. One could walk for miles along the beautiful rugged cliffs and scarce meet a soul. Here we sat in the evenings and watched some magnificent sunsets. Wait till you see my face – and that shall be on Thursday this week?

Your letter was one of the most interesting I have had from you. I want to hear very much more of the ILP and all that Mrs Shimmins told you. Wouldn't it have been splendid if we could have taken the work up together? I believe dear, that you are on the right road, though I would scarcely dare to hazard a guess as to the goal.

That *is* good news about your money! But you deserve more. You must value yourself a little more than you do.

I am sorry you have cause to worry over the home folk and hope all will lighten soon. Mother has been, and is, very cool to me, and I wonder sometimes what it all tends toward.

But now I must come to an end. Needless to say I had a grand time at Guildford. Details of that too must keep.

Your loving friend, Ruth.

Ruth's Diary   3 August 1908
Bank Holiday. Wal and I had dinner by ourselves, then took some papers and set out to find a comfortable and cool spot where we could sit and read. We found the spot, but the gnats gave us no peace. Wal brought up the subject of marrying again, and I suggested it should be next year. I thought of my promise to Elizabeth and tried to tell him I was feeling unsettled and could say nothing definite.

Ruth's Diary   Friday, 7 August 1908
Heard from Brompton Hospital that Daisy is now 75th on the list and that her turn will probably arrive early in September. I only heard about it through Dad. Felt terribly hurt. Mother cooler than ever.

Ruth's Diary   Sunday, 9 August 1908
Went to Ealing for day. Big discussion on Women's Suffrage, Free Trade etc. over dinner. Admired Mrs Randall's sound common sense. In the afternoon, Wal again mentioned the forbidden subject, so told him I have never been quite able to forgive his lack of straightforwardness with regards to this year. Then I would have considered his interests – now I am inclined

126

to consider my own. A new spirit has crept in. I did not want it – it came!

Ruth's Diary   Wednesday, 19 August 1908
Lunched with Nim [Miss Nimmo] who is bowed down with woe. Being unfortunate enough to have fallen in love with a short and ugly man, and a socialist to wit, she has incurred her Mother's strict displeasure. As they work in the same office, things are exceedingly awkward. Really, the state commonly known as 'being in love' seems more prolific of worry and misery than any other – especially to we poor girls, as witness the jaded specimens of 'engaged' girls at Kearley and Tonge's, and the bitterness of those who have been engaged and are now free. Men have so little straightforwardness, unselfishness or backbone nowadays, or so it seems.

Ruth's Diary   Wednesday, 26 August 1908
Spent a very eventful evening. Walked down to Fleet Street, found *New Age* Press Office, but as it was closed, found it in vain. Walked through Chancery Lane to Holborn, marvelling the while on the splendid buildings, all new to me. Was astonished to meet May. Stood talking for a few minutes, then proceeded along Grays Inn Road to Clerkenwell Road. Explored neighbourhood a little – Leather Lane etc. Entered little shop where heard Yiddish only. Place altogether reminded me of Whitechapel. Returned to Club Union Buildings, under the impression that a Women's Meeting of some sort was to take place. Could see no one about, so mounted stairs in search. Through open door saw lady seated writing – knocked – and was invited inside. Found I was talking to Mary Macarthur[10] Editress of *The Woman Worker,* and straightway became stupefied with glad astonishment. Nice chat, during which she asked me 'if I ever wrote', and to send a specimen to her if I did. Signed petition for reprieve for Daisy Lord[11] – my name coming immediately beneath Keighley Snowdon's. Am thinking of getting a petition. Came home in a state of high excitement.

Ruth's Diary   Thursday, 27 August 1908
Wal round very early. Went to Harrow for Brandy for Daisy. Wal imagining me getting thin and condemning his own selfishness. Busy dusting etc. Weather most stormy and strange.

Ruth's Diary   Saturday, 29 August 1908
Letter from hospital last thing for Daisy to go up on Monday.

Ruth's Diary   Monday, 31 August 1908
Said Goodbye to Daisy in the morning – thought of her all day
– returned home to find she was there again, the Doctor having
told Mother they could do nothing for her. Daisy herself
ignorant of it – told her Abbey Wood air was better for her
than Brompton. Hardly knew how to restrain ourselves. Got her
to bed early.

Ruth to Eva   21 September 1908
My dear,
I hope you will overlook a pencilled scribble – I want to send a
few lines.

Dear, the events of this last weekend have put me in a muddle
for this week, so that I want to put off our evening until Friday.
It is just cruel the way the weeks have slipped by without our
meeting – I have missed seeing you brown from the holiday –
had to defer the presentation of my birthday offering – am in
your debt – and yet the muddles and the difficulties of meetings
increase.

I have been working fast and furiously this last fortnight,
staying late, and rising limp and 'used up' each morning. At
the same time there have been big anxieties at home. Our
local Doctor says Daisy will most likely be gone before the
Spring unless there is a great change soon – a hopeless case.
Eleanor Fairfax wrote me a fortnight ago, urging me to see a
Christian Science friend of hers about her. I talked the matter
over with Mother, and we thought we might at least find out a
little more. This lady friend of Eleanor's lives not very far
from Hornchurch, so I decided to visit her whilst in that
direction. I am still unconvinced of their power over a complaint
like Daisy's, but I want Mother to meet her and see what she
thinks. Daisy was much worse than usual yesterday and I do not
like to be away three whole evenings in succession. Tonight Wal
and I are going to Manor Park. It is the Harvest Festival and
Mr Sunderland is to be there. Perhaps you will think it unkind
of me not to miss Chapel tonight, rather than our meeting
tomorrow, but for some unaccountable reason, I feel terribly
'Chapel-sick'.

Accept all love for yourself. Ruth.

128

This has been an ugly, unhappy fortnight. Perhaps I have suffered more than ever before, but now a reaction of dull indifference has begun and I can write quite calmly of it all. Daisy has been very bad at times and though I may often have seemed an inhuman monster towards her, these signs of increasing weakness have given me bitter pain. Among other things Wal told me he was going to live in a whirl of gaiety between now and Christmas – I could go with him to different things if I 'managed to get invited'.

On Saturday 12 September I arose in a happier frame of mind than I had known for some time. Arrived downstairs however, I found Tom was being taken to task over something and proceeded to take his part. Almost instantly I became the culprit and things quite foreign to the subject in hand were brought up. Dad remarked that in all his life he had never known a couple like Wal and I, compared us to Tom and Hebe – of course to our disadvantage. Mother said we should not bring our miserable faces home there, and Dad suggested that I either 'got married' or went somewhere else to live. This put me in a nice mood for meeting Wal. I tried to be pleasant when the afternoon came, but his manner made it difficult. The Exhibition was crowded – one had almost to fight for an entry. It is a magnificent place, but so vast and bewildering. Wal stalked round a yard or two in front of me, and I wonder we did not get parted several times. He was chillingly silent too. In the Women's Court we saw part of the original manuscript of *Jane Eyre* and a splendid portrait of George Eliot. Later I told Wal I had been wondering if it would not be better to give it all up and offered him his ring, but he would not hear of it. That night, so tired and wretched did I feel that I lay down in my clothes and awoke in them the next morning.

By 16 September affairs at home were not mending and though the thought of leaving Daisy was dreadful to me, I *longed* to get right away. The thought dwelt in my mind and the longing grew. It seemed that my poor sick mind would have an opportunity to recover itself and the others would benefit. That night I broke the idea to Mother, but although she still contended that I was all that was bad and undesirable, she threatened all kinds of things should I dare to put it into action, chiefly that she would not let me know how Daisy progressed, or have me near the house to see her. Of course I gave way, but I still think my plan a wise one.

Saturday 19 September was a memorable day. On leaving business I took the train for Upminster to see Eleanor's friend, the follower of Christian Science. The country was looking lovely and my sorrows seemed less as I drank in its charm. Mrs Morris greeted me most kindly and made me feel at home at once, but I did not feel drawn towards her in the way I was beginning to feel towards Mrs Horncastle – her friend. We had tea in their lovely garden, and I talked over Daisy's case, the wonders performed through Christian Science, etc., but I was not convinced. I could, and can, well imagine much being done for mental and nervous disorders, and some physical complaints but, perhaps it is lack of mysticism or imagination, I cannot see how they can mend decayed organs. I don't know that I should have been very impressed had I seen Mrs Morris only, but Mrs Horncastle fascinated me completely. She is a very beautiful character. I fell in love with her. I believe I fall in love with a certain type of woman as easily as some girls fall in love with men. This woman, I felt sure, was an artist to her very fingertips and I longed for an opportunity to learn more about her. Of course I set out for Hornchurch in an absurdly elated frame of mind. I know its dangers so I tried to put it down. I spent the night at Jessie's, and while Harry was out she and I had a very intimate talk together. I was pained to hear her say that she and Harry were agreed that marriage was not worth the sacrifice it involves. Poor Jessie – you might have thought so different.

Ruth's Diary   Tuesday, 22 September 1908
Spent the evening at home. Had been worrying all day as to whether I should have said anything to Daisy about the Christian Science, and half hoped she would refuse to have anything to do with it, but when I asked her, she said she would. On Wednesday 23 September I went as arranged to Sloane Square to meet Mrs Horncastle.

I got there much too early, so started out to explore a little of the neighbourhood. I did not get far, however, for a funny little quaintly dressed woman pounced upon me, and directing my attention to a notice chalked on the pavement to the effect that some suffragettes were holding a meeting in the Square that night, asked me if I had ever been to one. Without giving me time to reply, she told me she did a great deal of work for the suffragettes, pavement chalking,[12] etc., but she thought their

130

methods wrong. 'Now I'm a patriotic speaker', she continued, 'I have a talent for speaking, and I must use the gift God gave me. I appeal to the patriotic spirit, and talk about home and industries, but these Suffragettes talk about political parties, and immediately arouse a spirit of prejudice in the hearts of their audience.' She was by no means a fluent and coherent speaker, but she gesticulated wildly enough to arouse the attention of passers-by, and some small boys were soon heard jeering at the supposed Suffragettes. She told me she often spoke in Hyde Park and, 'You could hear a pin drop almost.' One painful thing she told me about the way girls are often treated in workhouses made my blood boil – if it is true. It was with difficulty that I got away – after a very hearty handshake and 'God Bless You'.

Back at the First Church of Christian Science I had some time to wait for Mrs Horncastle, in the Assembly Room. I watched the fashionable throng sweeping in – and wondered – and doubted; but directly Mrs Horncastle joined me I felt reassured. She promised to come to see Daisy next day. I said Goodbye and hastened away. In the Square the Suffragette meeting was in full swing. The moment I stood listening caused me to just lose my train at Charing Cross.

Ruth's Diary   28 September 1908
Daisy has been reading *Science and Health* and the literature that Mrs Horncastle has brought and certainly seems brighter. It may be fresh hope has arisen and consequently fresh life and power.

26 September – during the morning Wal rang up on the telephone and told me he was back too late last night to come round as he had promised to do. In the evening Mother and I went to Woolwich where I made some important purchases for Daisy. Then wisely or unwisely I told Mother more than she has ever known before about my trouble. I was weak and in need of sympathy. Mother thinks Wal wants to put an end to things and is acting in this strange way to show it, else he has someone else to attend to as well. How could she say such things to me?

Ruth's Diary   Thursday, 1 October 1908
Another hot day. Walk with Wal in the evening. Talked mostly of business. He was upset about one or two things which have happened lately where he works, and I told the story of the

131

indignation rising rapidly in the breasts of K and T-ites. The latest injustice has been in putting Miss Williams on very difficult and worrying work, at a wage of 18/- in place of a man earning £2 per week. Trade is very bad everywhere and the papers are already full of distressful accounts. One wonders what the winter will bring. Dad is working late every night through a lessened staff. Feel very depressed and strange.

Ruth's Diary   Thursday, 8 October 1908
Went with Miss Williams to City Temple in lunch hour. There was great applause at Mr Campbell's outspokenness on the questions which are troubling everyone just now – the terrible distress through lack of employment and the frequent 'war scares'. I had no idea before how much of the national income is yearly spent in preparing armaments, and in schemes for out-rivalling other powers.

Ruth's Diary   Saturday, 10 October 1908
Went with Miss Panting to Franco Exhibition. Had dreadful headache and the rooms were very crowded, so cannot say I enjoyed it much. Worst of all, I let Eva and Gertie pass by and I had expected to see them. What is the matter with me? I seem to be changing slowly but surely into someone else. On getting home I learned that a lady had been during the afternoon to see Daisy. She is a magnetic healer. Hypnotism and massage is practised and the 'healer' 'breathes' into the patient. I do not know what to make of it all – I feel just worried to death.

Ruth's Diary   Wednesday, 14 October 1908
Home in the evening. Mother still very poorly. Walked round Tower Hill in the lunch hour. Great meeting of 'Hungry Marchers'. What hundreds of wretched looking men! The day before had been one of great excitement. Unemployed riots. A lady actually got into the House of Commons, astounding the members who were sitting within discussing the Children's Bill, with the cry, 'Votes for Women'.[13] I could be glad but that she got there through a mean action.

Ruth's Diary   Thursday, 15 October 1908
Eva's. Very pleasant evening. Heard many funny ILP anec-dotes. Serious talk between Eva and I after we got to bed. Felt strongly that shuddering fearful sensation that has haunted me

132

of late – of terrible uncertainty. How strange that one can live their ordinary, everyday lives, eat, drink, smile, converse, and yet live another life so different, so foreign, so unsuspected by others.

Ruth's Diary   Wednesday, 28 October 1908
Spent a most memorable lunch hour on Tower Hill listening to Victor Grayson MP[14] who has just been suspended from the House for speaking out on behalf of the unemployed, while another measure, which he considered of less importance, was before the members. He is a fine looking young man, and spoke well and earnestly. It was glorious to be in such a crowd, though the sight of so many pinched and desperate faces made one very sad. A procession of Hunger Marchers, headed by Stewart Gray, joined us, each man brushing me with his clothes as he passed.

Ruth's Diary   Wednesday, 4 November 1908
Wal, Miss Nimmo, and I went to the *Woman Worker* reunion at Holborn Town Hall. Place packed, and an 'overflow' downstairs. Brief speeches by Robert Blatchford,[15] Mary Macarthur, Victor Grayson and Margaret Bondfield[16] – also music, singing and recitations.

Ruth's Diary   Thursday, 5 November 1908
Eva's. Victor Grayson meeting at Leyton Town Hall, Robert Blatchford in chair. *Wonderful meeting!!* Up *very* late, Eva and I smoked our first cigarette – a Woodbine! Were not sick! Found we have both been cherishing the same longing to one day explore London in men's disguise. Shall we ever do it? I *hope* so.

Ruth's Diary   Tuesday, 10 November 1908
Daisy again very bad.
    If I could see Eva's diary, would it be like this of mine, full of horrid little things, rubbish and stupidity, personal animosities? I don't think so. I imagine rather that it would prove to be a record of large thoughts, careful judgements, beautiful dreams for the future, with here and there perhaps an account of mental nightmare, or torturing pain, when either grew too intense to be borne without some form of expression!

133

Ruth's Diary   Sunday, 15 November 1908
Quiet day at home. Daisy very bad, Mother poorly and Dad far
from well. Took Mother tram ride in the afternoon. Music in the
evening. Daisy trying to sing. How my throat ached with the
effort to keep back my tears! Oh my sister! If only we could talk
our hearts out to one another.

Ruth's Diary   Tuesday, 23 November 1908
Met Eva in evening. Went first of four lectures on 'Parenthood
and Race Culture'.[17] Splendid! And to our ignorant, untrained
minds, most illuminating. Think I am beginning to understand
what is meant by Natural Selection.

Ruth's Diary   Thursday, 10 December 1908
Quiet evening at home. Talk with Daisy about Dad. She says he
irritates her so, that she feels she must leave the room directly
he enters it. I feel much the same. He actually said to me the
other night, and to Daisy later on that Mother's leg cannot be as
bad as it looks, or she could not get about on it! What a fearful
ignorance of woman's will. Poor man! He is making himself
wretched, yet is too blind to see the cause lies in himself, not in
outside things at all.

Ruth's Diary   Thursday, 24 December 1908
1 p.m. Xmas Eve. Am wondering whether the holiday will be a
happy one – I hope it will. Daisy has been much brighter these
last few days and Mother seems less harassed. Dad is in a little
better humour. I am always so tired that I could drop asleep
anywhere and at any time – now, even, it would be quite easy! I
never feel bright and alert.

Ruth's Diary   Thursday, 31 December 1908
Another Xmas has come and gone. We all, I think, spent it very
happily.

I left business at 2 o'clock last Thursday. I wandered through
Leadenhall Market, then, as some shopping was necessary, to St
Paul's Churchyard, where the crowds were numerous and
dense. Round Paternoster Row, enjoying wistfully a most
tempting array of literary jewels, and along Fleet Street. Here
an idea struck me. Why not once more explore the mysteries of
the *New Age* rooms, and see if it were not possible to satisfy my
curiosity about that certain article, 'The Rites of Astoreth',

published now some six months ago. I had the letter, inviting me to call, in my purse. The wish was sufficient, and soon I found myself in a little place more like a cupboard than a room – stuffy and unwholesome, reading what I sought. It added to my present perplexity and bewilderment very much. The writer, a woman by the way, pointed out the great difference between ourselves and the Eastern people in that the Eastern people deify their pleasures. They set aside certain women, trained as dancers, and keep them in their temples, while we allow women to become degraded and sell themselves in unsanitary corners. Every woman is not fitted to be a Mother and rarely does a good Mother mean a good wife. (The writer seemed to hint that we are in danger of making too much of the eugenic point of view.) Economic equality was also put forward by the writer as urgently necessary. She further said that children are not indispensable to the happiness of a home.

On Tuesday I returned unwillingly to business. About nine o'clock it commenced to snow and by the time we left for home it lay inches deep in the streets. It was dangerous work walking, and to watch the poor horses made one's heart ache. I saw one after another go down, We were wet through on getting home. The papers say we have not had such a fall for 28 years.

Yesterday morning we toiled through the snow to the station. The train crawled along and before we had gone far I was ready to shriek with the pain my feet were causing me. Arrived at business I had a day of rush, for Miss Panting was away unwell. Outside a black pall hung over the city, making the snow-clad buildings look most eerie. We were later than ever getting home. A quiet time by the fire, however, soon set us right. Daisy had had a severe fit of coughing during the day and seemed ill and exhausted. In the night I lay awake hours, and picture after picture of our life together rose in my mind. A great lump gathered in my throat – and I suffered as I thought of the change. As surely as I felt that night at Folkestone that she was very seriously ill, so surely did I feel last night that she is much worse. Today, the banks of snow are disappearing, running as water, like rivers.

I don't think I have another word to say about 1908!

Ruth's Diary   Tuesday, 7 January 1909
These early days of the new year have been very busy, and I have had no time to start my new book. The habit of keeping a

diary seems to have grown upon me, and though I fear its influence is not always good, I do not quite like to break it.

On Saturday we went to Eva's. Each of us read something of our own choosing and there was plenty of discussion after. Eva read Edgar Poe's poem, 'The Raven', her Aunt read 'The Pied Piper of Hamelin', Wal read a little poem. My contribution was enthusiastically received, although it was made up of oddments. A little selection from George Eliot, another from Victor Hugo. Eva commands my love and admiration more and more – she is splendid!

Ruth's Diary   Monday, 11 January 1909
Went to Club in the evening – spent an inspiring hour or so listening to Doctor Cobb. He was speaking of the condition of women now and as he imagined it would be under Socialism, drawing out the girls' own ideas as he went along. He is an ardent Socialist. Among other things the subject of heredity came up. Most of the girls seemed to think it probable that at one time women were as strong, comparatively, as men. I certainly think so. Skimmed Professor Forel's *Sexual Ethics* on way home. Think a *few* difficulties are lessening.

Ruth's Diary   Tuesday, 12 January 1909
Spent a wretched morning. Could have wept and wept from sheer weariness, weakness and despondency.

Ruth's Diary   Wednesday, 13 January 1909
Awoke in a worse mood than ever. Nodded all the while in the train, and crawled along after like an old woman, my mind busy all the time with ridiculous notions of writing a touching story founded on the events of my own life. The story was to move the hearts of the people so that justice and happiness should reign quite easily and all should be roused to usher them in. Myself in the book was to fade quietly away – an unrecognised genius, starved mentally and morally, yet clinging to the last to an exalted ideal!! By lunchtime I was more myself and entertained friend Nim with a humorous account of it all.

In my distress I had written Eva and she came up this evening laden with physic and port wine. We had a lovely time together, and the sole remnant of the morning's mood that haunted me were vivid pictures of Davy Hill and Sons [Ruth's first place of employment] – the sickly and evil odours, the filth and my distaste ever since for certain foods Mother used to prepare as suitable to take. Perhaps another was the stab of pain I felt as I noticed that not a single dustbin was without its ragged starving form turning over the contents, this morning.

Ruth's Diary   Thursday, 21 January 1909
Spent a 'red-letter evening'! Wal came up and together we attended a meeting organised by the Women's Labour League[18] on behalf of unemployed women. The meeting was held at the Memorial Hall, Farringdon St. However, we found room at the back of the gallery, and stood for preference, as that was the only way to see the speakers. There were so many speakers – Mr and Mrs Ramsay MacDonald, George Lansbury (Labour MP),[19] Esther Dicks, Margaret Bondfield and Mrs Despard[20] had spoken before we left and others were to follow. Esther Dicks spoke as a working girl. She had toiled in an Ammunition Works for 1½d a thousand bullets, seen fingers cut off and similar accidents, frequently; also women carried out of the factory 'black' through the effects of gunpowder – all for 1½d a thousand. She had tasted the miseries of tramping the streets in search of employment; the bitterness of seeing 'want' written on the home faces, without bringing in the means to alleviate it. She made a fine and telling speech.

Need I say I was ready to fall down and worship Margaret Bondfield and Mrs Despard, especially Mrs Despard, whose face and gestures have been in my mind ever since. *How* she pleaded, speaking of the inadequacy of the feeble effort made lately in connection with the St Pancras workrooms, and urging for wider scope and training for all women. It was a grand meeting, though so pathetic.

Wal, of course, was not so enthusiastic as myself, and spoke of Socialism as stirring up class and sex strife. Again I could not agree with him and said so, and this time I seemed able to let myself go and spoke with a fluency and fervour which surprised myself. I felt conscious of power, where it came from I know not. Perhaps out of this long chaos form is slowly shaping.

Ruth's Diary   Friday, 22 January 1909
Quiet evening. Library with Wal. I was a little upset during the day by a missive received from Nim. A letter I wrote *The Woman Worker* has been published – a little abbreviated unfortunately. Nim has misconstrued my meaning thereby –

137

hence this letter of concern.

Eventful day. Arrival of Miss Brown in the afternoon. She kissed me very tenderly – calling me 'a dear girl'. We did not have much opportunity for converse together but it *was* a treat to see her again. In the evening we went to meeting but I found it an occasion to doze peacefully.

Met Eva Liverpool St. 2 o'clock. Went to National Portrait Gallery and stayed till closing time. Of course we halted long in the little space devoted to pictures of eminent women. In the sculpture room we especially admired the grand bust of Sarah Siddons. Then proceeded to a Lyons for tea. Eva was present at the Memorial Hall meeting, so we had plenty to say about the speakers and speeches there; I had more to hear concerning the Rev. James of Walthamstow and the poor cases Eva is looking after in connection with Robert Blatchford's Bread Scheme. Then I had to tell her of Miss Brown's visit, and my sense of aloofness from things religious.

After that we made our way to the Duke of York's Theatre and took up our stand for *Peter Pan*. We had a long weary wait, but *it was worth it!* Pauline Chase (Peter Pan) was just exquisite and we felt sure she must be nice in real life. Eva came home with me. As we crept up to bed, we agreed that it had been a most memorable day of pleasant things. Confused images haunted our dreams. The portraits we had seen in the afternoon, the lissom form of Peter Pan, the crocodile, the pirates and all kinds of things.

Went lecture at Woolwich in the evening, 'Physical Culture and Hygiene'. Should rather have been styled 'Pathology and Disease'. The lecture was by a woman and for women only. It was extremely interesting, but extremely morbid.

I feel considerably disturbed because Dad thinks I ought to get time off from the City and stay at home while Mother is so poorly. I am afraid that would mean courting dismissal just now, and then what would we do? A little while ago when he might

have helped me persuade Mother to have help in, he could not
see any necessity for it; now, when Mother looks ill, he is
frightened. Why are men so dense?

Ruth's Diary   Thursday, 4 February 1909
Quiet evening at home – Wal at a party. Miss Panting declared
she believes in 'Votes for Women' – Oh, hard-earned triumph!

Ruth's Diary   Monday, 15 February 1909
Took a tram ride through Whitechapel, after leaving business,
and called on Eleanor. Found her harassed and dejected
through having sole care and responsibility of a boys' home.
Eleanor stated that she and most of her friends have studied Dr
Stall's books for young people and incline to his ways of
thinking. I have seen these books advertised in *Great Thoughts*.
It seems they advocate suppressing displays of emotion –
physical displays – as having a very injurious effect on the
moral character. They say, Eleanor tells, that many pure-
minded girls have sent young fellows to houses of ill-fame
through expecting and encouraging this show of affection,
thinking the young man must be cold if he is not demonstrative
– little dreaming that in so doing they set fire to a slumbering
volcano. Not only does this exciting of the sexual organs
undermine the moral nature, but it seriously affects child
bearing, so that a doctor can easily tell whether his patient is of a
sensual disposition.

I do not like a great display of feeling – it has always seemed
to me to cheapen things. But I am certainly not so ascetic as
when I first knew Wal. I have always thought that the value of a
caress is in proportion to the feeling behind it.

Somehow tonight I felt sick and almost disliked Eleanor for
putting such thoughts before me. What *is* truth? Has one to
leave sex alone to be pure? Is it such an *evil, ugly* thing? No! It
must be this dreadful all-prevailing ignorance.

Ruth's Diary   Friday, 5 March 1909
Wal round. Would not let me help him distribute Progressive
League literature, so we went for a walk. The snow-clad country
looked beautiful, and we saw some tobogganing which made
me long to try, but it was spoiled by a continuous fruitless
argument. Strange – but I do not get nearly such a heartache
lately; instead, a dangerous coolness steals over me – a down-

right 'don't care' mood. I asked Wal if he thought we should make each other happy if we married and told him I sometimes felt as if I never wanted to marry. He replied, 'So do I'.

Ruth's Diary   Tuesday, 9 March 1909
Wrote little note to Wal asking him to keep the ring until he could say he loved me and meant it and until I could say the same. It was very hard. Met Eva in evening. Went 'League of Kingdom'. Very interesting meeting on prison reform.

Ruth's Diary   Saturday, 13 March 1909
A stormy interview with Wal – a troubled, sad, sad walk – a more pacific ending. Wal told me what I *knew* but could never quite face. I cannot write of it here in case this book ever gets before other eyes than my own, but I went to bed smarting with agony for which there seemed no relief.

Ruth's Diary   Friday, 19 March 1909
Wrote farewell letter to Wal. Told him I wanted us to have kind thoughts of each other in spite of what has passed. Perhaps it was foolish and futile of me to write, but I do want us to try not to harbour bitter thoughts about each other and tried to make my last word a kindly one. I cannot say any more now – I think I hardly realise what has happened. After all, I do not know whether to be sorry or glad – it has been nearly all pain.

I could not face the thought of another quiet evening at home, so remained in the City and spent a memorable time. I had seen an announcement of a Public meeting to be held at St James's Hall in connection with the Fabian Society, and decided to go. The speaker was Dr Ethel Bentham.[21] Her subject, 'Socialism and Race Welfare'. She spoke on infantile mortality and taking the commonly accepted theories with regard to its awful and alarming extent, such as the decline in breast-feeding, the working of mothers outside the home, etc., the supposed increase in the habits of intemperance, showed that they do not in any adequate sense explain the evil. She then turned to a much less considered side of things and pictured the daily life of a woman with three or four children whose husband brought home thirty shillings a week – the fearful anxiety of making ends meet, the insufficient food, the washing and mending and all the housework, the lack of a bath or hot water, or of a sanitary storing place for food, and finally of the increasing

140

demand on the woman's strength and attention. I thought she struck right at the root of the matter.

Ruth's Diary   Monday, 29 March 1909
I am in a very different frame of mind to when I last wrote in here. There has been an awakening – horribly painful – but, will it seem strange to say so – I am glad. On Saturday morning I told Miss Panting my engagement had been broken, but I did not tell her the reasons. It was an awful shock to me to know I had been deliberately deceived and misrepresented. This has been the reward of my patience, and I have been patient. Little by little I began to realise that I have been duped and fooled and a dark anger has begun to rise. I was roused enough to contemplate acts of vengeance. I am not meek and he has tried me too far. Everyone at home is painfully kind. Mother has cried bitterly, reproaching herself for ever persuading me to encourage him. Daisy says she has known it all along. That is not very comforting, but I suppose I shall get used to it. Otherwise I have a feeling as of relief from some oppression, and already my thinking powers seem clearer. Certainly the worry and pain has deadened everything for a long while past. I have sat down and cried bitterly, but have not cried since. I cannot feel unhappy. After all I have done my best.

Ruth's Diary   Thursday, 29th April 1909
It is nearly a month since I wrote in my book – I have not had the heart. I have not missed Wal so much as I expected, but my pain and disappointment at his behaviour has increased each day. The weekend before last I left home very early for Purley, in response to a kind invitation from Elizabeth. She of course had no idea what had occurred and presently asked after Walter, and I was not surprised to hear her say, 'I am glad', and not once or twice only did she say it! She had never felt he was my equal intellectually and she thought it would be a good thing for my personality now to develop on its own lines.

Presently Mr Grubb came for us and we started on a delightful walk. The country about there is very pretty. Part of the conversation was between Mr Grubb and Elizabeth only, as when they spoke of Syriac writings, and again of experiments by some brothers Hubbard – I forget now what on. As I listened, the feelings of progress which have recently encouraged me seemed to leave me – I realised what a difference there is between the 'little knowledge' and broad culture. In my own circle lately, I have been conscious of a certain power – here I was dumb. During the evening meeting I could only think with a certain bitterness of that enormous difference and of the unfairness of unequal opportunity. 'I have the brains', I thought, 'and the willingness to use them, but I have never had the chance.' Even now every little effort of self-improvement has to be made at the expense of recreation. Why should it be so?

Tuesday was memorable as the last day Daisy was up.

Ruth's Diary   Sunday, 9 May 1909
In the afternoon I, with Mr and Mrs Garey, went to Carmel Chapel, where Isabella Ford gave a splendid address on 'The meaning of the Women's Movement'. I was glad to notice the enthusiams of the men present (they formed by far the majority of the audience).

Ruth's Diary   12 May 1909
Went to see about getting Daisy an air bed. The Doctor told us he thinks Daisy will only live a week or two longer.

Ruth's Diary   19 May 1909
Home all this last week.

Ruth's Diary   20 May 1909
Went Garey's. Walked to Plumstead Common where the 'Clarion Van'[22] was stationed. Large and enthusiastic gathering. Speaker Mr Moore Bell – a hard-hearted, stern, practical man. The discussion which followed was very stirring. The great crowd, the eager upturned faces, right out away onto the Common, under the starlit sky.

We had a nice talk on the way home, following the subject – economic freedom – up. Mr Garey asked me if I was coming back to the Progressive League. I said I thought not. He told me that Wal is very much taken up just now with Mrs Annie Besant[23] and went to St James Hall last Sunday to hear her lecture. A verbatim report of her speech is given in this week's *Christian Commonwealth*.[24] I think it contains some fine thoughts and splendid suggestions. Among other things she mentioned the 'iniquitous doctrine of sex inferiority, which has brought such infinite suffering on one half of humanity'. I wonder what Wal thought of that? He is not for equality and comradeship between men and women – he has not the soul of progress. In trying to subdue my will to his, he showed me that in his character.

Ruth's Diary   21 May 1909
Met Eva. Went Devonshire House to hear Beatrice Webb[25] on Poor Law Administration. She charmed our hearts thoroughly, besides appealing to our brains – a winsome, sweet faced little lady, with a very beautiful voice. Her plea that people should be helped before they reach the stage of destitution, instead of having to prove absolute destitution before relief being given, as until now has been the case, is surely the only humane way to deal with the problem. What a wide subject it opened out! One third of the total number of paupers, she told us, are sick persons – another third, children. How foolish then and wrong to wait until destitution can be proved! Her husband was with her. They must be two splendid persons. A discussion followed during which we had to leave. We were sorry, for a hard-hearted Guardian had just made a callous speech, Mrs Webb's reply to which we should like to have heard. He referred to the lying-in ward of a workhouse in which he was interested, and stated that nearly all the expectant mothers who came there did not wish their 'bastards' to live. Not a word about the conditions which make such things so common.

Ruth's Diary   Monday, 21 June 1909
At the time of making my last record I was rich in having a sister – now I am alone and desolate, bereft of sister and lover. I cannot pour out impassioned grief and regrets, neither could I describe myself as feeling like a stone. I am just dull, stupid and miserable. Right till the last she suffered and all our agonised prayers were in vain. Shall I say I felt near to hating God? It all seemed so wicked, so cruel and so unnecessary. The sight of it at last nearly maddened us.

I have been to the Tuberculosis Exhibition, showing at the Whitechapel Art Gallery. It was very interesting in a sad, sad way. One thought of the stories of suffering and heartbreak, hidden behind those cold and formal statistics, almost in despair. Of course there were many illustrations of the good work being done – model chalets, sanatoriums, hints as to food values, feeding and clothing. There were preserved specimens of diseased lung, making it all too clear why and how the poor consumptive suffers so. Samples of infected milk and meat made one loathe the thought of food.

The Exhibition was crowded and as it was not exactly the kind of thing to attract the usual sightseer, one wondered if their presence had tragedy behind it. After all, is it not strange to spend so much time and money and labour in wiping out a disease, when the chief causes of it are left unheeded? Why not try to prevent, even more than cure?

After Daisy's death, Ruth, feeling isolated and low in spirits from 'serious bothers' at home and another move further out of London, made only a few diary entries; but she and Eva exchanged some interesting letters.

Ruth's Diary   Saturday, 4 September 1909
I wonder what is the use of all my scribbling? As a revealer of myself it is useless – unless as a revealer of the small and foolish side of my nature. There are many, many things I dare not write; there always have been big reserves – yet the habit of recording the outside details of my life has a wonderful hold upon me. My diary must be as full of detail and self interest as was Pepys' – without its interest. Weary and sick at heart I must pull myself together and record that on Monday I did 'so and so', on Wednesday went 'so and so'. It soothes me – and I have no words wherewith to express and record the rest.

It is useless my trying to get up to date, at least as far as details go, and I do not feel either any wish to record in cold formal writing the inward experiences of the last two or three months.

A fortnight ago I returned from Cromer, where I spent two happy weeks with May. It is a delightful place and we had never a sight nor sound to jar us. May's company did me a world of good – she is so strong and sane, yet possessing a wonderful depth of poetry and romance. I am constantly filled with wonder as I meditate on the precious friendships life has brought me. I have not been so happy since, for there have been grave disturbances at home, involving both myself and Tom. Dad, it appears, and Mother also, think we have had far too much money to keep for ourselves and have been niggardly at home. He has said some very outlandish things and the attack is as unjust as it is uncalled for. We have both done our utmost to help. I was told that I had no business wanting to go out and that classes were foolish. I feel that things are tending to make me hard and indifferent in spite of myself. Tom is anxious to get married at Christmas, as Hebe is far from happy at home, and the thought of an added loneliness fills me with painful forebodings.

Ruth to Eva   3 October 1909
                            'Mostyn', Ethronvi Road, Bexley Heath
I am afraid dear, I shall *not* be able to come with you next Saturday. We are so upside down, there seems no opportunity plan for anything, and we are all aweary, aweary. But there is something else I want to suggest. You will have seen the announcement in recent *Christian Commonwealths* of a great Progressive League Demonstration being held at the City Temple on Monday 11th. (Among the speakers will be Bernard Shaw.) I would very much like to go to that and so, I expect, would you, and dare I ask it – may I come home with you?

I have just finished reading Blatchford's *God and My Neighbour*, and it has given me furiously to think. I can understand the magic appeal Blatchford makes to the working man – his writings read so pleasantly, like homely lucid conversation. I was prepared for a great many of his ideas – but some struck like sword thrusts. For instance, he speaks often of a certain Buddhist and says his character appears to have been nobler and sweeter than Christ's. I could never have dared such a thought, and yet I often wonder how much is just the unconscious clinging to systematic and thoroughly taught childish beliefs.

I was horribly selfish dear all through our last evening together – it was wrong to burden you with the tale of the skeleton which appears so often in my life. I get more and more oppressed with the sense of the terrible suffering so prevalent in the world.

You must come down to us as soon as we get fairly straight. My room is at the top of the house and looks quite 'comfy' already. I think we shall be happier here in many ways, but oh! I sigh for the town. Just now I should not mind living right in the heart of London. With much love. Your sincere friend, Ruth.

Eva to Ruth   21 October 1909

My dear,
I should like, dear, to say a little in answer to your letter. You speak of the suffering in the world and the sense of oppression it

brings one – I do not wonder that you feel so, Ruth, for you have just passed through a long period of close contact with the most terrible suffering – it has been an awful experience, I know, never to be forgotten. I must read Blatchford's *God and My Neighbour*.

I often think about you in your new home, Ruth, and wonder how the evenings pass with you. I am afraid you often feel lonely and sad, dear. I know what it is to move to a strange place and to see only strange faces. Could we meet some time next week, Ruth?

This is just a note. Let me have a card and take great care of yourself. Your Loving Friend, Eva.

Eva to Ruth   8 November 1909
Mine dear friend,
I feel in most excellent mood tonight and just in the vein for a chat with you before going to the meeting! There is really no very good reason for such good spirits for I only returned this morning from a visit to Kingston. The truth is, I think Mr Gallop and Miss Walmesley have roused what little fighting spirit I possess! Mr Gallop was in one of his worst humours the whole weekend, and the vials of his wrath (for my benefit) were emptied upon the Socialists in the Bermondsey Election and the Suffragettes – you know his opinion is that women are best at home darning stockings. I spoke up for women and tried to put matters in a reasonable light – but Mr Gallop will not reason. Cecil [Eva's step-brother] unfortunately joked in the wrong place, and Mr Gallop left the room roaring out that we were a 'damned ignorant lot' and he would like to 'clear us all out'.

We are, however, so used to these scenes, we are learning to take them quite calmly. Oh Ruth! He is *so* selfish, his attitude towards women seems to me so dreadful – Mother has to wait on him hand and foot – he does not even wish to ask for a thing and he cannot bear to hear you express a different opinion. I find myself more and more in sympathy with the efforts women are making towards liberty and equality. Oh, Ruth! One must press onwards and upwards, only sometimes it is all so difficult and dark and one longs for clearer sight and greater courage.

I only saw Miss Walmesley [a friend] for a few minutes but she clung to me as though she felt me slipping away – she said she could not bear that there should be any shadow between us, and I stammered out that I must be free to live my own life.

146

Your friendship, Ruth, is so precious to me – I always feel I can speak with perfect freedom, but with these early formed friends I have a strange feeling that I have wandered into regions to which I cannot take them and which they do not know. Your Loving Friend, Eva.

Ruth to Eva   22 November 1909

I expect you are wondering what has happened and when you were going to hear from me. There is not very much to tell, only that there has been another bother – more serious than its predecessors – and that I am going into lodgings for a time. I have thought and worried to the point of brain fever and this seems to be the only solution. I think you will agree with me. I must be either exceptionally lucky or exceptionally wicked, or both.

Next Monday I take up my abode quite near to business – my address after that day being 143 Commercial St. East. I think I shall be very comfortable there.

Excuse me not writing more now dear.

With much love. Your Friend Ruth.

Ruth's Diary   Sunday, 5 December 1909

This is my first Sunday in lodgings, tomorrow I shall have been here a week! I could not be more comfortable and indeed, if it were not for the worry of thinking of the home folk, I should be very happy.

6

The Free Woman
January 1910–December 1912

Ruth's brief note on her first Sunday in lodgings was her last diary entry for three and a half years – years that she was later to describe as being 'most full of interest and wonder'. With the absence of diaries, the course of events (until Eva's methodical records started in 1913) must be drawn up from the correspondence left from this period. Much of this consisted of 'hurried scrawl' on notes from Ruth, which nevertheless contained some intriguing information.

When Ruth left home, she was able to branch out into a more independent life, and extend her interests and activities. Through her lodgings at Miss Cloake's, she met other radicals, made new friends, benefited from life in the City and enjoyed coming into contact with 'modes of life other than one's own', living in the East End of London. Once recovered from the 'long strain' recently put upon her, Ruth sounded busy, more confident and, finding her company much in demand, felt she 'must have become suddenly fascinating'. At Commercial Street they were often 'as lively as crickets' with guests and visitors.

Ruth seemed at times to be in a whirl of activity – going to the theatre with Hugh or 'Brother Jones' (whom she met in January 1910); visiting a Music Hall (previously frowned upon as being vulgar); spending the weekend with a 'Russian lady'; seeing Miss Brown and talking 'all through the night with her'; rushing off to hear the Rev. Campbell in her lunch hour and attending Progressive League meetings; helping at Toynbee Hall, the famous 'settlement' in Whitechapel which was near her lodgings; involving herself in a women's circle; was considering joining the ILP; and was teaching at the Hoxton Adult School. She visited her parents frequently and helped them with yet another move, to

148

Bagshot, but a visit to them in summer 1911 reinforced her decision to leave home: 'this place stabs me with bitter memories' she said, 'and I cannot imagine myself ever being strong enough to live here permanently.'

Ruth's growing confidence renewed her determination to find better work – although she was to remain at Kearley and Tonge's until 1914 – but a note to Eva showed her feeling clear about the firm's exploitation of her:

Excuse a hurried scrawl in pencil dear, but I am frightfully busy and still more frightfully agitated. I have made up my mind to 'fling off the chains' and make a bid for better things, but they say here I *shall not go,* in words so emphatic that I cannot repeat them, and are prepared to give me almost anything I like if only I will stay, but I am determined to go. It is not *me* they care about here – only what I can do for them, and it seems the people who really do care, and will miss me the most, think I should be silly not to make the most of an opportunity which might not occur again. I have decided to go to Pitman's evening school every evening for a month (or nearly every evening) to get up speed – so altogether there is some hope for me.

On 21 December 1910, Ruth expounded upon an altogether 'new plan of existence' to Eva, which included plans to join the ILP:

And now – I have news for you! The battering rams of the Finsbury ILP have begun to play upon me and I have been invited in a charming little communication from the renowned Fenner Brockway (!) to go thither this evening to be 'welcomed'. I was all alone, as it happened, on Monday evening, when a young couple (a man and maid) arrived, saying they had heard that I was interested in the ILP. That is how it all came about. The young couple stayed some time – the young man, by name Mr Fenner, talking (*how* he talked) and the young lady looking on (not quite pleasantly I imagined). We knew personally, and by repute, ever so many people in common. The young man is one of the P. League 'Rebels' – knows Mr S. James and all sorts of people and things. I have firmly declined the invitation for this evening, but have promised to go after Xmas and am getting wondrous excited.

Judge not my frail flesh too harshly – I am meditating a new plan of existence for 1911, as follows. Shorthand – imperative! German – overboard for a time. This ILP will bring a 'live' interest into my life, for which I pine, and will safeguard me from the fiery darts of all sorts of 'mission workers'. Do you approve? I hear that Fenner Brockway is resigning his position on the staff of the *Christian Commonwealth* and joining that of the *Labour Leader*.

I shall go home on Friday. Both you and I, I expect, will just *have* to seem happy for other folks' sakes through this festive season. Write and let me know what evening you can come up here in the new year.

By 1912, Ruth appeared to have joined the Women's Freedom League, for she was on their mailing list, had been out selling flowers for them on Piccadilly Circus, and had leaflets to distribute for their International Suffrage Fair at Chelsea Town Hall in November 1912. The grand-sounding Fair had 'National Dances, Theatrical Performances, Concerts, Action Songs and Prizes' and was 'the chance of a lifetime to buy your Christmas presents from articles sent by Comrades All the World Over'! The Women's Freedom League had split from the WSPU in 1908 to form a more democratic organisation, which was less militant, but still took direct action.

At the end of 1911 the suffrage campaign was at a crucial point and a massive amount of activity and support had not produced 'the longed for result of the vote'. Even though the Conciliation Bill for Women's Suffrage had had two majority Readings in the House, Prime Minister Asquith remained intransigent. Between 1910 and 1912 the militants were almost at war with the Government, organising window-smashing raids and attacks on Government property. Large numbers of women were on hunger strike in Holloway Prison being brutally force-fed, and Asquith's treatment of the suffragettes was coming under criticism from many quarters, whether militant tactics were agreed with or not.

Eva's Aunt Edie and half-sister Gertie became militants. Gertie was possibly involved with some of the raids and gave her 'views on the subject of militancy' at Ruth's 'circle'. The circle seemed to discuss a number of topics and Ruth discouraged Eva from bringing her half-brother Cecil – 'I am being quite frank, and considering the subject, I think we can talk more freely if only the girls are there.'

Ruth's move away from home also brought with it the possi-

bility of investigating the alternative lifestyles which accompanied the idealism of the period (much like the communes of the sixties). Both she and Eva had contact with several rural communities that were being formed in an effort to create a more co-operative and spiritually fulfilling life. In September 1910, Ruth

Moore Place, 'A Christian Social Settlement' in Stanford-
Essex, which had a Holiday Centre 'where people
in Social Reform were received', and which was trying
non-profit-making industries. In the summer of 1911
Eva from the Whiteway Colony in Stroud, Gloucest-
nearer to perfect happiness than I ever remember
am actually dreaming dreams (keep them secret) of
to live ...' In August she and Eva spent three days at
nion Summer School of Religion, Psychology and
e at Letchworth Garden City – a model socialist
was built in 1906, in Hertfordshire. The summer
two weeks and had a very full programme, with
as 'The Bearing of Religious Ideals on Social
by Annie Besant, 'The Fate of the Nations: the
of the Position of Women' by Mrs Clara Bewick
on, and 'The Coming of Socialism'. In 1912 Eva
nmer school at Woodbrooke.

time when 'the talk of the day', as Ruth called it –
' and the 'Sex Question' – was influencing their
ationships. Early in 1910, Eva wrote to Ruth after
e Obscure ('an unusual book dealing with the Sex
uth, my views on marriage are altering to an
– I really believe some people would call my
ral!' In 1911 they both avidly read Edward
Carpenter's Love's Coming of Age, *which argued against 'the slavery of women', for the free union, and for 'people to express their sentiments quite freely, with love of the body, not shame, as a motivating force'. Carpenter also presented, in the controversial chapter on* The Intermediate Sex *(published in 1906), the idea that certain people could be attracted to their own sex, a position which isolated him from his more traditional socialist 'comrades'. While his attention was focused more on male sexual activity and his ideas about women's sexuality remained rather stereotyped,* Love's Coming of Age *was one of the pioneering books of the day, when discussing a free (heterosexual) union alone was seen by most of the population as immoral. It is not clear what all this meant to Ruth and Eva in terms of their own feelings except that*

*they were acknowledging a struggle around sexual questions and
the problems of physical expression.*

*Eva seemed to be experiencing longings for a relationship, and
felt in sympathy with the 'odd women' – single women who felt
frustrated and 'redundant' as a result of the position assigned to
them by society. In 1910 she seemed to have suffered a disappointment over someone and Ruth wrote to console her.*

Ruth to Eva   10 August 1910
You are so much in my mind – and your pain and struggle, but
I would not hurt you dear by touching your wound. Be brave
and true to yourself and there will surely grow up a wonderful
thing in your heart, which seems as yet to have no name, the
sum of all one's suffering, and which only those who have
suffered can know.

Eva to Ruth   15 August 1910
I have been in a very bad mood all day, so presently I shall
betake me on a solitary walk to the Library to return, I hope, in
a more cheerful frame of mind. The truth is I fell in with another
'odd woman' today at the picnic – Mrs Awes' sister [Mrs Awes
was a neighbour of Eva], a woman of about thirty-three or
thirty-four. On our way home she opened her heart to me and
told me the story of yearning and emptiness that you and I are
getting so used to hearing and feeling. I have been quivering all
day!

I am afraid the day is very far off when I shall cease to suffer,
indeed I am not sure that I should like to reach such a solitary
eminence, but I would like to lessen the suffering of the world
and sympathise and share the griefs of others.

*At the end of 1911, a longer exchange of letters between Ruth and
Eva was prompted by a sudden crisis in Ruth's relationship with
Hugh which, until that point, had been a comradely friendship,
but now seemed to verge uneasily on a sexual love relationship.
The letters show how difficult it was to talk about and deal with
anything relating to sex. But despite being shaken and agitated by
the developments with Hugh, Ruth was open to change. It was
Hugh, however, who dictated the terms of the relationship and,
with his abrupt changes of heart and tendency to crush sentiment,
would not allow it to settle into one thing or the other.*

The letters also show how Ruth and Eva continued to trust and

*confide in one another, and rely on each other emotionally, so
that they could 'reflect more and more on the beauty and comfort
of our love, which lives in spite of disappointments and yet does
not slacken conscience and the demand of an ideal'.*

*While responding to Ruth's problems with Hugh, Eva attempt-
ed to expand her ideas on relationships and mentioned for the
first time Minna (Mrs Simmons) who 'interested' her 'exceedingly' and with whom she would form a passionate friendship.
During this period Ruth moved to a room at 64 Lordship Road in
Stoke Newington.*

Ruth to Eva   30 November 1911
                                                  143 Commercial St E.

My dear,
You will be surprised to hear from me so soon. I have heaps to
do but it will comfort me to tell you a trouble – only I trust you
will not let it worry you. I feel in need of conscious sympathy
and spare kind thoughts occasionally and I know I can rely on
you for both. I am going to be horribly frank – casting decorum
to the winds in a way I could not do if I were talking.

You know how comfortably happy I used to be in Mr Jones'
company and how it seemed ridiculous to imagine anything
different. I think it must have been in May or thereabouts that
we were sitting talking alone here one day and getting on to
rather deep things when he very suddenly – as if feeling an
overwhelming need of sympathy – flung his arms round me and
leaned his head on my shoulder. Things have seemed changed
ever since. A similar thing happened the other night and I think
he said there was no such thing as Platonic friendship – I was
too agitated to hear properly. It is this, dear. I may be altogether
wrong but I think he is struggling with himself – against
himself. He has not wanted to love anyone – feeling that he is
meant for an ascetic – and prizing too his freedom, yet I know
this struggle is going on. You wonder, I know, how I feel, and I
dare not analyse myself. I have tried to prevent this – and now,
temptation though it be – I could not take one step towards
influencing him. I do not think he would ever know or consider
how shaken I feel, and upset. He then asked me to write. I have
written and Heaven only knows what, and I trust I wrote
nothing wrong or foolish.

Keep this a secret dear, and tear up my letter. I have written
very badly and I feel stunned and stupid. Do not bother to write

dear, unless you have time. I wanted to tell you of the little light that is coming to me after the long, long gloom. You spoke my intensest belief last night when you mentioned Love as the touchstone of life. With very much love, Ruth.

Eva to Ruth   7 December 1911
Ruth dear,
I have been pressed with work on every head since your letter came. I feel I can say so little dear – I have been thinking about it all since Friday. If only something definite could be arrived at – and perhaps by the time this reaches you things will be clearer. I can see plainly you will not be able to continue in the old way.

Your confidences sink very deeply in my heart – write *whenever* you feel the need – though I can help so little, be *very* sure, dear, of my love and sympathy. Would you care to come to our Local Parliament next Monday or to the Church Social on Thursday? I shall think of you until I see you – and *I want to see you*.

Mrs Ryan has lent me *Love's Coming of Age* and I am enjoying it – I find it full of suggestion, and as I read my mind wanders off along various lines.

I have been hearing from friends this week – Kate, and Miss Walmesley – and I have been thinking thoughts about Mrs Simmons this afternoon. They may not be correct, but what think you? She seems to me to be a type of the woman of the future – maternal, calm, sensitive, spiritual and strong. Nature has cast her in a large mould physically, intellectually and spiritually – she will always be averse to the modern Women's Movement because she has evolved so far beyond it. She interests me exceedingly despite certain faults.

Gertie and I went to see Galsworthy's *The Silver Box* on Saturday – it was a sermon. I think we both felt fresh inspiration to try to do our little part towards a juster, fairer life. Hardy has lent me the first copy of *The Freewoman* but I have not yet had time to read it. I do hope that all is well now – 'Blest be the tie that binds/Our hearts in kindred love.'

Ruth to Eva   9 December 1911
My dear,
Thank you for your letter, I was getting almost ashamed as the days wore on and nothing came. There is one thing I wish to say.

154

You will remember that a little while ago, when you were sleeping with me at Commercial Street, you said, 'Be careful to whom you give your confidences, for people do not see things as you mean them.' When I know, as I do assuredly, that however foolish and even wrong I may seem, *you* will try to see the motive behind, I can tell you what I told you in my last letter and what I am going to tell you now. Do you not think that the best love we know is that which endures in spite of faults, which sees the groping effort of the erring will – and beyond? So I am going to trust you.

The morning after I wrote to you I had a letter from Mr Jones. I could not open it dear for a long time – I felt so sick and trembling. Then I read '. . . I feel I should like to say, that at almost any price, we must keep our friendship . . . I have always tried to crush sentiment – just as I grew without personal effort so has this desire grown to conquer sentiment, whether for good or evil God only knows . . . You will be surprised to know that I have had my little love experiences whilst I was a Stoic philosopher . . . Just this, when I found that you had escaped from love, when you first came to Miss Cloake, I worshipped you.'

You have the substance of the letter. Then he says, 'Is it right that I should make a confidential friend of you and then perhaps throw in my lot with another?' and concludes – 'but when worship turns to lust I hate myself.' I cannot describe to you the anguish of my mind I felt – and still feel. Perhaps you can imagine it. I don't know what to do. I am beginning to realise Eva, that men too suffer and struggle a great deal.

I want to see you – I want to walk with you – and the only evenings you are free I am engaged. I want to say this, dear. If you think any definite thoughts about it all, will you tell me? If I do not agree, I shall take no notice. On the other hand, you must not worry – for you have your own troubles.

Thanking you for your love. Your friend always, Ruth.

Eva to Ruth   11 December 1911
I will come up on Wednesday – I wonder if you would consent, and if it would be quite convenient – to be my guest to tea at Lyons'? This way we should have greater freedom and opportunity to talk.

I do so long for happiness for you, Ruth, and I know how you must have felt over the letter you tell me about. Do you not think Mr Jones has made a great mistake in trying to crush sentiment? Now, he is, I think, experiencing a rebound, and so gives a harsh name (sentiment) to what is perhaps a much healthier and more lovely feeling. Try and think of it so dear, for I believe it is so – perhaps if he gave himself more time he would see these things in true perspective.

I shall look forward to Wednesday. My heart to you, Eva.

Ruth to Eva   21 December 1911
                                            143 Commercial Street

My dear friend

Thoughts of our talk together last week have been very much with me. I have been thinking today dear of our weekend at Letchworth when there was a curious unsettlement in our relationship – my fault I know – which might have done harm, but it passed. I think you understand the intensely brittle state I was in; do you remember what I said about my dreading people getting fond of, or even kissing me? The feeling has gone at last dear, and if you were here I should give a real hug to prove it. I am getting out of my spiritual and mental prison again and am going, I think, to breathe freer air. You will forgive me starting off with so much of myself but I do want to tell you what has happened.

On Tuesday Mr Jones came round, and strangely – for it is quite unusual, we were left alone. We talked about many things, and underneath it all I was wondering if this was a chance given to me to be brave – for, except for our letters, we had never *spoken* of the problem. And while I was wondering and worrying dear, he brought it up himself and told me he cares for me and felt he had been doing wrong in crushing his feelings so. We had a very solemn and precious talk in which the future was not forgotten, but about that I feel as blank and unsettled as ever. I do not expect dear, any calm, decided happiness for myself; looking ahead it seems impossible. But I feel myself again, and could be happily unhappy if need be – do you understand? It is no good dear, but if I try to be anything else the result is horrible. And while I am telling you so much I will tell you this also. When I first came here I felt I had to undergo every sort of suffering until I was purged of self – I do not think I was self-deluded, and I did not think an experience of this kind would again come my way. It has made me so happy, even if it should prove temporary.

156

Above
Ruth, aged 15, in 1899

Below
Ruth in York, circa 1917

Above
Eva circa 1915

Above right
Emma Clover, whom Ruth and
Eva taught from 1904 to 1907

Below right
Ruth at Woodbrooke, 1914

174 Albert Road
Leyton
6 Nov. 1906.

My dear Ruth,

I am so glad you can all come next Saturday! Yes, dear, you were quite right in thinking I meant that day. I am looking forward so now to seeing you all, & hope this will only be the first of many visits. You know Ruth, if someone

is going to run away with you one of these days, I don't mean to give up my share of you for anyone - so there! You don't know how I grow to value your dear friendship more & more - I don't know how I should have felt if your new friendship had made a difference between us - but it has not - you are just the same dear girl, & I am so delighted about you altogether. But I am afraid you will think this "utter foolishness" & that I am getting

Left

Sample letter from Eva to her 'dear girl' Ruth, 1906

Below

Extract from Ruth's diary 1908, describing the WSPU rally in Hyde Park, one of the largest suffrage events

Fri 19th Wal came round. Her knee was painful so we stayed indoors

Sat 19th Home. Adds to do. Wal at Hatford again

Sat 20th Mother took Daisy out to Forest Gate to see Jessie. + Mrs Newcombe. Jessie very bad indeed. I met Wal at Cannon St 3 o'clock. Went by train to Hayes. Ideal afternoon - weather superb. Enjoyed it very much

Sun 21st Up to City 12 o'clock. Met by Wal at Charing X. Hyde Park Demonstration by Womens National + Political Union. Most marvellous sight, out reaching the procession of the previous week in numbers. I should think by thousands, but my sympathies are more with the others. We joined the throng around Miss Pankhurst's stand for a time, but the crush was becoming dangerous, so we fought our way out. Miss Pankhurst was wearing her robes. College cap, + made an inspiring figure in an inspiring spectacle. I should very much have liked a picture of her as she stood, a smile on her almost beautiful face, a slender arm + hand outstretched, appealing for an audience, which a gang of roughs stationed right in the front, refused for some time to give her. It was all very wonderful, but I could not help thinking their object would not be half attained. The crowd seemed more intent on amusement than anything else.   I went on with Wal to Ealing to find Mr Reynolds. The young lady he is

Left
Woodbrooke 1915,
showing Ruth seated right

Above
Françoise Lafitte circa 1921

Below
Françoise with Havelock Ellis

Above
Ruth as welfare worker at
Rowntree's factory, 1917,
seated centre bottom row

Below
Ruth in later years

And dear, I will tell you what I dared not acknowledge to myself – the feeling of completeness I experience when I am with Mr Jones. Nothing has surprised me more dear, than this wonderful gift of love, where I had expected nothing.

Well dear, I must not weary you. Your own confidence was sweet to me. I had wondered a great deal but waited until you should tell me. I am sure there must be a real and great happiness in store for you somewhere – perhaps much nearer than we dream and then how I *should* rejoice. And dear, let nothing shake our friendship; even the cold spells that descend upon one's spirit at times. Have we not gone too deep for that?

I shall think of you through the holiday. How is your cold? Do take care dearie, and try to keep well.

Miss Cloake sends her love and best wishes – and I cannot put mine into words, but just sign – Your friend, Ruth.

Eva to Ruth   27 December 1911
My dear,
I wanted to answer your precious letter directly I had received it, but you know, dear, what it is like at Xmastide – how it is almost impossible to get even a few moments to oneself! Come on Friday dearest, and we will walk, rest and make merry just as you choose – *I* feel inclined to kill the fatted calf for you (where is he?) and to meet you with a robe and a ring, only it wouldn't be exactly appropriate, you not being a prodigal – but Oh, we will be joyful! I *am* so very glad for you dear – I sat in Chapel on Sunday evening and rejoiced on your behalf. It is your speaking about the sense of completeness, which makes me feel that probably whatever happens you will be more truly happy with than without this love. Your life too has been so changeful – so full of 'ups and downs' that a life of some uncertainty will scarce be strange for you. Love too is the great reconciler in many, many ways. How I *am* looking forward to Friday! I press my glad love on your heart dear, and kiss you in spirit.

There are just a few little things I would like to say about myself dear, and then I must close my letter. I sternly forbid myself to look forward to any great happiness, but I feel quite sure now that many friends will be mine, and I try every day to look on men, women and children as mine very truly, and I don't think the future will be uninteresting.

I think I am passing through an experience I have heard you speak about – I feel as though I have lost the power to feel in that way – something seems crushed and broken. It is very foolish – I expect it will pass.

I trust that the holiday has been happy in every way and that you had a real good time at May's. I had such a dear letter from Minna on Xmas day. I will try and meet you on Friday.

Very much love, Eva.

Ruth to Eva   1 January 1912
My dear friend,

Your Xmas letter is open before me and as we had so little speech together last evening I will write a few thoughts.

I cannot find any fitter words than your own to express my wishes for this New Year – may 'glorious thoughts, new hopes, faithful love and happiness' come to you – you deserve them all.

What marvellous changes there have been in our lives already! We have lived most in heart and mind and the few outward changes have been the result of that. I am confident that the future holds greater changes in store and for you my hopes run high. But I want to say too, how glad I am for the new friendships that have come into your life like rays of sunshine and fragrant as flowers. I am not afraid of being displaced for, as you wrote me once, there is something 'unique' in our friendship – the common bond of early struggles and mental suffering, which no one else will ever be able to understand quite in the same way.

For myself, after dipping (what joy it was) into a few pages of George Eliot again and observing her absolute frankness about moods, headaches, etc., I feel no compunction in telling you that I am having a hard struggle with a gigantic fit of depression, but do not worry about me, for I shall not succumb.

My dear, only to you can I confess such appalling ignorance! What is the 'anterior lobe'? George Eliot speaks of this often, I notice, in her description of people.

Did you notice this? After the strain there has been on our vitality just lately I thought it lovely. 'What a wretched lot of old shrivelled creatures we shall be by and by. Never mind – the uglier we get in the eyes of others, the lovelier we shall be to each other: that has always been my firm faith about friendship.'

I wanted to read you wild, splendid passages from Wells – how he stirs the rebel in one! I have just lived in the closing chapters of *The New Machiavelli*. You must read it one day – when you feel quite calm and strong and able to master the slumbering volcanos.

I think dear, I must realise my 'centre' before I experiment (I am thinking of the projected move) and then I shall be strong to face the issues. I shall find it here in the silence if I listen.

And now Eva mine – I must cease. With deepest love, Ruth.

At the end of the year the trouble with Hugh resurfaced.

Ruth to Eva   4 October 1912
I am sitting on the floor in front of the fire. Mr Jones has just gone. I think you have guessed that there has been more than just the home trouble on my mind of late, yet I could not speak of it. Much will have to work itself out in my mind as time goes on, but oh, my dear, the awful, crushing, agonising sense of failure! To begin with there will never be anything deeper between him and I – I am not a genius, with wonderful, strange appeal, I have not the thrilling power of beauty, no gifts, only foolishness – yes dear, let me say it to you, who will love me none the less. Sometimes I wonder how long I can bear my life as it is – so lonely and unnatural and empty.

I was impressed with the beauty of your story, dear heart. You can express so much where I am dumb. I thought that as I was reading that perhaps I might be useful one day just to write the story of your life.

I shall look forward to Wednesday as to a bright star. Do stay the night if possible. Your friend, Ruth.

Eva to Ruth   8 October 1912
Your letter and thoughts of you have been so much with me since Saturday. I feel I ought to have written differently at Xmas time, but I saw things in another light then, and was so glad for you. I cannot say anything now dear, but sympathy is deepest when we are silent. The words you sent – have we not both *proved* them to be true?

Dear, I shall not be coming to tea tomorrow as I am bringing Aunt Edie to the School, but I shall like to stay the night.

I could not help smiling over your idea about writing my life – I am much too much of an atom, dear, ever to call forth such a demand, but I'm glad you liked the little story; it is nice to scribble sometimes to amuse oneself and give one's feelings a 'vent'. I had a vivid and curious dream last night – so vivid that I awoke. It was the resurrection and I was united soul and body

159

with living and dead friends – I think the feeling of love and unity (even with relations for whom I do not really entertain affection) was the *most* remarkable thing about it.

Comfort and strength go with thee and my love. Eva.

In November there was a new interest in Ruth's life, when she met Françoise Lafitte (who she thought 'a second Olive Schreiner') at The Free-woman Circle, and they soon became friends. The Free-woman, which started in 1911 and produced a journal of the same name, was concerned with some of the women's issues neglected by the concentration on the vote. It attracted young women, 'stirred by the realisation of poverty and social problems, economic and sexual'. It also attracted Edward Carpenter, Rebecca West, H. G. Wells and other well-known radicals.

Françoise was a new influence for Ruth – more impulsive and outspoken than herself or Eva, less bound by a sense of female propriety and 'humility', and with what would now be called 'radical feminist' politics. When they met, Françoise, not long arrived from France, and trying to escape the restraints of her respectable family, had been living in a 'Tolstoyan commune' (frequented by some of the Freewoman Circle). She was pregnant from what had turned out to be a disastrous 'free union' and was in a fairly desperate situation. In November she delivered a lecture at the Freewoman on 'What Woman Wants' – a demand for the 'Complete Endowment of Motherhood by the Government'. This demand had been a feature of some socialist and women's programmes since the 1880s, and requested that the state pay benefits to mothers, recognise the labour of motherhood and, according to a Fabian tract, 'place this most indispensable of all professions on an honourable basis'. For Françoise it meant that 'Woman may then claim children without a man, in spite of man, apart from his so-called chivalry, which feeds her and her little ones only to keep her enslaved.' And from Woman's point of view she challenged 'the whole organisation of society, rather than compromise with it any further by aping man'.

Françoise's theories are described in full in her autobiography, Friendship's Odyssey, *published by Heinemann, in 1946, under the name of Françoise Delisle. In it she said of Ruth – 'This young sensitive woman of exactly my age, hard working and a dreamer as myself, I knew through the Freewoman and other meetings. We shared many views in common and remained friends our lives long.'*

160

7

'The Urge of the Spirit'
February–December 1913

*From February 1913, Eva's diaries provide a steady narrative of
events and give a welcome, much clearer idea of Eva herself (her
earlier journals have not survived). In contrast to Ruth, Eva,
disliking the 'rush and tear' of the City, was firmly rooted in her
local Walthamstow community, where her work and home were a
stone's throw from each other, and where she was part of a close
group of friends, connected by the Chapel and political activities.*

*The group included the rather austere Misses Leith – one
'mystical' and one 'an ardent suffragette'; the militants, Aunt Edie
and Gertie; Owen and Eva Awes, and Nellie and Brew, two
young socialist couples; the 'restless' Mrs Pettinger; the controversial figure of Mr James, the minister; Mrs Taverner, who
wrote children's plays; and Eva's 'daily more precious' Minna
and her family. Minna, who was married to Will, had three
teenage children, Winnie, Edie and Horace. In June she became
pregnant with a fourth (when she was 40). Eva particularly
enjoyed the warm and affectionate atmosphere of Minna's home,
and admired Minna's frank and unconventional views on politics
and domestic matters.*

*The diaries record the day-to-day life in the community, and
the lively political discussions, showing the Sex Question to be in
the forefront of the current debates, especially amongst the
women. Much of the discussion focused on the issue of marriage
and the free union, but at any opportunity – lunchtime, teatime,
Chapeltime – the women discussed a range of related topical
issues: the limitation of families; the vote; jealousy; monogamy;
men's and women's roles and natures; the relations of the sexes;
and the relationship between sexuality and spirituality. Eva
continued to be concerned with the status of the single woman and*

161

struggled with her longings for a relationship. But such a relationship would have to respect her independence and could not replace the 'loving friendships' which were fundamental to her life and were at the core of her political ideals. Eva used her journal to work through ideas and sort out her political theories; they displayed the intellectual thoroughness and ability so admired by Ruth and others. She described her basic religious philosophy of 'love and toleration' (love being a great, life-enriching force for change); and expressed her characteristic optimism for 'the immense possibilities of life', no matter how small the opportunities for change, or how depressing things seemed at times.

For Ruth it was still a time of 'event and development', though not without its ups and downs. A brief entry in her diary in May recorded that she had moved into a flat in Notting Hill with Françoise, where they enjoyed a happy companionship. Ruth, according to Françoise, 'displayed forbearance of my whims and fits of despondency', and with other friends, she supported her when she had her child, in August. In September, Ruth visited Chalice Well, a centre for Arts and Crafts in Glastonbury, run by the charismatic Alice Buckton, which was also a 'retreat for pilgrims and travellers'. There she met David Thompson, an American visiting England for the summer, who after their brief meeting wanted to develop a relationship with her. When he returned to America they began an intimate correspondence, discussing politics and their life histories. David was in many ways a positive influence in Ruth's life. He was Law Librarian to Congress in Washington, a job which involved preparing recommendations for legal reforms, and he knew and worked with well-known American suffragists on legislation affecting women. Earlier, he had worked in England; he was secretary of the Sheffield ILP in its revolutionary days in 1893, and there he formed an 'intimate friendship' with Edward Carpenter. He considered himself a 'thorough-going feminist', and was concerned with 'the free development of Ruth's life'. At the end of the year he offered her a loan, which she accepted, to pursue some line of study or writing. He also sent money to help support Françoise and the baby. The friendship with David produced a conflict in Ruth over her relationship with Hugh, which continued to be as ambivalent and as involved as ever.

Eva's Diary   Tuesday, 25 February 1913
Such an unpleasant incident at business this morning in connection with a very sad case – a young girl of nineteen has just
given birth to an illegitimate child – her life has been despaired
of, her nerves having completely given way. Mr Cunningham
had an interview with the father of the child this morning – a
bold, coarse-faced youth who denies the charge. They argued
loudly for some time – at last the father came out of the room
and sang at the top of his voice, 'I don't care what becomes of
me', and whistled loudly on his way down the stairs. Is it that he
really *does* care, I pondered, but is trying to hide that and all
fear under an air of bravado? I feel there was a desire to wound
in that man's heart – I doubt whether he will be faithful to the
compact he has entered into. It is hard to understand why so
much suffering, physical, mental and spiritual, should fall to the
lot of the women in these cases – why has nature so evolved
man and woman that the man has so small a part to play in the
generation and birth of the race? Perhaps there is some truth in
the view that woman evolved *from* man and is *greater* – if so she
would naturally suffer more in erring, *being* greater – perhaps
in the suffering, patience, care and tenderness of Motherhood
we have a fuller expression of the Eternal, and it should be to
our glory rather than our regret!

Eva's Diary   Sunday, 9 March 1913
At the Conference this afternoon the Rev. Wilson gave an
address on 'Work in terms of Life'. 'Work', said he, 'has been
described as the greatest privilege bestowed upon mankind.'
The remedy for a host of evils.
    I have been thinking over this problem of religion and work
– why is it that we do not now express our religion in our work?
Is it because expression by means of hand labour has so largely
passed away, and machinery has become the master instead of
the servant of man? In the olden days when men worked by the
hand many happy hours must have been theirs: as they bent
over the spinning, weaving, carving and fashioning they were
able at least crudely to express some child of the heart and
brain; but the conceptions of the mass of mankind were
probably very limited – only the few could express beauty,
originality, power. Machinery is now with us – it has removed
as well as imposed a burden! By its aid the printing press has
spread enlightenment and knowledge with a lavish hand:

machinery has lifted from the housewife the burden of much cooking and sewing. The public mind has probably become much more complex than in the past. For all this, however, machinery is our master, we are its slaves; we make it, feed it and serve it mechanically, and at times men curse it – we allow it to deprive us of interest in work, of labour and of bread. Surely the time *must* come when we shall see in machinery our great opportunity – uniting we shall force it to serve our ends, and with minds enriched, and horizons widened by our very struggle with and benefits from machinery, we shall bestow upon it the work of monotony and return to expression by the hand, to produce more expressive and truly beautiful work than the mind and hand of man has ever before been capable of giving to the world.

Eva's Diary   Tuesday, 15 April 1913
How nobly Minna has trained her children to think and view the body! Winnie is at home today in bed resting a sprained muscle – at Minna's bidding she showed me her budding breasts with fresh, innocent joy at their growth – if only all children could be trained to think so purely! Minna startled me by announcing her intention of joining either the Women's Freedom League, or the National Union – she praised the brave spirit shewn by Mrs Pankhurst. I felt her sympathies, broad and deep always, had widened wonderfully.

Eva's Diary   Wednesday, 16 April 1913
Am reading the essay on 'Fruitarianism' lent me by Cecil – it is very convincing. I should like to try again to do without flesh food, but think it hardly wise unless I first gain a proper understanding of vegetarianism.

Went to Miss Leith's this evening – seated around the fire we perused the two long tortuous introductions to Scott's *Quentin Durward* – I found it such difficult reading and comprehended but little. Oh! how wearisome are Scott's long sentences, and unnecessary padding! Miss Leith seemed to enjoy it all ! I felt so sorry for the two Miss Leiths: they looked so worn and weary. I felt it to be a rather 'odd women's' atmosphere – it weighed heavily on me. I found myself wondering whether they had ever really lived – ever 'abandoned' themselves to the joy of life! Their training seems to have given them so many mannerisms and so much restraint and reserve. Laurie (Miss Leith's nephew) remarked that the girls at School were taught to sing and shout at play – I said perhaps it was really better for them than so much restraint, but Miss Leith disagreed, saying she considered it made girls noisy and selfish. I think perhaps this is the danger in expression, but I do feel repression is a terrible thing and that we need to *allow* children to be natural, normal and healthy little beings.

When I came away I almost felt I wanted to run wild – to execute a war dance in the garden under the light of the moon.

Eva's Diary   Friday, 18 April 1913
I have been thinking today that many friendships overwhelm me and give me a *diffused* feeling – I feel myself longing for close companionship with the two or three my soul chooses, and who choose me – for the times of deep and earnest growth. After all, it is only the very few who come to one centrally, but it is my hope that by a wide outer circle of friendships the spirit of love and comradeship is extended and in time to come, my ideal may be realised as Walt Whitman has expressed it:

I dreamed in a dream I saw a city invincible to the attacks of the whole of the rest of the earth,
I dreamed that it was the new City of Friends,
Nothing was greater than the quality of robust love, which led the rest,
It was seen in every hour in the actions of the men of that city,
And in all their looks and words.

Eva's Diary   Saturday, 19 April 1913
Read a great deal of Wells' *The First Men in the Moon* today and enjoyed the imaginative description. Wells' conclusions with regard to the moon's surface, its growth of fungus, subterranean world and moon caves seem to me to be logical, but his description of the Selenites is not so convincing. I wonder whether such stories of the imagination will ever be realised – if one could reach the moon one would need a rarefied body to breathe the more rarefied air.

I journeyed to Kingston this afternoon, and found all well in health, but Mr Gallop out of work again. Mother, Mr Gallop and Cecil disagree so. Oh, how I *feel* the lack of love amongst them all – the atmosphere stifles me. We all went to see *Lorna*

Doone at the Cinematograph Theatre. It is a fine film.

Eva's Diary   Monday, 21 April 1913
Ruth came to Hoe Street this evening. We had tea at a
confectioner's – I felt concerned about Ruth; she did not look
at all well. Her father has taken another business in Bagshot.

The National Union meeting was well attended, and we
greatly enjoyed the lantern lecture on 'The Position of Women
in Hungary'.

Eva's Diary   Tuesday, 22 April 1913
Under pressure of desperate feeling I wrote this evening to the
Editor of *The Christian Commonwealth* to see if he had or was
likely to have a vacancy in his office – I did this with a reluctant
feeling – it seemed to me almost as though I had written a
'begging' letter.

Eva's Diary   Wednesday, 22 April 1913
A troublesome cough gave me a broken night–I felt but little inclined for business – but I am only one out of the many who must
often feel so. It was fortunate I went – I was kept highly busy.

Mr Wilson invariably now shouts and speaks uncivilly to me
over the telephone. I tremble with indignation and yet know not
what to do! I fear he dislikes me. He is a fair type of a certain
class of city man, possessing a shallow shrewdness, bluster and
wordly knowledge, perceiving quickly the kind of mind one
possesses.

Eva's Diary   Thursday, 1 May 1913
I thought my little talk with Minna today somewhat strange. We
discussed the Women's Movement, and Minna said she thought
if we could get an ideal man our difficulties would be solved. I
cannot see how we are to get an ideal man until woman is
spiritually and economically free – sometimes I wonder
whether such a man will ever exist; when character has evolved
to seeming perfection, may it not be that fresh vistas, greater
possibilities, will open up – we must go from strength to
strength. Oh! it is the urge of the spirit which should make
woman desire and claim equal opportunities with man; the
enlightenment which shows her the many avenues in life which
need to be purified by men and women – we should feel it is
our duty to shoulder the broader responsibilities of life. I long

166

for the day when men and women shall press forward in the battle of life, acknowledged and honoured comrades. If there is any truth in the possibility of an 'ideal man' – woman will not aid his development by meek submission – she will only create tyranny; she must compel him to recognise her as a personality, a soul, with right to freedom. The very fact that man has the *power* to *deny* the vote to woman is conclusive proof not only that he is in material authority, but that he does not so recognise her right to freedom!

We also discussed School Clinics – Minna said she thought they were of little use, as children suffering from incipient consumption after leaving the Clinic so soon lost in weight and health. She thought too we were in danger of becoming State-controlled to such an extent that loss of responsibility would be the result. I feel the good done by the School Clinics must far outweigh the harm. With regard to 'loss of responsibility' it seems to me we have already largely lost this; perhaps the Clinics are just what we need to arouse us to interest and understanding of the condition we are in. Poverty is more often the cause of sickness and neglect than ignorance, and one needs to remember but few social remedies go to the root of the evil – life in the country, good housing and a very much higher rate of wage would solve a great deal.

There are days when life presses in upon one with its worst aspect. I must get away from everyone, in quietness to brood upon 'Love' – if one meditates long it is wonderful how soon irritation and anger fall away. Love is the great key to life, the solution to every problem!

Gertie came home this evening with the news of the raid by the Government upon the WSPU[1] premises and upon their paper; one would think by now history would have taught its supposed scholars that suppression only leads to volcanic eruption.

Eva's Diary   Friday, 2 May 1913
Mr Cunningham asked me today if I would like my desk lowered. I replied that I should, it would be much more comfortable; so it is to be done. How I have altered! As Frost pointed out, two or three years ago I would have said it did not matter that the desk was much too high, or would have offered to bear half the cost of alteration. I suppose I have at last come to recognise that certain rights are due to every person.

167

Eva's Diary   Saturday, 3 May 1913

It was a long journey by tram to Red Lion Square this afternoon, through poor, sordid localities, teeming with struggling, unhealthy life – the city has always interested me keenly, but even interest seemed to depart from the part of London I passed through today. We passed a hospital – I could see through one of its windows a nurse busy with linen – a little child lay in a bed on the balcony overlooking the busy, dirty street. The endlessness of it all crept over me: these Doctors and Nurses heal, whilst daily the very towns they inhabit are creating fresh victims. I do think our modern city life with its ultra-organisation and rush is a stupendous problem; how to live more natural, simple lives and yet to progress is a question which so frequently presents itself to me – I should like to see little groups formed in different parts of the country cultivating the land and farming generally, also forming guilds of arts and crafts where women and men would be free to make and to study the useful and the beautiful. I should not care to see these groups trying to live without money because, after all, if one's heart is set in the right direction it matters little whether money is used or some other form of exchange. Besides, I do not believe in cutting oneself adrift from the world and one would largely do so by adopting such a method – of course these groups would disperse from time to time, but thus room would be made in life for the purely creative, apart from the political (which of course has its part to play). Large, generous rules might cover such communities – such as Co-operation, Equality, Brother-hood!

I must let this line of thought rest here. By the time I reached the Ashburton Club I was very weary, and but little inclined for social life. It *was* nice, though, to see the children in their pretty party frocks flocking in. I was impressed by the number of very dark Manx people – one little girlie interested me particularly. She was dressed in black satin, with pink sash and hair ribbon – a strange dress for so young a child, but it suited her dark beauty admirably! She looked just a little Southern peach – brown and sunkissed, with dark, liquid eyes and curling hair; I could have kissed every bit of her and lost myself in a rapture over the little 'brownie'!

Brew and some of the other adults acted *The White Boys* – dressed in white they fought with wooden swords. The vigour and activity of the men appealed to me in a most curious way as

168

they fought and leapt – I felt (I think almost for the first time in my life) distinctly attracted by the male body with its square-ness, sinew, muscle and vitality. Following upon this came the old heart sickness – the longing for one love and the bearing of children. Oh! it is not always easy to stand conqueror of the flesh and say, 'Though a lover be denied me, I will be a world lover – though children be denied me I will open my heart and arms to the universe!'

Eva's Diary   Friday, 9 May 1913
Frost asked me some questions this morning concerning Byron which led me to remark that I felt forced to admit some men and women possessed 'lover' natures, but did not make satisfactory husbands or wives, fathers or mothers – Frost at once said he had such a nature and did not intend to marry. He then launched into an angry denunciation of marriage, declaring that ninety-nine out of a hundred marriages were failures. I wonder whether 'free love' is really higher than monogamy? Sometimes I feel to live faithfully unto death with one man or woman is attempting in marriage (or sex) the ideal attained in religion by the conception of one God rather than many Gods, and I believe that somewhere in time and eternity a soul awaits us who will upon union give us a sublime sense of completion.

Lunch with Minna in depression: discussing 'bitterness' – owing to my then mood I said I thought it meant a hard battle to prevent oneself being embittered by life – Minna did not agree with me, but even now, I am inclined to think it is difficult.

I had an argument this evening with Aunt Edie and Gertie upon 'militancy' – I declared the imperishable could not be won by force – quoted the fable of the Sun and Wind – the failure of Puritanism etc. Afterwards I always fear lest I have not shewn toleration. I really am afraid at times that my hatred of force may blind me to the splendid qualities possessed by so many of these women. It seems to me the position of the militants is a difficult one – either (being scarce fitted for open warfare) they must go on with secret plots to even more violent deeds, or they must retreat – the latter course would need strength and dignity.

Eva's Diary   Sunday, 11 May 1913
An interesting little talk over the breakfast table with Gertie this morning – she thinks I am one who would love passionately. I

wonder if such an experience will ever be mine? Minna, Will, Stanley Pettinger and Lily [a close friend of Minna] came to supper – I enjoyed so *intensely* preparing all for them. Our time together was so happy – we sang songs until twelve o'clock. I had a brief talk with Minna – she is distressed at the thought of her Mother coming to be with her. She says I do not understand what struggles she has; it seems to her I find life's unpleasant duties easy and have a natural goodness. Sorrow crept into my heart when I heard this – I long so to be near to people, to share struggles and sins. Is it true that I find the unpleasant duties of life easy? I think of several and find that it gives me pain and effort to perform them. Minna is so large and noble and has such power of expression – she attributes to me that which I do not possess, or wish to possess. To strive and conquer is surely greater than never to feel the necessity for struggle!

Eva's Diary   Thursday, 15 May 1913
At lunch today Mrs Daisley was very emphatic that she never allowed herself to suffer from jealousy as it is a most fearful feeling, changing and embittering life. I heartily agree, but I think it plays a much larger part in life than is realised – is there not a great deal of secret jealousy? Minna said if her husband came to care for another woman she did not think she would be jealous – she would give him his liberty. I am afraid if I were married and really loved my husband but found he cared more for another woman I should suffer an agony. And yet if one loved in the highest truest way, one's love, I suppose, would be selfless.

Eva's Diary   Wednesday, 21 May 1913
I ran round to see Mrs Taverner in my lunch hour – we sat in the summer house and chatted. Mrs Taverner said she thought so many young married women shut themselves away from outside interests because at first the love of husband and children seemed all sufficient. She believed this was a mistake – but a mistake of ignorance. Ah! homes would not be closed at least to a single woman, if the married once realised how the hearts of their sisters yearn after companionship. Mrs Taverner also gave me a verse upon the lonely woman. It is a comfort to me to believe that we single women have a very definite part to play in the battle of life. If all women could marry would they have sufficient leisure and opportunity to study the position of

170

woman and to represent her cause to the world? This is work which single women can make their own. So enriched we can become world lovers – the companions of the lonely!

Ruth's Diary   Sunday, 25 May 1913

What extraordinary events have happened since I let my habit of keeping a diary lapse! It is a pity I have no record of the happenings of the last three or four years for they have certainly been most full of interest and wonder. I do not know quite what to say about development, for sometimes it seems that the heart of me has died since the great struggle and suffering of four years ago and the head (mind) of me has certainly become strangely dull.

But now I begin a new life. The joyous beauty of spring ushers in my new birth, and though I feel the pain of effort after the long lethargy and the grief over wasted years and opportunities, there is a new fount of love welling up within me telling me that in and through others I may yet experience happiness un-dreamed of.

Yesterday I moved into a little flat here at Notting Hill with my French friend Françoise, and we have spent such a delightful day together, putting our few things in order, cooking our dinner, writing letters and enjoying fellowship with each other. We really have a charming little place and feel we are going to be happy here.

Yesterday Eva, ever faithful, more loved if possible, and certainly more valued than of yore, came up to help us, also Hugh, who did some carpentering to our satisfaction, and we had much fun over our work.

How I have missed my diary! I gave it up chiefly through lack of time and partly because I feared becoming too introspective and interested in myself, but I have come to the conclusion that for me it is a good habit, seeming to deepen experience and certainly to clarify and link up thought.

Eva's Diary   Wednesday, 4 June 1913

Such a pleasant happy day! Read a good deal of *Katherine Frensham* during the morning. I am thoroughly enjoying this little romance, and find Katherine charming.

Tea at Minna's with much happy converse – we retailed romance after romance. Minna has read so *very* many romances. How wonderful she is! I feel that to me she has been a healer of the soul – my heart is full of thankfulness for her blessed friendship. We sat together on the kitchen step this evening and gazed up at the wall of ivy facing the doorway in pleasant greenness. Minna said as long as we lived we would share our trust with one another.

Aunt Edie met me at the Bank – she told me a suffragette had thrown herself before the King's horse at the Derby, receiving terrible injuries.[2] I cannot express what a shock this news was to me – can such martyrdom and sacrifice really be necessary? Will it hasten the longed for result?

Eva's Diary   Thursday, 5 June 1913
I called for Miss Leith this evening and we went together to a suffrage meeting at the Pioneer Cafe. Mrs and Miss Woodruff sang – Mrs Reeve was in the chair – she referred to the terrible Derby tragedy. Miss Thompson then addressed the meeting; I thought her personality dignified and striking. She wore a shot mauve dress with a V of white lace at the neck. She spoke with a pleasant simplicity of the need for the vote and especially referred to the great pilgrimage of women to take place during the summer to London and Edinburgh: they hope to riddle the country. I signed a 'friend's card'. Mrs Jones made a most amusing little speech: 'anti-suffragists', said she, 'get on platforms and tell us to stay at home. Why do not *they* stay at home since they believe so strongly in it?'

Eva's Diary   Wednesday, 11 June 1913
We wended our way to Hoxton Adult School – it was so nice to see the girls again – and my little addresses went off very happily. Françoise was not at home when we reached the new home. It is quite a sumptuous place now. 'Bobby' the cat met us at the foot of the stairs. Françoise came home so gay and winsome, and sang us a spirited little revolutionary song in French as we lay in bed.

Eva's Diary   Thursday, 12 June 1913
Ruth and I were up betimes this morning and went softly about our toilet lest we should wake Françoise. Françoise joined us at breakfast in cheery mood – she is so *very* attractive and lovable. I think she and Ruth will be very happy together and will do one another good. Françoise with her large, buoyant nature will cheer and widen Ruth, and Ruth with her fine

172

sensibilities and consideration for others will check and refine Françoise. I had much to tell Minna at lunch. She seemed rather tired of work and making ends meet. My dear Minna, poverty is hard to bear, and does rest upon one heavily. I do not wish to see anyone rich – but it seems to me a good many of us could do with more of this world's goods! Minna has such a large, life-giving nature – I think she would be better with some outlet outside the home.

Mr James called with reference to the Conference, and sat smoking and chatting whilst I lunched. He then asked if he might walk to the office with me which he accordingly did, and we discussed books we were reading. As I sat in silence today seeking the consciousness of God, it came to me almost overwhelmingly that if I did not deliberately run into temptation then the Divine Strength would be sufficient for my need – it would enable me to give whenever the call came, and to lift the most delicate and difficult experiences of life onto a spiritual plane. But oh God, how my nature is torn: the human in me cries out, 'Must I pay this price? Is it always to be mine to give – oh, how I *crave* to be the receiver of some deep and special love!' But this is weakness !

Eva's Diary   17 June 1913
An interesting conversation with Minna today over lunch. She tells me Mr and Mrs Pettinger have abandoned their scheme of co-habiting only when a child is wished for. The repression and strain have been so great upon Mr Pettinger, it has been making him ill. Mrs Pettinger has therefore agreed to co-habitation taking place whenever desired, provided Mr P. is willing to face the consequences. It has all interested me exceedingly; their plan has always seemed so strained and artificial to me. I feel strongly, however, spiritual and intellectual love should rule and be sufficiently strong to suppress physical intercourse during the weakness, ill health or pregnant condition of the woman. I would say, let love have full expression (with the above restriction) and be bold enough to face the consequences. Of course, I know the economic question is, more often than not, at the root of this evil: 30 or 40 shillings a week is not a strong income with which to face the prospect of a large family. Let life multiply that it may *demand* and *wrest* the labour, food and payment due to it!

Eva's Diary   Wednesday, 18 June 1913
Mrs Taverner's garden looked gay with white, pink, red and
blue flowers today. We had a long discussion upon the subject of
unlegalised marriage (arising out of the action of Mary Wollstonecraft.) I said I felt convinced that the highest form of
marriage is where trust in one another is so great it enables each
to accept the love of the other without legal or Church bond.
Mrs Taverner felt humanity was too frail for such trust. I wonder
if we should arrive at greater strength of character and wisdom
of choice if law (with regard to marriage) was destroyed, and we
were left absolutely free to form, dissolve and reform unions?
Society would be in a curious state of chaos for a time, but at
least without deception. Would the result be strength or utter
failure. Our Mary Wollstonecrafts and George Eliots are surely
the pioneers.

Tea at Minna's – Horace is a dear boy, I am very fond of
him. I believe sex is felt unconsciously in the relationship of
children: hence the girls adore Stanley; Horace has, I think, a
special corner for me.

Some pleasant music at Miss Leith's this evening, and a quiet
reading. Miss Leith is an ardent suffragette. I am afraid I felt
rather weary of it all – not because I have not the cause of
women at heart, but because I notice the militant suffragettes so
seldom discuss the fundamentals of progress amongst women –
it is always 'the Vote'.

Eva's Diary   Thursday, 19 June 1913
Minna said today she thought we built up a great deal of
romance around the idea of marriage, and often the less
romantic marriages, built upon kindly, friendly feeling and
trust, were the happiest. I feel that to some extent one lowers
one's standards unless one can feel in some degree a three-fold
attraction – physical, mental, spiritual. I do not think I could
marry unless I felt this! The committee meeting this evening was
well attended – Owen and Eva came. Eva seemed so pleased to
see me; she looked well, and as always, pretty! She says she has
had a good holiday and the children are bonny. Owen seemed
delighted to have her back – I realised to the full how inevitably
we single women are 'outside the heart of things'; our friendship
with happily married men and women after all only touches the
fringe of their lives. I am so *deeply* grateful to Owen and Eva for
the love and kindness they have shewn me. When Owen said I

174

came as inspiration to their home I was glad I could express the gratitude I feel. Tonight I asked myself, 'Could I pay the price of this friendship?' Every love, friendship and experience of life demands a price. I think Owen's is a nature which absorbs all one has to offer, and draws largely upon one, without realising that suffering might follow.

Eva's Diary   Friday, 20 June 1913
If I am to take Frost seriously he really made me an offer this morning – to me it seems so ridiculous. He said he had heard of stranger things happening – I replied, 'If I accepted you, you *would* be in a fix, Frost', to which he answered, 'No, although you may not believe it, I should be delighted, really delighted'. I have felt a little uncomfortable. He furthermore said that if I were in some wild and desolate place with only him near I should be glad then of his companionship. I said, 'only as a brother'. 'Oh, hang brotherhood', said he, 'it nearly drives me mad; it is as much as I can stand now! I suppose he really has grown attached to me – we have worked together for nine years now. I like Frost very much in a comradely way, but that is all.

Minna informed me today she believes she may expect another little life. While my heart leaps with joy for her, it leaps with fear too, lest she should be lost to us all – I know she suffers terribly at such times. Mrs Pettinger thinks she is also in the same condition. How daily more precious Minna's friendship becomes to me – a pearl of great price!

Eva's Diary   Saturday, 28 June 1913
I am reading *The New Machiavelli* – it appears to me a brilliant but shallow book. Wells reminds me of sherbert which when shot into water causes it to effervesce – he is stimulating, but, I think, transitory. I dislike the manner in which early sexual episodes are related – I am perhaps fastidious, but to seize opportunities for sexual intercourse merely for self-gratification appears to me to be the attitude of the drunkard and glutton. Even in my most rampant moods, when nature *thunders* in me and almost *demands* expression I feel in the depth of me that unless as an expression of love and completion the act would have but little satisfaction for me. The book would, I think, give young men the impression that such conduct was a proof of virility and manhood. *Is* there any truth, I wonder, in the view held by many that passion is too strong in young men for

restraint? We need books which strengthen in the minds of men the conviction that liberty should not lead to licence – lifting sexual intercourse onto a higher plane than the animal. At the same time I am most dissatisfied with the conventional attitude towards the question. It is horrible hypocrisy and false morality which binds many (especially women) to continence, leading oft times to madness and intense suffering. We ought to be honest enough to recognise that to some natures this experience is imperative.

Eva's Diary   Sunday, 29 June 1913

Aunt Edie and Gertie went to a demonstration in Trafalgar Square this evening, so I trudged alone to Conference. It was very hot in the lecture hall, but it was pleasant to find friends in the shape of Mr and Mrs Taverner, Owen and Eva! I sat with Minna in Chapel this evening. I experience such a sensation of completeness at times when with Minna – I could not help telling her so this evening. We had one of those moments of loving unity when ordinary life was transcended. Mr James preached a stirring sermon against the militancy of the Women's Movement, and the continual use of the word 'martyr' – he pointed out the immense powers and possibilities of the movement, but deprecated the deliberate provocation of those in authority – such action he termed 'immoral'. What a brave soul he possesses – he makes his stand for the truth as he sees it, and relies very much upon the sympathy of the few.

Eva's Diary   Wednesday, 2 July 1913

I find *The Suffragette*[3] does not impress me! It is a somewhat witty and exceedingly sarcastic magazine. I cannot get over the cool manner in which the militant actions (burning of homes, wrecking of pictures, etc.) are reported. How much the Government are to blame for this attitude on the part of the women: militancy has been greatly provoked. Nevertheless my sympathies are in other directions.

Tea at Minna's. There is a possibility of her going North for the month of August: how I shall miss her, but anything for her good, and I do think the bracing air of the North would strengthen her – she does not seem *at all well*. I told her that if she were a man, I should feel absolutely completed; Minna says I rest her so, and that I am a robber and a thief, for I have stolen her heart.

Eva's Diary   Monday, 7 July 1913

I finished reading *The New Machiavelli* today. Margaret's letter to Remington impressed me greatly. She contrasts their two natures – she is quiet beauty, anxious to progress, yet willing and eager to remain within laws and convention which appear to be good and of service. He is hot passion – reckless, turbulent, pressing on towards the ideal, yet ever dissatisfied with realisation – bursting asunder the bonds of convention.

How one recognises these two forces playing through life – and how the world needs each force. I am essentially constructive, but I have enough of the rebel in me to enable me to appreciate and value the bold, reckless souls who destroy the fictitious peace of society. They disturb us, annoy, irritate and shock us; they are the volcanos of social life, the preventatives of smug self-satisfaction!

Mr James called to see me at Minna's today – I think he was feeling the need of sympathy. He lays great stress now upon the Church, its importance and government. He stated the Conference would have to abide by the decision of the Church. I said how anxious I was that as a Church we should not become over-organised – we had been exceedingly free, dipping into many social and intellectual problems. Was there not a danger now of orthodoxy and over-organisation? Mr James stated he did not attempt to please all. I had a queer feeling that Mr James (whom I love and honour) could, if he chose, be almost tyrannical; I suppose opposition tends to develop this.

Eva's Diary   Thursday, 10 July 1913

I found Minna too unwell to think of accompanying me to London this evening. Aunt Edie and I reached Westminster a little after 8 pm. I was delighted with Caxton Hall. The moment I entered the room I had a sensation of being amongst my own people – most of the ladies wore pretty pinafore gowns and reminded me of Letchworth! Mrs Despard wore a grey dress, with a scarf of heaven's own blue around her shoulders. I met a member of the Labour League, and such a nice little woman brought me refreshments and enrolled me as a member [of the Women's Freedom League]. Mrs Despard made a moving speech upon the need of love – love as the core and motive of all our actions. We must never forget we are out for men as much as for women, nor must we look upon the vote as an end in itself, but press on to ever nobler ideals. A money present was made which Mrs Despard handed over for the use of the League. Following upon this came an entertainment – a lady sang most beautifully, and we had a good humorist, who sang a song he had composed about Mrs Despard – we all joined in the chorus: 'For she is our own great lady, And this is her birthday eve!' A Hindoo performed upon a strange instrument used for many years by the Yoghis and mystics of the East. Then came the glory of the evening – Indian dancing by a beautiful young girl: she gave us a slave endeavouring to free herself from her chains, spring and joy dances etc. I could have kissed every part of her – I felt intoxicated by the beauty of the human body, the joy of motion. Here was dancing expressive of body, mind and soul – my idea of 'redemption' exemplified – harmony is unity!

Eva's Diary   Saturday, 9 August 1913

This evening my dear Ruth came, looking so pale and weary – she has had an exhausting, worrying time. Françoise has a baby boy! Such a terrible confinement – she was in agony and then four hours under chloroform – room in a terrible condition, and the Doctor almost in despair. Terrible as it all was, there were some touches of humour. Madame Lafitte (who arrived on Thursday with an ocean of luggage, three umbrellas, three parasols, six costumes, blouses, etc., and without being able to speak a word of English) rushed about the room whilst Françoise was in labour, clapping her hands and crying, 'Ma pauvre Françoise, ma pauvre Françoise!', then seating herself she would scribble upon paper, 'Sacrifice the child, but spare the Mother'. At last the Doctor turned her out of the room! Just as the nurse was about to plunge the baby into the bath, in rushed the dog, whereupon the nurse waved the baby at him in such a frantic manner that the dog turned and fled!

I think her friend Mrs Camebus, has been exceedingly good to Françoise – it has been a big undertaking to see her through this trouble. Dr Eder and the Doctor who attended Françoise have both offered from sympathy to become responsible for the expense of the child for the first year of its life: I do not know if Françoise will accept – it is all so wonderful! I am afraid I feel somewhat envious; so many girls suffer in loneliness. Help and friendship has just poured in on Françoise – is it all, however, good for her? She seems already inconsiderate and almost to demand things as her right!

Eva's Diary   Sunday, 10 August 1913
I gave my little address upon Galsworthy's *Little Dream* this
morning at the Men's Adult School. Only a small gathering –
but such adverse criticism. Mr Stannard [a member of Chapel]
objected to the whole play as immoral and my interpretation as
wholly wrong: in his opinion, it was rightly named – 'the little
dream of a little soul. I thought at the close of the school his
remarks exceeded criticism and courtesy – he could not let the
subject rest, and ended by asking me whether I had been
studying Pneumonics or memory training, as it did not sound at
all impromptu. The whole morning stabbed me – but I have
been reading myself a little lecture: what about my fine phrases
with reference to 'love to humanity'! Now here is my test! I have
certainly been brought much into contact lately with the cynical
and cruel side of human nature; can I rise above it and gain a
really comradely spirit towards those who hurt me?

Eva's Diary   Tuesday, 12 August 1913
A surprise for me at Minna's today. She had called at Mr
Stannard's, and he informed her they had a fine time at the
Adult School on Sunday morning – they *did* enjoy it, and
thought I (as a single woman) dealing with the questions I did,
was very plucky. I *did* go up in his estimation. They *had*
criticised me, but that was what they went there for! It was a
great relief to me to know they had enjoyed the address – I
shall not take them so seriously again. Criticism is good – its
power is destructive, but too much criticism, I am sure, destroys
and prevents one gaining inspiration!

Eva's Diary   Saturday, 16 August 1913
Aunt Edie and I left this morning and set off on our journey.
Paddington was crowded with passengers en route to sea and
country. The day was brilliant and we passed rapidly miles of
typical English scenery – the ground rising and falling gently in
a soft greenness. At last we entered the black country, stopping
at Birmingham, Wolverhampton and Shrewsbury. At these
stations the atmosphere was almost suffocating – a pall of
gloom, of yellow mist, overhung the cities and the surrounding
country, caused I suppose by the smoke of the manufacturing. If
there is anything worse than living in London it must, I think, be
to live in one of these towns! After leaving Birmingham I began
to feel so much leg and head throbbing and a sensation of

179

sickness. We reached Llangollen – such a lovely spot; then we dashed through truly striking scenery, mountains rising precipitately on every hand. But I felt too unwell to appreciate it all: I am ashamed to say the glorious mountains I have for years yearned to see I now only longed to escape – my Heart's desire being to find a darkened room and couch whereon I could lay my aching head and body. We have such a comfortable room at the Midland Temperance Hotel in Barmouth.

I read a good deal of Grant Allen's *The Woman Who Did*[4] in the train – I am enjoying it; it contains many thought-suggestive sentences, and deals with the problems of the free union. I do not agree with Grant Allen when he makes Hermione say, 'I wouldn't have spoken my inmost feelings to another woman.' Have we not here Grant Allen the *man* speaking? Do I not know from experience the deep, tender friendship and heart to heart communion possible between women? Indeed the sex Grant Allen alludes to as 'a magic link' I have often felt to be a barrier to continuous intercourse between men and women.

Eva's Diary   Monday, 18 August 1913
This morning we packed our lunch and set off for the Panorama Walk! Climbing a hill we found ourselves amongst the mountains. On and on until we came to a heap of stones marking the spot from which the best. view of the Panorama could be obtained. Here we lay until late afternoon, stretched upon the heather, the sea glittering mysteriously in the distance, the estuary some way below, and the mountains heather and gorse clad all around; such thoughts came to me, lying there amidst such indescribable beauty!

In the evening we listened for a time to a suffrage meeting upon the shore – a lady member of the Freedom League was speaking and a large crowd had gathered to listen. She answered all questions so bravely – I did admire her! A young fellow near to her aroused my ire by shouting, 'Get down! You'll never get the vote!' Some rough natives would, I thought, have tipped over the little stool upon which the speaker was standing: we stood near, and were glad to see her get safely away.

Eva's Diary   Tuesday, 19 August 1913
Incessant sunshine is our lot here day after day! I have finished reading *The Woman Who Did*: the book has interested me

greatly. I agree with Hermione that in present day marriage we live too closely with one another – we do not give each other room to breathe, to develop, to possess our own souls. I should like, if I were married, each to possess a bedroom and sitting room – each to continue their development in service to the community – the one to invite the other to evenings of work and enjoyment as in the days of pure friendship. I see grave difficulty in women continuing to support themselves by employment, at any rate during maternity. For one thing it appears to me too great a demand upon physical and mental strength, and for another, the cares of a family are very absorbing; at the same time I feel the necessity for women to keep in touch with the work of the world, in order as her children grow and pass from her absolute care she may fill a place again in the active life of the world.

Eva's Diary   Tuesday, 26 August 1913
This morning we took the train to Fairbourne – such an open, sunny little place – hills at the back. I lay prone upon the shore for three or four hours, my eyes closed, the heat of the sun and music of the waves lulling me. Almost I lost consciousness of identity and personality; I seemed one with nature – part of the breeze, the sand, the restless waters. I dreamily imagined the water lapping softly around me until I should be borne out to sea; on and on to some Isle of the Blessed where tender love doth reign and divine companionship!

Eva's Diary   30 August 1913
Returned home!!!

Eva's Diary   Thursday, 4 September 1913
Lunch at Minna's today when Minna again expressed, I thought, original views. We were discussing *The Woman Who Did:* Minna said she thought Hermione gloried in martyrdom and that thus martyrdom lost its value and point. She also thought the tie of affection between Mother and child very much overestimated. Minna thinks as children grow older, unless there is sympathy of nature and temperament, the love between parent and child does not necessarily grow stronger: it may even decrease. It is quite possible for a friend to be loved more fervently than a son or daughter. How I admired Minna for her frank statement – I believe she is right.

181

Eva's Diary   Saturday, 6 September 1913

This month's copy of *The Labor Woman*[5] arrived this morning, containing some very good little articles. I was so glad to see the question of the limitation of families dealt with. The wording of the article very strongly resembled my own thoughts expressed a little while ago on the same subject in this journal – it proves how electric thought is: it is a current ready to touch like minds in different parts of the world. It interested me too to read the reference to Queenie Gerald,[6] procuratress – one longs that this frightful practice should cease.

Eva's Diary   Tuesday, 9 September 1913

Lunch at Minna's when we talked much of the days of our childhood. I do not like to dwell on them – they depress me so. My daily more precious Minna! She says if it were not for her friends her life would be so barren; what she misses in Will she finds in me and Lily! She says she thinks a man unsatisfactorily married suffers and hungers more than a woman because a woman can find comfort in the depths of another woman, but very seldom a man in another man – and sex is the barrier to prevent him finding it in another woman. Yet I believe it is possible to transcend sex.

Eva's Diary   Wednesday, 10 September 1913

Tea at Mrs Awes' – much fun and laughter. Mrs Awes says she has never known anyone get as excited as I do – when she first knew me she thought me very calm and intellectual. Eva told me Owen thought my work in life would be to tell people stories and write books for children. It is nice anyone should think I could possibly do anything beautiful; sometimes I feel so numbed and the way dark, yet if I only press on, work will come. Then we chatted a little over our work – Eva said how glad she was I had taken up embroidery – so I am, since it binds me closer to other women – to get even closer to men and women day by day is my great longing – such a passion for tenderness, to understand and be understood possesses me at times: is there *one* heart somewhere to love and love?

Eva's Diary   Thursday, 11 September 1913

A nice, cheerful subject came up for discussion at lunch today, viz., my appearance! It appears so many people think me prim and proper, and that I look so fearfully learned and good – Oh

182

dear! How it does add to the burden of life to have such an appearance, and how many pangs I have received through it! I *should* like, not only for my own sake but for that of others, to have a pleasing appearance. I met Ruth at Liverpool St. Station tonight. She seemed in a rather curious mood: I felt chilled but I think, poor girl, she is thoroughly run down.

Ruth to Eva   16 September 1913
                                            Chalice Well, Glastonbury
My very dear friend,
You have been so much in my thoughts since last Friday (or was it Thursday?) evening, when I fear I appeared somewhat quiet and absent. But I *did* enjoy the play. I hope you had a pleasant journey home and did not feel unduly tired next day. How is that leg?

Well dear, you will be wondering about my holiday, I know – what manner of place 'Chalice Well' can be, what sort of people congregate here, etc., etc. I seem only just to have arrived, but in a quiet sort of way am feeling very happy (though physically I cannot get warm!). Of course, things are at the beginning stage and nothing here can be compared with Woodbrooke, but the atmosphere is beautiful and soothing. As I came down in the train I felt more than ever before (and that means a *great* deal) how I am becoming a Commercial Product – and in that too, typical of hundreds of others. I do not mean willingly – I feel that life and circumstances seem to mould many of us into patterns we ourselves dislike and shrink from: physically care-worn and undeveloped, where we had dreamed of beauty: mentally timid and ill-equipped, where we had visioned culture and capacity; and spiritually – ah, what of that? A choking pain seized upon me.

There is a beautiful girl here, kneeling busily engaged on the floor of this room as I write, who has gone through Kindergarten training and is going to have children here. She is quite radiant with life and confidence. There is another girl who simply fascinates me. She has a Rossetti type of face, most striking and lovely, and she has been a pupil of Raymond Duncan's and is going to teach weaving and Greek dancing. Miss Buckton is here and her personality seems more rich and wonderful than ever.

This morning we went over the Abbey ruins – it was very beautiful, and I hope to get some nice walks. It is early yet to write much about things. And when shall I see you, dear? I would like it to be soon, so can it be next Monday?

With my fondest love, dear, and hoping all is well with you. Your friend, Ruth.

Ruth to Eva   September 1913
                                                                 Bagshot
My dear,
A little flutter and excitement and suspicion of romance! The very nice man from America, whom I met at Glastonbury, has written me a charming letter (confessing the he stole my address from the visitors' book) and invited me to go to the theatre. I have thought things over and am wondering, dear, whether it would suit you as well if I came on Friday. (What next is going to happen to your queer little friend?) I will bring his letters for your approval, when I come.

I wanted to tell you the other night, only words failed me, of the last evening I spent at Glastonbury, when I sat beside Miss Buckton, just in the firelight, and she put her arms about me, as we talked. It will always be one of the most holy memories of my life.

On Friday Madame Lafitte returned to France, so we expect to get into more regular ways again. The baby is a continual joy.

I am having rather a depressing time at home: Dad seems even more melancholy than usual and talks constantly of madness.

There is much my heart would fain share with you now, but I am wanted to make tea – so, dear Eva, Goodbye for a little space. Ruth.

Eva's Diary   Sunday, 21 September 1913
It was strange to awake this morning in Aunt Emily's house, Bromley! Aunt Emily seems full of energy and is so industrious too. I fully sympathised with her when she said the Women's Movement was far from satisfying her – yet I know the necessity of it. I reverence the courage and devotion which it has called forth, but oh! how great gatherings – movements in the mass – oppress me now! It is the individual who appeals to me – the building up and development of character.

We went to see Aunt Emily's friend Mrs –. I do not know when I have felt so uncomfortable and secretly amused. I was greeted and treated almost as a celebrity. What can that Aunt

Emily have been saying? Mrs – said she had long looked forwards to meeting me, and what a busy life I must have with my wide interests and literary attainments!!! (Query – what and where are they? I do not know, said the Great Bell of Bow!) I had a horrible sensation that she was absolutely hanging upon my words; as Gertie said to me afterwards, 'Anyone would have thought you were H. G. Wells!' It appears Aunt Emily has been sharing my letters!

Eva's Diary   Wednesday, 15 October 1913
Mrs Awes called at the office this afternoon to invite me round to tea. I ran round to Minna to tell her I should not stay to tea – she looked so fine I thought. How I admire the largeness of her form, her hands so perfectly shaped, the well-poised head with delicately curling hair, the unusual cast of countenance: she always represents to me woman past, present and to come; she retains all the primitive instincts of the past – sex, maternal instinct, love of home; she lives in the present, for she has borne and now rears a family; she is a type of the woman of the future because her thought is deep, her sympathies wide!

Eva's Diary   Thursday, 23 October 1913
Lunch at Minna's today. She tells me the little unborn baby kicks and turns a great deal. How wonderful it all seems. Shall I ever know such an experience? This has been a day of castles in the air – of plans and schemes. Mrs Gibbs kindly sent her Froebel book over for me to look at, but does not advise me to try the work as teaching is already frightfully overcrowded, women holding certificates being obliged to seek work in tea-shops.

Eva's Diary   Tuesday, 4 November 1913
Quite a merry lunch hour with Minna today. In the evening Aunt Edie and I went to London to the Cripplegate Institute to see *Hiawatha*. We found the Institute easily – it has a fine hall with gallery and stage. How I enjoyed the play! Not a man took part in it: at first, I thought the Indians were men – they were specially fine women. I admired them so, and the war dances were splendid. My mind travelled back into the past – to the ages of conventional, stilted movement. I rejoiced that the corset is being gradually thrown aside – that Chinese women are seeking a natural growth for the foot. Life seemed full of

185

promise as I watched those fine athletic women, leaping, dancing. I thought too of the redemption of the art of dancing which I feel is taking place, through Greek dancing and such expressive movement as I was then witnessing.

Ruth was there. She looked so nice in her art dress, but she seemed much disturbed in herself and has, I think, been fretting a little. How I wish some wonderful love would come into her life! But I feel sure that something joyous will come to her some day!

Françoise has secured work for the *Citizen*.[7] One pound a week for an article, with the possibility (if her writing is satisfactory) of another pound for another article! I am afraid (although glad Françoise should have the good fortune) Ruth and I felt just a little envious – so many years have we been 'gathering up the fragments'.

Eva's Diary   Thursday, 4 December 1913
Lunch at my dear Minna's – she says she feels better, but I do not like the dark rings around her eyes. Mrs Awes has refused to start an Adult School, saying she wishes to concentrate on being a good Mother and she would rather meet others to *do* something than to discuss. I feel there is time to discuss and a time to work – a time when one cannot work until one realises one's mental position, and a time when one is ripe for action, and mere discussion seems waste of time! I feel so sorry for Mrs Pettinger: she is full of restlessness, Minna tells me – going to Liberal meetings and reading the lives of great women, whilst her children need her so. Poor woman! It must be terrible to feel one has great abilities which one's own home life prevents one using – yet, after all, little duties done in the spirit of love and faith are truly great.

It was so cosy at home this evening – the shop closed, we sat and worked. Gertie came home with the news that Mrs Pankhurst has again been arrested – militancy will thus receive a fresh impulse.[8] I admire Mrs Pankhurst, and feel she has fought a good and brave fight. I know how terribly hard it is for the human spirit not to retaliate – yet I think if even one retaliates oneself it does not seem right to incite others to violence.

Eva's Diary   Tuesday, 9 December 1913
Ruth spent the night with us and prepared this morning to return to business after two or three days' absence on account of

186

sickness. However, I drew such a tempting picture of the pleasure of a day at the Tate Gallery that (although I hardly expected to persuade her) she agreed to take another day and complete her cure at the Gallery! Hoorah! It will do Ruth good and it serves her niggardly firm right.

Have finished *The Life of Josephine Butler* today – the book has been an inspiration to me.

Eva's Diary   Wednesday, 10 December 1913
Mrs Taverner tells me Mr Taverner is very disappointed in Mr James – thinks he has *gone back* – does not believe in appealing to the emotions but to reason. I believe in appealing to both: emotion is of the soul, reason of the intellect. I fear we should be poor creatures if reason ruled, and emotion (is not love emotion?) sat shivering without! There are so many whose reason assents to social reform, to the necessity of the vote to women; but it is emotion's holy passion which propels to labour and conquest!

Eva's Diary   Saturday, 20 December 1913
A day of *work* at the office and at home! At the end of the day I became very weary – my side and legs gnawing and aching badly. These pains make me anxious at times, and I wonder what is before me in the years to come. Read a little more of *Ann Veronica*.

Eva's Diary   Friday, 26 December 1913
I enjoyed my journey to Kingston – went by omnibus to Waterloo – the river looked a mirror of silvery grey in the deepening twilight, and the buildings upon the Embankment an uncertain blue, whilst lights twinkled amidst it all! On my journey I was able to read a little and enjoyed some fine extracts in *The Conservator*. I do not agree with Margaret Sanger[9] that under capitalism it is impossible for young men and women to live beautiful lives or to have strong bodies – impossible for prostitution to cease as long as there is hunger. Partly all this is true, but poor creatures we should be indeed if we allowed circumstances wholly to shape us. We must be strong, become masters of our fate and circumstance.

Eva's Diary   Wednesday, 31 December 1913
Went to see Ruth this evening. Françoise, I thought, looked

beautiful. She is recovering her vitality – baby too has such a colour and laughs so prettily! Some poor children were there for a party – Françoise lit lanterns and hung them upon a line, turning out the gas – then the Xmas tree was brought in gaily lighted and hung with toys – it all looked so bright and pretty. Françoise and Ruth marched the children round whilst they chose their toys – afterwards we had games and then goodbye to the children.

Ruth and I sat together talking until almost midnight, and then saw the old year out and the new in together. Shall we, I wonder, be near enough to one another at the end of this year, to do the same? I feel that this will be a year of great change, and sadness presses on me! Ruth looked so fine, I thought, as she sat and talked to me – like one of William Morris's beautiful women! She had another letter of delicate sympathy from Mr Thompson – she has thought much about his offer, and feels if it will make her a more useful woman to her fellows she will accept it as a loan; it seems to be a door. She feels probably Mr Thompson may wish her to go to America, and it is possible she may do so!

The attitude Mr Jones has taken up in this matter has, I think given Ruth much pain. He thinks it is all a splendid opportunity for her – does not wish to stand in her light; he has also become very interested in another young lady.

How *young* men are! I feel so impatient with them at times – they seem blind to the treasure life offers them and place emphasis upon those things the least essential. I do feel at times Mr Jones has not been an altogether healthy companion for Ruth: she needs a robust, bracing mind to wed her own!

8

'Almost Too Precious to Pen'
January–July 1914

At the beginning of 1914 there were two quite different, but important changes in Ruth's and Eva's lives. Ruth, with financial help from David Thompson, secured a scholarship for full-time study at the Woodbrooke Settlement; Eva was drawn into a closer relationship with Minna, when Minna's husband Will suddenly died.

For Ruth, Woodbrooke was a 'unique opportunity' after all the years of longing for more creative and politically useful work. Established in 1903 as a 'settlement for religious and social study' Woodbrooke was set up by leading Quakers anxious to tackle the 'increasing economic and social problems of the modern world'. Religious study was not compulsory, and students could, as Ruth did, pursue only, or mostly, social subjects and the basics of social work itself. The settlement was international – 'students from Europe, Asia, Africa, America and Australia claiming their share of Woodbrookers', according to the log in 1914. There was a majority of women students and some subsidy was offered in cases like Ruth's, when students had no private income. Situated at Selly Oak, in pleasant countryside just outside Birmingham, the settlement directed much of its work towards the oppressive industrial conditions of the City. (Woodbrooke still exists as a Quaker study centre and community.)

For Ruth, the change was momentous. The combination of interesting academic study and progressive social work, in the co-operative atmosphere of Woodbrooke, suited her perfectly, and she gained confidence and skills. Before long she was writing to Eva – 'My thoughts are inclined to run into plans for Utopian changes and think of the millions for whom such rest and change should be possible.' Her letters were full of descriptions of

189

lectures and Woodbrooke activities, and she tried to pass on much of her learning to Eva. She continued to correspond with David Thompson and see Hugh, who was working as a gardener at Chalice Well.

For Eva, there was a more intense and physically passionate relationship with Minna, when she moved in to help with the birth of the baby after Will's death. The experience of living in what she called the 'love-atmosphere' of Minna's house was exhilarating and she began to expand her ideas on physical union and relationships generally. The baby added a new dimension to Eva's life although there were times when she and Minna were overwhelmed with the difficulties of domestic life and the problems Minna faced supporting herself and her four children. Eva and the Walthamstow friends rallied round, organised relief and raised money which eventually paid for Minna's nursing training.

The birth of Minna's baby aroused complex emotions in Eva. Despite her closeness to Minna she sometimes felt rather 'out of it all' and 'longed for a child and lover' (not seeing Minna as a lover) of her 'very own'. She also felt threatened that Minna might need her less as time went by. Minna herself experienced a conflict, wanting to rely on Eva more, and yet holding back at times, feeling 'afraid to love, afraid to trust herself'. With her increased responsibilities, Eva, at times, felt 'mentally hungry' and 'destitute of ideas and initiatives' (although she started a Girls' League at the Chapel). She missed Ruth, and hoped she would not seem 'too primitive' when Ruth returned from Woodbrooke.

Eva's Diary   Tuesday, 6 January 1914
Lunch at Minna's, when I was much amused by Minna's account of a conversation with Stanley. He considers education does women a great deal of harm, and thinks if I were married to a poor man and had children, I should be wretched, my intellect struggling to escape my surroundings; if sick, my children possibly dirty and neglected. How heartily I laughed at it all. Stanley is quite mistaken in his opinion re.education. Neglect of honest, wholesome labour does not arise from too much, but too little education – from insufficient education upon the meaning of life and labour!

Met Minna at Dr Eliot's at 9 pm and we had a lovely chat together on various subjects – Mr and Mrs Awes' kindness, the possible changes in Ruth's life, etc. Minna spoke of the wondrous interchange and merging of soul she had often experienced with Lily and me. I felt so honoured when she said there were some things she had said to me – confided – which she could tell no one else; but she felt I understood. I pray that I may grow more and more worthy and meet more fully the needs of others.

Dr Eliot said the pain in my leg is local neuritis. I had to lay on his surgical couch while he tested the nerve and then applied a blister. I hope I shall soon be free from the pain.

Eva's Diary   Wednesday, 7 January 1914
Tea with Minna. She looks very frail, and Will's throat is troublesome. Had to defend Mr James at Class this evening. Miss Mansfield referred to him as a 'rotter' and said she thought it was a fearful thing that he should so have upset Trinity. He should have started a church elsewhere. I informed her that I was a member of Trinity Church, that I knew and admired Mr James, and that he had acted quite rightly in remaining within the church as he looked upon his work as part of a new reformation coming from within the church. The suffragettes were then discussed, and I felt impelled to announce that I was a non-militant suffragette. My little testimonies left me in a trembling condition, but I could not stand by and hear Mr James and righteous causes maligned.

Eva's Diary   Thursday, 22 January 1914
Finished reading *Modern Women* by Laura Hanson this morning. It has interested me very much but I think it is biased and sometimes even cruel. It seems to me to be small and show narrow sympathies when a writer can speak of George Eliot as a 'moralising old maid'. I do not agree with L. Hanson that marriage (love) is the supreme end of a woman's life – it is most certainly one of the great fundamentals of life, without which one is the poorer, but I think it is a morbid and unhealthy view to take that a woman's life is a failure because she never experiences love and marriage.

Ruth came this evening, and we sat at needlework, I teaching Ruth some embroidery stitches. Her affairs are in abeyance just now; Françoise is very worried – she wishes to form another free union, this time with Mr Hoffmeyer, and fears the effect of the news upon her Mother.

Eva's Diary   Friday, 23 January 1914
Lunch at Minna's. Will seems better, but the Doctor says he has been upon the verge of consumption! How I hope all will be well.

Eva's Diary   Sunday, 25 January 1914
Tea with Owen and Eva, then all set off to Adult School. The meeting was packed – mostly working men and women. Mrs MacKenzie was so good; she spoke of 'Fellowship' – the value of love and comradeship.

Then we returned to Owen and Eva's and all sat round the fire and talked. Owen urged me to write – was sure I could do so. I once feared lest this friendship should cost me too much; that petty feeling has gone – tonight I felt all three were hallowed by sympathy and love, and all I long is to give and give! I walked home – I could not sleep, I was so excited. I lay awake almost the whole night – Oh, how my legs ached!

Eva's Diary   Wednesday, 28 January 1914
Met Ruth in London – she is off to Woodbrooke in a fortnight's time! I can scarcely believe it! I am so *very* thankful and delighted for her – but oh! I shall miss our weekly 'communes'. We have been friends now for almost thirteen years, and I don't think have missed meeting for more than a fortnight or three weeks!

We met Aunt Edie at Liverpool St. and then made our way to the Hoxton Adult School through the busy sordid streets. Such a big school – I *was* scared! I got through my little address on 'Christ and Woman' rather lamely, I am afraid – I spoke of the call of the past to woman to marriage and motherhood – and Christ's call to the future to citizenship with men, to make the world a home, a kingdom!

The girls were so nice afterwards, especially Clara and Rose. Ruth and I found the flat in darkness – Françoise in bed – so we stepped quietly about to get supper and then rest!

Eva's Diary   Thursday, 29 January 1914
Only half an hour for our toilet this morning, we just scampered! When dressed, I ran in to say goodbye to Françoise: she was in bed with baby at her breast – she really is most attractive and has such a charming manner. I do not wonder she is so much admired!

192

Eva's Diary   Monday, 2 February 1914
Lunch at Minna's. Will looked so ill, and his face was burning
when I kissed him. Minna said he almost died in the night on
Saturday – he choked so she had to push him out of bed and
fling open the windows. Dr Shone had sent round for Minna to
call to see him this evening – I felt at once she ought not to go
alone, for I felt convinced Will was *very* seriously ill, indeed I
suspected consumption. We went to the surgery and Minna saw
Dr Shone. When she rejoined me, she was weeping, and I knew
at once my fears were confirmed. We walked about the dark
streets – Minna telling me between her tears that Will must go
away to a Sanatorium before the baby is born. Minna asked me
if I would sleep with her each night whilst Will is away, and I
said at once how I should love it – what a joy it would be!

Eva's Diary   Wednesday, 4 February 1914
Edith called at the office this morning and asked me to go round
in the lunch hour. She assured me all was well, but I wondered
what Minna needed me for. When I reached the house, I
noticed the blinds were down, and a pang went through me; but
I thought, the sun is so bright, it is because of that the blinds are
down. When I saw them all, however, the truth came home, and
Minna murmured, 'He is dead, dear.' After a time I hurried
back to the office taking Horace with me to tell Frost I should
remain away for the afternoon.

Lily came and stayed the evening, and did us all good with her
kind sympathetic presence. We prepared the sitting room, and
the undertakers came, and brought Will downstairs.

I slept with my darling, or rather lay close beside her, my arms
around her, for we scarcely slept. Minna asked me between her
tears if I would make a home for the children if anything happened to her, and I said I would; I *know* God would help me.

Oh, these last few days – I cannot write of them in detail. I
have *lived* at my Minna's, and at night she has wept in my arms,
and I have started from a tiny doze to hear her murmuring 'My
comfort!' Once she threw her arms around me and whispered,
'Oh Eva, I should have *died* without you.' I write these things
that I may never forget them. I felt I had not lived in vain.
Yesterday dear Will was laid to rest.

Baby *does* kick me at night as it lays under its Mother's heart
– I *love* to feel it. Minna moved my hand over it and before I
got up I bent and kissed it, that it might receive its first kiss

before it was born. I feel it will be specially 'my baby'. How I *should* like it to have a name for me, other than Eva. Little Mother would be lovely, if Minna would not mind! I want to be present when it is born, and on mentioning it found Minna wished for me too, but was afraid to say so lest it should be too great a strain. But I do not feel fear: I only pray my darling may have strength to be free from unnecessary pain!

Eva's Diary   Thursday, 12 February 1914
I was glad to find my Minna brighter this lunch hour. I went to meet Ruth this evening. She looked so nice in her green frock. She has had another letter from Mr Thompson saying he will be sending more money and probably will be over in the summer and take her to see Edward Carpenter – I quite longed to share this latter experience! She is off to Woodbrooke on Saturday. I bid her 'Goodbye', and I think tears were near! Strength for each day – love and trust: these things I need!

Eva's Diary   Sunday, 15 February 1914
Minna and I went quietly about our work this morning – chatting a little. I notice grief falls heavily upon my dear when she is left alone. I ran round to the Chapel at the end of the afternoon hoping I should catch Mr James, but he had just gone home! Owen, Mr and Mrs Taverner, Gertie, Cecil and others were all in the vestry discussing *A Midsummer Night's Dream* which some of them have lately seen – I cannot express how strangely it all affected me: after the tender home atmosphere, the depth of death and sorrow, the merry talk shook me strangely and the tears seemed near!

Eva to Ruth   Tuesday, 24 February 1914
My dear,
You will have received my post card I hope, and now will be looking, I know, for a letter. How *much* you have been in my thoughts and how I have longed to write – now I am just snatching moments, but if I am incoherent, I know *you* will understand!

Dear, do not worry about me – I am wondrously well and happy. I think a miracle has been performed on my life – and this house is fresh and open. Minna's nature is so large and easy that she is delightful to live with! You will be relieved to know, deary, that Minna seems stronger and calmer, but it does not do to leave her long alone, and some hours and days she is very depressed. We are hoping baby will not arrive before the 28th, when Nurse MacIntosh will be free to come to us.

What subjects have you decided to study? May I imagine you dining in the Conservatory and going to lectures in the little hall? You must tell me about the lectures soon!

Thursday: I *must* finish this letter tonight for tomorrow night is your birthday. *Many, many* happy returns of the day, dear. I am sending you *Lovery Mary*, because it is so delightfully light – just the kind of book for you to read twixt heavier, graver subjects.

I am so happy here with Minna – this home is blessed with a 'love atmosphere', the extent of which I had not fully realised until I came to stay. It is so beautiful to see Minna and the children together – to see them bathing freely without false modesty, and the way in which the girls revel in the body – indeed, dear, I have come to think that for the most part human beings live divorced from the body – that too much physical expression is reserved for marriage, not expressed in relationship and friendship! You would like Horace – he has such a refined nature. Edith too is a nice capable little girl. Winnie just twines round your heart. She has one of the sweetest natures – a little passionate soul with a genius for loving.

Mr and Mrs Awes have called several times. Mrs Awes is just beginning another baby (I know you will laugh at my way of putting it!) – I tell her I feel dreadfully out of it all.

Are you reading any special book, dear? How I hope you are really feeling better dear, and I trust you are not feeling lonely! Yes – I *must* come soon to see you – so much already I *would* say. Minna and children send their love. Minna says she is trying to take care of me. I certainly look the picture of health.

My deep love, dear, Eva.

Ruth's Diary   Wednesday, 18th February 1914
                                                    Woodbrooke
After an interval of over four years – years more full of event and development surely than any before, I plan beginning a diary again, for I have missed it very much. My life has been so full and I have been so tired at the end of each day and rushed at its beginning, that I was obliged to drop a habit I had thought of giving up on account of its making me introspective. But against that danger I now weigh many advantages, the chief of which

seems to me to be a calming influence, along with a sifting and clearing of thought.

I arrived here in the depths of depression, on Saturday. The depression arose chiefly, I suppose, from my dislike of change, even while I love it; and my fear and doubts concerning the future of the precious friendship surely established between myself and Hugh Jones. Furthermore, I was tired to the point of exhaustion. A fortnight ago I was spending my days at the office teaching Miss Nimmo my work as far as possible; and the evenings entertaining many visitors who called in, incidentally trying to make preparations to my coming departure. On Saturday I said farewell to my 'cage', as Mr Thompson called it, almost without emotion – and I have hardly given it one thought since. Hugh saw me off at Waterloo to Bagshot, where I stayed until Tuesday evening. Somehow Hugh and I did not get as near to one another – sometimes things happen like that, and we both really had hoped so much.

There has been a tremendous change in Mother. She is so patient and sympathetic now and full of real pluck, but Dad, I am grieved to notice, gets more and more steeped in hopeless melancholy. They both seem delighted, however, at this prospect of change and rest for me.

On Thursday I went over to Walthamstow, to Mrs Simmons, with whom Eva is still staying. Mrs Simmons is expecting a child any day, and a fortnight ago her husband died from galloping consumption, leaving them very, very poorly off. I am full of concern about her – she looked so spent and ill, and I fear she may be having a complete breakdown unless she is very careful. It hurts me to think of all that Eva is going through while I am having a good time. I went on to the flat and when I saw it again – my little odds and ends all teeming with associations, Françoise and the dear babe – my heart clave to it and I did not want to come away.

Hugh met me again on Saturday and after some lunch took me to the station and finally saw me off into the train. What a battle I had with my tears all the way down, and I could not prevent a few rebels trickling down my face.

Ruth's Diary   Saturday evening, 21 February 1914
I begin to feel very much better, and friends are remarking on the improvement in my appearance, yet I think it will be some weeks before I am able to give my mind to prolonged study.

In narrating the little events of last week I forgot to mention that on the Friday afternoon, when wandering through the City, I called in at Stackpool O'Dell's and had my head read. I had no intention of such a thing when I started out, but on the walk I mused on my development, concluded that it had been degenerate, and went in (as I happened to pass) to have the verdict corroborated. But the reader told me only nice things. She said my intellectual powers are well developed, but not so my self-assertive and self-protective qualities, which accounted for the narrowness of my head in proportion to its length. She said I live in a world of my own, a world of ideals, and am exceedingly conscientious. Directly I wake I am thinking, reasoning, planning, criticising – am never satisfied, always wanting to learn. Should succeed at literary work, be good at languages and (if I could gain confidence in myself) in speaking and debating. Suggested music as a recreation. I am inclined to think very highly of the thoughts of others and undervalue my own – need more self-assertiveness all round. Would never be happy in domestic life if married – should avoid commercial life. Have ability and should succeed.

Ruth's Diary   Monday evening, 23 February 1914
All my soul has been shaken this evening by tidings of Grandma's death last night. I can scarcely bear to be away here amongst strangers, without the presence of even one that I love.

Poor old Grandma. We must all feel profound relief that the end has come for her; it has been so terrible to watch her gradual decay and this awful change in old people has become a big problem in my mind. And yet I remember a few months ago, sitting quietly beside Grandma's bed, watching and thinking, thinking that as we live so do we determine our manner of dying. I may be quite wrong, yet I think of old people who have had beautiful deathbeds, and I think most often it has been because their spiritual life was so strong.

My heart is also yearning over Eva in her tender care of the sad, expectant Mother, and over Hugh, who is again unsettled and seeking fresh work for himself.

Ruth's Diary   Friday, 27 February 1914
My birthday! A month or two back I was reading reviews of a life of Florence Nightingale, published recently, and came across an extract from her diary which ran thus: 'My thirty-first

year, oh God! And I see nothing desirable but death'; and she went on to speak of the monotony of her life and the dread she felt of the probable 30 more years she would have to spend on this planet. When I read this I felt in a mood keen with sympathy, and yet what a change has come about in so short a time! Today has been the happiest birthday I have known for years. Partly because my pigeon-hole was so packed with letters this morning, the news leaked and I have had showers of good wishes.

But I have also received a shock. A letter I have been looking for all the week from Hugh came this morning, from Glastonbury where, it seems, he has gone. I am full of rejoicing for him, for I know this change will give him new vision, life and hope, but my intuition tells me that it may also herald a change in our friendship. Is he not bound to meet there some incarnation of love and beauty who will kindle undeveloped powers of affection? Well, today I have 'crossed the Rubicon' dividing ill-smothered hopes and dreams from stern reality, and I must brace myself to walk alone. We have had an exceedingly rare and beautiful friendship and I do not regret it, but sometimes I wonder if he realises how much I have really given him.

And to think of the fierce struggle which waged in my own heart before I decided to come here. Glastonbury was pulling all the time! My yearning for art and beauty made me long for Chalice Well, but practical considerations pointed to Wood-brooke as a unique opportunity of training and study. I only feared I should feel stifled here, for after the general impression I have gathered of a curious lack of imagination in Friends, I was inclined to dread having to mix with them exclusively. But I have been greatly relieved, for not only is there a fair sprinkling of non-Friends, but the atmosphere is so free and tolerant. It is true that Mrs Braithwaite is decidedly evangelical but she does not directly attempt to influence any of us. She is really a most delightful and lovable woman.

Ruth's Diary   Friday, 6 March 1914
I think I should begin to record some of the interesting visits I have made, before they get hopelessly numerous.

I have been, with small parties, over two Rescue Homes in Birmingham. The first was a very small one, worked in connection with the Free Church Council[1] – a fine, cheery woman at the head, but the place so dull and poor that I felt hopeless about good reformation work being done there. The other was under the management of the Salvation Army. Here everything was bright and pleasant, but it was painful to know that the inmates were not allowed any privacy all day. I was also dubious about the wisdom of putting a text, 'The soul that sinneth, it shall die', inscribed in great black letters, over one of the beds in the room where the worse cases slept. Somehow, as we went through the Home, the girls and women rising up as we entered any room where they happened to be, I felt full of shame and wanted almost to apologise to them for my presumption. In this home there was accommodation for a few babies and we saw some dear little mites.

Last week some of us went over a school for the Deaf, which was both wonderful and encouraging (Gem Street, Birmingham). I marvelled at the infinite patience of the teachers.

One afternoon I renewed my aquaintance with the Art Gallery, enjoying once again the tapestries of Burne-Jones and the paintings of Holman Hunt.

Eva's Diary   Sunday, 22 February 1914
I went to Conference in the afternoon leaving my dear Minna resting – although so *very* happy in the dear home circle, yet it was a pleasure to see Conference faces again. Mr James touched upon the subject of modern Utopias – after a little they weary him – make him feel the necessity of hardship. A few days of Letchworth make him long to introduce smoking, etc. Almost thought I could hear Owen speaking here!

Minna and I had a delicious two or three hours together – the girls had gone out to tea, so we were quite alone. We discussed the difference between passion, sensuousness and sensuality, and decided that we were both passionate and sensuous. How I love the body – I feel for the most part we humans live divorced one from the other. Too much spiritual and physical love is reserved for sexual union. We ought to be able to mingle soul and body, woman with woman, man with man – brothers, sisters, parents and children glorifying, caressing, embracing with the whole body – not simply the touch of hands and lips. Minna had been reading *Dorian Gray* whilst I was out – I asked her if she did not agree with me that much of the writing of Oscar Wilde and Bernard Shaw resembled sparkling champagne – their books flash like meteors through one's brain, but it is to the George Eliots, Emersons, Brontës, etc., one turns for never failing strength and comfort.

Eva's Diary   Wednesday, 25 February 1914
I found Lily at tea with Minna. She brought a box of lovely baby
clothes sent by a lady for our little one. We all had a cosy
evening together. Still Minna and I passed a restless night. Once
in the night Minna murmured, 'How *close* we are, we can never
grow apart now – we were near before, but not so near as *now*.
We clasped one another, and Minna said, 'It is worth living to
love thus.' Oh precious love, dear words. I treasure you in my
heart and here, but you seem almost too precious to pen!

Eva's Diary   Saturday, 28 February 1914
Such a bright, springlike day. Baby was expected, but did not
arrive. I found Minna looking so nice having prepared for a visit
from Nurse MacIntosh, who arrived during the evening. Such a
fine-looking woman – tall, big, and as fresh as a daisy, full of
affection and sympathy too. I thought as she sat by Minna I had
seldom seen two finer women; they gave one the sensation of
strength both of body and character. I longed to be big too in
physic and nature, with just such large well-formed hands and
arms, such calm strength of will.

Eva's Diary   Sunday, 1 March 1914
Such a longing has possessed me today to be quite alone! I have
felt mentally and spiritually sapped and *yearned* to be renewed,
refilled with divine energy. I suggested to Minna I went on a
little walk in the afternoon, and she at once advised my taking
Horace. My desire for a walk at once vanished, yet I *love* to
have the dear boy with me. Aunt Edie, Aunt Emily, and Gertie
came to tea. It was so lovely to be with my dear Aunt Edie – we
had a cheery tea-table.

Eva's Diary   Monday, 2 March 1914
The Relieving Officer called this morning to see Minna. He was
very kind and will endeavour to get as much as possible for her
each week. In the meantime, she can have tick for grocery.

Eva's Diary   Tuesday, 3 March 1914
I was awakened in the night by Minna's bitter crying – for the
first time since I have been with her she turned from my
sympathy – I just lay still and quiet, knowing that grief is

200

sometimes too sacred to be shared even by one's dearest! I realised too, that she was now becoming less dependent on my sympathy and would perhaps need me less in future in that special way.

Eva's Diary   Wednesday, 4 March 1914
Good news in the lunch hour – parish relief to the extent of 7/6d in food has been granted whilst Minna is ill – I am so glad. Although so *very, very* happy with Minna, such a longing for Aunt Edie and home has possessed me today.

Ruth to Eva   Monday afternoon, 2 March 1914
                                                              Woodbrooke
My very dear,
My heart inclines to talking with thee just now as the most faithful and understanding of all my friends. A little matter is causing me much soreness of that most sensitive organ, but do not worry about me: I am getting stronger to endure and duty alone must enable me to push aside personal feeling just now, when such real kindness has come my way.

Thank you very much dear for your lovely letter and for the gifts. I am looking forward to a treat in *Lovery Mary*. I have had so many letters to write. Later on, when I get into the swing of things, I shall not be able to write so many, but you and I dear must keep close together and write often even if we cannot manage much at a time.

I am full of wonder about the baby and shall be so very relieved to hear of its safe birth. How I envy you such nearness to the gates of life! Have you not realised a wonderful expansion of soul? I am not yet quite easy about your health, in spite of your statement that you look 'the picture of health'. I wish you could have a real holiday when the strain is passed, and I am wondering whether you could spend Easter down at Bagshot with me.

And now to write of myself. At present I am writing in the little Barrack's sitting room, where there is a fire. It seems quite a little home here, and we can get to know each other quite well.

Shall I tell you about my immediate companions? In the room next to mine is an American, a woman getting on for fifty, I should think – tall, stiff, and a little reminding me of Miss Leith, though not *so* difficult to get near. She has been very ill and is terribly deaf. The warden, Mrs Braithwaite, has been very kind to her and gone to a great deal of trouble to get her electrical ear trumpet contrivance, which would help Miss Small to hear the lectures, but the specialist in Birmingham says that nothing can be done and in a few years' time she will be quite deaf. Is it not sad?

Next to her is a spirited Scotch woman, just 40, named Janet Kelman. She is very artistic too, and has done some pen and ink illustrations and margins for nature books, poetry, etc. which I thought exquisite. She has also been ill and is here for rest and refreshment. She quite Mothers me and though not exactly demonstrative is, I feel, quite fond of me.

Then comes Bessie Cannon. It is good to see a girl of that type here, though she is the sole representative, and everyone is interested in her. She is such a Cockney. She calls everyone 'dear' most freely. Occasionally she will fling her arms around one, or seize one's hair, and she remarks on people's clothes and ornaments with a total disregard of the personality of the particular wearer! She has been a hard-working organiser for the Workers' Educational Association in her spare time (she has been working in a shirt factory!) and when I hear of what she has done, and of the books she has read, I feel full of shame. I am getting very fond of her.

The other inmate, Jessie Marsh, is a difficult person to describe, though perhaps I like her best of all. She is not very attractive in appearance, at least I thought not when I first saw her – but I am beginning to find even her face quite compelling. She has the drollest wit and something of Ann Stevens's faculty of seeing 'all-round, inside and outside' of every argument. I find her company most stimulating.

I have been to some very interesting places, dear, but will tell you about them and also about my studies, in my next letter. Oh, to see you my dear – my news and thoughts pile up every day, but I will write as often and as much as I can. Goodnight! (and the babe?) My deep, deep love, Ruth.

Eva's Diary   6 March 1914

Our little baby girl was born on Friday morning, at 9.30 am. We had been up at 4.30 on Wednesday and Thursday nights. Dr Eliot was not there at the time of the birth, so Nurse called me in. It was so wonderful to see the baby, attached to Minna by a cord. I was able to help a little with Minna. Oh, I felt *stirred to the depths* – joy, anxiety, sympathy – and deep down tears

202

that could not be shed!

I found Minna looking *so* exhausted this lunch hour. Baby had
been 'yelling' gloriously in the night. Minna could scarcely speak
to me for weariness. I *do* feel the children are in the room a
great deal too much. Nurse is so wise, but perhaps she thinks it
comforts Minna to see them. Aunt Edith came and I went
upstairs and had a few sweet moments with my Minna. She said
she did miss me from the house – felt I ought to be there, we
had grown so together.

I have felt so terribly depressed today – suppose it is reaction
– so lonely. Baby and all this experience has made me realise
the pains and joys I am missing – longings to love and be loved
– to be the dearest to some one person – to hold in my arms a
child of my very own; these feelings have been pursuing me and
making me wish to stay quite away from Minna's for a time, but
of course I put the wicked selfish feeling and thought behind me!

Eva's Diary   Friday, 13 March 1914
Nursed baby awhile this lunch hour – such a dear little bundle
pressed against one. A quiet evening – I washed Winnie's head
and sat with Minna. I think Minna's physical suffering has
affected her personally for she seems cold to me. Perhaps
however I am in a sensitive stage just now and notice things
more, and also *imagine* a great deal.

Ruth to Eva   Tuesday afternoon, 10 March 1914
                                        Woodbrooke
My very dear,
I feel much easier about you all now that Baby is actually born,
and I do hope, very fervently, that all will go splendidly now. I
look forward to your story of it all. My love to Minna and
congratulations for producing such a little Amazon! I hope she
had less pain than usual but fear the size of the child [9½ lbs]
must have meant considerable suffering. How I long for wings to
fly to thee! I wonder why I did not receive a telepathic
communication of the news?

I look forward very greatly to Mondays, there being two
treats on that day! The first lecture in the morning is given by Dr
Rendel Harris, and is always exceedingly beautiful. He has been
taking the teaching of Mystics such as Madam Guyon. We

always have music before and after the lecture. In the evening there is the lecture on Social Philosophy at the university – just like a breath of mountain air!

Then I go to one lecture a week on Economics and Industrial Legislation, which I enjoy least of all, but which are of course very useful. The lecturer on these topics is a demure little man with no fire about him, which adds dullness to his themes.

But then I very much enjoy one lecture a week on Comparative Religions by a fine young fellow named Brown. Just now he is speaking on Mystery Cults, such as Mithraism in Persia, once a fierce rival to Christianity and from which we borrowed an amazing number of rites and ceremonies; also another lecture each week on Hebrew religion.

Again I look forward to two lectures each week given by a woman, Mildred Field, one on the lives and methods of great Educators, and the other being a sort of combination of elementary Logic and Psychology. She gave us an extra lecture last week on the science of Fairy Tales and oh, my dear, it was wonderful! Among other most interesting and suggestive points she mentioned that the prevalence of the 'witch' in fairy tales is probably a relic of the Matriarchate period.

I would like to tell you a little about this lecturer, especially after your remarks about Minna and Nurse Mackintosh. Miss Field is tall and finely proportioned, wears her hair short (but it is thick and suits her head well), and has a keen bright face. I felt full of envy when I first beheld her! Judging from some remarks she made the other day I think she must be a little older than fifty, but she doesn't look anything like that age. I ought to mention her healthful sense of humour!

From the foregoing you will see that I have plenty in hand. In addition to all that I have two Care Committee Cases in Birmingham to look after – a boy and a girl, each just on the point of leaving School. Further, a visit of 'Investigation' is made every Tuesday afternoon to some Institution, in order that any budding Social Worker may become acquainted with the machinery now in motion.

This is really quite an extraordinary place! One could work tremendously hard, or one could be absolutely lazy! There is no compulsion of any sort, and one really needs good powers of concentration in order to benefit by the opportunities given. So you will see I was wrong in fearing that everything would be cut and dried. On the contrary, there is a freedom which may easily become a temptation. Above everything else, though, there is such healthfulness and sanity about the place – it is quite healing to me.

Last night we had a very gay time out on the tennis courts in the moonlight, holding a farewell festival in honour of the Norwegian, who leaves tomorrow. We feasted, played delightful games and sang, and some of the masculine students sent off fire balloons.

The mention of these young men reminds me of your question as to whether Woodbrooke is a settlement for women only. No, it is not, but the men students all sleep away in some of the other houses, coming over to meals, etc. There are few of them, however, in comparison with the women, but some of them are exceedingly nice. As Bessie Cannon rather wistfully remarked the other day, 'There's a wonderful purity about this place.'

Now I may not write any longer – my loved one. Let me hear as soon as you can how you are all faring. Soon, very soon I shall be seeing you again, which is a glorious expectation. What did you think of my Easter idea?

The sun is so beautiful today and the birds are warbling their sweetest. Yes, it is good to live and love! Goodbye for a little space. My fond, fond love to all of you, Ruth.

Eva to Ruth   17 March 1914

Dearie, I *do* feel such a culprit! Over a week and not a page have I written to you, and I intended to write so very much after baby's birth, but as usual, there have been obstacles with which I had not reckoned. The first few evenings were spent playing 'London' and 'Dominoes' with Edith and Winnie, that Minna might not be disturbed – then when the evenings came during which I might sit with Minna, there were little interruptions, little things to do, and a subdued light, a drawback to writing and working.

Your description of your companions interested me deeply. Then your account of subjects and lectures, I must confess made me feel 'mentally hungry' – in fact, I may say, 'ravenous'; but there, I shall just rely upon you to pour your reservoirs of knowledge into my empty brain when we meet!

The first of your unanswered letters, Ruth, reached me the night before baby was born. That night, after reading your letter, I crept to rest beside Edith and Winnie, and lay there feeling the contact of Winnie's warm limbs, and gazing out of the window at the sky, listening to the wind in the ivy and watching the branches wave to and fro. The night seemed tense with expectancy, and I thought much of you! The doctor came and went – it was so weird waiting through the still, dark hours and dawn. I could not leave the house, and at 9.30 Nurse called me in – baby was *just* born, so after all I did not see her actual arrival, but she was not separated, and as the Doctor was not there, I held back the afterbirth whilst Nurse cut the cord – it was a strange wonderful sight. I cannot describe my feelings, anxiety, sympathy, joy and deep down, tears! Minna had a normal time in spite of baby's size – but had to have one stitch. She is going on splendidly now, and the baby is so pretty and good. Yes dear, I have felt, as you say, an expansion of soul. I am *so* grateful for the experience – only I find things so difficult to realise this year – big events have followd one another so rapidly.

If dear, you find you will be spending Easter at Bagshot, I shall be delighted to accompany you. How I look forward to seeing you again, and how we will talk. There is a strange emptiness in the week without the evening 'set apart'.

Warm kisses dear, and *deep* love, my *dear* friend. Eva.

Ruth to Eva   18 March 1914
                                                          Woodbrooke
My very dear,
It was with welcome joy that I hailed your letter this morning, for I was on the point of getting anxious about you all.

I am going to be a little pig and say how happy I feel at the prospect of our spending Easter together – 'all by ourselves alone'! It will be just lovely to wander through the pine woods, talking out our thoughts and news, or sitting by the fire quietly thinking together in the evenings. And not only will it be specially good to have you thus, but it helps me simplify my arrangements very much, I find – for my brains got quite confused this morning in trying to plan the holiday so that I missed no one out, and yet contrived to keep a clear fortnight for home, which I badly want.

And now to come again to your own letter! I am so hopeful about your future and inclined to think, dear, that this long time of patient drudgery means that it is an extra big work which you have to do. Do you remember Josephine Butler's remarks about the 'period of gestation' which some lives experience before

206

their work and power is born?

Last week, dear, we went over a 'Lock-up' and I felt depressed for days by the thoughts and feelings this visit called into life. I will not write about it but *tell* you – how nice to say *tell* you.

Isn't life rich and wonderful though, in spite of its pain, when we have learned to respond?

And now dear, I must bring this scattered little message to a close. It brings a heart-full of love, though it says little about it. Goodbye my own friend, for a tiny while. Ruth.

Eva's Diary   Tuesday, 31 March 1914

Minna greeted me today with the news that Edith had this afternoon to go before the Guardians[2] – an ordeal! But fortunately Edith is very courageous. When I called in to tea I found the Guardians had granted 6/- a week and tickets for food – Hurrah! this at least will meet the rent. Edith is a brick! She now realises perfectly her rights as eldest daughter and evidently means to hold them both as regards baby and the house. It is, of course, quite natural, and I think after Easter they will manage very well without my staying there altogether. Mr Gregory called re. a concert he is organising on Minna's behalf. I have felt so thoroughly tired today, the weather has been glorious too – it has made me long for freedom; the routine of life and of the office has weighed heavily – I positively crawled home after sitting with Minna!

Eva's Diary   Wednesday, 1 April 1914

Baby has been looking around today with quite a 'criticising' air. Minna came downstairs this afternoon, but the change has, I can see, depressed her afresh, and brought back many memories; she is still weak and ill. *Snatched* a cup of tea and then off to the Girls' League[3] – about 20 girls gathered – not a bad number with which to start. I made a little speech (being Superintendent) about doing our best to make the League a success, and asked the girls to suggest a motto – 'Always merry and bright' was suggested, which I thought was not at all bad! Then followed jumping and games. I see possibilities of raising an Adult School from this League and splendid work might be done! Had to hurry off to Committee Meeting – Mr James has now full particulars re. training as nurse (for Minna) – only seven weeks necessary in the home, which seems to me an

207

absurdly short time, and hardly likely to place Minna in good monetary position in competition with more highly trained nurses.

Aunt Edie came to meet me – she had a nasty accident in the shop today – a boy fired a pistol and ran away, leaving the shop full of smoke. This boy and others are always insulting Aunt Edie about being a suffragette – I feel so angry and yet I wish it was not so generally known that Aunt Edie and Gertie are militants.

Eva's Diary   Thursday, 2 April 1914

I took up my abode with Minna again today – she is very depressed. I know she will miss Nurse. She seemed heartbroken in the night, she said it all seemed so cruel, she felt as if her heart would break, and if she had seemed at all cold during the past few weeks, it was because she had been afraid of affection, afraid to trust herself. My poor darling, my heart aches for her – if only I could bear the pain and grief for her, but I can only stand by in love and sympathy.

Eva's Diary   Saturday, 4 April 1914

This evening I ran round to the Lecture Hall with the concert tickets – I was glad to see the hall filling well. Mrs Pettinger came in and commenced hurling words at me with the force of a battering ram. She informed me I might not think Minna was worrying but *she knew* Minna was – that her mind was in a terrible state, but if I did not realise it, it was because she was hiding it from me – that from long experience of Minna she had found her a *very* helpless woman, unused and unable to plan. With this I do not agree – Minna is neither unable or incapable. It has been want of opportunity, and necessity rather than want of ability. Perhaps owing to a lack of sufficient sleep I felt weak, anyway tears were dreadfully near the surface after my encounter with Mrs Pettinger! Lily said that she thought Petty's ideas were mistaken – that she imagined a great deal and was jealous. I was glad to see Minna make a good supper. I saw her to bed and asked her if she had been worrying about the future and she admitted the dreadfulness of being left with the children had overwhelmed her at times.

Eva's Diary   Sunday, 5 April 1914

A busy morning – Minna very depressed at first, but after a

time she brightened a little and began to talk of the future. She said she thought she would take a larger house with Lily and take in lodgers, and when baby could run about would go in for training as a maternity nurse. (This proves Mrs Pettinger's opinion incorrect – Minna evidently can plan and has planned very effectively.) Minna said in time the house might come to be the home of several lonely women, and be a centre of refuge to them.

Such a sensation of loneliness swept over me as we talked – wonderful possibilities seemed opening up before Ruth, Minna and Lily of lives of wider service and development – whilst I remain a little 'filler in of gaps' with my legal work day after day! And then the little baby will be Lily's – I cannot let it go without a pang; and Minna and Lily will be so much to one another. Minna said she could not shake off the presentiment that a great change was close at hand for me – she felt I would shortly pass out of her life to a place like Woodbrooke itself. I too have felt change impending all this year.

This evening I held baby in my arms almost naked. She is such a bonny girl! Whilst I hushed her to sleep, Minna and I discussed ways and means for the future. As we settled down for the night I could not help saying what a wonderful friendship ours had become – 'So wonderful', said Minna, 'that at times I am almost afraid.' Yes, we have experienced exquisite moments together!

Eva's Diary   Thursday, 9th April 1914
I felt parting from Minna even for a short holiday, but she seemed much brighter and better, and to be alone will test her strength and resources! Although I started in good time from home this evening the train simply *walked* to Liverpool St. and I lost the last train to Bagshot. I felt very distressed and after sending a telegram to Ruth, determined to catch the first morning train to Bagshot, returned wearily home.

Eva's Diary   Friday, 10 April 1914
I hurried away this morning in the hope of catching the first train and jumped into a taxi from Liverpool St. to Waterloo – alas, no train to Bagshot until 6.10 pm!!! I hurried from porter to porter to ascertain if it were possible to get anywhere near Bagshot, but did not meet with any success – I do not know when I have felt so weak and helpless – the atmosphere of

death and grief in which in which I have been living for some months seemed suddenly to make its influence felt. I felt incapable of caring for myself, of meeting even the difficulties of getting to Bagshot. Waterloo bewildered me with its throng of holidaymakers, soldiers and porters, but I found it was possible to send a telephone message from Charing Cross. Accordingly I set out on foot, crossing Hungerford Bridge, feeling as though all London were upon me, crushing me – I met so many people, and the materialistic aspect of human nature struck me very forcibly, and it seemed to me a tremendous task indeed to spiritualise London. All around me was the work of the hands of men – great bridges, buildings, ships; it seemed hard – in some way, stupendous.

I returned to Waterloo with the fixed and firm intention of not moving from the spot until the 6.10 pm train arrived. It was a great pleasure and relief to find Ruth and her father at the Station ready to receive me with open arms! *So* good to be with my dear friend tonight!

Eva's Diary   Sunday, 12 April 1914

The sun in all its glory greeted us this morning – Mr and Mrs Slate had left early for town so Ruth and I were alone. We hastened with the few household duties, packed our lunch and set off for High Curley. How I enjoyed the walk – the road led through the yellow gorse and pine woods; at last we came out upon the hill tops and away rolled the country before us, as I love to see it – blue in the distance. Upon the summit of High Curley we laid down to rest – here we partook lunch. Afterwards Ruth read me the story of Circe and Odysseus from the *Odyssey* and the music and rhythm of its language and the warmth of the sun almost lulled me to sleep. Then I read aloud from my book upon 'Dreams', we discoursed of many things, and read a few of Ella Wheeler Wilcox's poems. Ruth had much to show me in the evening – photos of some of the women staying at Woodbrooke (one very fine head interested me especially) – letters and a paper written by Mr Jones upon 'Wonder'.

I mentioned to Ruth Minna's strong feeling that some great change is before me – that I shall go to Woodbrooke or to some place like it. Ruth then informed me she had written Mr Strain [a Woodbroke colleague] telling him I had been much with a friend in trouble lately, and she felt such a change as she was

210

then experiencing would do me a great deal of good. I felt quite amazed!

Eva's Diary   Monday, 13 April 1914

The day somewhat overclouded, but we made our way through the wood to the lake and there at the still water's edge we sat long and talked. The heaviness and stillness of the day made the woods seem strangely oppressive; they looked like scenes of possible dramas and mysteries. A quiet evening – Ruth read aloud a little from Edward Carpenter – his poem on the Urnings [probably 'O Child of Uranus' from *Towards Democracy,* published 1883] led us to talk of the 'intermediate sex'; we wondered whether the great teachers Christ and Buddha belonged to this category, having in themselves the experiences and nature of either sex – then we talked of the procreation of children by the intermediate sex either naturally or by thought and ended in a confusion of ideas, having lost the thread of our discussion.

Eva's Diary   Tuesday, 14 April 1914

I parted from Ruth at the station, feeling how precious our dear friendship is. Some enchantment seemed to have fallen upon me for it seemed ridiculous to believe I was really returning to the office: visions of Mr Strain, study, useful work and happy love filled my mind, so that I arrived home in quite an exhilarated and exalted mood!

Eva's Diary   Friday, 17 April 1914

Such a happy time with Minna this evening. We discussed *The Mother* and I was impressed by Minna's memory of the wise, witty and tender thoughts in it. I had difficulty in recalling some, but Minna lives so in a book – reading it again and again, until it is her own. Minna said she sometimes thought how much she could do if there was no baby – it is true a baby fills one's time, yet, I said to Minna, we cannot read the future – it is a struggle now *with* baby, but often the children least desired, and who come at seemingly unfortunate times, in later years, prove to be the greatest blessings.

My Miss Leith then came in – she wanted to know whether I had become engaged, I looked so well and happy. I felt highly amused; I fear curiosity is one of Miss Leith's little weaknesses.

211

The girls came to the League tonight possessed, I think, by the very spirit of mischief – a feeling almost of despair about maintaining order came over me at once. Afterwards I found Miss Smith thoroughly upset about the girls, and I promised to speak very seriously to the League next Wednesday.

I felt very happy with Minna this evening – we all bathed, I with the scullery door open and Horace in the kitchen. I felt I had made progress – but Horace is such a dear, pure-minded boy – Minna said he did not once glance in the scullery!

Ruth to Eva   28 April 1914
                                            Woodbrooke
My very dear Friend,

I feel I must have a little chat with you before I go to bed tonight – so much in the beauty of the day, and more especially of this evening, has made me feel very near to you.

Wasn't it lovely being together at last on Saturday at Euston? We were a very jolly little party in the train and all indulged in tea on the way and much chatter. Jessie Marsh told me some interesting things about a day and two nights she spent in a cheap lodging house for women during the holiday. She had managed to learn quite a lot about the inmates, and most of the stories were sad ones. Arrived in Birmingham, and seeing that most of us had things not easy to carry, we took a taxicab between us and rushed here in state! Oh, the delight of coming up the drive and seeing the daffodils nodding amidst the grass! Then the hearty welcome of the Wardens and students who had already arrived!

We have two newcomers in the Barracks. One, named Dorothy Rutter, is distinguished looking, very intellectual and a little difficult, but I think she is going to thaw. She comes of Quaker stock but seems to have been very much influenced by Roman Catholicism whilst abroad and I think her parents have been upset by this and desired her to come here to be cured! I moreover imagine she came rather under protest which made her not very amicable at first. She has visited Chalice Well several times, liking it very much and admiring Miss Buckton. Last night she donned sandals and a Grecian gown and gave us a little demonstration of dancing in the sitting room downstairs. She is wonderfully graceful and I longed for a little expression in that sort of way.

The other girl, Theodora Isaac, is tall and handsome, very refined and pleasant in manners, rather quiet. I think I shall like her very much. On Saturday evening we had a little music and introduced ourselves generally. There are so many new students, a fair proportion of them foreigners.

Yesterday morning I went to the first of a course of lectures on Co-operation (Industrial). It was very interesting. In the evening we outlined the Social Work programme for the term and the person responsible for each branch made a little speech. I am to be responsible for assisting a trained organiser with Organised Games for children in the local park, so that *I* had to stammer out a few broken words!

This afternoon I spent an hour trying to play tennis but with ill success. I got into such a state of heat that I came up to my room and sat sewing, minus all clothes!

I enclose Mr Strain's letter for you to read. I have been so full of thought and excitement and do wonder what is going to happen. I am sure, dearie, something good is coming along and oh, how you deserve it! It came over me today the work I really could do given knowledge and training and which I should enjoy. Book reviewing and the writing of semi-philosophical articles such as one gets in good literary journals such as the *Nation*. I have not your gift of imagination so that I could never do original or creative work, but I believe I could gather up threads and present intelligent digests of things. But such a thing needs study of language and literature to a despairingly wide extent.

Goodnight and warmest kisses! I missed you so the first night I slept alone after you had been at Bagshot. My love to Minna and the children including the little babe, and your own huge share, dear. Always your friend, Ruth.

Eva to Ruth   Thursday, 30 April 1914
My dear,
I meant to be the first to write this time, but you have again forestalled me – I always feel gladly excited when a packet from you falls through the letter box. Don't you thank the Lord for the postal system? But I must not talk flippantly!

Now for a nice clear evening and a long talk with you, dear, during which I expect I shall be quite lost to the outside world!

Yes, it was just splendid getting an hour together on Saturday, and I am so glad to have seen the Woodbrookers.

I feel very interested about tennis – for my own part I have a horrible feeling I should miss the ball every time if I attempted the game, and perhaps bang someone in the eye. And dear, it is lovely to sit without clothes, but do be careful. Don't go and get a chill or sit in a draught – I thought at once of Beethoven whose deafness came through exposure to draughts after great heat.

Thank you for sending me Mr Strain's letter, dear, which I now return. I wonder what the coming month will bring forth – I feel I must now allow myself to dream.

Yes, I feel sure your gifts are literary, and perhaps dearie you overrate the knowledge necessary for the work you mention. I believe you could write as you say, gathering deeper culture on the way. For myself, I had meant this year to think *seriously* about more expressive work and to give a good many evenings to *trying to write,* but events and responsibilities have come along which have made writing difficult. And now, dear, before turning to other matters – have you come to any decision about going in for the Social Diploma, or do you think of making just for the literary work?

As for the Girls League, I think the work will really do me good, and I hope develop that which is very feeble in me at present – power to rule when necessary. I am *not* sure – but I believe the troublesome one, Doreen, is inclined to like me – if so, half the battle will be won. Next week, I have to call them together and talk to them *very seriously!!*

Minna seems better too, and baby is a darling, laughs and talks to us, and is getting such rosy cheeks and bright eyes, looking at us from her shawl for all the world like a little bird!

You ask about Miss Brown – Yes, I saw her again at the Centre last week. Mr Alan Leo was lecturing upon Astrology – I was particularly pleased, as I have often wished to hear a lecture upon this subject and I believe he is quite an authority. He said we must remember the true Astrologer was no fatalist. Astrology did not fix the spirit or development of the ego – it only prepared the environment for the soul, whether the circumstances ruled the soul, or the soul the circumstances depended upon each individual. The whole of nature is so linked with the stars – not only the earth but we ourselves containing within us iron, atoms, flowers, such as may be found in the stars, that as the months pass, we are greatly influenced by the movement of the stars. Thus souls born under the influence of

214

Virgo (I believe I am a 'Virgo' so felt special interest) often inherit analytical tendencies – the 'chemist' mind. The influence of the stars is, however, both coarse and fine – those responding to the coarser vibrations of Virgo will become fault-finding, hypercritical, whilst the finer vibrations would develop keen criticism, a fine discrimination twixt good and ill – indeed most Virgo people are very susceptible, not only to atmospheric changes but to temperaments of the people they come into contact with.

Now 'Goodnight' dear – angels guard and bless thee always.

Your loving friend, Eva.

Eva's Diary   Friday, 1 May 1914
After lunch today Minna gave me a letter to read during the afternoon – from herself to me – this letter I shall treasure all my life, for its words of love.

Eva's Diary   Wednesday, 6 May 1914
Minna decided this afternoon to pay Mrs Awes a visit, so handed baby over to me that I might change her gown and dress her! A very new experience for me! Baby, however, is a substantial darling – she looked at me in such a knowing way as though she knew all about it being my first attempt to dress her, and enjoyed it as a huge joke.

How I have today inwardly fought against the limitations of my life – the limitations of love and service. Oh, to love and be loved as I feel myself capable of loving. It does not seem possible I was intended to spend a great part of my life writing about investments and petty quarrels in a lawyer's office. Sometimes I am affrighted lest I spend my time on things which matter but little, neglecting 'the *one* thing' I may have been sent into the world to do! What if I should miss the gate?

Eva's Diary   Tuesday, 12 May 1914
At lunch I found Minna preparing to go before the Board of Guardians. I ran round to hear the result after leaving business. Hurrah! The Board have now granted 10/- a week and food tickets.

Ruth to Eva   7 May 1914
                                                     Woodbrooke
I was very glad to get your precious letter last week – it already

215

seems such an age since we were together and I miss you and other friends, I think, more keenly this term, when the strangeness of the new order of living has begun to wear away and my mind is not so occupied in trying to adjust itself to the fresh conditions (though it stll gets a fair amount of such exercise!).

We 'Barracks' people have grown into a fond little group. Jessie Marsh's eyes trouble her very much so that we often read to her. After she is in bed we sometimes read her *The Hound of Heaven,* of which she never tires, and last week we had some Christina Rossetti poems. The newcomer, Theodora Isaac, proves most lovable and nice. She was secretary to Sylvester Horn[4] for several years and to R. J. Campbell for a time, and says he is wonderful to know in private. She also is quite familiar with St Ethelburga's. We are going together next Sunday evening to hear the Rev. Gertrude von Petzgold.

Dorothy Rutter, the very intellectual girl, also gets more likeable every day. Yesterday afternoon we went to the Theatre together – a luxury I may not really allow myself – but we were able to book our seats for 1/-! The play was produced by a Repertory Company and is attracting attention as it was written by a promising young poet named John Drinkwater, who comes from Birmingham. It is called *Rebellion.*

One afternoon last week I had a nice walk with Miss Pelton. She is very keen on a movement hailing from America called the Camp Fire Girls and I wondered whether its ideas would help you with your League. It is thought to be having a very good influence in America.

How I have rambled on! Your own dear letter un-noticed!

I was *very* interested in your account of Mr Leo's lecture. I heard Bessie Cannon telling someone that she was a 'Virgo', so I read her the part of your letter describing the tendencies of people born under that influence. Is it not wonderful to think we really are linked in divers ways to sea, and sky – indeed, to everything!

I see I have not answered your question as to whether I am going in for the Social Service Diploma. That is not yet settled, as the course always begins in the Autumn Term – but, as you will see, I am taking mostly Social subjects.

My fond, fond love to you, and a very warm kiss – my love also to Minna and the children (how I long for the birdie-babe!). Ruth.

Eva to Ruth   Tuesday evening, 12 May 1914
Last week I just *hungered* to hear from you, and watched the
post for a letter. I miss you so *very* much dearie.

I feel very interested in your reference to the Camp Fire Girls.
I grow more and more interested in this new work, and the
numbers increase weekly. I have felt so delighted lately at signs
of affection amongst the girls, although of course, dear, I have
moments of absolute despairing weakness, when they create
pandemonium! Last Wednesday I spoke to them very gravely
about the need for a certain amount of order, and that if the
League meant anything it meant that we must stand by and help
one another. The effect was magical – a comparatively model
League all evening. We have skipping, drill and sometimes
Gymnasium going all the evening, whilst I take embroidery,
games, folk songs (your book, dear), tell stories and get them to
recite. Last Wednesday I told them Oscar Wilde's *The Happy
Prince* – it made a great impression.

Perhaps, dearie, the enclosed list of the International Theosophy Society Lectures will interest you. Last night's lecture on
'Work in Sleep' was particularly interesting to me – how you
will laugh when I tell you my last vision – very practical and
material; a new article of clothing – think I must patent it –
nothing less than a 'reform' corset for women who have been
Mothers and feel the need of something!! Evidently, my past
experiences, maternal, etc., are playing upon my mind!

Minna is a great deal better in health – I am so glad. I stayed
all night with her on Saturday. Baby is such a *dear,* darling – all
smiles and goodness.

I have just finished reading *Broken Earthenware* by Harold
Begbie – it has interested me deeply – it should be read by
those who believe in reform through social changes and material
environment. Such books make one long for bigger sympathies
and work *ringing* with earnestness – do you not think so, dear?
Is it not difficult sometimes not to 'faint upon the wayside'?
Write to me soon dear – how nice to have a 'heart to heart' talk.

Much love and many thoughts from Your loving friend, Eva.

Ruth to Eva   Sunday afternoon, 17 May 1914
My dear,
I wonder what *you* are doing today? I must tell you the
delightful time I am having.

Immediately after breakfast this morning I put a few biscuits,

217

one or two little books, some letters and this writing block, into a basket, slipped unnoticed out of Woodbrooke grounds, and walked straight along the road where *we* walked together one Sunday evening (you will remember), continuing it for about four miles, which eventually brought me up on the Lickey Hills. I chose a lovely spot, under a spreading ash tree, just now full of scented blossom, and overlooking peaceful pasture land and a reservoir urged into gentle ripples by the breeze and reflecting the intense blue of the sky. Moreover I cast off my shoes and pressed my feet on the lovely grass. So, I mused and wrote letters home to Hugh. Then I ate my biscuits, and beginning to feel a little chilly sought out a warmer, though less beautiful spot, where I might sit and talk to you.

I wondered if I were unsociable to creep away thus, but you will understand me when I say I feel it a necessity to be utterly alone sometimes.

Little things, such little things, excited me last week, and I fear dear, you will think your friend growing woefully emotional. For one, I seem to have stepped over the hazy border-land into real friendship with Jessie Marsh. I have spent some time with her nearly every night this last week, and we have had some lovely talks, or more correctly she has talked and I have listened. And on Monday she asked me to kiss her Goodnight!

I have also had some interesting talks with Dorothy Rutter and am trying to get some knowledge from her of the Roman Catholic faith and the source of its power.

I am enclosing several pages from a letter I had from Mr Thompson which at the time disturbed me greatly. Again I asked myself whether I ought to pass on such a very personal confession, but again I say that it is to me just a telling to another self – intimate and true. I thought about it a lot dear, and while I do not judge him at all – I think he acts from high principles – the idea is repugnant to me. I could not enter into sexual union with a man who was not *My Lover,* either to satisfy desire or curiosity, or for the sake of having a child. It seems to me I should suffer more thereby from starved longings. Again, dear, what do you think? I am beginning to get a new conception – the thought of Society as a *Whole,* in the light of which much burden bearing and suffering seems a duty which may be nobly fulfilled and which may be cheerfully acceded to if one sees it is for the well-being of the majority. You know I have often tried to explain to you the difficulty I feel (and which I

218

think you feel also) of reconciling the desires of the individual will with that of the larger will of the community, or nation, as expressed in its customs and laws. Wells, it seems to me, pleads for individual freedom and even in his own stories one sees this leads to chaos, unless a larger motive than the satisfaction of self underlies the individualistic action taken. It is true that to find oneself one must lose oneself and somewhere I think there is a meeting place between the self will and the General Will – I am groping after an understanding of this and I think it holds in the world of sex. You and I have endured unsatisfied desire – with stronger antidotes of change and opportunity of expression we might have suffered less. We have endured and have been slowly learning to command ourselves and to take up other interests when something we cannot have torments for indulgence.

But I have not thanked you really yet for your own lovely letter, which I was very, *very* glad to receive. Thank you for the little notices and for *Brotherhood*.[5] I am sending a book about Parsifal to read, which I brought from the Theosophical Stall at the Simple Life Exhibition.

I did greatly admire and enjoy Miss Petzgold last Sunday evening. The Town Hall was full and the congregation (containing a surprising number of men) very quiet and attentive. She spoke of our modern civilisation – how it seeks gain through unholy ends, supporting white slavery[6] and the drink traffic. She recited very beautifully that dream of Olive Schreiner's. The hymns were sung with fine spirit.

I was very amused to read of your latest vision – how strange! And what next?

Talking of things extraordinary, we have a Norwegian maiden here who can see people's 'auras' and she doesn't mind a bit describing them and what she thinks they mean. Mine is mostly dark blue, she says, which is a good colour. I am quick in mind, *too* sensitive (alas), possess large powers of influence (?), literary ability, and great capacity for dealing with children!?

I have to learn a rather large part for a sketch which is to be given on Friday, and haven't begun it yet! Life is very, very full here.

Kiss the baby for me – also give my love to Minna and the girls, and to Aunt Edie and Gertie; and your own share ever increases, dear friend. Ruth.

219

Eva to Ruth   Sunday evening, 21 May 1914

First dear, thank you from my heart for Saturday's message of love and for your letter of such deep interest – both were more than usually welcome, for I had been wishing so to see you and had felt I must push everything aside and rush to Woodbrooke and snatch a few hours with you.

I return the pages of Mr Thompson's letter. You know, dear, do you not, how *deeply* I value such confidence? In this matter I feel with you and all you say about your conception of 'Society as a whole' interests me greatly – it is such a big subject. It does seem to me the moment we snatch at and demand an experience here and now we act as though we and life are *finite* – we have lost the sense of the 'fullness of time' of 'unfoldment'.

On Friday I went to see Miss Martin – she is lodging in a humble part of Canning Town. We had tea together and chatted of many things. She does not appear, Ruth, to have any daily work – she said she did not care to work through a settlement,[7] but liked living as at present, *amongst* the people, and making friends of them. She had that day been taking a poor woman about London–giving her a day's pleasure–when I arrived she had the landlady's baby in her arms. Miss Martin asked after you, dear, and when she is again at Bourneville will try and see you.

Isn't May a month of beauty? The May, Lilac, Laburnum and Chestnut trees in the roads around have been such a joy to me lately. Dear, do you find this less harassing life is renewing you in every way? I feel you were *very* tired when you first left London.

I will try not again to be so long in writing, for I enjoy deeply this little communion with you. Your loving friend, Eva.

Ruth to Eva   10 June 1914
                                                 Woodbrooke

My very dear,

I have chosen to commune with thee rather than go to Mr Woods' lecture tonight. It is a beautiful evening. From my little window I see a soft, clear sky, with fine trees silhouetted against it and a beautiful meadow, while a thrush is singing his sweetest up above.

The weather seems to have set fair again but during the weekend and continuing right up to this morning we have had torrential rain, which was an especial disappointment to me as Mr Jones was here. He cycled away again to Glastonbury on

Monday. I thought him looking ill and depressed. He thought Woodbrooke a very beautiful place however, and was much interested in things.

On Monday evening Dr Harris was very beautiful. He spoke of the Sufis (a Persian sect) and told us the two symbols of their religion are Wine and Love, and seemed to suggest that in many ways Tagore's teaching resembles Sufism – which has for its keynote ecstasy, intoxication, abandonment. He showed us how Christians have gradually dispensed with the first symbol and how they have also tried to expel erotic language, quoting as an example the hymn, 'Jesu, lover of my soul, Let me to thy bosom fly' – which the unitarian hymnal renders – 'Jesu, refuge of my soul, Let me to thy shelter fly' – as though Christianity had no place for any whose temperature rose to summer heat. He then quoted from the Song of Solomon and early religious writings and hymns, to show how passionate our religious language has been, and pleaded for life and fire today. It would be better to have the sense of God in a Tavern than to dwell in temples and Churches where life and thought are shut out, to have a pantheistic view of God than a joyless creed.

You ask about the vacation and my plans. I had made tentative efforts to get temporary work in the City, but Mother says she would like me to go home as Dad is causing her such anxiety. And of course if I am going in for exams next year I shall really need the quiet change to get some preparatory reading done. My money shows signs of getting low so that I shall have to be very careful indeed, but might I not come down to see you for a few days before going on to Bagshot? I am being simply deluged with invitations!

I can get no word of Françoise though I have sent beseeching cards and letters, and Mrs Camebus says she has no idea where she can be as she can get no news. It is trying of her to treat us so.

I am so interested to know you are reading *The Mystic Way*. I am hoping to read it myself one day. And have you still got that book by Lucy Re-Bartlett[8] on Sex, that once belonged to Mrs Shimmin? I believe I could appreciate it much better now. How are the Shimmins?

It seems certain that Mr Thompson will be coming over, probably at the end of July, and he speaks of settling down at Cambridge for nine or ten months in order to study for an extra degree! I wonder if I shall see much of him?

I have to go to Birmingham, so dear I will post this letter. I wanted to tell you more about the Care Committee work and to describe the Open Air School[9] and other places to which I have been, but it may have to wait until the holiday. Last week I took one of my cases to the Labour Exchange and am taking her to some mills this afternoon and getting her a 'place', and then bringing her here to tea.

You *know* you live deeply in my heart *always*.

With my very very fond love. Your own friend, Ruth.

Eva to Ruth   12 June 1914
My dear,

How I look forward to this weekly talk with you, and to receiving your letters. I can assure you they are perused many times!

Thank you so much for the account of Dr Harris's lecture – strangely enough, Mr James' sermon on Sunday dealt with a similar subject, viz. the secret knowledge of the Greeks.

With reference to the holidays – mine are not yet fixed. You must come and spend a few days with me before going to Bagshot – stay as long as you like.

I had a rather curious dream a little time ago, amd I will tell it to you:

I dreamed I came out of a house, and found myself in a square, surrounded by shoeing forges. I walked through a narrow valley and came upon a country – I commenced to walk along a *very* narrow lane, but was at last prevented by several horses who were leaning over the hedges. As I had not the courage to push aside their heads, I turned and began to retrace my steps, then a voice (my own or another's) cried 'Remember me to all', and as I walked I heard footsteps pattering at the side. At the end of the lane I turned and faced my follower, a splendid white horse, with lustrous eyes. I at once exclaimed, 'I know you – you are Pegasus, the winged horse.' As I spoke, the horse changed into a Prince in ancient dress of silvery blue satin. 'And what are you going to change *me* into?' I cried. The prince flung a feather into the air, and I exclaimed, 'I know, a skylark!!' As I spoke I felt that I diminished in size – became birdlike, and flew up and away with the sunshine – then I awoke!

I feel almost ashamed to send you such a fanciful 'rigmarole', but was it not a dream a little out of the ordinary?

On Tuesday evening I went to a meeting of the 'Women's

222

Labour League' – Nellie accompanied me. The meeting was held at Cliffords Inn Fields. Such a quaint, old world place – a cobbled yard, grass grown, large shady trees, and the Tea Rooms, so old, low-ceilinged with many many windows with deep window seats. We were quite a jolly party at tea – Dr Latter was there in boisterous spirits, emphatically refusing to support the Baby Clinic, declaring he could deliver an address proving it to be an iniquitous institution! Dr Ethel Bentham joined us, and Miss Mary Longman[10] gave an address. I wish you could see Miss Longman – she has such a beautiful expression and wears simple, artistic gowns. She told us a good deal about Germany and the Baby Clinics there, which appear to be badly organised. She also told me a great deal about a 'Young Socialists' League' which is known there under the name of 'The Young People's League'; in this league young boys and girls get much instruction, political and otherwise, and in the summer go on long tours – the girls wearing a similar dress to the boys, with the exception of a full blouse. At almost all German gatherings a great deal of *beer* is consumed, but in this League cocoa and soup are the beverages. I think one always finds temperance in a movement presenting ideals, but it seems to me a weakness in the Temperance Movement that it dwells much on the *pledge,* not enough upon the future.

If I am to see the dressmaker tonight, I must draw to a close.

Heart's love, my dear friend – Love from Aunt Edie and Minna. I miss you more than words can express! Eva.

Ruth to Eva   17 June 1914
My very own,
Oh it is a wonderful afternoon and I cannot bear to think of thee pent up in a little stuffy room while I am so able to enjoy the sunshine!

I have spread a rug in the garden, for the long grass of my favourite nook still holds the damp of the last fall of rain, and over me spread the branches of a large fruit tree – just enough to shade me from the sun's intensest beams.

I am in the queerest frame of mind today, for a letter came from Mr Thompson this morning hinting at the chance of my going to Newnham for a year! Now, don't laugh dear. I know quite well that it's utterly absurd and out of the question, but somehow the thought of there ever having been a connection between Cambridge and myself, so slight as just to have been in the mind of another, is strangely moving. It is now settled that Mr Thompson will come over, and he expects to arrive in England towards the end of July. Do you think it will be very odd meeting him again after such a short acquaintance in the flesh and intimate correspondence?

On Friday afternoon I went to tea with Miss Martin in the little house you will remember we visited. She gave me a very cordial welcome, and while I do not think she is so interested in the modern trend of mystic thought, her conversation was thoughtful and stimulating. We spoke mostly of Women's Suffrage and the Labour question, and when in connection with the latter she told of many interesting little movements going on in B'ham, I felt, as I told her, like an old war horse hearing his old call to battle. At this she showed some alarm and begged me not to mix in too many things whilst at Woodbrooke, which I was compelled sadly to admit was sound advice.

I had a lovely walk with Dorothy Rutter on Saturday, out on to the Lickey Hills. We skipped dinner, satisfying ourselves with biscuits, bananas and the exquisite beauty of the scene. On the way home Dorothy told me how she and a brother disguised themselves a few years back and took out a barrel organ, playing and singing in the streets at night, putting up in Common Lodging Houses, and once in the Workhouse! As I write I see her, a most exquisite little figure in white, playing tennis with her cousin, John Harvey, brother to the well-known Thomas Edmund Harvey, MP. She told me more about her mental evolution, which much resembled ours and included a most ardent Socialist phase, during which the experiment with the street organ was carried out. This last was told to me in strict confidence, but I thought I might tell my trusted friend. That night, came a timid knock at the door and a ridiculous question, and finally the real purpose came out – a goodnight kiss! I think I told you what an unwilling frame of mind she came here in – she says now how glad she is about it. Dear, I do pray that I may be always kept humble and sincere in my relations with other people. I seem to get quickly near to people and sometimes I feel this is my snare.

On Sunday I had quite another experience. I was invited to lunch with the Cadburys! Occasionally a few Woodbrookers are invited and this is considered an honour. The house they live in is magnificent – I have never seen anything like it before, but it impresses me as being very like a museum! On the great landings were trophies of jungle hunting, great oil paintings of ancestors – I could never describe it all. Seventeen of us sat down to lunch, mostly Americans, who extolled Bournville through a good part of the meal.

On Monday evening we had the woman who organises the work for the girls at Cadbury's and looks after their welfare generally, to tell us about it. Among many strange statements which she made was one to the effect that the girls liked monotony and resented change in their work. I made bold here to interpose a comment and said that I thought the piece work system of payment accounted for this, as naturally the girls could earn more on work to which they were accustomed. She did not agree with this at all, but persisted that the love of monotony was part of the mental make up of the girls – what *do* you think of that?

Yesterday afternoon I called a Committee of the people who are helping to organise games for children in the public Park, so that we might get a clearer idea of the aim of the thing. I thoroughly enjoy my evening's play every week and am getting to know a lot of the children.

In the evening a huge party was given here, the students from settlements around being invited. It *was* a crush and everybody was clad in their choicest garments. We crowded into the lecture hall and listened to a wonderful American woman who is here for a few days, while she told us, with a dramatic force amounting to genius, stories of American working girls.

Your letters dear, as you say of mine, get read many times – they breathe always so much of you and keep you near to me.

I do think the dream of the horses decidedly out of the ordinary – very poetic and romantic.

And now dear I must say *adieu* and go in. I am getting utterly devoured by insects and many varieties seem to be swarming on my body. Fond love to thee, precious one. Ruth.

Ruth to Eva   24 June 1914
My very dear,
I will make a commencement on this week's letter to you, though I am afraid I shall not be able to write to much length during the next few weeks. So many festivities are being crowded in, it appearing that the Summer term is the time for these.

On Saturday week between 150 and 200 children are coming

to a party and we are already getting preparation forward for this. On Tuesday next the Wardens are giving *us* a party and we are wearing fancy dress! I am going as a 'Vegetarian' unless you can write quickly with a fine (and simple!) idea. As for tea parties and strawberry and cream suppers! This morning Bessie and I were whirling off in a taxi into Birmingham at half past six, with the deaf American who today sailed for home.

You ask about Jessie Marsh. She is a very unusual girl – some people here think she is a genius – but I hardly know, though I have grown to love her and see that she possesses uncommon characteristics.

My Care Committee girl has left the place I got her and I was busy all morning trying to get her another.

Today I have been looking through Christabel Pankhurst's book, *The Hidden Scourge,*[11] but I cannot read it. Have you, or Gertie, read it?

It is late dear, and I am tired, so I will say Goodnight and post this straight away in the morning.

A deep well of love and a warm, warm kiss. Ruth.

Eva to Ruth   26 June 1914

Dear, I *know* your days will be very full during the next two or three weeks and if you have only time to send me a page, I shall *quite* understand, and feel that all the more is reserved for telling when we next meet.

Oh, I wish I *could* help you with some brilliant idea as to a fancy dress, but alas, never was there such a 'wooden head' as mine at present but I think you will look ever so nice as a 'Vegetarian'.

I have not read *The Hidden Scourge* but I believe Gertie has. She is very well – busily practising on her violin and attending suffrage meetings.

Oh Ruth – when your letter came I had just finished reading Elizabeth Robins' *Where are you going to*. It is the story of two young girls paying their first visit to London to an Aunt – at the terminus they are met by a fashionable lady whom they think to be the Aunt they have never before seen. They are hurried into a taxi and driven to a house of ill-fame – they are in the hands of the White Slave people. Dear, the book upset me, made me long to move heaven and earth to lessen this evil – it seems to me a problem beyond the power of mere legislation. I was so glad to find this terrible and sometimes morbid book ending with a cry of hope.

Minna, the children, Aunt Edie and I went in a party yesterday to Woodford. We climbed on the top of the tram and had a refreshing ride along the country roads, trees and fields bathed in golden sunshine. At Woodford we descended into the near forest. I gathered wild roses with the children until the sun sank (a crimson ball) as though falling into a grey ocean, then we turned homewards and were whirled rapidly back to Walthamstow – arrived there I piloted the whole party to an Exhibition of Art needlework at the Library. I think all enjoyed it for the work was extremely fine, some having been brought from South Kensington Museum.

Aunt Emily has sold the business and comes to us next week! She seems very depressed. I feel so sorry for her – it is difficult to take a leap into a new life at 30; what must it be like at 44!

How I long to put my arms around you dear – the time will quickly pass now – so much I *would* say – a heart of love to you. Eva.

Eva's Diary   Monday, 22 June 1914
I had tea with Minna and nursed baby a great deal, carrying her about the garden. Then I sat quietly watching Minna undressing her – we both went upstairs to put her to bed, a little rosy cherub – bending over her. Minna said she did not know how she lived through the time of Will's death – she thought it was a good thing the birth of the baby came only a month later. I thought so too; the transcendent strength which upheld us through that month would not perhaps have sustained us longer.

I have been indulging in much day-dreaming today, a thing I seldom do now, and which is not good for me, the dreams being so often of domestic happiness, unlikely ever to be realised. I have vigorously been endeavouring to shake myself free of these moods, and turn *firmly* to the *practical*.

Eva's Diary   Friday, 3 July 1914
A letter from Ruth this morning – raising a doubt as to whether she will spend the whole of the promised week with me (she is anxious about home) or come for the August Bank Holiday. I was foolish enough to allow this to cast me into depression throughout the morning.

At lunch Minna and I again discussed plans for the future. I intend to try and still my restlessness, and yet not cease to knock

227

at every available door for more expressive living – surely at last a door will open and I shall hear a voice say, 'This is the way, walk ye in it!' What a 'home spot' it is to me there with Minna the children and baby. I stayed to watch Minna undress Joan – I love to bury my face in her fat legs, body and neck, to feel her tender arms and to hear her gurgle and laugh – she is a 'dinky darling'.

Eva's Diary   Saturday, 4 July 1914
Aunt Edie met me at Hoe St Station and we journeyed to Kingston together. We walked in the magnificent night far along the river, the water darkly glittering and gliding, the trees in almost bleak silhouette trembling, the moon riding high, until at last we came upon a sudden widening of the river and a sky of deep orange, the afterglow of sunset. There we rested and watched the beauty fade, a boat gliding silently by now and then, or a swan. We talked of many things. Talking of the influence of women, Cecil [Eva's half-brother] said there were women in whose presence one felt inspired, refreshed – women who keep up the ideal of life. I felt so *close* to Cecil tonight. Oh these communings with those one loves, how they stand out in life, stars in one's existence; I live more and more for such hours!

How full of desire life is – *my* life is. Often I have felt as though on the very verge of infinite beauty – whether in friendship, nature or art – yet it has never quite revealed itself to me, neither have I ever *quite* succeeded in unfolding into its essence – ever it eludes me, hovering just at the extremity of one's grasp, luring one on and on. Methought today I would value anew the opportunities which come to me – sing my song of life as best I can, and if sometimes tenderness and beauty in their fullness, because of wearisomeness of body and mind, become blurred, yet it will not always be so, for love and beauty must at last yield to my persistency.

Eva's Diary   Monday, 6 July 1914
Aunt Edie and I journeyed through the rain from Kingston to Walthamstow this morning – it was a scramble to catch trains and to get across London. We met men and women pouring into the City, and a great thankfulness came over me that my work lay in the quiet Hoe St office, and not in the huge commercial houses of London, yet for an ideal how much one would

228

sacrifice; but commercial London with its rush and tear terrifies me.

Lunch with Minna was a real communion; I told her about Kingston, read extracts from Tagore and then we fell into a discussion of men versus women. I said I thought fundamentally there is a sex antagonism just as there is a racial antagonism. I thought this arose largely from differentiation, leading to pride, which can only be eliminated by more and more perfect unions, by blending of interests.

Arrived home, I found Mr Turner had visited Aunt Emily in our absence, and had asked her to live with him – she is now in a very restless condition, unable to decide. To my mind, the fact that Mr Turner's wife is a confirmed invalid should decide one at once: loyalty to another woman – a sick woman. She should be shielded from deception and desertion; then again does this man *really* love Aunt Emily – does she really *love* him? Aunt Emily is of a jealous temperament – if she took the step, I cannot but feel after some feverish pleasure, she would awaken to insecurity, doubt, all enhanced by her position in the eyes of others.

Eva's Diary   Thursday, 9 July 1914
After tea with Minna we all made our way home to Aunt Edie. We discussed Aunt E's trouble, and all agreed that nothing should be done without Mrs Turner's consent, and this I think neither Aunt Emily nor Mr Turner would face. I have promised to write to Aunt Emily about this matter – I shrink from the task so, yet feel something must be done. It is all *so* pitiful!

Ruth to Eva   7 July 1914
                                                        Woodbrooke
My very dear,
Your letter as usual made your own precious self most near and dear. And to think that this time next week we shall be on the eve of meeting!

I am wondering about your Aunt Emily. Yes, indeed, it must be a crisis in her life and I hope she will pull round and find a niche where some peace and happiness may befall her. When you were *quite* young dear, did it seem to you that the lives of middle-aged women were all cut and dried and that even any changes they made in their circumstances were not very exciting? It used to seem so to me and I was almost impatient with them, but you and I are getting near the borders of that time

229

ourselves and what strange things are being unfolded!

Now about Wednesday. I am expecting to meet you at Liverpool St at 6 o'clock and then we are to go to Hoxton for tea. Bessie Cannon also wants to come to the School and we must arrange to meet her somewhere. Am I to go home with you? If your Aunt Emily is there and you are full up, do tell me and we must make other plans.

We had a very festive weekend here. On Saturday at dinner we drank toasts to the Americans – it being Independence day – and at ten o'clock we had some splendid fireworks and processed round the pool, singing and bearing lighted Japanese lanterns! On Sunday Miss Buckton came to tea, but so many people gathered about her it was difficult to get any consecutive conversation.

Tomorrow some of us are going to Cradley heath to see the Chain-workers[12] and we are also going down a coal-mine!

I have been reading Lady Constance Lytton's book,[13] and oh! dear, it is a book to read – *do* read it.

I am wondering about all the friends – the Taverners and Awes – and hope all is going well with them. Minna is always specially in my thoughts, and I am just longing to see the baby.

Eva's Diary   Saturday, 11 July 1914
I started for Mrs Taverner's garden party this afternoon freshly clad from head to foot. Alas! a motor bus came lumbering through a newly watered road, and bespattered me with mud from head to foot! I felt vexed at first as I had to return home and change, but was able to laugh afterwards when I realised what a spectacle I must have presented!

The garden party was a great success – tea in the garden, followed by skipping, swinging and games – then music in the sitting room, very pleasant to listen to from the cool garden! When it grew dark Mr Taverner sent up a fire balloon ornamented with the legend 'Votes for Women'. The garden, lighted by Japanese lanterns, looked so picturesque – we had supper there in quite a 'dim religious light'. It was midnight when I reached Minna, with whom I spent the night.

Eva's Diary   Monday, 13 July 1914
A night of almost suffocating heat! This afternoon I read a great deal of *My Little Girl*. I do not agree with the views expressed on women. I do not think men are nobler than women – there

230

are noble men and noble women – ignoble men and ignoble women. Also, while I believe, broadly speaking, there is work specially woman's in the world and work specially man's – there should be no barriers to education or service; men and women should be left free to do the work they are sent into the world to do. We must not crush our Joan of Arcs and Rosa Bonheurs behind a code of 'women's work' – or male nurses behind a code of 'men's work'.

Eva's Diary   Tuesday, 14 July 1914
A letter this morning from Mr Strain, saying he is within sight of land and will meet me in September. I did not feel so excited as over his previous letter – I suppose because expectation has been long delayed, but I expect Ruth will be excited. When I gave Minna the letter to read today, I thought she changed colour, but she only said, 'You will make an effort to see him then?' She seemed weary and depressed, and said she thought she was not only tired but mentally hungry. I must take her some books.

A quiet day at business with absolutely nothing to do, at any rate not on the firm's behalf. I wrote to Aunt Emily begging her not to take the step Mr Turner suggests, but I feel worried and anxious now, lest I have not been sympathetic enough, lest I have said too much.

Eva's Diary   Wednesday, 15 July 1914
I met Ruth at Liverpool St Station this evening – she looks ever so well, and seems so brisk and businesslike, I feel quite slow and heavy beside her – I must endeavour to be more practical! Then on to Hoxton Adult School. We all had tea together and Ruth had to answer many questions as to her life at Woodbrooke. As there were so few of us, school was held in an informal manner. I gave a little address on Michael Fairless.[14] The guests then severally excused themselves – this led to a discussion of how women could be induced to attend the School which is in a very unsatisfactory condition just now.

Eva's Diary   Thursday, 16 July 1914
At lunch today Minna asked me if I would write to Lily, as she did not want her to get jealous of me. I said I would do so, but such a wave of unhappy feeling swept over me. Trying to analyse it, it seems to me I felt lonely, jealous and uneasy as to

231

my own actions – had I taken too much for granted, been too much with Minna?

Ruth came to my office this afternoon and sat quietly by me whilst I worked. I had three quarters of an hour leisure and then Ruth read to me notes on the Friends' Weekend Conference she had attended.

We then made our way to Minna's for tea – Ruth thought baby was very fine. Aunt Edie joined us and we spent a good time in the garden. I enjoyed most the undressing of the baby – she was so good and looked such a beauty. When all the children had gone to bed we had a wonderful conversation. It began by Ruth describing a visit to mass at a Roman Catholic Church. Then I gave an account of the lecture I heard on 'The Duty of Happiness' at Centre, and the lecture at the Theosophical Society dealing with race, sex, and the causes of racial prejudice, and the discussion on dream life. Ruth then told us a little about the 'Origin and Meaning of Taboo'. When supper came we felt food was not for us, we had travelled far away into the region of revelation.

Eva's Diary   Saturday, 18 July 1914
I had to say 'Goodbye' to Ruth this morning – it has been so splendid to have her, but not so real to me owing to business.

Walking up and down the garden with Joan today, Minna came and questioned me about the little cloud which had arisen. Soon my foolish fears were all dispelled – and shame came that I should have been so weak. I went to the League with my heart bursting with thankfulness for the love of my dear friend.

Eva's Diary   Wednesday, 22 July 1914
Oh, the rest and blessedness of Minna's home this evening! We talked softly of marriage – Minna does not think the sex relationship would be well for me. She thinks that after a time it would become distasteful to me – I do not know; at present I feel union with one whom I *deeply loved* would give me great joy.

Eva's Diary   Friday, 24 July 1914
I made two foolish little mistakes in my work today, and came home burdened with a strong sensation of failure. Shall I *ever* make a good legal clerk? I am not prompt – I dream when I should concentrate; I do not throw my heart into the work, but

live for the best part in an ideal world, consequently I work mechanically and do not feel the *live* interest I should. I will try to take an active interest in my work!

Eva's Diary   Sunday, 26 July 1914
Minna and I have been so happy together today, and have longed that we may never be separated. It is very rare to find a soul with whom one can absolutely blend. I feel my friendship with Minna to be an exquisite gift.

9

'Man's Militarism'
July 1914–August 1915

On 31 July Eva noted in her diary that 'the possibility of a European war has burst upon us today!' and at the beginning of August war was declared. The First World War was a great shock to Ruth, Eva, Minna and others like them who were working in a spirit of fellowship and co-operation for progressive change, of which internationalism was a fundamental part. Much of the buoyant spirit and intense idealism of the pre-war period was shattered by 'nation against nation slaying and destroying' in an upsurge of 'cheap patriotism' and aggressive militarism.

Solidarity was further shaken when the progressive movements themselves split over the war, with only 'a small number of men refusing to join up,' and many of 'the splendid women of the Women's Movement' taking a patriotic stand. Emmeline and Christabel Pankhurst, who had so opposed the government, called off the militant campaign and toured the country making recruiting speeches. But other suffragettes and many suffragists actively opposed the war, and the ideals of the pre-war years were not abandoned. Many of the women whom Ruth and Eva particularly admired, such as Charlotte Despard, Isabella Ford, Maude Royden and Olive Schreiner, worked for pacifism and rallied, as a Votes for Women reporter put it, to 'protest against the time-honoured methods of brutal force by which men – regardless of one half of the race – have seen fit to settle national disputes'.[1]

Most of the Christian Churches supported the war, with the exception of the Quakers, who had long traditions of pacifism, and even the Rev. Campbell started to recant some of his radical ideas.

Ruth, Eva, Minna and Françoise were all pacifists. In the

234

Quaker atmosphere at Woodbrooke, Ruth was quick to join the Fellowship of Reconciliation, which was started by Quakers and some Nonconformists in December 1914. Eva joined later. Françoise went to the scene of battle in France 'to nurse soldiers of all nationalities', and returned convinced that 'no cause is so sacred as to justify such appalling suffering'. Back in London she wrote to the papers and delivered her 'simple tale of war', as she had seen it, to the study circles of the Union of Democratic Control (another pacifist organisation) and to 'Sylvia Pankhurst's little groups'. She was more than once accused of being a German spy and was raided by the police.

Gertie seemed to have had contact with Sylvia Pankhurst's East London Federation of Suffragettes in Bow, a pacifist group which had separated from the WSPU in February 1914 over political differences. There was a high level of militancy amongst East End women, but unlike the WSPU the ELFS concentrated not only on the vote but on the desperate living conditions of its working women. Pacifist activity centred on relief work with war refugees, support for conscientious objectors, and for Germans in England who were experiencing racism and discrimination. It had a political platform of internationalism which attacked the 'race hatred and national jealousy' that led to 'militarism and the ruin of all progress'.

Eva's diaries described the day-to-day effect of war on London life, and showed a narrowing down of interests and opportunities for those women who did not support the war effort. She was, however, elected superintendent of the Chapel's Women's Conference, which was a great success.

The war seemed, as Ruth wrote to Eva, 'to have overshadowed every other thought in the minds of most people'. It was a time when 'hopes and ideals trembled in the balance'. Eva felt 'stranded' by the developments going on around her, with Ruth at Woodbrooke for a second year, and Minna starting her nursing training. She was also not in good health, and went on holiday to a summer retreat in Hove. The arrival of Lily at Minna's to look after the children caused domestic tensions and some jealousy on Eva's part, but it did not in the end lessen the bond between herself and Minna. It was a 'strange time', she wrote to Ruth, when we 'must all keep close, close in love, and all will be well.'

A second year at Woodbrooke brought Ruth more confidence. She did exceptionally well in her exams and was one of the first women to receive a Diploma in Social Studies from Birmingham

University. When David Thompson visited England in the summer of 1914, Ruth considered his offer of marriage, feeling she had 'given Hugh every chance'. By the following summer, after much deliberation, she decided she could not marry him. Although the only reason mentioned was her parents, who had got into a 'hopeless' state, the letters from David suggest other problems. There were differences about 'fundamental questions' such as 'the relation of the sexes', and Ruth's relationship with Hugh remained a tie. She was rather overawed by David's social connections and his interest in 'an insignificant little person' like herself.

In the summer of 1915, Ruth succeeded in getting a scholarship for Eva to go to Woodbrooke, which after all the years of hoping, seemed like 'some beautiful dream'.

The beginning of August finds Eva preoccupied with the war.

Eva's Diary   Sunday, 2 August 1914
I went to morning service – the threatened war was dealt with by Mr James, he spoke of the possibility of God having lessons to teach all nations by this terrible war; in times of war a palace became a camping ground – elemental things entered into life. The whole world had been blessed with prosperity for some years, but how had we used the wealth? To build dreadnoughts, and prepare for war! Had the money been spent on social, intellectual and artistic reform, and advancement, how different would the condition of the world now have been.

Throughout the day and throughout this service my mind had been seeking to grasp a new conception of the kingdom – what, in its fullness, *is* the new life? I longed for a new vision, a new ideal.

As though in answer to my desires, at close of service Mr James asked if I would like to go to his house, as Mr Jones was also going. My heart leapt – I sent Winnie home with a message to Minna, and went away with Mr James and Mr Jones.

In the house Mr James was his old, delightful, impetuous self. He said how often he had longed for something closer, more intimate than ordinary Church fellowship, something in the nature of an 'engagement' betwixt man and woman, or woman and woman, and man and man – that could be relied upon, even though separated, for fellowship and inspiration: should we not form such a fellowship now – a Church within the Church: should we not strive after this old brotherhood – this

236

life which is life indeed? We talked long in this way. Then, in conversing, Mr James said to me, 'Do you know I was just going to call you Eva – Miss Slawson seems so formal after tonight.' I replied, 'Well, call me Eva, then – all my friends, everyone, does – I should like you to do so.' Nevertheless, I was startled when, later on in the evening, looking through his books, I asked him if he would be wanting a certain volume, he answered, 'No, Eva'; I experienced such a thrill of joy, such a sense of added kinship and friendship and reverence as I shall never forget.

I found Minna waiting up for me – we hastened to bed, but sleep was not for me. I sat upright in bed for a long time, gazing at the moon, and thinking of many things.

Eva's Diary   Wednesday, 5 August 1914
A day of great excitement – batches of territorials leaving Hoe Street – the people hanging out flags and filling the streets; one begins to feel the enormity of this war. I found Minna full of the same subject, and she read a good deal of war news to me while I was at lunch. I was too prostrate, however, with excitement and fatigue, to grasp very much. After baby had gone to sleep, Minna went out and returned with the report that goods were going up to famine price.

Minna and I were very quiet for some little time, feeling the shadow of a great calamity.

Eva's Diary   Friday, 7 August 1914
This afternoon we were startled by an air ship passing over Walthamstow. Frost and I ran down into the road, and gazing up saw it above our heads. It made me realise very vividly the fresh implements and dangers which have entered into warfare.

This evening I went to the Awes'. We discussed the war at great length. Owen is planting carrots, turnips, etc., in the back garden, and invited me (should I become skin and bone from famine) to come and share the carrots with them!

Eva's Diary   Sunday, 9 August 1914
Aunt Edie and I went to Minna's this afternoon. We all had tea in the garden in spite of the gloomy weather. Since war has been declared the sun has forsaken us!

Stanley called to bid us all goodbye as he expects to be sent out tomorrow. Stanley looked very pale – he has been working

237

tremendously hard on the *Telegraph*, and said he did not feel fit for a march. I mentioned it seemed strange to me that German *defeats* were reported – surely there must have been some victories? I could tell from Stanley's face that I was right – I feel certain much important news is being suppressed, and that things are more serious than they seem.

At such tense moments one either weeps or becomes wildly excited; we chose the latter course and drank Stanley's health and wished him God speed in apparent high spirits. Minna declared she and Lily would go out to the war – a sensation of desolation of course at once swept over me! But Stanley declared he should look for me in the hospitals with a red cross on my arm, and we made absurd appointments to meet in Brussels. We went to bed tonight with a realisation of the awfulness of war heavy upon us!

Eva's Diary   Monday, 10 August 1914
I called for Minna after leaving the office, and we all made our way over to Leyton. We had just settled and were chatting, when Ruth arrived, flushed and excited! I was *so* delighted to be with her – she was very excited and upset over the war and discussed it at great length with Minna.

Ruth had dressed her hair in a very classical style and looked so handsome. Minna thought it would be nice if I could do *my* hair in the same way, and nothing would satisfy but that I must then and there let Ruth comb and fasten my hair, which she accordingly did! Of course I knew from the first that the style would not suit me – it was a dismal failure! Gertie and Minna then attempted to dress *their* hair, and there was much laughter. At last Minna and the children departed homeward and Ruth and I settled down for the night after talking plans over for the coming day.

Eva's Diary   Wednesday, 12 August 1914
Lunch with Minna. I felt such closeness when she drew me with baby on to her knee – precious moments when soul blends with soul!

Then Stanley rushed in to say he was off in the morning to Belgium and expected to be in the great battle on Friday. He told us much of the horror of war, of living for days in the trenches – the ghastly things which happen made me cry in my heart, 'war is *diabolical,* it is *devil's work!*' I felt I could have

238

cried 'Peace' at the street corners!

I found Minna quite unwell today after yesterday's excitement, nevertheless she was preparing to go into the forest with the children. Before leaving Minna, we experienced again that merging of spirit. I came away stirred in my whole being – but I tremble to even write of such moments in their sacredness and intensity!

The thought has been with me today that it is terrible to sit safely at home, whilst thousands are suffering!

Eva's Diary   Friday, 14 August 1914
I believe baby Joan expects me to walk up and down with her each lunch hour now. What a darling she is!

I was deeply impressed this afternoon by a passage in *The Life of St Francis* stating the reason for the poverty of the Franciscans – 'If we possessed property we should have need of arms for its defence.' In this time of war this statement appears to me full of significance; indeed, the older I grow, the more I am convinced that the less we possess, the better it is for us; only I would like all useful and beautiful things conserved by all for the benefit of all.

Another passage stabbed me to the heart: 'Friendship among men, when it surpasses a certain limit, has something deep, high, ideal, infinitely sweet, to which no other friendships attain. There was no woman in the Upper Chamber when, on the last evening of his life, Jesus communed with his disciples.' I do think it should be recognised, there are women, as well as men, capable of the finest friendship. If there was no woman present in the Upper Chamber, there was no man to witness Christ's first spiritual revelation of himself after his death!

Ruth met me at the office this afternoon and we made our way to Finsbury Gardens, intending to talk and rest there, but found it packed with horses and gun carriages – it all looked very warlike! After inspecting it all we made our way to the Relief Committee meeting at Devonshire House. First was the silence which I always find so helpful and strengthening – I often long for the same in our services. Then a gentleman spoke of the great calamity of the war, more pictorial perhaps, and yet not really more awful than the great industrial struggle and distress. Might not we hope that out of this terrible war might arise some great blessing.

Then Miss Fox Howard spoke on the need of helping in our

towns – all could not rush off to do Red Cross work, etc. We could best help the world often by remaining at our posts, by spreading the spirit of peace, and checking panic.

The suggestion made as to relief work was that Friends should band themselves together to assist the alien Germans in this country – they were in danger of rough usage and want, and we might hold out a friendly hand at this time.

I think this proposal is a very fine one – it appeals to me as being 'international' and likely to help establish a relationship of friendliness with Germany in days to come. I want to suggest to Mr James that perhaps this is a way in which our church would help here in Walthamstow.

From the meeting house we made our way with some difficulty to Mary MacArthur's house in Caroline Place – the drawing room windows were wide open and we could see groups of men and women chatting – it appeared to be a friendly and rather private gathering; then Ruth declared she could not go in – it all seemed *too* private. I felt quite amazed about it at first. I do not know whether I am very gauche, but I felt the occasion such a momentous one, and the need to help so great – also I could not understand Ruth's timidity since Mr Thompson was there to greet her, and expecting her! It all ended in our walking up and down until nearly 10 o'clock when we made our way to the Thackeray Hotel – saw Miss Thompson and explained matters.

On our return home we retired to bed and then Ruth told me she felt Mr Thompson cares for her – that she had written to Mr Jones today saying she would be visiting Glastonbury to see him. She feels if she can only get the assurance of spiritual union (from Hugh), though she remain single all her life she would be content. I quite agree with her plan, and think it best for her peace of mind.

Eva's Diary   Monday, 17 August 1914
Mr Hazlegrove has found fault with microscopic errors lately, this morning he seemed more trying than usual and it does *wear* me so. His attitude towards me seems to vary with his impressions of the war! I felt depressed almost to tears this morning over my efforts and failures. At times my ten years' service here seems long.

Minna and I called on Mr and Mrs Taverner this evening. Mr Taverner's firm closed for half time and Elsie's firm are deducting 10% on wages! If this war continues there must needs be poverty!

Ruth told me tonight she had decided not to go to Glaston-bury, but to wait. We talked a little of office life and she said how she had suffered at the Alexanders [the Kearley and Tonge managers] by constant petty fault finding. She thinks change *will* come to me, and opportunity, and that I shall find the value of the thinking and reading I have been able to do in my abundant leisure at the office. The question arises – have I thought and read to much purpose?

Eva's Diary   Wednesday, 19 August 1914
I ran round to Minna's to lunch today, just burning to talk with her and discuss some problems. Lily has asked Minna to dissuade me from taking a holiday, as she thinks a hard time is before us.

In reading St Francis' parables I am very much impressed by his practice of 'The Lord's Table' – all surplus wealth placed in a common fund for use of all in need. I cannot tear myself from my faith in communism – it seems to me superior in every way to any political or even socialistic system.

Eva's Diary   Thursday, 20 August 1914
I am 32 years old today! I can scarcely believe it – I certainly don't feel my age. I am sure I felt 32 at 22, and 22 at 32!! If I go on in this way and live to be 60, I shall then probably *feel* about 16!!

Minna and the children spent the evening with me at home very quietly. Minna read aloud several of Ella Wheeler Wilcox's poems – I like to hear her – she has a melodious voice well suited for poetry! I had to show my presents. We had some fun after supper, over a story I attempted to write when I was a girl. I saw my little family to Knotts Green, and then to bed!!

Eva's Diary   Saturday, 22 August 1914
I had a pleasant journey to Hove, catching trains and buses in quick succession – plenty of people at London Bridge Station holiday bound, so evidently the panic is abating. I found St Michael's Hall, Hove, without any difficulty. As I walked up the drive to the entrance, and caught glimpses of white-robed figures at tennis, a wild longing for home came over me lest the School would prove too stylish! However, I overcame this

feeling – the Hall is a large, old building, with a cosy entrance hall and wide staircases and landings. I was just in time for dinner, and sat next to two nice girls, who did their best to make me feel at home. At my table were several French women – they reminded me of the French Revolution – they looked so wild and distraught! Another lady in very low evening dress and rather startling ornaments, made me wonder – she seemed so 'out of place' at the School!

The evening was devoted to dancing and music. I enjoyed several waltzes: as the men are *very* much in the minority, about 9 of them to perhaps 40 women – we women just danced amongst ourselves.

How I hope that this little holiday will give me a fund of life and strength that the winter may overflow with love and service!

Eva's Diary   Sunday, 23 August 1914
I hurried down to the service this morning – reminding me again of Woodbrooke and the Quaker services. Mr Bain prayed that the hearts of all might be turned to love and peace and the war ended. At breakfast I sat next to the lady of fashionable and startling appearance, who informed me she is a member of the Actresses' Franchise League,[2] so I presume she is an actress. She said she felt half starved on the vegetarian diet, having come for the benefit of the fruit only. Looking around nervously she whispered, 'And what a *holy* look vegetarians seem to get after they have practised it for a time!' I felt immensely amused!

I spent the morning on the seafront reading, and the afternoon in the garden.

Ruth to Eva   Sunday evening, 23 August 1914
                                          High Street, Bagshot, Surrey
My dear,
We have just come in from a long walk and I have been wondering whether to write to you or to re-commence my diary. Eventually I decided that the poor diary might as well be postponed yet a little longer, for I much want to talk with you.

I am glad you spent such a happy birthday. I thought a great deal about you. We must both go on growing younger in mind and spirit each year! Is it not a wonderful experience?

I have pictured you today in the vicinity of the much loved sea and I hope you have been enjoying yourself and not bothered at all with feelings of loneliness.

Well dear, it's about myself I'm wanting to talk! I wrote to Mr Thompson, declining his invitation to the Fabian Summer School; but I have said if it still seemed worthwhile to him I would join them somewhere, as I feel I would like us to talk things out together. I shall carry out my intention of seeing Hugh first – it seems otherwise impossible.

I am meeting Jessie Marsh tomorrow evening. She is evidently in distress again and wants to see me. I never told you dear – it was an experience curiously humbling somehow – that I really seemed to have a little healing influence with her. I spent a lot of time and thought over her once or twice last term, when she was in a very strange state. I knew by an intuitive thrill when she had got out of bed. One morning very early I went into her room and a sound of agony I shall never forget came from her lips, though she did not cry, and I just slipped down beside her on the bed and held her in my arms. I knew she was better when she just rested her head on my shoulders and drew the bed clothes over me. One day she brought me a great bunch of carnations and that night, after I had gone to bed, she crept in to talk and she told me then that the sort of feelings she had with me were the only things that made God seem real to her. Another time she frankly said that if she got better it would be my doing.

Now dear, I do not think you will misunderstand why I tell you all this. While it was a rich and wonderful experience to me, it made me feel more humble and unworthy than perhaps anything else in my life has done. I could not tell you about it in words. Then, dear, I thought of the expression of affection I showed her, a newcomer into my life, and I remembered all my awkwardness with you. It seemed almost as though I had given the flower which had bloomed on your stem, to another. Yet you know full well dear, how I love you and how precious you are to me.

The days have passed very quietly here and I have contrived to get some study done. I have been on one or two solitary blackberrying expeditions and we have made much jam.

My father is causing us great anxiety. I would that I had some healing power to use over him – his condition (mentally) is, I am sure, getting serious and it seems impossible to influence him. My brother has had his salary reduced, otherwise we have no news.

Much love, my own. Enjoy thyself and drink in beauty and

strength to your fullest capacity. Your friend, Ruth.

Eva to Ruth   Friday afternoon, [28] August 1914
It was a great delight to me to get your long letter – I went into
the garden to read it – but the breakfast bell rang and I had to
reserve my pleasure until I was safely on the sea front.

I feel perhaps it would be well for you to see Mr Thompson
again, and if you see Mr Jones first, things will surely be much
clearer. I am so *very* glad dear, you should write just as you feel
– you know I could not bear to feel you were keeping anything
back through thought of me.

Thank you dear, *deeply*, for all you have told me of Jessie
Marsh and your influence with her. It may be, dear, that you
have the gift of healing, and she is awakening and calling it
forth. I no longer believe we should fear or neglect gifts and
powers which *appear* supernatural – perfect growth means not
only gifts of body and mind, but of soul too! I know how you feel
about the expression of affection dear, it has filled me with
wonder sometimes, some of the experiences I have had with
Minna. I think such are exceedingly rare, sacred and unusual
too – perhaps because she is Platonic. You and I dear, became
friends when we were so much younger and inexperienced – we
love and approach in a different way – is that not so? Yet we
know and understand. Your words of love are so dear to me –
my *heart's* love is here for you!

And now, mine dear, you will want to hear about the School.
St Michael's Hall reminds me very much of Woodbrooke only it
is less stately. Almost all the rooms have names on the doors
such as 'Harmony', 'Sympathy', 'Welcome', 'Hospitality', etc.,
and the house is ringing all day to music and song, for there are
several good musicians and singers here. My room mate, a Miss
Pyne, and I are becoming companions. At first she seemed
awfully reserved and quiet, and had a screen placed across the
room – after the second day the screen was removed and she
informed me she felt so thoroughly at home with me. I
discovered she was an artist and miniature painter, and she
showed me some of her work – the miniatures were exquisite.
Her sketches were of Hampstead Heath, where she has gone for
another week's sketching.

On Sunday I had a long and interesting talk with Mr Richard
Whitewell, who contributes to *Brotherhood*. He expressed a
wish that we might meet again and gave me an address for a

244

meeting in London where he and Bruce Wallace hope to start a fellowship.

On Tuesday a party of us walked over the Downs to Rottingdean. How I love a wide expanse of swelling country, the blue sky overhead. I, with two others, took my shoes and stockings off, and it was lovely to feel the cool earth and grass! We lunched on the Downs overlooking Rottingdean – puff balls blowing hither and thither like summer snow flakes – the sea below bathed in silver light.

Dearie, I must close, it is almost tea time – the vegetarian diet, by the way, is excellent – delightfully prepared. I long to see you and to talk over our various experiences.

A warm kiss and heart's love, mine dear. Eva.

Eva's Diary   Friday, 28 August 1914
Miss Beale, the actress, informed me this morning she is staying here trying to re-organise a shattered life. At dinner I sat next to an elderly lady, a suffragette wearing the prison badge. She looked worn and weary, also I have an impression that her mind has suffered in some way.

Then came the lecture on 'Irisology', the science of diagnosing disease from the eye. Dr Anderson not only believes the eye is the mirror of the soul but of the body. He does not believe in cold water, we are not fishes and have not webbed feet – we are creatures of the sun and air and should take sun and air baths, and a warm sponge at night. He believed in nature cures and a fruitarian diet. It seems feasible that a great deal may be learned from the eye, but I am surprised that so much can be located on such a small surface.

Eva's Diary   Saturday, 5 September 1914
Morning packing – journey home all afternoon. Saw Minna in the evening.

Eva's Diary   Sunday, 6 September 1914
I miss the large house, fresh air and dainty food. I suppose I shall get accustomed to all, in a few days – that is the worst of it – that is the worst of it – one *does* get so horribly used to cramped and unhealthy conditions.

Eva's Diary   Monday, 7 September 1914
Business seemed strange today after my changeful holiday, but I

245

felt pleased to see Frost, and he seemed very glad to have me back. Frost heard Mr Cunningham say over the telephone that the great thing was keep us all employed, even if it had to be done on half wages!

Ruth arrived this evening – how delighted I felt to see her. We had a good deal of fun over my adventures, then we went for a walk, and Ruth told me Mr Thompson has asked her to marry him, but her friendship with Mr Jones is such a tie.

Eva's Diary   Tuesday, 8 September 1914
Aunt Edie went to London this evening to hear Christabel Pankhurst. I was not long alone however, Ruth was early home, and we were able to have a long talk together. She and Mr Thompson have decided to go to Whiteway for a fortnight, in order that they may know one another better. As Ruth says, Mr Jones has been very like a child to her – this makes her position very difficult. I am afraid after Ruth has gone home I shall be overcome by a sensation of 'flatness' which at present I am keeping in abeyance – I suppose really I have had such a *good* time, so full of change.

I slipped away from the League tonight to get up to town to meet Ruth and Mr Thompson. I met them at Liverpool St. and we went to a French Restaurant for dinner. Such a quaint place – it had once been a cellar but was now glorified with paint. A lady was playing the piano, the place was lighted by lanterns, the waitresses were French, also the dishes provided. The people present were very mixed – some suggested 'young rakes' to my mind, whilst a girl sitting opposite to me was smoking a cigar! We had a three course dinner.

We reached the theatre just as the play was about to commence – front seats in the dress circle. The play, *The Little Minister,* was delightful! On the way to the station we met a man who lives with Edward Carpenter – because of that I looked at him with interest! I like Mr Thompson very much – he looks quite forty, very trustworthy, and there is a gentleness about him which I like much.

Eva's Diary   Thursday, 10 September 1914
At lunch today Minna suggested if Ruth married Mr Thompson and went to America, we should all go too! During the afternoon the idea flashed into my mind – would it be possible to get a training as a teller of stories and make my way in America?

246

Aunt Edie and Aunt Emily went to the Picture Palace this evening, and Ruth and I sat quietly talking. I mentioned my idea – Ruth thought it splendid – the very thing, and thought she would be so willing to go if we would all go as well! We grew very excited picturing a new life.

Eva's Diary   Sunday, 13 September 1914

We all arose in high spirits this morning. After Minna had bathed Joan, the lodger brought *her* baby down and bathed it in the same water. The little baby had, I thought, a very distended stomach – the Mother said in the father's opinion this proved the child had had plenty to eat, but of course, it cannot be right. Minna tried to prove this, but the Mother replied *her* Mother had brought her children up that way. Minna pointed out that since the Mother referred to had lost *five* children this was scarcely a good argument. I could not help thinking what good work Minna is doing – it seemed like a Co-operative kitchen.

We talked a little of the really wonderful love that exists between Lily and Winnie: Winnie said she could not *possibly* love anyone better than Lily – then I said Joan seemed more *my* baby. How much I have experienced through her.

Then Minna and I talked a little of the possibility of two wives to one man – jealousy would be the stumbling block. Still Minna felt she could share a man with me – neither of us felt we could share a man with Lily or Ruth – I think because we recognise they are essentially lovers, and I suppose would in some way possess a decided advantage over us!

Eva's Diary   Thursday, 17 September 1914

I feel *angry* with the *Daily Mirror* – I consider it to be full of cheap patriotism! What a hero it makes of any stripling who shoots a German however treacherously. It has a crude notion of heroism!

After tea Aunt Emily and I set out on a visit to Mrs Taverner. Once there, of course, I had a long argument with Mr Taverner over the war – he gave me a horrible article by Maeterlinck to read, in which he said the subconscious mind of Germany could never be altered – we must be so pitiless that there would be no further need for pity. I felt terribly disappointed in Maeterlinck – we are always (for good and evil) increasing, influencing, the subconscious – what is possible to the individual is surely possible to the national!

As for being so pitiless, I feel this is a *ghastly* proposition and if we act so we shall be of all nations the most pitiable!

I ended by saying I would rather help and shelter a German even than a Belgian because I should feel in this way a more brotherly feeling would be encouraged between rival countries!

Ruth to Eva   17 September 1914
                                                       Whiteway Colony
                                                       Near Stroud, Glos.

My precious friend,

I cannot write thee the long outpouring I would like for I have an unavoidable heavy correspondence just now, but I must thank you for your helpful letter and tell you a little bit about myself.

Well, dear, I have become a new and interesting study to myself! I met Mr Thompson at Paddington and away we came! I could not describe my feelings. It seemed to me that the audacity of my propositions was amazing and I began to admire Mr Thompson's courage in so cheerfully submitting. I am more and more sure it was an inspiration which suggested this place to me, for it is a great thing to see persons in relation to their fellows. In this respect Mr Thompson has been a revelation to me and I cannot tell you how much I admire him. He has made himself quite at home, fetches and carries water, etc., is simply wonderful with the children, and has an astonishing fund of quiet and intelligent humour. Everyone likes him.

I am writing, seated at the window seat, with the most gorgeous sky all around – one of the loveliest I have ever seen. I should learn to paint if I lived here long.

I am glad you are finding out about the classes. How I wonder what *is* in front of us. You *must* come to America if I go, and somehow – somehow – I believe I am going.

I spent two sleepless nights dear, after a letter from Hugh – but even that is clearing up in my mind and I think he must come too and we form a trio – you know I believe in my bravest moments in the possibility of the impossible!

Dear, I love always to think of you – you are to me so much that is inspiring and beautiful. I must say goodbye now. With love right from the bottom of me. Always yours, Ruth.

Eva's Diary   Friday, 18 September 1914

A letter from Ruth – she seems very happy at Whiteway, and I really think it will all end in her marrying Mr Thompson. The idea of her union with Mr Jones has always seemed to me unwise and unsuitable.

I had a quarrel with Frost this afternoon over the war. Frost maintained *his* Mother was a patriot and willingly sent her sons to the war, but he supposed if *I* had any I would send them to *Church*. Very angrily I replied he had no right to sneer at my religion – I was as great a patriot as any woman, only my patriotism would take a different form – if I *had* sons I would send them to the street corners to teach peace, and into the firing line, not to destroy, but to save life, to rescue and tend the wounded! Finally, however, we had to laugh and shake hands over our difference.

Eva's Diary   Wednesday, 23 September 1914
'*Nine miles of dead and wounded being trampled into the ground*' was the news which greeted all readers this morning in *The Daily Citizen* – it filled me with horror – this war is hell let loose – one's very faith trembles. Oh! that the governments of all nations could be prevailed upon to make war *illegal*!!

We carried the news to Minna at lunch – she was aghast, and we grew very quiet as the consciousness of the awfulness of the war deepened.

Eva's Diary   Thursday, 24 September 1914
I met Ruth at Liverpool St. this evening, and we made our journey by way of the escalator to Lancaster Gate. Then came dinner at the Lancaster Hotel. Afterwards we spent a little time with Mr Thompson in a vast but pleasant drawing room. My last letter to Ruth was mentioned, and Mr Thompson enquired whether I was in the habit of forwarding other people's letters to my friend to read, as he had seen that done. He looked very keenly at Ruth and at me – we both felt very guilty as that is exactly what we are in the habit of doing. I suspect that Mr Thompson has a fund of knowledge of feminine ways, also that he is, in his quiet way, a keen observer.

We were not long in retiring. I shared a bedroom with Ruth, large enough for a family. Ruth had much to tell me, of her stay at Whiteway, etc. She told me she intended to complete her (next) year at Woodbrooke – that she had given Mr Jones every chance, but his lack of hope and courage had prevented him from taking same. She now believed it would be bad for him if she sacrificed her life to him, so she intended to go forward and test life. I could tell from this and from much she said that she will probably marry Mr Thompson next year. I am glad – he is a good man, and with him I think her happiness will be assured. Nevertheless, I laid me down with a heavy heart, for marriage with Mr Thompson must mean *America* for Ruth, and this time she made no reference to the possibility of my taking a journey there too, neither did she enquire as to my plans at all – so the future looked dark enough for me as to change of work! Miss O'Dell was perfectly right when she read my head – she said I relied too much upon the opinion of others. I must learn to find advice and encouragement within myself – must make my own plans, and take my own risks! This reliance upon the advice of others has become my great weakness!

Eva's Diary   Saturday, 26 September 1914
How strange it seemed to wake this morning in a West End Hotel, within a stone's throw of the great mansion where years ago I was for a week fourth housemaid! How delightful it was to walk down the wide, carpeted staircase to breakfast. Then came 'Goodbye' and a scamper off to Liverpool St. Station.

Work is *frightfully* slack at the office. It makes one wonder what the result will be if this continues!

Eva to Ruth   9 October 1914
There is no need for me to tell you how welcome your note was, as I wanted to know you had arrived safely.

I am still working in the city, my dear. However, I am at grips with the work, and dread and fear have departed – it is just 'want of confidence', you know, dearie, that is the plague of my life! I find the journeys, the bustle of London and the longer hours take away a good deal of freshness – still it is only for a time, and I am sure the experience is good for me!

The excitement of the war seems to stir London – enormous notices across the Mansion House – 'Citizens of London, we must have more men' and 'I rely upon the loyalty of my subjects in this hour of need, etc., The King'. Does this not suggest the seriousness of the situation? At Walthamstow the rooms below mine have been turned into recruiting offices, and the men are always up and down the stairs.

I asked the office boy what *he* thought of war. What do you think he said? That life would be so *dull* without, and that the whole of life and the world *turned* upon *war*! I felt a good deal amused at all this dear, and saddened too, for it is the military spirit, fostered and allowed to grow, which means the continuance of war.

Now for a confession – I went to the City of London College on Tuesday evening, and, my dear, before the first lesson was over, realised I had made a mistake. I cannot learn at such a place with my slow mind – it is nothing more or less than a great commercial centre – no individual attention – the teacher endeavouring to 'cram' as much as possible into the class. There is nothing for me to do but to plod patiently on at private lessons, watching and waiting.

Thank you dear for the lovely thoughts and wishes, I do not deserve them – but I know you understand how I long to be of real use. I think for me it is the duties and paths that *open up* that are *right*. I seem to fall to the ground when I plan and scheme. My arms around you dear. Eva.

Ruth to Eva   13 October 1914
My dear,
I should be studying this even, but I feel particularly restless and wishful to write to you. It was lovely to get your letter.

I am so sorry about the classes dear, but hardly surprised. You know Pitman's School was a revelation to me. A College, surely, should not be quite so obsessed with the commercial spirit.

Your news about the notices extended across the front of Mansion House made me shiver! People here seem grave and I should not be surprised if we are squeezing in some refugees before long. They are coming over in such numbers that it is difficult to find accommodation for them.

Our liveliest man student is leaving almost immediately. The Society of Friends is organising a body of people to go out to the most devastated areas to make them habitable again and this young man is a sanitary engineer and will therefore be a very valuable asset. We shall be sorry to lose him.

The days are very full, but it is so much easier and nicer beginning *at* the beginning and I feel in much better trim than formerly. I am enclosing a lecture programme so that you can see the extent of my studies. I have been elected as one of the students who form a Committee to manage things generally for the term. Then of course there is the Care Committee visiting.

What about our meeting, dear? For six Saturdays this term,

251

we Social students have to go into Birmingham to visit Slaughter Houses, Water Works etc. Could you come on a Friday evening?

Oh my dear, I would give a good deal to see you just this minute and should want to kiss you very specially. Your Ruth.

Eva's Diary   3 November 1914

Minna spoke today of Lily's plan that she look after house and children whilst Minna had the nursing training – I think it is a splendid idea.

This evening I went to tea with Lily at Stoke Newington – the journey reminded me of the many times I had been there to visit Ruth, and I felt again keenly the gap in my life which has come in her absence. Yet how full of gratitude I feel for the past – for the friendship which brought such richness and breadth into my life, and for the future – it has ever deeper joys for those who expect!

Lily and I chatted for some time – Lily telling me how she had grasped after knowledge, and felt she knew so little. She undervalues her powers. She then talked about her plan for helping Minna, saying that there would, of course, be *some* sacrifice in it – comfort and convenience which she would miss, but she felt it was a work which had come into her life and that she would have strength to do it. It would help if I still went into lunch, and if Aunt Edie came sometimes. Dear Lily – I believe a larger and fuller life will open out before her.

I feel rather anxious about the nerves of my legs – they pain me so – I get depressed about it all, and today have been more than usually conscious of discomfort.

Eva's Diary   Wednesday, 4 November 1914

The amazing news greeted us this morning that German war-ships had been within a few miles of Yarmouth, dropping bombs and mines which shook the windows of the homes. I had a talk about it all with Mr Cunningham: he talked in a much more reasonable way about the war. He spoke a great deal about *policy* – the policy of keeping nations ill friends so that 'the balance of power' might be maintained. I begin to feel I *hate* the words *'policy'* and *'diplomacy'* – why can government not be a question of *right*, not *policy* !

Eva's Diary   Saturday, 7 November 1914
Minna and children arrived just as I laid tea – it was so nice to
have them all. We talked a little of Ruth and her wish that Mr
Jones should go to America. Minna thought this a very unwise
plan – the change to married life is so great that she thinks for
the first year it would be better that Mr Jones should not be
near Ruth. I feel that Minna must be right, for I am sure she
speaks from her experience of marriage. I walked with Minna
to Lea Bridge Road – she was very impressed by the dim
lighting.

Eva's Diary   Thursday, 26 November 1914
Tea with Minna, as we had arranged to go to the Kents to
discuss plans for Minna's future. Minna said she does not mind
what she does, nursing, letting or shop-keeping. We hurried
home through the rain, and Minna persuaded me to spend the
night with her as the weather was so rough. I tucked in with
Winnie, but alas! not to sleep – I tossed the hours away, the
nerves of my legs aching, and sad thoughts flitting through my
mind.
   I thought of the keys of life which experience has yielded me
– keys which quickly open the doors for me now from sorrow to
joy. They are:

   Not to fight evil, but to *create love and beauty*
   Not renunciation, but *redemption*
   Not *doubt* but faith (*pessimism v optimism*)
   Not stagnation but *venture*
   Not facts but *symbols* !!

Eva's Diary   Friday, 27 November 1914
I felt almost too weary to get up and go to business this morning
after my wakeful night. However, Joan's bright little face was
peeping at me over the bedclothes, and I remembered work
waiting for me at the office.
   At lunch I rested in Minna's big chair, and wished that I might
remain there for some hours. Minna talked about certain
characters in certain books – she thought that I was like
Caroline in *Shirley* and possessed a forgiving nature – this
made me smile, as I often feel very *unforgiving*! I asked Minna if
she was satisfied with last night's arrangements – and she said
'Yes'.

253

This has been a day of depression – it has been difficult to feel the beauty and wonder of life, and light and love have seemed far off. On my way home this evening, I upbraided myself – I recalled my richness: Aunt Edie, Minna, Ruth and Miss Walmsley to love and love me; Mr James; my little baby Joan – and so many others. Why, I have a second home with Minna! When I reached home I found Aunt Edie so brisk and bright, my own spirit revived.

Eva's Diary   Saturday, 19 December 1914
I met Ruth at Liverpool Street – she looks so well and so full of vitality as usual. We talked over our coffee, but after separation it is always difficult in a short time to get below the surface! Ruth had much to tell me. Françoise has been reported in a newspaper as helping in a hospital at Lille and escaping in a butcher's cart through Mauberge, by way of Holland, Antwerp and Brussels!

Bessie Cannon has been tempted to form an alliance with a married man, who used the usual arguments about more women than men, and lessening the suffering for women, etc. Really sometimes such arguments appear to me to be evil masquerading as light! I am glad Bessie had the strength to resist!

Then there have been suggestions at Woodbrooke that a party of Quakers and Labour people should proceed to the seat of war – march between the opposing armies as a protest, and thus possibly end the fighting. I admire the courage, but doubt very much whether such sacrifices have an immediate effect. Differences of opinion on religion twixt the Quakers and Socialists, however, appear to have quite knocked this plan on the head – I thought this *very* funny!

We talked about the lady who is supposed to resemble me in appearance, Ruth says, because she has a *powerful nose*! Alas, my poor nose! And in disposition because she depreciates herself, and yet is very capable and masterful. Of course, Ruth tried to explain away anything not quite pleasant; but I could not help feeling secretly amused at this accidental peep into hidden thoughts. I should not be surprised if Ruth really *does* think me capable and masterful, etc.

It was so like old times, and so lovely to see Ruth!

When I reached the school, the League girls fell upon me in a body and absolutely tore my clothes off: we had a *glorious* evening.

254

Eva's Diary   Sunday, 20 December 1914

The service this evening was very beautiful. The choir sang special Xmas anthems. Mr James preached upon peace: in the midst of war, it is difficult to feel there are forces working for peace and for noble issues, yet, may we not hope for great things from the alliance of so many nations against what *is said to be* military despotism? Do we not find men of every class standing shoulder to shoulder in this great war – and Catholics, Anglicans and Freechurchmen, are sinking all differences of dogma that they may join in a great day of intercession!

Ruth to Eva   21 December 1914
                                        High Street, Bagshot

My dearest,

You have been in my thoughts so very, very much since Saturday. What a joy it was to see thee again! It seemed such a brief snatch at this time but we must have a much longer and fuller talk before I return to Woodbrooke again. I wish we *were* going to spend Xmas together somewhere!

I have been thinking of the lovely Easter we spent here together. Shall we try to have such another time this year?

I have been busy since getting home – dressing an Xmas tree, helping with a bran tub and serving in shop, besides performing household tasks and writing letters.

I have a selfish request to make, which I meant to have put forward on Saturday. Next term I am to take part in a debate at Woodbrooke on present methods of social service – both state and voluntary – debating whether they at all interfere with the liberty of the individual. I am expected to speak on the grounds that they *do*. Now do think of this dear and help me with some suggestions!

I shall think of you often during the holiday. How many Xmases has our friendship known? My thoughts run back to a year when you brought me a little card of your own making, which I have now somewhere – brown, with a church sketched in ink – and again the copy of Thomas à Kempis, in which I often turn up my favourite passage about the love that 'when sleeping, slumbereth not' etc. What wonderful development our lives have known! In looking back over the past year I see a time of noble love and service on your part which makes me even prouder of you than ever, and certainly even more humble before you.

Mother is urging me to go to bed, and as I am sleeping with her tonight and I know she is tired and anxious to get to bed herself, I will do as she suggests.

Goodnight, dear dear friend. Love me always as I shall love you. Ruth.

Eva's Diary   Tuesday, 29 December 1914

I said 'Goodbye' to Ruth this morning, after an all too brief time together – I shall not see her again until March. Our time together this Xmas vacation has been very unsatisfactory but must hope to make arrangements next holiday.

This evening passed so happily: we were *all* at home, and busy with needlework – Gertie has a number of toys to take over to Bow for the children's party. We discussed Sylvia Pankhurst a little. I think she must be such a lovable character. Gertie says she is always bringing in from the streets children, dogs, cats to be fed and cared for – in this she reminds me of Michael Fairless.

Such a number of pleasant things have happened today – a letter of love from Lily, and Mother sent 5/- by Gertie towards Minna's training. Mother's loving act and goodness touched me deeply – she has been trying to make it up to 10/- and I know what a sacrifice it all means, and what overcoming!

It has been very quiet at the office today, and I have missed Frost. I have felt burdened by life's many chains – but that will pass, I know – I shall come up again on the crest of a wave!

Eva's Diary   Wednesday, 6 January 1915

I have been reading to Minna today from Rev. J. Campbell upon the power of love, and Minna has read to me from Jerome K. Jerome upon 'the power of laughter'. She says I have so much more laughter in me, and seem much younger than when she first used to see me at the Conference – then I looked very quiet and serious. Yes, as Minna says, I have a big sense of humour, and I am so glad – it is a precious thing to possess! It was one of the gifts which came to me through pain – sometimes I think it was only after suffering acutely I knew what it was to laugh truly!

A free afternoon!! My work finished, I was able to go through my little address on 'Symbolism', write a letter etc., and enjoy my leisure.

The journey to Hoxton is always full of memories of Ruth,

now tinged with sadness for times that are gone! There was a good school and I think I got on remarkably well. As usual, at first I was inclined to be overawed by Ann Stevens [who was involved in running the Adult School], then I thought, 'I won't give way to this feeling, if the *school* is true to its *title*, its members will bear with imperfection!' Bearing this in mind, I managed to speak easily, and was pleased to notice the girls seemed interested; Ann made one or two slightly critical remarks.

Eva's Diary   Tuesday, 19 January 1915
Today I have read my first copy of *The Dreadnought*[3] and enjoyed it. I admire Sylvia's courage in referring to the ineffici-ency of rich and titled ladies as nurses after only a brief training. It is not fair either to the trained nurses or the soldiers that such women should be sent to hospitals on the front! I was *very* interested in Sylvia's articles on France.

Eva's Diary   Wednesday, 20 January 1915
At lunch today Minna said that she has made up her mind to go the the City of London Hospital for training – then we discussed ways and means, uniform etc.

Eva's Diary   Thursday, 28 January 1914
I found my dear Minna bright and brisk today with the prospect of hospital life opening out before her. As for Joan – it is almost impossible to hold her, she struggles so to get from one's arms to the ground.

A pleasant evening at home – I planned and carried through several tasks – worked at my child's frock: gave a lesson in shorthand to Edith, washed my head, wrote to Ruth and finished reading *The Nest of the Sparrowhawk*. This book has a repellent plot and gruesome ending. I shall not mind if this is the last I read of Baroness Orczy's romances.

Ruth to Eva   27 January 1914
My dearest,
I have just half an hour to spare for letter-writing, and you have my very first thought. I will try to give you a brief outline of my life since I last wrote.

We have been very busy here starting a wee club for our Care Committee children, so that we may get to know them better. It

257

is going to be a delightful venture. We have taken two rooms in the house where Miss Martin's friend Miss Randle lives, and we have furnished them very simply ourselves and made them wonderfully 'homey'. We have use of one scullery and gas stove and can hold little tea parties and have fine times generally, though the primary idea is to hold small classes on such subjects as History, Geography, Literature, etc.

I wonder if Miss Martin told you anything about her friend Miss Randle? She is such a mysterious looking being and makes me think sadly of the Odd Women. She nearly always wears *white*, is shod with sandals, and though her hair is a deep grey, has it tied back in her neck with a huge bow! She is tall, *very* thin and nervous looking – I often feel reminded of stories – you know the kind – where the bridegroom elect dies on the eve of the wedding and the bride lives in her wedding dress evermore. She lives with a woman friend, and was very pleased to have the children at the house – indeed, she was heard to say that no house is complete without children and a piano! I want to know about her, if that's not being unduly curious.

I dare not begin to tell you about the lecture today – instead I will tell you how we went over a Brass Factory and got thoroughly depressed. We saw men and girls working in dark, close rooms amidst most horrible smells and noises, and once more there rose up within me the old longing to understand – sufficiently to attack it – this unjust social order. The war seems thoroughly to have overshadowed every other thought in the minds of most people.

Thank you dear for the Folk Song book – I am to sing at a Mothers' Parlour! The debate in which I am to take part is not coming off for two to three weeks, but I hope you are going to tell me what *you* think on the matter.

I have had such a yearning for you lately – yet a little scribble brings considerable comfort and joy, does it not?

My deep, deep love to you dear – and a kiss! Ruth.

Eva's Diary   Friday, 29 January 1915
I have been reading the newspaper today. I feel so indignant at the suggestion that children should be taken from school and put to work on the land. If this is done, I can see many old battles for reform will have to be fought over again, and it is all because of this terrible war – to suit man's militarism! Also it is suggested women should work upon the land. So we may take a

258

share when the world is at war, but in time of peace we are not considered worthy of political freedom!

Eva's Diary   Monday, 1 February 1915
I had just begun my lunch and Minna was discussing the events of the weekend with me, when a knock came at the door and in walked Mr James. He called to return my book on 'Symbolism'. He said he saw no reason why everything should not be symbolised. He referred a good deal to the Roman Catholic religion, and with evident favour. He thought that one grew to see the very great value of *convention*. As I sat and listened I could not help feeling the great change in Mr James – the old, dear, warm personality is there, breaking through in flashes; but oh, the crust of formalism, which is growing up around him! I feel his development should have taken more the road of Whitman and Carpenter. Has he not a tendency to 'run an idea to death'? For instance, to symbolise everything would be wearisome. As to ritual – I love all that enriches and ennobles life, but it must be from a conscious desire and choice. I think if it were imposed on me I should feel stifled and only long to break loose from forms and ceremonies. I feel the time will come when Mr James will break away from Nonconformity. I felt very disturbed after parting from Mr James.

Ruth to Eva   6 February 1915
My dear Friend
I feel you will have been looking for a letter during the last day or two, but the Club has taken up a good deal of our time.

Are you seeing signs of Spring in London? Here we have snowdrops out and green things peeping up everywhere, whilst the song of the birds in the mornings is just lovely to hear! For myself the inward symptoms are unmistakeable – the same queer restlessness of mind and body that I know so well from past experience has begun to stir within me and I wonder how it is with you? Yet we remind ourselves that spring is fickle and that there may be snow and bitter cold before us yet. Our joy in the beauty of the new and sweet things will be dimmed this year.

Do you remember reading in the paper that a woman at a watchnight service when the clock struck twelve, called out, 'O God, end this war!' – it affected me so when I read it and I often find thoughts of her passing like an echo in my own brain.

You ask me how I am getting on with the lectures and which I like best. I am enjoying the lectures on Social Philosophy most of all, but they are very difficult and the idea of an exam fills me with terror.

I am finding the lectures on Industrial Legislation very hard – so much memorising of dates and facts necessary. I have six essays to write dear, so that if I only send a p.c. next week you will understand. They range in subject matter from the Law of Diminishing Returns in Economics to methods of settling Industrial Disputes, to a resumé of the Factory Acts since 1802! Also (do not laugh my dear), I have to sing at the Infirmary tomorrow afternoon! I no longer wonder that Emerson criticised our University methods and likened them to puffing out a balloon!

In my own peaceful room I am happy just now. I know what you mean so well dear, by the silences which come into one's life with these changes and I fear you will miss Minna terribly – but think of further ahead, when we may all be near each other again, working and loving with more intensity than before. Don't forget, dear, to keep Easter open!

I am sending you a heap of literature but I think you will be interested in this Union of Democratic Control. Does Mr James ever mention it?

Dear, I kiss you with all the feeling I would like you to know I have for you. Your friend, Ruth.

Eva's Diary   Friday, 19 February 1915

I found alterations going on at Minna's today – Horace whitewashing the garden wall and Minna has rearranged the bedrooms – in preparation, as Minna laughingly remarked, for 'the bride' – viz. Lily. I feel, however, really concerned about the house, and shall be glad when they can move – I went upstairs and the ceilings are stained with water, the doors will not shut, and the floors seemed crooked and rotten in places.

I am disturbed by the old longing to love and be loved – perhaps I feel the stirring of the approach of spring – I wonder if such love will ever thrill my life again?

Eva's Diary   Monday, 22 February 1915

Dr Shone's advice to me, 'a complete change of life', as a cure for neurasthenia, has been very much in my mind today, making me scheme and plan for the future. I discussed some of my plans with Minna, whom I found at work on her hospital aprons. She sent me away with comforting words.

My dearest one,

I am very conscious today of a strong heart-hunger for my friends and especially would I like a real *real* talk with thee!

I am sorry not to have written sooner but this week has been exceptionally full – as there is only another month between us and the exam. We had our first test exam on Tuesday morning but nobody came out very well. I think it was partly because the previous day was half-term holiday and we had a party in the evening and charades which needed a good deal of preparation during the day. I was in one scene, as 'Ophelia', and looked the part very well, I believe, in a nightgown tied round the middle and adorned all over with greenstuff and flowers. My hair was down of course and similarly ornamented so that you can imagine I looked mad enough to please even Shakespeare himself, but when the time came my heart failed me, and instead of behaving frantically and tearing my hair I just walked up and down once or twice like an animal in a cage, sang 'Hey non ninny'(!) instead of 'Hey non Nonny', tore up one or two sweet flowers, then fled. It was a horrible experience!

There is such a dearth of talent here that I am being pressed into all sorts of things. My singing at the Infirmary went off well.

Yesterday four of us went to Cradley Heath to see the Chainworkers and had a really wonderful time. Though the work is so hard there and the surroundings so bad, I felt I would rather work there, if need forced me, than in some of the factories we have visited, notably the Brass Works I mentioned in my last letter. The greatest evil of the chain trade is the low rate of wages paid but in the outhouses in which the women work there seemed such a spirit of friendly intercourse which almost always is lacking in factories. But oh, dear Eva, the whole district depressed me. It is of course situated in the Black Country and all around are great chimneys belching forth their awful smoke. I felt it was all a sacrifice upon the altar of greedy industrialism.

In the afternoons I go visiting and in this way am getting some insight into the working life of Birmingham. It is an ugly city.

The Social Philosophy lectures at the University are still to me as a breath of mountain air, but if I attempt to give you even a digest of the last two I shall be writing for another hour. I must just tell you this: the question of individuality came up and we agreed that the aim of progress is to make self-realisation – fullness of life – possible to *all*. We then saw that the tendency of modern times is to specialise, which narrows the functions of each one, and seems to be contrary to this ideal of progress. How are these facts to be reconciled? Professor Muirhead thinks the solution lies in our having a view of the Social *whole*, and entering into and sympathising with this. I agree with him, dear – it is what I used to say to myself in simpler language on especially dull days in my office life – but I think it is not a solvent for suffering until we all *see* this, consciously *feel* it, and *share* the burdens of life. How do you feel?

Now do try and tell me what you think about my debate, in your next letter, as it comes off on 1st March. My ideas are still jumbled. I shall lay stress on the fact that current social legislation maintains class distinctions and if my opponent says in reply that people have power through their voting capacity I shall try to show that it is not yet an equal power. The fundamental thing I believe to be knowledge and education, and until these are open in equal measure to all, as part of humanity's natural heritage, I believe social legislation to be prejudicial to the individual. When legislation is the *conscious* expression of the *whole* community, then it will be free from an element which at present makes most of it objectionable. How's that? All out of my own little head! Do give me some of *your* thoughts, which are always more profound than mine.

I must tell you that the result of the simmering which has for so long been going on in my mind is that I have determined to make my future work the effort to bring some light and happiness into the lives of Dad and Mother.

I am sending a pamphlet about the Fellowship of Reconciliation, which I am joining. I am wondering whether a branch could be started at your Chapel?

And now dear I am going to work hard for the next month, else I shall never get through, and may only send postcards. I shall think of you even more, if that is possible, and send you love currents.

Tell me when you next write how that leg is now? And if you have *quite* got rid of that cold? With a very big heart full of love dear. Your own friend, Ruth.

P.S. Could you let me have a p.c. with the quotation from Walt Whitman about 'The City of Friends'. Don't bother dear, if it means a hunt, but I feel I would like to wind up my part of the debate that way.

Eva's Diary   Monday, 15 March 1915
Lunch at Minna's – she seems so much brighter and better
since Lily came. Lily seemed a little worried I thought, telling
me not to get married – that there was a great deal of work to
be done in a home.

Eva's Diary   Thursday, 25 March 1915
At lunch today the house seemed strangely quiet and empty
with Minna ill at the Hospital and Lily visiting her.

The evening passed very quietly. Winnie came for her lesson,
then I sat on a stool reading and leaning against Aunt Edie's
knee. In this way I read in a desultory way a good deal of
Eldorado by Baroness Orczy – but I think I must be thoroughly
tired of her writing, for I cannot get interested in this book – it
seems but a repetition of *The Scarlet Pimpernel* and is at times
weakly sentimental. One wearies of such sentences as 'the
beautiful woman with great sad eyes fixed on the far distant
horizon' and 'her lovely face had in it a look of sublime self-
abnegation'!

Throughout the day I have been battling against anxiety and
depression, caused by the knowledge that Minna is ill, and by
the fact that Lily has gone to her whilst I must wait. Oh, how I
upbraid myself for these thoughts and feelings – I *am* glad
Minna has someone to be with her, and to love and care for her
– I know I shall conquer these unworthy feelings – it is
because I have been so much with Minna for the past year, and I
have tried to be some help and comfort to her. Now that
another has the *first* right – I suffer; sometimes I dare not look
into my heart for the pain there – I feel stranded. I have no one
in great need to devote myself to – yet I *do* give thanks for the
past deep and happy experiences. Oh, I feel sure strength will
come to me soon – strength to love and be strong and calm.

Eva's Diary   Friday, 26 March 1915
My first question when I went to lunch today was 'How is
Minna?' Lily said she seemed very unwell – could I go and see
her in the evening. I did not remain long after receiving
instructions how to get to the City of London Hospital. The
journey lay through crowded, sordid streets. I found Minna
better than I expected. She talked a good deal about the work
which is fearfully hard – no soap to wash the babies' clothes
with, much scrubbing and cleaning. Minna said the nurses all

263

seem hard, superficial women. Evidently nursing is not chosen by many as an *ideal*, but as a profession, by women of strong nerve rather than strong sympathies.

As for the patients – the poor things have a hard time. The nurses are not supposed to talk to them, but Minna has managed to speak to a few. One poor girl wept a good deal, and told Minna she was not married, but was so glad she had 'taken to the baby'. Another woman, because Minna helped her to sit up, said, 'Oh Nurse, I began to get better directly *you* came.'

In my mind the whole system of hospital work and training is wrong – it is hard and soulless. Nothing will convince me that nurses would not train better with less to do and opportunity for *real* study.

I think Minna was pleased to see me, though it was hard to tell, for she seemed listless with her illness; but she said we must never be parted. Yet when she said 'Goodbye' she said 'thank you for coming up dear,' which made me feel suddenly distant from her. Indeed I think this training will change her, and make her more self-reliant; she will look less for sympathy, and oh, I know I shall miss giving it.

I climbed on top of a tram crowded with rough men, laughing, talking and smoking, and finding a seat in a dark corner, sat and gazed into the streets, whilst burning tears kept falling. I seem *so* unstrung, and after seeing Minna my heart seems full to bursting.

Upon reaching home I hurried to bed. Gertie was so kind in many little ways, I felt very grateful to her.

Under all the pain I feel there is a strength growing which will surely uphold and save me – if only I could get rested and well nervously, I feel sure I should suffer less and gain the mastery. Now I am prey to unhappy memories, to doubt and to longing. My *trust* is evidently not as great as my *love*!

Eva's Diary   Wednesday, 31 March 1915
The League Social (*my* suggestion) was a great success this evening. Charades were much enjoyed – Doreen was really fine in her acting. I spurred myself to effort with the children this evening and feel I succeeded with them. Mrs Taverner came in – afterwards we went a little walk together, and she talked a great deal about her little plays. She is writing another, and said she *would* like to know Mr Taverner's opinion, but he is silent about them. She said she had found it so hard to launch out in

this way, because in the home she was always told she had nothing of the artist in her. I was so tired, and my thoughts scattered, that at this juncture I made a remark which would certainly not have escaped me otherwise: I said, 'Don't let them crush you – work on; *I* feel sure you have a gift to use for children.' Of course she would not have it that she was crushed – all the same, I feel that it *is* so!

The thought has come to me today that perhaps I do wrong to shrink from the work of a Superintendent. I feel that I am ill fitted for a leader in any way, yet lately the call to such work has come, not only from the League, but from Mr James with reference to a Women's Conference – what if such work is a new responsibility from which I should not shrink, but should strive to rise to the demand made? In the future I shall so regard the work, and do my best to make it a success!

Eva's Diary   Wednesday, 7 April 1915
It was so lovely to be with Ruth – my dear old friend. Ruth talked to me a little about Mr Thompson – she thinks he is treating her refusal to go to America just now as quite final – but I have hope that in time to come things will right themselves.

Ruth has arranged to write to Mr Grubb about Woodbrooke scholarships, whilst I am to write to the warden at the end of the week.

Lily gave me a letter to read today which she had received from Stanley. I thought it coldly and even unkindly written, and I could see Lily had been hurt by it, still she said she would write again. I cannot but question whether it is worth it – Lily gives too much; some men are blind – pearls scattered before them are wasted. What they need is a surgical operation.

Eva's Diary   Thursday, 8 April 1915
During my lunch hour today I seemed to meet 'just everyone' – first Miss Leith and her sister, then I ran twice into Mrs Taverner, and had not long settled to lunch when Minna came in, almost breathless, and with only twenty minutes to be with us. I was glad to see Minna looking so much brighter and better – she was full of her hospital experiences, and talked almost all the time very rapidly. A Doctor complimented her on her answers at the lectures. I hurried back to the office in a flutter of excitement over my friend – she looked so fine and grand in her

uniform that I felt quite timid before her – I feel that she is working nobly – she will grow to her full stature now!

I have read another 'war pamphlet' by Maude Royden. I think it very fine, but feel we *must* recognise that all people are not ready to see a nobler vision. Still that must not prevent those who *do* see from striving to realise their ideal, working for and preaching it day by day!

Eva's Diary   Saturday, 17 April 1915
A very busy time! I ran in and out of the shop, striving in the brief intervals to read a little of L. M. Rossetti's *Life of Mrs Shelley*. The book contains an outline of the lives of Mary Wollstonecraft, William Godwin and Percy Shelley – the Mother, Father and Husband of Mrs Shelley. How really *great* Mary Wollstonecraft must have been! William Godwin has never had any great attraction for me – he is too coldly calculating, too philosophical in his relationships – his ideal man does not excite me.

Eva's Diary   Sunday, 18 April 1915
The preliminary meeting of the Women's Conference: we were five in number, but so enthusiastic that I am full of hope that it will be a success. I had felt some difficulty about introducing myself as leader, as Mr James wishes, but this difficulty was quite overcome by those present voluntarily choosing me as leader. I early discovered how necessary it is for a leader to have plenty of tact, sympathy and patience, for different views and conflicting suggestions were made.

Later, we were just ready for Church when in came Minna, tired as usual, but overflowing with news about the hospital. Several of the patients have made her nice presents – a handbag, a brooch, a pair of scissors and a bunch of primroses.

Minna says the Matron and Doctors are so disagreeable – the Matron saying to a staff nurse who happened to rest her hand on her desk – 'How *dare* you place your hand on my desk – how *dare* you!' Whilst some of the doctors commence their lectures to the nurses with, 'Now my dear idiots!!' It *cannot* be necessary to be so offensive!

Eva's Diary   Monday, 19 April 1915
One of the delightful old days of leisure fell to my lot today. I conquered the work at the office, and was free to spend the

afternoon reading. I am so deeply interested in the life of Mrs Shelley; so full of romance and tragedy.

Home was in a nice pickle this evening, and I fell to spring cleaning the wash house – cleaned the paint, walls and windows, and was overflowing with ideas for our Women's Conference.

Ruth to Eva   18 April 1915

My very dear,

Thank you for your loving letter – it was *specially* welcome, for I have been getting very downcast about matters at home, but we will not dwell on that subject!

I am going back on Saturday and am sure to have my talk with Mr Wood [the warden of Woodbrooke] soon. His letter was very kindly, kindly written, so altogether I am very hopeful for you. I will write you the result as quickly as possible.

After that I shall not be coming to London again – for the sake of the expense entailed I am glad – but I *should* have liked another evening with you before I go.

On Thursday I went over to Farnborough, to see Eleanor Fairfax at the Orphanage. I arose quite early, walked in the delicious morning atmosphere to Camberley and finished the journey with a 6d motor bus ride. I found Eleanor and her assistant engaged on a formidable pile of mending, but was welcomed by Eleanor with great warmth. I was allowed to contribute to the work of mending, which was steadily pursued till 12.30, when the boys belonging to Eleanor's 'Cottage' trooped in to dinner, over which she presided with commendable zeal and expedition. Then she took me across to the staff dining room, where we had our own meal. I looked round the table, and dear, my blood was chilled: I do not think I have ever seen a more repellent set of women's faces and each one looked as though smiles were unknown! There was no attempt at friendly chatter, such as makes Woodbrooke meals so delightful – indeed, each Sister seemed hostile to the others. I told Eleanor how terrible it seems to me, and suggested she tries to warm the others up by inviting them to a cocoa party! No wonder she gets miserable and lonely.

After dinner we went for a long walk across the common and seemed all the time to be in the heart of military preparations. The beautiful common was disfigured all over by paraphernalia for mock battles – 'dugouts', barbed wire entanglements, mock forts, etc. – whilst aeroplanes whirled above our heads. Presently we got tired and sat down to rest on the grass, in a spot which commanded a very wide view, I should think miles – and before long we distinguished moving specks which proved to be soldiers, and gradually they developed into a mighty marching column, the like of which I have never seen before, and the sight weighted my head down with a sorrow I could hardly bear. As I came away home I longed more intensely than ever that light and strength may quickly dawn on all thoughtful people sufficient to remove this awful thing.

Eleanor looked much older, though very well, and she is now fighting out *her* battle dear, with maternal instinct and longings, and it has roused and stirred her greatly, though rather painfully. She longs so much for a child of her own flesh and blood and feels the time for this to happen to her is now almost gone. Her work at the Orphanage is so restricted by rules that it does not give her feelings in this direction all the space they need.

It is getting late dear so must say goodbye to you now. Give my love to Aunt Edie and tell her I hope she is not being scared by fear of aeroplanes and bombs!

With my fondest love to you and responding to your dear embrace. Ruth.

Eva's Diary   Tuesday, 20 April 1915
Owing to yesterday evening's exertions I overslept this morning and had a scramble to get to business. There I found Frost – it was so nice to see him again. He told me the firm had suffered but little through the war, that Miss Bone considered they had taken advantage of me in every way, first by substituting a bonus for an increase in salary, second by stopping the bonus owing to the war, and third by giving me Frost's work to do as well as my own.

Just after Frost had finished speaking, out came Mr Hazlegrove and informed me that I had used the telephone to the City *twice* yesterday, thus costing the firm *4d!!* Horrors! I felt inclined to point out that at present I am saving them considerably *over 4d* a week! It is such incidents which cast a bitter drop into one's cup – I must try however to rise above a rather sullen feeling which threatens to take possession of me after these experiences.

Kate came this evening and kindly commenced to make me a hat. We had much bright chatter – Kate said to Gertie she often wondered if our lives would ever be written about in a book, and how *interesting* they would be.

I am surprised at the revelations made about Sylvia Pankhurst and Bow – Gertie very truly remarked, 'Nothing seems ideal when you get near to it.' Well, one just has to live to create the ideal; if we could *find* it, we might express approval, but I doubt if we should experience happiness.

Eva's Diary   Wednesday, 22 April 1915
I managed to get through a little shopping in my lunch hour today, so I had only a little time to spend with Lily. I am afraid she has battles before her with the two girls – she complained of Edith's 'withering glance' – and Winnie remarked at break-fast, 'We shall have to get a microscope soon to see the bacon', and 'I don't want it always pushed down my throat what I *shall* have to go through!' Poor Lily, she is doing her very best, I know, to economise.

At tea Edith and Winnie were all excitement – during their Mother's absence they have found *sweethearts*.

Eva's Diary   Thursday, 23 April 1915
We really had a very nice home evening tonight. Mr Taverner came, also Una, Nelly and Kate. I played, Gertie gave two selections on the violin and Kate played and sang some 'rag-time'.

This afternoon I finished reading *The Life of Mrs Shelley*; as I read it seemed to me that never before had I realised the *very* real companionship and friendship that a book can give. How specially helpful biographies are – helping one to bear one's own troubles bravely, and to more fully enjoy all that life has to offer of good.

Eva's Diary   Friday, 24 April 1915
Lily told me today that Edith had informed Horace she 'did not intend to mind Joan *every* evening so that Lily could go out!' Lily complained of Edith and Winnie's wasteful habits and lack of modesty. I *do* feel that the girls fail to appreciate all that Lily has done and is doing for them. On the other hand, I think there is a *little* to be said for the fact that Lily has lived so long with an elderly lady and is very fond of giving advice, and that is very trying to young girls.

Gertie went to the Social this evening, and I had a *very* busy time with the business – in and out to a seemingly never-ending stream of customers.

At nine o'clock there was a sudden cessation of customers so that I was able to sit down and commence *Eliza Brightwen, The Life of a Naturalist.* I was so charmed that I read on and on until 11.30 pm The fact that Eliza Brightwen commenced at *60* years of age to write her books encouraged me greatly – if one at that age could be so painstaking and enthusiastic, surely *I* at *32* ought to be overflowing with energy and hope.

Ruth to Eva   Tuesday, [28] April 1915
                                                      Woodbrooke

My dearest,

I have about 10 minutes before post and a lecture, but have news and feel I must scribble it off *at once*.

I have just had my talk with Mr Wood and he seems delighted at the thought of you coming here. He says they are practically certain to give you a half scholarship for the whole year and probably *more*, though this must not be counted on and is not likely to amount to the whole £60. He thinks the best course would be to bring the matter up at the next Bursary Committee and then he will write to you, so I expect you had better wait a little while. In the meantime dear, get well and strong and begin to develop a strong interest in social matters! I will advise you what books to read in preparation soon, if you would like me to.

I am wondering about Aunt Edie dear. What will she do without you? Are you sure she will be willing for you to come here? Think the whole thing out *carefully*.

My dearest love – I may not write more now. Ruth.

P.S. Mr Wood only asked if you would be as capable of tackling the Social Course as I have been. I told him you had *better* – if a *trifle* slower – brains – so you must come and do me credit!

Eva to Ruth   3 May 1915
My own dear,

I have been *wanting*, and wanting to write to you, but have had a load of work and excitement which prevented me doing so until today.

Dearie, your news about Woodbrooke seems like some beautiful dream – I remember you thought in the same way when the change first came to you. Not that I imagine it all idealistic – only, dear, even the *possibility* of this change and opportunity for growth for *me* seems *miraculous*! It does indeed! If the Committee *do* decide to grant me a Bursary – it will be to me a deeply sacred trust, and you know Ruth, my best efforts would go to the work. I have really prayed, dear, about this – that I may *desire* only in order to *give* more richly.

Aunt Edie is delighted at the thought of this change for me. I hope Gertie will remain with her if I go, and if not, I am sorry to say Aunt Emily has lost her situation with the artist Mr Tonks, and I should not be surprised if in the end she came again to us.

About my *brains* ! How *dare* you assert they are *better* than your own! Nothing of the kind – you have always been able to give me points and to open new vistas of thought!

Yesterday seemed a momentous day in my life. I could hardly explain why, but for one thing my Women's Conference is 'in swing' at last – our third meeting yesterday. At the first we numbered *5*, the second *10*, and the third *11*; so I am very hopeful. We intend to give a social this month. I was only half way through the life of Margaret MacDonald[4] yesterday when it was time to stop. Mrs Campbell was present and made the time deeply interesting by the personal touches she was able to give by her friendship with M.M.

Then in the evening, Mr James stated that a Women's Class had been formed, and that the Church had called me to its leadership and responsibility. If I *do* leave here in October, it will be a great joy to me to do what I can until then.

Throughout today I have been thinking of the wondrous 'ball of life' at your feet dear, and at mine – longing to live more worthily – to make pain and loneliness yield a rich harvest.

My arms around you dear, and the depths of my love.

Your ever loving Eva.

Eva's Diary   Sunday, 9 May 1915

I have felt such a 'loneliness of soul' lately – I miss Ruth and Minna – I shall be *so* glad when both are home again. If I am to take flight this Autumn I want to spend the summer in binding my friends more closely to me.

Conference seemed such a success today – we numbered 12. I think I spoke with greater ease than formerly – a thrill of horror went round when I mentioned the sweated workers, their work and their earnings, whilst some women began to weep at the reference to Margaret's sorrow over the loss of her child. I

271

felt very touched and almost broke down too. Mrs Campbell was again a great asset and told us much that was interesting during the discussion. She said that M.M. visited *18* public houses in each of which she sat drinking ginger beer and studying the conditions under which barmaids work. She was very indifferent to dress and once appeared in a costume she had had for *16* years. An Indian remarked to Mrs Campbell, 'We admire and respect Mr M, but we adore Mrs M.' She was the first Englishwoman to make Indian women feel they were sisters. Upon one occasion she had come from a bed of illness to speak at a meeting. How I wish she had for the world's sake treasured her health more, that we might now have had her with us!

Mr James dealt with Israel Zangwill's play *The Melting Pot*: there a young Jew and a Russian girl grow to love one another, when suddenly the Jew discovers that the father of his betrothed was the man who led to the arrest of his father and mother in far-off Poland. Racial hatred and personal enmity assert themselves and all threatens to end in disaster, but love at last again prevails.

Then Mr James referred to the National situation. We are in the Melting Pot – the progress of science, telephone, electricity, commerce, travel, have brought the world practically under one roof; but this kind of progress will never unify humanity. The progress of love and co-operation are needed to weld the world with strong bonds. Only a universal religion will solve our problem – but we cannot impose upon others our creed, our dogmas – no, it must be the religion of love which must unite all.

Ruth to Eva   9 May 1915
My dearest Eva,
Your last letter was exceedingly beautiful. I rejoice with you over the Conference and feel guilty as a recollection of discouraging you from taking it up flashed through my mind. But you do know my reason was only a very natural anxiety lest you should overtax yourself. (By the way, do not omit from your next letter a full and faithful account of your present *physical* condition. How are those legs, etc., etc.?)

Then your summary of Mr James' sermon came to me with vivid suggestions. There is, and will be, such need dear, for faith in God and *living*, with such intense misery about us, and the social workers seem to me to have a unique opportunity of doing high missionary work in this direction. Perhaps one day you and I will be living out a dream together!

I am almost afraid to tell you that I feel harassed in regard to the approaching exams, for you may take fright! I have had rather more than I anticipated put on my shoulders by being elected Chairman of the Students' Committee for this term. It is an honour of course, and I am very pleased – but it has left me rather behind with my studies. You would be surprised to hear me in my official capacity, presiding at Students' meetings. I wonder at myself! In such ways the life here is really doing wonders for me.

I have been writing letters today about posts and I am making enquiries in several directions hoping something comes along for me in London. Bessie has gone to Newcastle to organise a big girls' club there for an armament manufacturer's – I am sorry she attempted such a thing for such a firm. Her last letter told of hideous accidents frequently happening, and made us feel she must not stop here.

Shall I tell you a little incident which happened to me last week, exciting beyond words? You will remember Mr Brown gave us a topic on which to write an essay during the Vacation. I felt in despair of getting anything done at home, as you know, but one evening dashed off a very stupid composition, with Mother talking at the end of the table. Judge my amazement then – sharer of all my experiences – when Mr Brown said he thought I had a gift for speaking and writing and should think out a way of using it! Furthermore he asked me to adapt the said essay into an article for a Friends' journal in which he has some responsibility! I am full of the thought that if they think *I* have a little gift, what will they think of *you*?

I have told Miss Kelman, the organiser of our practical work, of the possibility of your coming here; of course, your Girls' League and Conference will count for a good deal. I feel I have scarcely *begun* to write to you, but time proves otherwise, and I must draw to a speedy close. It is very lovely just now – nature's beauty is exquisite and people are kind – indeed, if it were not for the war, life would seem most rich!

A warm kiss to you dear one, and *tremendous* love.

Your own friend, Ruth.

Eva's Diary   Wednesday, 12 May 1915
It was really delightful at League tonight. Then came the
Committee meeting at which several of my points were carried.
I called at Lily's before going home – she and Edith were
seated at supper with very glum faces. I cannot imagine how
things have got into quite such a bad state. Lily *will* make the
mistake of talking *at* the girls. I remarked tonight how difficult it
had been to get discipline amongst the League girls, and Lily at
once said with marked emphasis, 'I *know* it has been dear, *very*,
very difficult.'

On my way home I ran into Nellie and Brew. The rioters are
out tonight looting the shops of German people. Oh! for a
working faith and movement which shall reconcile *all* nations,
which shall be led by *love* and not by *force* to co-operation and
reconstruction!

Eva's Diary   Thursday, 13 May 1915
Gertie arrived in great excitement over the East End riots –
and convinced that our house stood in danger of an attack! She
had seen people hurrying from looted houses carrying cornice
poles, overmantels etc., one woman remarking, 'I ain't half got
a lovely home now!' Another woman was dragging a sack of
flour through the wet streets. How senseless to wreak vengeance
upon the innocent.

Eva's Diary   Friday, 28 May 1915
Today I have read Longfellow's poems on slavery. Further I
read an article upon the limitation of families – matter for
grave thought. Are we wise to plead for prevention – to spend
our strength upon palliative? If, as stated, frequent sexual
intercourse is made necessary by the highly flavoured food we
eat, why not work for food reform? If a small family is made
necessary by financial conditions which prevent proper care of
the woman's health, why not clamour for adequate pay for
adequate work? Yet I feel the urgent need for the *present!*

Returning again to Aunt Emily's letter (she is very unhappy
and has no work or money) – it made me think seriously, for I
too grow older every day. If I go to Woodbrooke it will be a
venture – and *after* Woodbrooke? Will the world give me 'the
cold shoulder' I wonder?

Eva's Diary   Monday, 31 May 1915
Tonight after we had retired, we were soon aroused by 'boom,
boom, boom': nearer and nearer came the sound, until it
seemed a road or two away – then we sprang out of bed to go to
Gertie, but met her in the kitchen on the way to us – looking
out of the window she had seen what must have been a bomb
flash through the air. We dressed in the dark and I must confess
I was trembling in every limb although I tried to be calm and
quiet. Aunt Edie and I went to the door – some neighbours
were in the street, and policemen were putting all street lamps
out – the darkness was intense. At last we came indoors, made
a bed on the floor in the kitchen and all slept (or tried to sleep)
together in our clothes. It was a nightmare of a night, and it was
a relief when morning broke.

Eva's Diary   Tuesday, 1 June 1915
Aunt Edie went out this morning to see what damage had been
done. The Zeppelins must have passed over our heads – a few
roads away eight houses had their windows shattered. We all felt
very upset and disturbed by the events of the night.
   During the morning Aunt Edie and I walked over to see
Minna. Minna and Lily were busy washing – they were
surprised to hear about the raid. Minna made me laugh by
falling on her knees and imploring the powers that we might be
together always whatever might happen – she has had her
photo taken in her nurse's uniform and looks a picture.
   I have commenced reading *The Three Brothers* by Eden
Philpotts. I am interested to find that the three brothers are
three old men – it is seldom that romance centres upon the
aged. I think it is a good idea when novelists make age
interesting and poverty rather than youth and wealth.

Eva's Diary   Thursday, 3 June 1915
Minna and Lily accompanied me to Yardley Hill – we had such
a splendid time. The day was fine but dull, the country wide and
hilly. We had tea and fresh eggs on the hillside – a cat, a cock
and some hens came to share it with us. Some young bulls and
cows also gave us a passing glance. After tea we read a little
Ruskin and laughed heartily over his inconsistent and rather
dogmatic reasoning. Then we walked through the woods gathering wild flowers and talking of Shelley – of his love of nature,
the heart that had beaten so passionately in life! When alone,

275

Minna told me she made the girls beg Lily's pardon, and all were reconciled now, but she found Lily very hard to live with – so brittle and dogmatic – will not let Minna have her own way in anything.

Minna was *so* irresistible, full of good spirits; we sang hymns and songs until the sun sank, a deep orange in a grey sky. Minna said to me 'Oh, I *do* love you dear,' so *my* heart was full – life seemed well worth living with so much joy and nature – in spite of very real suffering and terror.

Ruth to Eva   11 June 1915

I have been just *aching* to sit down and write to you, my own, and this is my first real opportunity.

I am very thankful the exams are over. Some people meet them with all the zest of battle, but for me they mean actual physical and mental torture. After the first one I was foolish enough to shut myself up and weep. We have already heard the result of the Economics exam which, along with Social Philosophy, is reckoned as the stiffest of the year. Judge my absolute amazement dear, on learning that I have come out on top! I really cannot believe it *yet*. But the fact is that I have been gaining confidence all along and have done better with each exam. Little successes by the way have done a great deal towards spurring me on. Everyone seems very pleased and congratulations have been sweet. I am glad, dear, not so much for my own sake, but because I feel such little triumphs as mine may do much towards vindicating the intelligence of those who have not had many opportunities – you will, I know, see what I mean.

Later: Since writing the above I have taken another step towards emancipation from shyness and self-consciousness. I had to propose a toast at lunch today on behalf of the students, for our Economics lecturer, who is off to France to do War Relief work. It was rather an ordeal as the tables were thronged with Woodbrooke Councillors, but I have grown fond of our little man and this helped me to rise to the occasion. A propos the Council, dear, I expect your destiny is being discussed!

With this very disturbing item of news off my mind let me say how glad your letter of last week made me. All your revelling in the open air and the delightful expansion you were feeling, I know so well. When I first came here the very mooing of cows and clucking amd crowing of chicks filled me with ecstasy! I hope your confinement in that ugly little office is only for a short time!

As to the Conference dear, I will certainly come if I can. I should like to speak on the following subject: 'Is War necessary to progress?' and I will try to make it really *intensive*.

I wonder whether Mr James or any of the Chapel folk have yet evinced an interest either in the Union of Democratic Control, or the Fellowship of Reconciliation? I went to a very inspiring meeting of the Fellowship in town last Friday. The movement seems to be making headway in this neighbourhood. A very interesting Church of England clergyman took the chair and told us a little of the struggle his step had cost him as the only male member of his family who was standing apart from the war party. He was so honest and refreshing that my heart went out to him.

I may not write more dear, for I am due at a First Aid lecture in a few minutes, as there will be an exam for it shortly.

I really must say goodbye to you for a little while. With my very, very fond love, dear friend. Ruth.

Eva's Diary   Saturday, 3 July 1915
A quiet day – I sat in the garden in the afternoon writing to Ruth and reading. In the evening I went to Minna's to stay the night. It was sweet to be together, but a melancholy fell upon me and in bed in the darkness after Minna had fallen asleep I could not help weeping a little. I felt that I stood upon the verge of a new life full perhaps of greater opportunities and possibilities, but Oh, the wrench to take the step into that new life – but in my soul I hail the new possibilities and bless them!

Eva's Diary   Friday, 9 July 1915
I went to tea with Minna. Walked to Shernhall in the evening, enjoyed the sunshine and trees. Minna was very quiet during the evening. I told her I felt sure she worried and she admitted that she felt troubled over Lily, who did not seem happy. They did not seem able to talk together now as formerly. Minna wept a little and leaned against me. In bed Minna said she wanted to give me a ring if I went to Woodbrooke – I felt so happy then and ashamed of former feelings – it is not the *ring* really, but it is such a symbol of *love*. I felt *so* close to Minna tonight, and our love so deep and precious!

277

Eva's Diary   Tuesday, 3 August 1915

It was good to be at my old Walthamstow post this morning, after a fortnight's 'hard labour' in the City! Mr Cunningham said he was glad to see me back, and that he had missed me very much. This remark gave me quite a dreadful pang when I thought of the revelation I had in store for him!

Woodbrooke was the great topic of conversation at lunch today. Lily said she believed I would end by going as a missionary to Timbuctoo – Gertie has said she would miss me, and Minna said she did not believe I would settle in Walthamstow again, but that the whole course of my life would be altered – she thought it quite possible that I would one day go to America. Well, my heart has been bubbling and singing throughout the day, but there is a deep undercurrent of sadness, and unwillingness to break from familiar scenes and ties.

Eva's Diary   Friday, 6 August 1915

My thoughts today have been not only of the future but of the past – I wish I had loved people more truly and worked more thoroughly. It reminds me of the boy in Dickens' *Our Mutual Friend* who, upon the death of his grandmother, wished he had turned the mangle better for her, and, as Dickens remarks, at such times we all wish we had turned our respective mangles better.

Eva's Diary   Sunday, 8 August 1915

This has been such a happy day – I am afraid I began it in rather a frivolous manner, talking much about dress, and trying on various articles, suggesting alterations which would make the same wearable in my new life.

Then I settled down to the study of my book on Economic Organisation. I found it so fascinating, and when I read of the evictions by lords of manors of their tenants, in order that the land might be reclaimed and used for sheep farming – the people turned away to 'live miserably' – my heart ached. I felt what very real wrongs the poor have compared with the rich, and hoped to endeavour to right some of the wrongs of the world.

We went over to Minna's to tea – the tea table was a picture, and Joan so loving to me throughout the meal.

Eva's Diary   Monday, 9 August 1915

This morning I told Mr Cunningham of my new prospects – I

278

think it was a great surprise to him. He looked at the books on Woodbrooke, and said he felt it would be a splendid thing for me, and that it would be selfish of him to try and dissuade me, although he did not know what the firm would do, as it would be very difficult to fill my place. I feel an inconsistent creature, and I cannot help laughing at myself, but he did not seem *grieved* enough to satisfy me.

Eva's Diary   10 August 1915

Mr Cunningham again opened up the subject of my leaving this morning. He thought typewriting so monotonous – he had wished to see me settled at work with more scope than his office could offer. He had sometimes wondered why I had not launched out. He also remarked that Miss Bone thought I had been very 'wide-awake' or 'lucky'. I saw at once how it had appeared in the eyes of the City folk – 'That *quiet* Miss Slawson – yet she had her eyes open for her own interest!!'

I do not think Minna looks well, and she seems so quiet – I wonder if she is feeling the thought of our approaching separation?

I met Ruth this evening at Liverpool St. and after tea we had a fine ride on top of an omnibus to Hyde Park. We walked and rested in the Park – I enjoyed the space, the trees, and beds of lovely flowers, especially a bed of lilies!

Ruth had much to tell me – she is staying with Françoise in a great house almost destitute of furniture and yet comfortable. Françoise had a most thrilling time in France, nursing the wounded German soldiers, sometimes she was on her feet 40 hours at a stretch. She only got back by travelling with a Dutch Jew trader, and passing as his wife – she found the position exceedingly trying, as the Jew was very familiar.

Ruth's affairs are still in abeyance – she has written again to Mr Thompson, and is awaiting his answer.

I have been wondering today whether in the past I have been too patient – too meek. Mr Cunningham's remarks and the adventures of Ruth and Françoise have led me to these thoughts. Have I been too content with the by-paths of life and with bad conditions? I *will* try to expand and improve!

Eva's Diary   Friday, 27 August 1915

Today I have been studying the subject of food values, and although not dealt with from the point of view of vegetarianism,

I certainly think that it contains a good argument for the vegetarian, for *meat* is held to be *less nutritious* than many other foods. I am surprised to read of the value of *cheeses* as a food! When I think now of the ILP meetings, I blush to think of the ignorance in our midst on these important questions. How often we spoke publicly upon subjects which we understood but little.

Eva's Diary   Sunday, 29 August 1915
This evening Mr James said that he wanted a long talk with me, and that I must come to his house one evening. He said that his feeling for me had been of a special nature – more like that of a brother for a sister – he had always felt he could come and tell me *everything*. He wished there had been more opportunity for our friendship – to meet and to know me – now that I was going he felt all this. I felt overwhelmed with gratitude for the gift of this noble friendship. I spent the night in a state of ecstasy.

Eva's Diary   Friday, 3 September 1915
By the last post came notes from Ruth asking if she could come and stay with me – evidently she is dreadfully unhappy, and she has decided *not* to go to America. I wrote at once telling her to come. I feel anxious about her – something has happened, I feel sure.

Eva's Diary   Monday, 6 September 1915
I met Ruth this evening at Liverpool Street – it was glorious to be with her again, but I thought she looked tired and over-strained. We walked and talked as usual. Ruth is in great anxiety about her Father and Mother. Her Mother is far from well, and her Father's mental condition seems well nigh hopeless. She has cabled to America that she cannot go, although she had received a fine letter from Mr Thompson inviting her to become his sister's guest until she felt she cared enough to marry him. I feel that this is not the end – that Mr Thompson will not pass out of Ruth's life, but that one day she *will* go to America.

Eva's Diary   Thursday, 16 September 1915
How different it all seems at Minna's now! The lunch hours pass without the old comforting chats and times together. Lily seems so disappointed in the life, and is either very sharp, or very quiet, whilst Minna looks ill and distraught. There seems to be a

280

barrier just now between myself and Minna – I think because she is so unhappy. I wish I could go away feeling that all was well. I have longed for Minna today in quite the old way.

Eva's Diary   Sunday, 19 September 1915

A quiet time at Minna's – we talked about our idea of heaven; Lily hoped it would be a place with nothing to do and plenty of beautiful music. Minna asked me what I would like Heaven to be like. I said I never really thought about it or believed there was such a place, but rather a state; but I hoped for loving intercourse and comradeship – communion with kindred minds. It seemed to me it would be a great thing to talk with George Eliot! From this subject we drifted to friendship generally – Minna said her great weakness was being able to love the few, feeling indifferent to the many. She wondered if there was not also a great danger of trying to love too widely – desire for appreciation and popularity could so easily be at the root of it. I think Minna is right in one sense, but everything depends upon the motive – the ideal; if it is to spread comradeship and break down barriers that we try to love widely, I think we are right; but always a motive, an ideal, needs watching and cleansing.

I came away feeling *so deeply* my need of humility – longings too deep for words were in my heart – that I might be kept from falling into the snares that all ideal brings with it. Oh! I longed that I might grow in depth and *patient* love with each day.

10

'Better Fitted for the Battle of Life'
August 1915–April 1916

The roles of Eva and Ruth were reversed when Eva went to Woodbrooke and Ruth returned to London. Eva was at last experiencing that much longed for 'growth and expansion' while Ruth was feeling isolated and low in spirits. After gaining so much confidence at Woodbrooke, Ruth found it hard to establish a new life away from its supportive community, especially when faced with the realities of wartime life in London. She was soon 'pressed in upon' by familiar home troubles, which caused her a great deal of anxiety.

In October her father's mental condition was pronounced 'utterly hopeless' and Ruth took him to a sanatorium, and helped settle her mother in yet another home with a small business attached to it. She was also depressed by the fact that Hugh had enlisted, by having no permanent home and by her search for work. She managed to find temporary jobs – a week in the offices of the Friendship of Reconciliation in Red Lion Square – and some work for the Friends' Committee for Distressed Aliens (helping war refugees) which seemed to be a 'noble and splendid thing, but the sheerest piece of drudgery' she had ever known. She had interviews with organisations ranging from the Fabian Society to the YMCA, and hoped 'to find a safe anchorage on the happy medium ground between these two'. David Thompson continued to offer financial help in an attempt to encourage her to write, but she was 'not sure how to set about things'. In November she accepted a job as Welfare Worker at the Rowntree's Factory in York, which indicated that her capabilities for social work were highly rated.

Paid welfare posts had existed in factories for some years, and at the time of Ruth's appointment there was much debate as to whose interests they most served – the factory owners' or the workers'. In the case of a philanthropic firm like Rowntree's, Ruth believed that the job was intended (as she wrote in an article to the Daily News *in May 1917) to 'bridge the gulf between employers and their workpeople ... build up a sense of industrial co-operation ... and investigate working conditions in sympathy with the principles of trade unionism'. It was some time, however, before Ruth felt her work at Rowntree's to be effective.*

At Woodbrooke Eva gradually adapted to her new life. Less used to socialising than Ruth, and more intimidated by the college atmosphere, she was sometimes 'tired and bewildered by the people and by constant listening'. Academic work did not come easily to Eva and she failed the first test exams. By February with an increasing sense of optimism, she wrote 'everything is becoming clear to me – subjects are linking up – I feel I have really started work!' With her full programme, Eva found her diary was 'slowly but steadily going to the wall' (as Ruth's had) and she made only a few brief notes. She and Ruth continued a close correspondence, feeling the effects of their ongoing separation, and anticipating the time when they would be living and working together.

Eva to Ruth   7 November 1915
                                                                              Woodbrooke

My own dear,
I am sitting in Miss Albright's beautiful little drawing room – it is Sunday afternoon and some of the party have retired to rest, but a few remain here, writing letters or looking at books.

I feel, dearest, it is so long since I have sent you anything like a coherent letter, but I know that you will understand the sensation of pleasant bewilderment which possesses one during the first few weeks of life at Woodbrooke.

In spite of your warnings, dear, when once I arrived, I felt convinced that everyone was tremendously clever, and that I had much to do to make headway. I still feel those around me are more *accustomed* to college life, and there really are some clever people here this term. I am anxious dearie, for your sake, and because of everyone's kindness, not to disgrace myself, but the new-ness has been a little against me. Also, I think the year's study will be even fuller than usual, as three exams are to be given at the end of this term.

A Women's Afternoon Meeting is to be started soon, at which

Social Students will have practice in speaking, and then there are the extra household duties.

I find Industrial History fascinating, and am interested in Sanitation, and feel the importance of it – but Local Government I fear I am very stupid over, and I feel quite afraid to receive my first paper on it, back from Mr Cunnison.

I have not, as yet, formed any friendship – but am just friendly in a general way. I have felt it rather a difficulty dear, such a *big* pull to be much with people and to be very sociable, and yet I feel so much depends upon my earnest effort – it would mean a great deal to me, however, if I could feel some special bond. I am so very happy in the Woodbrooke life, dear, and feel it is doing me so much good in *every* way. It is indeed a *rich* experience which you have helped me to share.

There is a lady here, a Miss Sunderland who is very keen upon my becoming a Deaconess – she tells me they are *born* and not *made,* and she is convinced that I am a *born* Deaconess. I do not think I *am* cut out for a Deaconess – I would like to *harmonise* life, not cut sections off. The more I learn at Woodbrooke, I feel I would like work combining the religious and the social, but of course everything must be in abeyance for some months.

I turn to your own dear letter. My heart went out to you when I read of your father – this seems such a cruel time for you. If only I could be near to share it with you – but I do share it with you in spirit at least.

I feel anxious about your work – the hours seem too long. Have you thought any further about Mr Thompson's suggestion? I really think you should, Ruth. I feel sure it is not just the desire to help you which prompts him – he recognises that you can write and wishes to help you along that line. I am certain it is work you are fitted for and can do; give it earnest consideration, dear, – don't let any imaginary difficulty stand in your way.

I am so grieved about Mr Jones – I know, dearie, what a pain this will be to you: it is one of the unexpected things which shake one's faith.

When I think of Christmas time dearie, my heart leaps forward to meet you. I think I shall work much better during this coming half term – it has taken me until the present to adapt myself to my very changed life.

My heart's life, dear, with a strong desire to be with you.

Your ever loving Eva.

13 November 1915
40 Granville Road
Welling, Kent

My dear one,

I did badly want to send you a note for Sunday but I have been almost distracted these last few days. Mother is rushing all over London in search of a business. I urged her to give up the idea until the Spring, and suggested that we took up a little place together, thinking that she could there nurse up her shaken nerves. But her heart is set on it. We also came to the conclusion that the Sanatorium is doing my father more harm than good. We have decided to let him remain there for a month, and in the meantime Mother hopes to find another home. Today she has seen a business at Wood Green and seems very excited about it. I do not like the sound of it at all, but I expect she will have her way and take it if possible. But if the seller is speaking the truth, it is, in Mother's words, 'a little gold mine', and she feels too poor and harassed to consider any other point of view.

I have found it well nigh impossible to concentrate on my search for work. I have written to heaps of societies and people, which I hope is seed sown to good purpose, but sometimes I am tempted to lose heart. Most days I get to the library and scan the papers, but there is little doubt that competition for posts in London is very keen.

With regard to Mr Thompson's offer, I have read his letter many times and it always renews my courage, but I feel not quite sure how to set about things, and also positively certain that I should never *earn* (in the real sense) what he would pay me. I feel so pressed-in upon by home troubles that sometimes I wish I could sleep and never wake again. But that is sheer cowardice and I think of my good friends and of all the good that has come into my life and take heart again – only just now the world seems pitched to a note of agony.

Your last letter was such a treasure, and has not Stevenson said that, 'so long as we are loved we are indispensable'?

I hope you feel much rested for the change at Miss Albright's and braced up for those rapidly approaching exams. I sympathise with you keenly over Local Government. I never could understand it and seem already to have forgotten most of what I learned. As Mr Cunnison says – English Local Government has just muddled along, and it's pretty bad stuff for brains to digest. You must not bother to write much now dearie, as your time is most precious. After all, Xmas will soon be here. Think how gladly we shall hug each other – and will there ever be time for us to say all we shall have to say?

Françoise and babe are getting on splendidly, but their financial position is daily becoming more serious and I cannot see what they will do.

Mother looks at me in wonder and thinks I intend to scribble all night, so I forbear to write more.

My truest love to thee and a fond kiss. Ruth.

Eva to Ruth   21 November 1915

My own dear one,

I know you must be looking for a letter from me, but I know you understand how full the life is here.

I feel so anxious about you Ruth, and about your Mother and Father. It is the fact that I am not near to see you and talk things over which makes me dissatisfied. You do not say, my own, if you are still working for the Distressed Aliens Committee. Oh my dear, I *do* understand all that you are feeling just now. I press close to you, dear, in my heart, with deepest love and sympathy; remember you *are* 'indispensable'.

Test exams begin next week – we depart for home on 18 December.

Have you heard anything of Mr Jones since he enlisted? This has been a blow to you I feel sure. Oh, this war! I have had two letters from Cecil since I have been here, which make me feel very anxious. A recruiting officer persists in calling at the house to see him and from Cecil's letter I fear he has given a half promise. He wrote to me saying he had never before felt so strongly the need of moral support, and begging me to write. I have written urging him to be firm and true to his convictions – to join the FOR [Fellowship of Reconciliation] – I do not know what else I can do. Cecil's letters have touched me very much – he speaks of me as his 'beloved sister' and there is a note of suffering in each one.

I am *longing* to see you dear. I wish you could be here, sharing the life of Woodbrooke with me. Miss Robb, a Scotch-woman, and myself have the reputation of being the hardest workers. I wish I felt more *particular* and less *general* knowledge – but during the next few weeks, I intend to get certain points and sides of each subject more definitely into my mind. I feel so attached to some of the women here.

I have long intended to tell you that 'Fircroft' [a neighbouring men's college] has been taken over by the Government for wounded soldiers, and the 'Fircrofters' have been for some time installed at Woodbrooke – I like some of the men very much.

I must not continue to write, as I must do my unruly hair again – I washed it last night, and today it resembles 'Struwwelpeter's'. My heart's love dear, and a warm kiss and embrace from your ever loving Eva.

Ruth to Eva   23 November 1915
                                                        10 Waterlow Court
                                                Hampstead Garden Suburb

My dearest,

I cannot tell you what a joy it was to see your dear handwriting last night. This evening I am determined to spend another happy time with you, myself being spokesman on this occasion, in fair order.

You will now wonder why it is I should not have written sooner. Well, I have really been very busy indeed. My work with the Aliens Committee only lasted a week, but the week following I did some investigation work in the East End for the Women's Industrial Council, thinking it might perhaps lead me along the direction suggested by Mr Thompson. It would take too long to tell you all my adventures, but I found the work extremely tiring – though of course most interesting, but as my share was but a portion of a very large whole, I can hardly work up the information I gained into articles for America. It took me a considerable time drafting my reports to the Council and as I wanted to be scouring the papers in search of a post, I was not sorry when I had completed my task. Then came a letter from the FOR confessing muddle and asking me to go along to give a little help, which I am now doing. Next came an exciting letter from Seebohm Rowntree asking me whether I would consider taking up a post as Welfare Worker in the Cocoa Works at York, and suggesting that I should meet him in London this week to talk the matter over. The work sounds interesting and the salary offered is good – £120 p.a. rising to £150. Will it surprise you to hear that I am actually considering accepting the post if deemed suitable? The prospect of leaving London is very painful to me, yet many considerations press me towards the post. I have seen Tom and have talked things over with him, and tomorrow evening I shall see Mother. The shop at Wood Green is taken and Mother is already there getting her insight into the business with the former people. You shall hear as much as you want to know when you come up for Xmas, and perhaps things will have cleared by then. I just have a feeling that for me the warmth has gone out of life, but do not worry my own, I expect the fire is only low.

I am glad you are getting specially fond of a few of the women. Do you not find that your common study forms quite a bond? I do sympathise with you over those *horrid* exams, and am only vexed to think that you are cramming for three all at once. And now, sweet one, I must say goodnight, promising to write to you again with news of my decision, as soon as ever I can.

My heart's deep affection to you, beloved friend – may you always be richly blessed! Ruth.

Ruth to Eva   23 December 1915
                                                        60 Station Road
                                                        Wood Green, N

My sweetheart! I have thought so much about you since Saturday and do hope you have ceased to bother anything about those foolish exams. What *does* it really matter, dearie, whether you get through or not? I have been feeling concerned about you, for I knew from Miss Kelman about the exams, but I hoped you would not hear until after Xmas. I am sure that Wood-brooke people are very fond of you dear, and I do not think in the end that the exams matter one bit.

I can only write a short note, for I am particularly oppressed with a sense of blankness – almost despair. It is so unhappy here – and so utterly hopeless.

I am going to disappoint you, my own, but I know you will understand. Mother reminds me that next Sunday will be my last at home for a long time [because Ruth had accepted the job at Rowntree's] and wishes to keep me here. I had looked forward to seeing all the good Chapel folk, especially Mr James and Minna, but I am putting home before everything else just now. But I will try to get down quite early on Monday morning.

Dear, I do hope that I have not seemed cold lately – sometimes I fear it may be so, but be patient with me, my friend, as you have been before, and I shall one day glow again.

And now beloved one, goodbye for a little while. I shall be with you in thought all the time until we meet – and send now a warm kiss of love. Your friend Ruth.

Eva to Ruth   22 January 1916

My dearest,

Although I have not written it is hardly necessary for me to tell
you how much I have been with you in thought, how often I
have *longed* for your companionship. I have read your two
letters – my dear, what an anxiety and trouble it all is! My
great wish is to get where I can be with and near everyone whom
I care for – and I quite understand your loneliness in York. My
own, wait until I am home again, and settled once more; we may
then pick up the threads of the old customs and know times
more strengthening and glorious because of our experiences of
pleasure and pain. Let us look forward to and live for that time.
People here talk to me of Deaconess and YWCA work, and I
feel rather a hypocrite because I listen and ask questions,
knowing all the time that I intend to get either secretarial or
welfare work of some kind. I cannot bear the idea of living *in* an
Institution or Order for all time!

I am glad, dearie, you have grown to know at least a few York
people, but they none of them sound particularly like kindred
spirits!

I do not know that I really feel as you say 'calm and strong'
about other matters, I am afraid I do not – but I am not anxious
or worried now.

I enclose a timetable. We are now, as you see, helping in the
garden once a week. This week I helped to roll the lawn and
thoroughly enjoy it, but also find it very tiring.

Indeed, several things have happened this week to help me.
Miss Fox told me how she had failed when she first sat for her
exams – she said she wanted to tell me how brave I was (you
will smile) then she showed me how to make a synopsis of each
chapter of a subject and recommended different methods of
study. Miss Blomfield spoke so finely too at Devotion the other
morning on the subject of failure – it is not the failure which
counts, but the efforts, the aspirations.

I am still working at the Play Hour, teaching singing, games,
etc. Last night I had twenty-eight children in my section, but I
find no difficulty controlling them.

I feel, my dear, that it is so *very* long since we had a heart to
heart talk. I have come to the conclusion that you and I do not
transplant well, but our friendship should be all the richer for

our parting and absence from familiar scenes, and I believe (about *you* I feel sure) that we shall be better workers in our little world because of our wider experience.

I don't deserve a letter *soon,* I know, but I shall just wonder and wonder until I hear from you.

My heart's deepest love, dear, and tenderest sympathy. How I wish I could be with you! Your ever loving Eva.

Eva to Ruth   6 February 1916
My own dear one,

Have I kept you *so* long without a letter? My dear love, I *wish* I had written sooner just now when you stand in special need of letters. When I read your letter I just wanted to put my arms around you and give you the love and silent sympathy which I feel, but although I cannot do this in the body, just *now* and *always* the love and sympathy is yours.

Sunday morning. After all I was unable to get this letter finished yesterday as I have promised to go to a big 'No Conscription'[1] meeting in Birmingham. I also went for a walk in the afternoon, which sounds as though I had not my letter to you on my heart. That was not the case, however, dear, but I hope I am now more fitted to write to you clearly than I should have been without the exercise. The truth is I have slept badly and in consequence have been troubled with neuritis again – I feel the effects of the years I spent in that gloomy little office far more than I ever thought I should do.

Last night's 'No Conscription' meeting was so wonderful. So many of the Fircrofters here intend to resist, and they need all the encouragement and support it is possible to give them. Quite a big contingent from Woodbrooke turned out to the meeting – Clifford Allen, Fenner Brockway and Miss Catherine Marshall were speaking. I thought Fenner Brockway greatly improved since I last heard him. Clifford Allen interested me – such a clear cut, determined face – and such keen, clear thinking. He dealt very fully with the Act dealing with conscientious objectors, and pointed out that it certainly was a concession from Parliament to recognise conscience at all – such a thing had not been known before except in regard to Quakers. Still, the Act was very subtle: exemptions from military service on the ground of conscience would only mean that the Government would put men upon work which would make it more possible for them to continue the war. The only really effective action to take in order to get the Act repealed would be to claim *absolute* exemption, but this not alone upon personal grounds, but from the even higher motive that the future greatness of our country depended upon our action.

My own dear, will this letter convey to you I wonder the deep love and tender sympathy I feel? Oh, I *hope* that it will!

Have you heard from Mr Thompson lately? Oh! I have so *much* to say – and I long to see you. Write soon dear.

My *deepest* love. Eva.

Ruth to Eva
7 February 1916
60 Station Road
Wood Green, N.

My dear,

Your letter when it came this morning was indeed food for the hungry. I am sorry dear to have seemed so impatient but it *did* seem a long time to wait, especially as rumours were rife in London that fearful damage had been done in Birmingham by Zeppelins. I even heard that New Street had been completely destroyed! You know the papers gave no hint of the actual places attacked and Birmingham is one of the important 'Midland Towns'. I even pictured you escaping from Prof. Muirhead's lecture, with bombs in foul pursuit!

You *did* manage to convey a wonderful lot of feeling in your letter, dearie – I am only sorry you had the strain of writing it when you were feeling tired. I become more and more convinced that we can never be freed from the effect of those long years of dreary labour. I find the confidence which I seemed to gather at Woodbrooke only *really* holds good when I am with friends – I am still meek and timid with strangers and those in authority. There is such an abundancy of spirits, I notice, in those who were at school until their twenties and then began on a 'profession' – which tells me plainly that in our cases a reservoir has been sapped. I was particularly struck at Rowntree's with the tired, faded look of the forewomen there, most of them a little over thirty but had been working at the Factory since they left school. The social workers on the other hand, who had a jolly school-time and lots of choice as to the work they would take up, looked smooth and fair and healthy. Reflections such as these take me back to socialistic thoughts again and make me feel even that I could write a treatise one day.

291

You will be sorry to hear that I have succumbed to a partial collapse which, after all my struggling, is rather disheartening. Perhaps it was unwise of me to rush off to the Dentist so impulsively, but dearie, my teeth seemed to be dropping to pieces. By Sunday morning I was prostrate with the worst headache I have ever known and during the day violently sick. The worst thing of all was my inability to stop crying. Mother was very kind. I believe it is just that my nerves are completely unstrung, and that nothing but a rest somewhere will put me right. I am just suffering from an awful sense of disappointment, but once the depths have been plumbed I shall rise again!

I was glad to hear about the 'No Conscription' meeting. How are the Fircrofters faring? I think Clifford Allen's point was right and that it will have to be much more bravely and openly emphasised in the near future. Even Friends, many of them, are shaky here and willing to accept questionable 'alternative service'.

Well my own, I have obeyed you and answered you very quickly and as Dad is just going out to post I will stop writing so that you may get this tomorrow.

I feel your very real embrace my dear one, and answer it with one as ardent and as true. Always Yours. Ruth.

Eva to Ruth   10 February 1916
My own dear,

It *was* so lovely to get your quick response to my letter, but I fear you were in no fit state to write, and I feel so anxious about you. Oh my dear, I am very tempted to run up and see you this half term, and yet I *know* I must be careful, but if I do not get a better report soon you will have me paying you a weekend visit. Dearie, I really think you had better wait until I am home to have the rest of those teeth seen to, and you need a thorough rest and nursing up. What is the sense of disappointment which is depressing you so? Are you troubled, dear, about America?

I am feeling so much better nervously – last week I got into a tired overstrained condition, but I pulled myself together and determined I would do all in my power to cure these mental conditions into which I frequently get! I must tell you that in pursuance of this determination I commenced to learn tennis on Monday and as a result dear I have slept and felt well; indeed, I begin to feel a new creature. The life here this term is meaning so much to me. When I think of all that you have rescued me from I am full of thankfulness. I do not know what I *should* have become if I had remained many more years in that cramping office.

For the first fortnight after my return to Woodbrooke I felt very depressed over those exams, and had a daily battle for a little self-confidence. Now I am determined, dear, that if possible the life here shall yield me *some* confidence and at any rate a fresh supply of physical energy. I am very much impressed with what you say about the girls who are able to remain at school until they are twenty – their 'abundancy of spirits' – and, may I add – 'energy'! This was very noticeable during examination time – I worked and worked beforehand and when the critical time arrived, had not any reserve strength to fall back upon. Many of the other students also, as they call it, 'swotted up' and still were able to sail calmly and gallantly through the tests – so much for the advantages of the college girl compared with our own! I do think though we have the advantage in a much more intimate knowledge of the suffering side to life – of those who toil – and, I think, perhaps, a deeper appreciation of friendship.

Oh my dear, I just long to be in your presence – get well quickly for *my* sake. My tenderest, deepest love. Eva.

Eva to Ruth   27 February 1916
My own dear,
Tomorrow will be your birthday, and I hasten to send you my deepest love and warmest wishes for a happy day, and a new year in which I trust all clouds will roll away and a more definite future will open up before you! I think I must send my little gift separately as it is Sunday, and I want you to get this letter tomorrow.

You ask about the Woodbrooke men – this is a very trying time for them. Most of them are claiming 'absolute exemption' – some are willing to take alternative service; all are waiting to go before the tribunal, and I believe some are to appear this week.

Woodbrooke is just now surrounded by a white world. Day after day the snow has been falling. It is such an experience for me to spend the seasons of the year in the country dear, and I get such joy from the country, sky and sunshine. Indeed, this term is meaning a very great deal to me. I am throwing myself more into the *life* here, for I feel I need the *social* element quite as much as anything else. On Thursday I gave a little tea party in my room which was a great success, and next week I intend to give a cocoa party. Then things have gone well with me so far as my work is concerned. My first essay on 'The Law of Diminishing Returns' Mr Cunnison said was good and well thought out; then I got 75 marks for my test answers to questions on practical social work. I tell you this dearie, because I feel you will know how encouraged I am – I wish I had not been so absolutely *scared* last term. I sincerely trust it will not happen again. I am growing so much better in health that I think I should have considerably more reserve strength when the testing time comes.

Already there is talk of work in the air. Four of us were having tea in Miss Sunderland's room on Friday, when Miss Kelman appeared with the news that a lady Welfare worker had arrived with information about work at Gretna Green – it appears that a huge ammunition factory is to be erected there which will mean the employment of a great number of girls, and Welfare workers will be needed. I declined to entertain – the mere thought of an ammunition factory and Gretna makes me shiver! Something much more possible has opened up today – another lady, a Miss Wilson, is spending the weekend here. Such a pleasant, fine face – she wears art dresses and is a *vegetarian* . She came up to my room this morning and told me a great deal about her work. It appears she was once a student at Woodbrooke, and went straight away to a mixture of Welfare and Club work in connection with a Hosiery Factory in Nottingham. At this Factory 100 girls are employed. The Club is open three or four nights during the week and Miss Wilson organises classes in needlework, cookery, debates, and I was specially interested in her *Art* evening. Beautiful music is played, Greek stories are told, poetry is read, and lantern slides are shown. About 20 girls attend and find it helpful and on Sunday afternoons a 'Snowdrop League' is held; its special aim is to deepen purity of thought amongst the girls. Miss Wilson also visits amongst the girls – tries to get them to think for themselves – and although she does not *lead* strikes, yet these do occur, and are often the outcome of the influence of new thoughts introduced at the club. The girls are also taught to act, and have performed *Eager Heart* quite wonderfully. Morris dancing is also taught. No, my own dear, if I *cannot* get work in connection with a Labour or Co-operative movement, I really think I would like this kind of work.

My letter writing was interrupted this afternoon in the shape of a throbbing headache which made me feel I was writing nonsense to you – at last I gave in and rested on my bed. I think it was merely the result of the intense cold and dazzling snow. The headache has quite gone now, and I am scribbling away in the Common Room to the accompaniment of rich music, for *at last* a musician has arrived, a Mrs Sheldon, who *composes* music to some of her songs!

On Wednesday a good number of us went to a big tea and meeting of the FOR in Birmingham – Dr Hodgkins was very impressive and dwelt upon the two attitudes we may adopt towards life – the evolutionary attitude which says little by little, and which only too often means that reform is postponed because we say 'we are not yet ready for it', or the attitude of Christ which was that of reckless daring, attempting now to do the will of God. Should not all Christians adopt this attitude – range themselves on the side of Christ and *dare?*

In a month's time, dearest, I shall be home, and then we must meet. I hear frequently from Mr James – queer little notes of sudden thought and impulse – he urges me to try and write – says I have such a graphic way of expressing myself! I hope dear, I may do a little in that way some day, but it is difficult when there are so many demands on one's time.

I feel anxious about your health Ruth, and those teeth – are you really feeling better, and are you less troubled with those wretched headaches?

It is almost supper time, my own, so I will not write any longer as the people are trooping in.

My tenderest love, dear, and many blessings come to you.

Your loving friend, Eva.

This letter was the last Ruth received, for on 4 March Eva died suddenly from undetected diabetes – a condition which would have accounted for her feelings of tiredness, the throbbing headache she mentioned, the neurasthenia which was diagnosed earlier, the recurring pain in her legs and possibly many of her other ailments. The sheer unexpectedness of Eva's death was devastating to Ruth and Minna – central as she was to their lives – and to the 'fellowship' of friends and comrades in Walthamstow.

It was also painfully ironic that Eva died on the brink of that fuller life that she had wanted for so long. She was buried at

Woodbrooke after a funeral service in the Common Room attended by family and friends.

Continuing her diary to make what were to be her last entries, Ruth attempted to express some of her feelings and pull herself together through her writing, although she felt the inadequacy of words. In the Woodbrooke Chronicle *for the Spring Term, she managed to write 'a fitting memorial' to Eva.*

Ruth's Diary   Monday, 13 March 1916

Now that I am likely to be thrown so much on my own resources I feel it might be good and helpful to begin once more to keep a diary. My thoughts just now lack grip and coherence and I feel that to attempt to write should aid in altering this.

I can scarcely believe that I am actually back in York and have set myself to this work which in prospect promised so much, but which in reality has so far proved most dreary. Yet I am determined to give it a fair trial.

How I shall miss my Eva here! At times it seems that the very foundation of my life has been shattered, but I am saved from despair by the loving way in which I have been made one of the little circle, or family, of friends which Eva left in Walthamstow. Mr James calls himself my 'brother' – and I feel this to be no empty word. I think of us as a 'Beloved Community' and share the hope of Mr James that we may some day be shown the way to corporate action in the direction Eva would have loved, and for which surely in this dark sad time, there should be an opportunity. I do not yet feel my heart close to God in the way in which I believe Eva did – my mind seems more restless and sceptical than hers – but this human love is leading me on towards the other and one day I too shall know rest.

Ruth's Diary   Wednesday, 15 March 1916

I have had some wonderful letters, which have shot through my pain with an exquisite joy. I still feel a queer, ordinary little sensation of surprise that Eva could have gone without my knowing it – that there is actually an experience unshared – and it seems to me she *must* soon come back to tell me all about it. Oh, would I were a Tennyson, that could weld his love for his friend into a wonderful poem, but I have no expression save in deeds, but with God's help I mean to make these a fitting memorial to her I love.

Ruth's Diary   Thursday, 16 March 1916

I am not so conscious of fellowship this morning and the dreary weather and surroundings all tend to depress me. So far I do not like York as a place to live, thought I have heard it highly praised. No doubt it is very interesting to visit, and one is of course always under the charm of its glorious Minster and quaint survivals of antiquity; but the air and people lack exhilaration and one meets with very little which touches the imagination – at least, such has been my fate hitherto! I suppose one never realises the extraordinary stimulation of London life until one misses it.

The Cocoa Works are situated on the outskirts of the City, about a mile from the Minster, and the distance between is covered with mean and ugly streets. There is a marked absence of trees and the flatness everywhere is depressing.

The Works are of course enormous – great red brick structures which rear their heads boldly to the skies. There could be no mistaking them, even if their towers did not bear inscriptions such as 'Elect Cocoa'. But in my dislike of modern industrialism I must not be unjust. There is less advertisement here than there might be and the approaches to these monuments of prosperity are not without artistic merit. There is plenty of clinging ivy and green shrub. Inside, the downstairs corridors are adorned with large hanging trays of ferns and even some of the workrooms are ornamented with hanging pots of Creeping Jenny and the like.

In many ways I feel exactly as if I had gone straight away back to Kearley and Tonge's, except that my surroundings here are much more crude. I climb stone stairs to this room, about the same in number as those which used to tire me so, years ago; and the little office, when reached, is very similar to the section partitioned off in K & T's saleroom. Even my books are reminiscent, except that they deal with wages instead of 'takings', and my task here of discovering discrepancies is wonderfully alike, except that here I shall have myself to deal with the difficulties, instead of merely providing figures for a more responsible person.

I was shown over the factory when I was here in January. It is a wonderful place, and on the whole is well planned and equipped, but I do feel somehow that most of this industry is rather disgusting. Surely, as a civilised race, we should have got beyond wanting elaborate sweetmeats, all gay with tinfoil and ribbons? Though I think too that life should have its gala days and feasts. It is a hard problem! But there are tiny boys here who spend their whole days preparing nuts, and one poor little wretch sits in a *cage* cracking nuts all day! All the work is intensely monotonous and I wonder greatly what boys and girls think about as the hours pass by. I find it hard myself, when my work is dull and tedious, to keep down a tendency to a morbid undercurrent of thought, and this sets me in a curious mood concerning other people. If I get a chance to investigate this subject while I am here I shall certainly take it, but I fear it would be almost impossible to win a candid statement from the girls.

Ruth's Diary   Monday, 20 March 1916
I am beginning my second week's work in a more hopeful vein. On Wednesday I summoned up courage and asked the Director for an interview in order that my prospective work might be discussed. The result is that I now have a type-written statement of my duties, which is quite fairly and hopefully stated, and also I shall very shortly be installed in a private office of my own, where I shall be able to interview the girls, and work to greater advantage.

The weekend passed very quietly. I roused myself yesterday morning and walked to Leeman Rd meeting, but it was not particularly helpful, though I enjoyed the singing of 'They who tread the path of labour' – one of our Woodbrooke favourites.

The buoyancy I experienced during the past fortnight has ebbed away, as I knew it must, and I am coming to grips with that sense of desolation which is so hard to bear. No one was so close to me as Eva, and at times I feel that the very foundation of my life has slipped away. Our lives, with their similarity of thought and experience (though Eva's nature was much more profound than mine) were so interwoven that a separate existence seems unthinkable. I had counted much on her too, I find, for the future – which looks so dark – and had felt that with her sure friendship I could face it. I sometimes feel her very near me, but how one aches for the human word and touch.

Friendship has been the breath of my life and Eva was its crown. I must now learn to be more self-reliant and single, for Eva's death brought me a great sense of responsibility. I was so sure that she had a special work to do in this world and I used to picture myself as her righthand helper – her amanuensis and secretary, perhaps; but now I feel that I must carry on the work that she had in mind, and learn to be brave and honest.

Ruth's Diary   Tuesday, 21 March 1916
I am feeling especially anxious about Hugh, for it is now over a week since I heard from him. I posted him a note this morning; for a mind like mine, that has been tamed and taught by sad experience, has little use left for pride and anger. In his last letter Hugh referred to life (thinking of my loss) as a necessary disappointment until one had hardened oneself, and said that although it might seem awful, very few things could really move him. My friendships with men seem disappointing things, though I think much of the reason must lie in myself. I have known almost ever since I knew him, that Hugh's heart was frozen in his youth, but it is a cruel realisation that after all the wonder of our intimacy it should still be so. His letters have been the only ones which have not brought a warm glow of loving sympathy with them, yet I believe I am more to him than anything in his life. It was a keen disappointment to me when he enlisted, and I thought him not looking improved when I saw him the other day at Oxford. He could help me so much now if only he understood!

Ruth's Diary   Friday, 24 March 1916
This week has brought me a sense of loneliness and depression which has threatened to overwhelm me. I heard from Hugh on Wednesday but it was a letter which chilled my heart and made more realise more than ever what very different worlds he and I live in.

Then I had a wretched letter from Mother, in which she tells me things which confirm my fears that Dad is relapsing into his former condition. And yet she still thinks he suffers only from bad temper and laziness and tries to goad him into an energy which is not in him. This worry of home is like a millstone to me. It breaks my heart at the same time. I would like to plan a happy little home for their later years, and see them knowing some real peace and joy, but the obstacle to all this lies in themselves and I cannot see what is to be done. I have sent Mother's letter on to Tom and asked him if he has any suggestions to make.

Wednesday was a day of important letters. One arrived from David Thompson making a last appeal for me to marry him, but I wrote back at once telling him it is utterly impossible and urging him to find someone else. He is not happy living a single life and it worries me to feel so responsible for it. I am sure our friendship would continue and I could be glad in his joy, but I feel many pains to find myself so surely hastening on into spinsterhood.

I have had loving letters from Gertie, Minna and Mr James, and feel their affection and sympathy my whole support just now. Physically I am very tired and feel the long days at the Works a great strain. The sickening smells and terrific noises are a trial to my nerves, but why should I be exempt from what is the daily lot of hundreds of others?

I was pondering yesterday on the stress everyone at Wood-brooke seemed to lay on Eva's 'humility'. How little they understood either of us! Much of that humility was the lack of self-confidence which both Eva and I have felt to be the curse of our lives, and which has been unduly and unhealthily fostered in us by mistaken religious training and hard circumstances. I never before *quite* realised what a very different world Eva and I represented there – yet I should find it very difficult to explain myself to an ordinary Woodbrooker. Alas! these things cannot be explained but only divined by the sympathy of rare loving.

Ruth's Diary   Monday, 3 April 1916
I have been invited out quite a lot to the homes of several kind people, but I do not want to get inveigled into numerous acquaintanceships. I would rather wait a bit and find one good friend, and it almost seems that I have already found one. A week ago I was beguiled into going to a small Sale of Work, got up by the Friends in aid of a Belgian fund, and there met a girl who has come to York as recently as myself to take up professional gardening. Conversation revealed the exciting fact that she has been living recently at Whiteway – also that she possesses an ardent and attractive personality. Our hearts went out to each other at once, and last Wednesday I went to tea with her at her lodgings. In my painfully conventional and ugly clothes I felt ashamed, and fearful lest she should fail to recognise a sister spirit, but we did really meet and know one another. After a happy scramble tea we walked to the Library together, talking of many things.

Yesterday she came to me. It was a perfect day – the scents and sounds of spring were in the air and the sun shone bright and warm, though only a week ago a blizzard swept the country and we were nearly perished with the extreme cold. We went out for a walk in the afternoon and found some delightful meadows, in one of which we seated ourselves on the trunk of a fallen tree. I enjoyed her physical beauty too and loved to watch her boyish gestures. Such a lovely healthy face and figure; the face very delicate and intelligent. She was wearing a pretty, soft green hat, devoid of trimming and independent of hatpins, and ever and anon she lifted it and passed her hand through her hair in a delightfully expressive manner. There was a painful moment when we confessed our respective ages. I was dismayed at first to learn that she is only 22 – and she actually thought me 24! – but the qualm soon passed. She came to my lodgings to tea, and in the evening we sat telling each other the story of our lives, and as I felt the beauty of her a wonderful sense of healing and comfort stole through me.

I had also beautiful letters in the morning and a box of flowers – human love, and surely God's love through it, is seeking to uphold me. I crave that my life may not be *all* little and worthless, but sometimes I am tempted to drift – I am very tired.

Woodbrooke Chronicle   Spring Term, 1916
Eva Slawson

As one of Eva Slawson's oldest and closest friends, I have been asked to write a tribute to her memory for this 'Chronicle'. I feel my power of expression too limited to give more than a glimpse of her beautiful spirit – I was too near her ever to analyse her character in phrases, but I hope that I may be able to say enough to kindle anew in the hearts of all who read this the longing to love and to serve which was the passion of her life.

Of the students who come to Woodbrooke, term after term, representing varied environments and outlooks upon life, I think it is true to say that the majority may look back upon a life which, in regard to its circumstances, has been comparatively easy. There has been the prolonged education at an age when appreciation is ripening and social instincts are beginning to expand; there has been leisure for outdoor sport, art, personal hobbies; and above all the development of a healthy self-confidence has been encouraged, ensuring escape from the torments of hyper-sensitiveness and the chance of success along some desired course. To these, Woodbrooke is a further school where facts about the great world of problems and suffering are

301

learnt for the first time, and where the instinct for service is roused and directed.

But occasionally there comes to Woodbrooke a soul which has striven and suffered much – a Student whose life has been handicapped by meagre opportunities and worn by the effort to fulfil itself in the narrow margin of long days of toil. To these Woodbrooke is as an oasis in a desert, reviving health and energy, and above all the capacity to dream dreams and see visions of the things that are to be. To this small company Eva Slawson belonged, and those who knew her intimately know how her lovely faculties were blossoming out in the new world (to her) of released energies and opportunities. A week or two before her death, she had written to some friends – 'This term at Woodbrooke is meaning so much to me, and I am endeavouring to make it yield me more self-confidence, that I may come back to you all better fitted for the battle of life. There is so much I just *long* to help in – so much evil to combat – so many ideals to try to bring into being!' She was full, too, of the joy of living through the seasons of the year in the country, and described for her friends many panoramas of sky and fields with which other Woodbrookers will be familiar.

The motive power of her life was love – enriched by a profound intelligence, and a sympathy wonderful in its depth and perception. Shy, and fearful of obtruding herself on the notice of others, I feel that Woodbrooke was only beginning to know her when she was taken away, but the little fellowship of friends which she has left behind in London know from long experience the power she possessed to inspire others and to radiate a spirit of goodwill and joy in high endeavour.

The following quotation from a letter has a significance all its own: 'The life here makes me feel more strongly for *labour* than ever. I feel upheld by the hope that the time spent at Woodbrooke may fit me in even a small way to understand the problems of all poor and oppressed people. It is even worth while to *fail* if it gives one a deeper understanding of others and brings one nearer to the suffering side of life.'

Perhaps the highest tribute to her memory lies in the fact that the small company of her friends feel themselves bound together in a sacred unity, pledged to live and work for those ideals for which she lived and worked; not resting even to grieve.

(Ruth Slate)

302

Appendix

'This Ever Perplexing Sex Question'
Letters to Ruth from Minna Simmons 1916–17

After Eva's death Minna and Ruth drew closer together for a time, having 'found each other, though it were through a great sorrow'. Minna, who had never written a word in her life, was prompted by the loss of Eva to write not only letters, but poems, and 'accounts' of her own and Eva's life, which she sent to Ruth to 'see and criticise'.

Reading the letters, we can appreciate Minna's warmth, humour, passion, honesty, radical ideas, and the generous nature that Eva had described. In one letter to Ruth she says of herself, 'I am such a primitive creature that sometimes I am afraid of you seeing too much of me, else I should shock you and you wouldn't love me as I want you to.'

Minna described the intensity of her feelings for Eva and the process of dealing with the loss, writing to Ruth on 22 March 1917, 'I had to go to the doctor, I felt so ill after Eva died; I have lived in her and pined for her so much it has made me ill.' In an undated letter she said: 'I used to love to feel Eva and wish now I had been more demonstrative.' In one of her 'accounts', she wrote, 'O Eva. Never to feel your arms around me again. Never to hear you say, "O Minna", never to sleep with you again and hear you say, "I do love you", this is really to suffer.' Minna managed however, to be optimistic, energetic and idealistic.

Minna to Ruth   *undated*
My dear,
I feel I must tell you dear how my heart is overflowing with love for you. I have not felt so warm since Eva went. I have read your article in The *Chronicle* and I think it very beautiful.

How delighted I was to find my letter was of some use to you. Let me say my darling, let me, in my small imperfect way, be just a little to you of what Eva was. I feel her so very near tonight as I came home – the sky was the perfect picture even the factory chimneys. There is something so strengthening to me in the sunset, somehow even more than the colour; it thrills and calms me so.

It is so nice to be with the girls, I feel so young with them.

I felt the singing as I came along and the words, you know them: 'Though the cause of Evil prosper/Yet the *truth* alone is strong.' We must have some walks in the forest and grow into one another much, much, more. I feel with our kinship and our beautiful ideal before us, who knows what heights we may attain.

I just felt I must write before going to bed. I do hope you find things not so acute. I know just how you feel dear, even prayer seems of no avail.

My love dear, and a goodnight kiss from your reborn Minna.

Minna told Ruth about her affair with Mr James (SBJ):

Minna to Ruth   15 July 1916
My Own Beloved,
Never never speak of you disappointing me, do I not love you dear and hold you close to my heart. I hope the time may come when you will need me, so I may prove my love. Are you not Eva's gift to me?

I must be frank and truthful dear to you and so I will tell you what no other eye must ever see. What I now confess is with the deepest shame and humiliation. Yet, dear, with joy, that one can feel as I have felt, is to know the very consciousness of reality. Ruth can you love me after this.

After I had received that letter I showed you and had gone home from my case, *He* [SBJ] came to see me. We had a most lovely talk. We had been to Maude Royden's meeting and it had been the means of one of those soul talks.

Well dear we went into the front room alone and he kissed me, opened my dress and kissed my breasts too, and he said how he felt I was his. He was just going away when he came back and pleaded with me dear to give him everything a woman can give a man. I told him I was sure we should regret it but no dear anything that would make me his. 'Well dear, I did'. The tears I have shed have quite washed away any wrong I did.

My dear Ruth I can never tell you what I suffered. I felt I could never look at anyone again; how I have sat in Church I

304

don't know, it has been simply agony. Well dear I met him out again one evening when I was with Lily and the strangest meeting it seemed, though we never even shook hands. We just mingled together. Then dear he promised to come to Stroud Green to see me, and to write. He did neither. It was simply brutal. Think of me there dear with my tormenting thoughts, my hatred of myself and yet dear I do love him. I knew I was determined it should never happen again.

In my letter I told him there could not be passion between us. If it was to be anything it must be higher than that, told him I knew it couldn't be right or I wouldn't have been so miserable about it. When I asked him if he didn't agree about the latter, he said he had come to the same conclusion.

He said I was more attractive than ever and he simply dare not kiss me or he didn't know what might happen. So dear, I do feel if it has to be anything it must be a pure and noble spiritual bond.

Ruth you do understand dear, all my life I was tied to the tragedy of mated loneliness, if it hadn't been for Eva and Lily and my kiddies I simply couldn't have borne my life. Then to have seemed to have found your mate, and yet dear if I felt he was true and worthy, my life would be a great joy.

I feel we haven't mixed enough with men to know their minds because, dear, he told me he felt like this towards Eva and wished he had given her everything. I can understand him loving you, dear, you are so pretty, but me? Somehow too I feel there is a lot in what he says in his letter. Giving Joan to Eva and Lily has made me see that in Motherhood and Fatherhood the bond is mostly physical and not nearly what has been written about it. You see dear, God showers his gifts on us all and I feel we have only touched the fringe of love.

It will be a hard struggle for us women; men will walk, dear, over our broken and bleeding hearts, but we must love them still in spite of everything.

The strangest thing is, dear, that I haven't felt I wronged Mrs J. No, I felt, dear, what love he gave to me was mine, and never was hers, nor could be. Don't worry about me dear, I have quite regained my self possession.

If he had only written and told me he felt the same and we had blundered, but to be silent and to shun one was bitterly cruel.

I do hope I haven't wearied you. My heart's love dear and my life's devotion. Your own Minna.

*Minna revealed more of Eva's feelings for SBJ and showed that
he had been involved with many women but without sustaining
much commitment to any of them. She decided in the end that
SBJ was 'what we call a dipper ... My love, let us thank God for
our faithful hearts, it is a priceless possession.'*

*Minna gave Ruth advice about Hugh, David Thompson and
volunteered information about contraception, urging her to resist
the security that marriage might appear to offer. She wrote: 'I do
feel, Ruth, marriage isn't enough to fill many lives, either men's
or women's. True friends mean so much to me that I'm sure for
myself I'd rather remain single and somehow I'm beginning to
feel it isn't, after all, the biggest thing to be oneself to one – we
must release ourselves from this, someone must begin.'*

*Minna's letters are also full of news and chat about the splits in
the Chapel, her nursing work, herself and Lily, the war and the
'dreadful raids', her 'account' of the Irish Rebellion which SBJ
had witnessed as a reporter for* The Christian Commonwealth,
and the goings on in Walthamstow.

*For her the Sex Question was still of vital importance and
something she felt an urgency about, wanting to progress beyond
the boundaries that existed. 'This Sex Question', she wrote to
Ruth, 'does pull at me so: it follows me like the Hound of
Heaven. That people are so ignorant of their own being and the
Laws of God seems to me simply awful. Do you know, since I
have been nursing, I have only nursed one woman who wanted
her baby – they are all accidents. This most precious thing, this
glorious sensation, that fuses two people in one, and creates a
third, is then to be degraded. No wonder we have a war.'*

Minna to Ruth   *undated*
My own dear,

Thanks dear for your letter, I felt I wanted to answer it at once,
so very strongly do I feel your question as to what I think of
women's part in the war. I have been more than disappointed in
them dear Ruth; sometimes I even despair of them. I, too, have
felt I wanted to speak from the street corners, or anywhere; a
passion which is hard and, I feel, wrong to stifle.

And war means so much to us women, the fruits of our body.
How they can so lightly give up their sons and husbands I cannot
think, especially after you see how they suffer to bring them
into the world.

I have been trying to grapple with the sex problem. I get so much of it. You know how Eva was so interested in it. I did think of writing my impressions of it but things occur to baffle one. However, we must talk over these things.

Must close in great haste. My heart's love and greeting soon. Your loving Minna.

Minna saw that women needed their own support systems and their own lifestyles. In January 1917 she wrote: 'In our dreams, we spoke of the other evening, we had planned that at some future date we might move somewhere distant nearer the city and so form a small colony for lonely women. There they could at least live free and if they ever felt they wanted to obey a divine impulse and have a child, it would be made possible for them in every way. Also it would be a fellowship for all who had been hard knocked and needed love and tenderness. I feel like you, dear, it may in some way help on the cause of humanity.

Among Minna's poems were 'The Joy of Life', 'Thoughts on Looking into the eyes of Ruth and those women I love', 'Sonnet to Trinity', and her poem on 'Friendship':

A sage he said to me the other day, you are a woman
Tell me which is the greatest love this world can hold
The love of man for woman, Mother for her children
Or Friend and Friend. I searched around for proof
And came at last to mine own heart, and looked inside
I have been wife, I am a Mother, I dream oftimes even of a
    lover
There is one now in my life a woman friend
For all she is to me I owe a debt to her and through her
    womankind
For seven short years there was given to me a love,
A Woman too, she was my life, and soul, words fail
And desolation fills me, Life itself seems nought
And it is night forever more without her.
The greatest love this world can hold is soul affinity
Linked together from the foundations of the world
No end and no beginning, one and yet separate
Their home the throne of the eternal
O blest indeed who meet them on this earth
Their earth is Heaven.

Epilogue

'As we Live so do we Determine our Manner of Dying'

Ruth seemed to be moving in a different direction, not having shared Minna's experiences, and Minna remained rather isolated in her views. Minna's letters make up the last part of the intense writing or correspondence in Ruth's collection.

From 1919 until 1953 Ruth made regular but brief notes in small pocket diaries. Those notes, and conversations with friends and relatives, give some idea, although not a very complete one, of the rest of Ruth's life.

In December 1918 Ruth married Hugh for, despite their difficulties and her disappointment that Hugh had enlisted, they drew closer during the war and by 1918 had become lovers. Although they would have preferred not to marry ('how happy and more ideal we should be if unmarried', wrote Hugh, who 'would rather not sacrifice principles'), they gave in, it seemed, for the sake of their families and to avoid 'scandals'. When planning to marry, Hugh spoke of 'that useful and rational life we separately have visions of, and which we can only attain as a mutual affair.' At first they lived separately, but in 1921 moved to Blackheath, where they lived for the rest of their lives. Their relationship was not easy and was as full of contrasts as ever, for Ruth mentions 'delightful days', and 'dreary days', and times when Hugh was often 'moody', 'disagreeable' or 'restless and depressed'. They had no children and it is not clear why, except that Hugh was known to think children 'unnecessary' believing 'it was an unfit world to bring them into'.

Ruth continued to have an active life, seeing many friends and working hard. She had a series of social work jobs and seemed to be the main breadwinner, Hugh being in and out of work.

After leaving Rowntree's in 1918, she was Senior Administrative Officer for the Trade Boards Section at the Ministry of

308

Labour, Whitehall (she had to resign on marriage, as married women could not work in government posts). For nine years she was Organising Secretary for Woolwich Invalid Children's Aid. When she left in 1930, the local paper reported that 'the children of Woolwich have lost a much-beloved friend by the departure of Mrs Hugh Jones.' She then worked for the Metropolitan Society for the Blind (again 'terminated owing to the marriage bar' when the work was taken over by the London County Council), and for the Save the Children Fund.

She kept in touch with Minna, who continued nursing and moved out of London. In 1943, when she was 59, Ruth read Eva's diaries and visited her grave at Woodbrooke; she then contacted Minna and they 'had much talk of Eva and bygone times'. Minna died in 1946.

Ruth also saw and wrote to Françoise, who was living with Havelock Ellis and her two sons, teaching, writing, and campaigning for birth control, the 'endowment of Motherhood', and for peace. She wrote to Ruth in 1930 that her life 'was indeed one of much happiness these eleven years with Havelock'. She published three books: Friendship's Odyssey, *her autobiography, in 1946, described by one reviewer as 'a determinedly and courageously feminist volume';* The Return of Havelock Ellis; *and* The Pacifist Pilgrimage of Françoise and Havelock, *in 1974. Ruth recorded that she had 'delightful and happy times with Françoise, HE and the boys'.*

Ruth continued to work in pacifist groups, attended meetings of the Fellowship of Reconciliation, the Women's International League (founded during the First World War), and the Peace Pledge Union. She mentions a 'No More War Procession' in 1923. During the Second World War, she worked in the Blackheath Peace Shop which, amongst other things, arranged 'Circles for the Study of Foreign Languages and gathering of Peoples of all Nations'; she did much work with war refugees, and was particularly involved with a group of women refugees in Blackheath. On one occasion she wrote of being 'devoured by refugees most of the day, one calling after the other about their problems'. During the period of some of the 'terrifying' air raids she helped to evacuate blind people from London.

In the early 1950s, her health, which had never been very robust, began to deteriorate. In 1953, when she was 68, she suffered a stroke and was bedridden for some time. Hugh wrote to a friend that she did not have enough strength for 'tidying up her things' and 'looking after herself' and 'this depressed her as she liked to be independent of others'. On 28 March 1953, Ruth recorded a 'serious talk' with her doctor, after which she was very depressed. He told her that she would have a further stroke and angina. On 9 April Ruth decided to take her own life and took an overdose of sleeping pills, dying peacefully in her sleep after spending a quiet evening with Hugh and a friend.

After Ruth's death Hugh received many letters from friends and colleagues, which all paid tribute to Ruth and her work, showing the deep impression she made on many people.

Edwin le Bas, who had known Ruth since her teens, said 'Ruth's influence will live on in the lives of all who knew her ... she did a great work and was one of the pioneers in those days [at Rowntree's]'. The Fellowship of Reconciliation appreciated 'her steady and loyal support of all the peace efforts through many years'. One of the refugees wrote, 'her high spirited nature and genuine sense of humour made her splendid company and a great help in times of distress. She was one of the people who made us feel at home in this country.' A friend 'knew she wore herself out helping other people', and another said 'one cannot imagine Mrs Jones inactive and not helping others'.

After Ruth's death, Hugh read the diaries and was impressed by the quality of the writing. He asked Margaret Johnson to 'do something with her writing': the result 35 years later was Dear Girl.

Notes

Introduction
1 *There's Always Been a Women's Movement This Century*
  (1983), by Dale Spender.
2 Ruth's diary, 10 November 1908.
3 Letter to Ruth from Charlotte Despard, 27 July 1909.
4 Isabella Ford's speech for the Woolwich Fellowship, at the
  Carmel Chapel, 9 May 1909.
5 Eva's diary, 1 May 1913.
6 Charlotte Despard, 'To the Women of Great Britain',
  Women's Freedom League leaflet, December 1909.
7 Letter to Ruth from Charlotte Despard, 27 July 1909.

Chapter 1
1 Wanstead Flats, part of Wanstead Park.
2 The Christian Endeavour was a widespread international and
  interdenominational organisation founded in America in 1881
  'for the purpose of promoting spiritual life amongst young
  people'.
3 The day school was probably the Manor Park School Board.
  Free compulsory schooling was introduced in 1890 for
  children until the age of 13.
4 The British Women's Temperance Association, founded in
  1876, was part of the large Temperance movement which
  advocated total abstinence from alcoholic drink. The BWTA
  concentrated more on helping women in their daily lives than
  on the 'pledge'.
5 Joseph Hocking, a novelist who advocated practical Christianity.
6 The 'khaki' election which returned the Conservatives amidst

a great deal of war sentiment.

Chapter 3
1 The Band of Hope was the youth wing of the Temperance Movement.

Chapter 4
1 The journal of the Society of Friends (Quakers).
2 The Sweated Industries Exhibition, was promoted by the *Daily News* as a result of agitation from Mary Macarthur and the National Federation of Women Workers. This exposure of appalling conditions in such industries resulted in the formation of the League for the Abolition of Sweating.
3 Renan's *Life of Jesus* (1863), with its critical examination of the Bible stories and its imaginative interpretation of Christ, was highly controversial in the nineteenth century.
4 Phrenology was a popular science of the mind, which argued that a personality could be read from the contours of the skull.
5 Dr Campbell Morgan was a Liberal Nonconformist preacher.
6 Dr F. W. Cobb, the rector of the Anglican Church of St Ethelburga within Bishopgate, was an ardent socialist, a defender of the militant suffragettes, and a member of the Church League for Women's Suffrage.
7 Marie Corelli (1855-1924), a writer of romantic melodrama, lamented the decline of England and the suffragette's disrespect of womanhood.
8 Josephine Butler (1828-1906) campaigned, with other middle-class feminists, against the Contagious Diseases Acts of the 1860s; they were often called the 'social purity' campaigns. Under the Acts, women could be picked up and examined on suspicion of prostitution, poor working-class women being particularly affected. She also campaigned to raise the age of consent to 12 years of age. The campaign antagonised some eminent politicians because it threatened to expose their use of prostitution. The Acts were repealed in 1886.
9 Millicent Garrett-Fawcett was president of the National Union of Women's Suffrage Societies (NUWSS), the non-militant constitutional section of the women's suffrage movement.
10 Mrs Bramwell Booth of the Salvation Army supported Josephine Butler's campaigns for reform. She was married to

312

Bramwell Booth, son of William Booth the founder of the Salvation Army.

11 Deaconesses or Sisters were trained women Church workers, usually attached to an institution or local parish. Sisters could undertake teaching, nursing, missionary or social work, and many worked in poor communities. There was a growth in the movement during the late nineteenth century.

Chapter 5

1 The Woolwich Arsenal, where armaments were manu-factured.

2 *The Woman Socialist* (1907), by Ethel Snowden, a prominent Labour Party member and one of the founders of the Women's Labour League. The poem, she said, 'echoes the heart-cries of ten thousand women'.

3 Mrs E. Pethick-Lawrence was an influential leader of the militant suffragette movement.

4 *A Vindication of the Rights of Woman* (1792) by Mary Wollstonecraft, was one of the first books to plead for sexual equality.

5 *The Story of an African Farm* (1883), by Olive Schreiner, a South-Africa-born writer active in the suffrage, peace and anti-slavery movements. The book caused a scandal; the heroine abandoned her religious background, formed a free union and became pregnant.

6 The 'Votes for Women' procession was organised by the constitutional suffragists. About 13,000 women joined the demonstration.
Black Agnes of Dunbar was a fourteenth-century Countess who defended Dunbar Castle from the English Earl of Salisbury, who returned in 'ignomiy' to England after 19 weeks of seige.

7 The *New Age* was a radical literary and political journal not-able for its coverage of a wide range of controversial subjects.

8 *The Woman Worker* was the journal of the National Federa-tion of Women Workers, founded in 1906 to act as a central union for women.

9 Probably the Anti-Suffrage League, founded in 1908 by Mrs Humphry Ward, author of *Robert Elsmere*.

10 Mary Macarthur was the leader of the Women's Trade Union League and subsequently the National Federation of Women Workers.

11 Daisy Lord was a young servant who was sentenced to death for killing her baby. Cases of women driven to desperation by poverty and their inferior social status were taken up by Labour women and suffragettes.

12 Pavement chalking was a popular form of suffragette propaganda and notices of meetings were often chalked on pavements.

13 On 13 October 1908, hundreds of suffragettes converged on Parliament Square to rush the House of Commons in a symbolic attempt to get women into Parliament. They were surrounded by cordons of police, but were triumphant when Margaret Travers Simmons, Keir Hardie's secretary, managed to enter the debating chamber.

14 Victor Grayson, the Independent Socialist Member of Parliament for Colne Valley, took his seat from the Liberals in a surprise by-election victory in 1907 with a strong women's suffrage platform.

15 Robert Blatchford, an early Independent Labour Party member, was editor of *The Clarion,* a socialist newspaper founded in 1891. *The Clarion* promoted Blatchford's romantic, family-based vision of socialist England and the glorious 'New Life' under socialism. The Clarion movement was famous for its practical schemes and recreational activities.

16 Margaret Bondfield was a trade union organiser for the Shop Assistants' Union, a leading member of the Women's Labour League, and one of the first 3 Labour women Members of Parliament, elected in 1923.

17 Parenthood and race culture, birth and population control, and eugenics, the planning of the race, were contentious issues in the early twentieth century. Socialists and feminists adopted a variety of political positions on the subject.

18 The Women's Labour League, established in 1906 by leading Labour women, became affiliated to the Labour Party in 1909. The constitution stated that members would 'work with the Labour Party ... to secure the full rights of citizenship for all men and women', and 'strive to improve the social and industrial conditions of working women'.

19 George Lansbury, Labour Member of Parliament for Bromley and Bow, resigned his seat in 1912 in support of the WSPU suffragettes. He fought a by-election as a Women's Suffrage candidate and was defeated.

20 Charlotte Despard was president of the Women's Freedom

League, a member of the ILP and a pacifist. She was 67 when the WFL was established in 1907. Widely idolized by feminists, she was 'a striking figure with white hair, upright bearing and a costume which usually included a black lace mantilla and sandals' (*Feminist Encyclopedia*).

21 Dr Ethel Bentham, a pioneering woman doctor, prominent in the Women's Labour League and the suffrage campaign, devoted much of her time to the WLL's first baby clinic opened in Kensington in 1911.

22 The Clarion Van was a horse-drawn caravan which toured the country delivering the socialist message of Robert Blatchford's Clarion movement.

23 Mrs Annie Besant campaigned for many causes including trade unionism and birth control. In the 1870s she was prominent in the secularist atheist movement. In 1888, as a Fabian Socialist, she championed the famous London match-girls' strike. Late in the 1890s she converted to theosophy, becoming the centre of the Theosophical Society in Britain. A number of feminists at that time became interested in Theosophy.

24 *The Christian Commonwealth,* a Nonconformist magazine which, after 1901, particularly supported radical Nonconformists and the activities of R. J. Campbell's City Temple.

25 Beatrice Webb, was a leading Fabian socialist who endorsed the value of motherhood and family life, and was concerned to better women's domestic and working conditions. For some time she was known to be an opponent of women's suffrage but later changed her views.

Chapter 6

1 Sylvia Pankhurst in her book *The Suffragette Movement* explained why some young suffragettes were attracted to the Freewoman and dissatisfied with the WSPU's focus on the vote.

Chapter 7

1 The suffragette premises were raided and the leaders arrested and charged with conspiring to commit malicious damage. *The Suffragette* was seized as a 'danger to society'.

2 The victim of the Derby tragedy, the suffragette Emily Davison, died five days after the incident. She became a martyr of the suffragette movement and her coffin was

escorted through London streets by 2,000 uniformed suffragettes.

3 *The Suffragette* was the newspaper of the WSPU.

4 *The Woman Who Did* (1895), by Grant Allen, dealt with the Sex Question and the New Woman. The book was much debated and was intended as a protest against the subjection of women. The heroine refused to marry her lover, believing marriage was slavery.

5 *The Labor Woman* was the journal of the Women's Labour League.

6 Queenie Gerald was sentenced to three months' imprisonment under the White Slave Traffic Act for procuring young girls for prostitution. The case caused a sensation and was taken up by the suffragettes, in particular Christabel Pankhurst, who exposed the well-known men involved and argued that prostitution was another example of women's degradation by men.

7 *The Citizen* was Britain's first socialist daily paper.

8 During this period many suffragettes, particularly the leaders, were in and out of prison, temporarily discharged under the 'Cat and Mouse Act' when their hunger strikes weakened their health, and re-arrested as soon as they had slightly recovered.

9 Margaret Sanger (1883-1966) was a life-long campaigner for birth control.

Chapter 8

1 Rescue homes of this type were for 'fallen women' (often prostitutes or single mothers). The Free Church Council was the more radical wing of the Nonconformist Church.

2 The Poor Law Guardians were administrators of the Poor Law. Many socialists and reformers had campaigned against the severity of the Poor Law which only granted relief if destitution could be proved.

3 Girls and Youth Leagues of an educational and recreational kind were often a feature of the activities of socialist feminist and religious groups.

4 Sylvester Horn, was a well-known Nonconformist and Liberal Member of Parliament with strong Labour sympathies.

5 *Brotherhood* was the journal of the Alpha Union which stood for 'freedom through truth' and operated from the Letchworth Garden City Community.

316

6 The White Slave Trade was a term for the exploitation, and sometimes the abduction, of young girls for the purposes of prostitution, which feminists and moral reformers campaigned around in the late nineteenth century.

7 Settlements were primarily education centres set up by middle-class radicals in working-class areas. Some women's settlements were set up in the nineteenth century.

8 Lucy Re-Bartlett was a staunch WSPU supporter. In her writing about sexual relations she attacked the subjection of women in marriage for men's sexual needs, argued for sexual union to meet only 'the actual needs of creation' and for spiritually fulfilling relationships.

9 Open Air Schools were for consumptive children.

10 Mary Longman was a prominent member of the Women's Labour League. The baby clinic referred to is probably the WLL clinic in Kensington.

11 *The Hidden Scourge* (1913) by Christabel Pankhurst argued that the 'scourge' of venereal disease was a result of men's promiscuity at women's expense. The vote, she claimed, would free women from their sexual, economic and legal oppression.

12 The Cradley Heath women were known for waging a successful strike in 1911, in conjunction with the National Federation of Women Workers, against the appallingly low rates of pay for women in the chainmaking industry in the manufacturing areas around Birmingham.

13 Lady Constance Lytton's book *Prison and Prisoners* was published in 1914. She was a militant suffragette and frequently imprisoned for her activities. Being a well-known figure, she received preferential treatment in prison, particularly in receiving a medical test before force-feeding during hunger strikes. In 1911 she disguised herself, was arrested, force fed without a test and with such violence that she was partially paralysed from a stroke. Her identity was then revealed and the case received much publicity.

14 Michael Fairless was a woman, Margaret Fairless Barber, known as 'the fighting sister' for her nursing work in London's worst slums during the 1890s.

Chapter 9

1 *Votes for Women,* 1914, reporting on a rally at Kingsway Hall, attended by 2,000 women on 4 August, two days after war was declared.

2 The Actresses' Franchise League, founded in December 1908, was an active part of the suffrage movement, involving many well-known actresses. The League staged suffrage plays and 'The Pageant of Great Women' in 1909.

3 The *Workers' Dreadnought*, edited by Sylvia Pankhurst, was the paper of the East London Federation of Suffragettes. It was also a paper where workingwomen generally 'might express themselves and find their interests defended'.

4 Margaret MacDonald, president of the Women's Labour League, a tireless organiser, much respected in the Labour movement, was married to Ramsay MacDonald.

Chapter 10

1 The No Conscription Fellowship, founded in 1914 by Fenner Brockway and mostly Independent Labour Party members, was more socialist than the Fellowship of Reconciliation. When national conscription was introduced in 1916 it became the focus of the conscientious objectors movement.

Select Bibliography

Cain, Barbara, 'Beatrice Webb and the Woman Question', *History Workshop Journal*, Issue 14, Autumn 1982.

Davin, Anna, 'Imperialism and Motherhood', *History Workshop Journal*, Issue 5, Spring 1978.

Delisle, Françoise, *Friendship's Odyssey*, Heinemann, 1946.

Faderman, Lillian, *Surpassing the Love of Men*, The Women's Press, 1985.

Fernbach, David and Greig, Noel (eds.) *The Selected Writings of Edward Carpenter*, Vol. 1, Gay Men's Press, 1984.

Heasman, Kathleen, *Evangelicals in Action*, Geoffrey Bles Ltd., 1962.

Horn, Sylvester, *Nonconformity in the 19th Century*, The National Council of Evangelical Free Churches, 1905.

Jeffreys, Sheila, *The Spinster and Her Enemies*, Pandora, 1985.

MacKenzie, Midge, *Shoulder to Shoulder*, Penguin, 1975.

Middleton, Lucy (ed.) *Women in the Labour Movement*, Croom Helm, 1977.

Mitchell, Hannah, *The Hard Way Up*, Virago, 1977.

Oldfield, Sybil, *Spinsters of This Parish, The Life and Times of F. M. Mayor and Mary Sheepshanks*, Virago, 1984.

Pankhurst, Sylvia, *The Suffragette Movement*, Virago, 1977, first published Longman, 1931.

Payne, Ernest, *The Free Church Tradition in the Life of England*, FCM Press, 1944.

Raeburn, Antonia, *Militant Suffragettes*, New English Library, 1973.

Rowbotham, Sheila, *Hidden from History*, Pluto Press, 1973.

Rowbotham, Sheila, *Women, Resistance and Revolution*, Penguin, 1972.

Rowbotham, Sheila, and Weeks, Jeffrey, *Socialism and the New Life,* Pluto Press, 1977.

Samuel, Raphael, 'The Vision Splendid', *New Socialist,* May, 1985.

Spender, Dale, *There's Always Been a Women's Movement This Century,* Pandora, 1983.

Sylvester-Smith, Warren, *The London Heretics,* Constable, 1967.

Taylor, Barbara, *Eve and the New Jerusalem,* Virago, 1983.

Tuttle, Lisa, *Encyclopedia of Feminism,* Longman, 1986, Arrow, 1987.

Vicinus, Martha, *Independent Women,* Virago, 1985.

Weeks, Jeffrey, *Coming Out,* Quartet, 1977.

Weeks, Jeffrey, *Sex, Politics and Society,* Longman, 1981.